Empire and Nation

D1082494

Anglo-America in the Transatlantic World

Jack P. Greene, *General Editor*

Empire and Nation

The American Revolution in the
Atlantic World

Edited by Eliga H. Gould and Peter S. Onuf

Johns Hopkins University Press
Baltimore

© 2005 Johns Hopkins University Press
All rights reserved. Published 2005
Printed in the United States of America

Johns Hopkins Paperback edition, 2015
9 8 7 6 5 4 3 2 1

Johns Hopkins University Press
2715 North Charles Street
Baltimore, Maryland 21218-4363
www.press.jhu.edu

*The Library of Congress has cataloged the hardcover edition of this book
as follows:*

Empire and nation : the American Revolution in the Atlantic world /
edited by Eliga H. Gould and Peter S. Onuf.
    p. cm. — (Anglo-America in the transatlantic world)
  Includes bibliographical references and index.
  ISBN 0-8018-7912-4 (alk. paper)
    1. United States—History—Revolution, 1775–1783—Influence.
2. United States—History—Revolution, 1775–1783—Social aspects.
3. West Indies—History—1775–1783. I. Gould, Eliga H. II. Onuf, Peter S.
III. Series.
  E209.E45   2005
  973.3's—dc22   2004011135

ISBN-13 978-1-4214-1842-1
ISBN-10: 1-4214-1842-8

*Special discounts are available for bulk purchases of this book. For
more information, please contact Special Sales at 410-516-6936 or
specialsales@press.jhu.edu.*

Contents

Contributors

Maurice J. Bric, Director, Clinton Center for American Studies, University College Dublin

Trevor Burnard, Professor of American History, Department of American Studies, University of Sussex

Robert M. Calhoon, Professor of History, University of North Carolina at Greensboro

Edward L. Cox, Associate Professor of History, Rice University

Eliga H. Gould, Associate Professor of History, University of New Hampshire

Marc Harris, Associate Professor of History, Penn State University, Altoona College

David C. Hendrickson, Robert J. Fox Professor of Political Science, Colorado College

Don Higginbotham, Dowd Professor of History, University of North Carolina at Chapel Hill

Keith Mason, Lecturer in History, University of Liverpool

Peter S. Onuf, Thomas Jefferson Foundation Professor of History, University of Virginia

Ellen Holmes Pearson, Assistant Professor of History, University of North Carolina, Asheville

Richard Alan Ryerson, Academic Director, The David Library of the American Revolution

Steven Sarson, Lecturer in History, University of Wales Swansea

Mary M. Schweitzer, McNeil Center for Early American Studies, University of Pennsylvania

James Sidbury, Associate Professor of History, University of Texas

Melvin Yazawa, Professor of History, University of New Mexico

Empire and Nation

Introduction

Eliga H. Gould and Peter S. Onuf

When did the American Revolution begin? Was it the commencement of hostilities on Lexington Common or the imperial reforms of the 1760s? Is the Revolution best seen as a political accident, the result of contingency and miscalculation on both sides of the Atlantic, or did it reflect deeper forces that had been gathering strength for years, if not decades? Like many apparently simple questions, this one admits no easy answers. But of the various original moments one might choose, none would appear more decisive than the Peace of Paris (1763), which marked the conclusion of a series of wars among the European powers in North America, Europe, the Caribbean, India, West Africa, and the Pacific. For the British victors—in America no less than Britain proper—the Seven Years' War gave rise to vaulting hopes for a new era of peace and prosperity. Having vanquished France and Spain, Britons everywhere could hope for a transatlantic *pax Britannica,* an epoch marked by the rule of law, liberty, and commerce. As Massachusetts patriot James Otis exulted in 1763, Britain would be the first "universal monarchy" in history "favourable to the human race," an empire for liberty.[1]

But there were clouds on this horizon. West of the Appalachian Mountains, in the vast region seized from France, Indian nations contested Britain's conquests, resisting the westward movement of settlers, speculators, and imperial bureaucrats. On the seas, France and Spain were rebuilding their navies, fortifying their colonies, and preparing for the opportunity to avenge their losses. In Europe, Britain had to contend with a widespread conviction that its triumph had been too complete: the alliance with Prussia was in tatters, Austria was pledged to France, and prospects for new alliances were dim. Most troubling of all was a stunning expansion of the national debt, which led to unprecedented levels of taxation on both sides of the English-speaking Atlantic and prompted metropolitan Britons to search for new sources of revenue.[2] Although the American Revolution eventually touched every aspect of domestic politics in Britain and the American colonies, its origins lay in the diplomatic uncertainties and strategic pressures wrought by this rapidly changing world.

Despite general recognition of this overarching fact, the Revolution's global context has been too often neglected. Under the aegis of the new social history, scholars looked to local conditions in the American colonies for explanations of revolutionary discontent and mobilization.[3] While rejecting attempts to reduce the Revolution's origins to material conditions and social factors, members of the so-called neo-Whig school agreed that the Revolution's "ideological origins" were to be found in idiosyncratic provincial understandings of the British constitution.[4] Even historians of eighteenth-century Britain—whom one might expect would produce a broader perspective—tended to conceptualize British politics in narrowly particularistic, parochial terms.[5] Underlying these oddly complementary perspectives was a sense of the distinctive and divergent character of the small political worlds within which colonists and metropolitan Britons moved. During the revolutionary crisis, these approaches all suggested, the protagonists became increasingly and acutely aware of the differences that divided them, making the final break with Britain seem predetermined and inevitable. As historians dug deeper for its origins, many of the Revolution's broader accomplishments—especially America's independence from Britain—came to seem decidedly unrevolutionary, at most a recognition and confirmation of pre-existing realities rather than a movement with profound implications both for Americans and for peoples elsewhere in the Atlantic world.

The contributors to this volume take a different approach. Eliga Gould demonstrates that the British policies that inaugurated the revolutionary crisis—the decision to keep 10,000 soldiers in America, new revenue measures to pay for these troops, and reform of the Navigation system—represented an effort to come to terms with the changes wrought by the Seven Years' War. The conventional interpretation of the Revolution emphasizes the haphazard and shifting course of British policy, dismissing the possibility that successive ministries were inspired by any coherent conception of the empire. But Gould suggests that colonial patriots were not being "paranoid" when they discerned a consistent determination to reconstitute provincial government. Conscious of the vulnerability of Britain's newly extended empire, policy makers sought to incorporate American colonists into the system of military finance that had been established in the years following the Glorious Revolution (1689). Patriots erred in seeing the Stamp Act (1765) as a deliberate design to "enslave" provincial Americans, but British reformers did believe that the best way to secure British liberty was by *enhancing* the government's power throughout the empire.

Gould also reminds us that, far from being an act of exclusion—as American historians have often suggested—American taxation was meant to include the colonists more fully in the British nation, placing them on the same footing as men and women in metropolitan Britain. In challenging the traditional rights of colonial assemblies, Parliament's defenders used the same rhetoric of law, liberty, and peace that colonial patriots embraced in their resistance to British imperial authority. Obviously, this implicit conception of citizenship, which the British referred to as "virtual representation," proved unacceptable to American patriots; to Britons, however, taxation without representation seemed entirely consistent with a metropolitan system that denied even the wealthiest women the right to vote and that left some of the most economically dynamic cities in Britain—including Liverpool, Birmingham, and Sheffield—unrepresented.[6] Despite their destructive effects, British policy initiatives were driven by a desire to secure peace and prosperity for all of the king's subjects, in Virginia and Massachusetts, no less than in England itself.

As they responded to imperial policy initiatives, cosmopolitan colonists were no less mindful of fundamental changes taking place in the Atlantic world. Where the British were convinced of the need for imperial consolidation, Americans believed peace and liberty both depended on preserving the empire's character as a looser consortium of quasi-autonomous polities.[7] This did not mean that Americans were groping toward a sense of themselves as a separate people or nation. To the contrary, they understood their own world as being ever more deeply embedded in the British Atlantic. Readers of colonial newspapers were fed a steady diet of news about foreign commercial conditions, politics, and war; thousands of colonial sailors and soldiers served in the king's forces; Protestants of all denominations participated in transatlantic revivals and missionary enterprises, corresponding and traveling across vast distances; ordinary men and women purchased goods from around the world: Jamaican sugar, East Indian calicoes, tea from Asia, manufactures from England.[8] Despite the looming controversy over colonial taxation, Anglicizing provincials thought of themselves as more English, not less.

If the colonists claimed to be British, however, they also recognized underlying tensions in their situation on the North American seaboard. On the eve of the Revolution, Americans and Britons alike regarded the western and southern reaches of the Atlantic as inherently colonial parts of the world, beyond the pale of civilized Europe.[9] Although the more cosmopolitan colonists—Benjamin Franklin is the classic case—assumed that it was possible to replicate European social and political norms in North America, most also assumed that their societies were situated in chronically warring space—a brutal state of nature—that could only be governed by subjection to one of Europe's principal imperial powers.[10] Far from objecting to the provincialism implicit in this view, Americans embraced their status as loyal subjects of the British king, grateful for the protection he afforded them in a dangerous world. They believed that their safety and prosperity depended on the vigorous projection of imperial power, both on the high seas and along the frontiers of empire. The most visible expression of this benevolent power was the Navigation Acts, which limited colonial trade to British ships and ports but in so doing sustained Britain's naval supremacy and secured lucrative markets for enterprising colonists around the world.[11] Even after the Stamp Act crisis, when precocious patriots explicitly denied Parliament's sovereignty over the internal affairs of the colonies, Americans continued to profess their willingness to submit to the Navigation system. "And though some of these restrictions were grievous," wrote the Continental Congress in its "Address to the People of Great Britain" (1774), "we looked up to you as to our parent state to which we were bound by the strongest ties: And were happy to being instrumental to your prosperity and grandeur." "Place us in the same situation that we were at the close of the last war," Congress concluded, "and our former harmony will be restored."[12]

For citizens of the independent United States, preserving the prosperity and individual freedom they had enjoyed as subjects of George III required fashioning a new kind of empire, based on a fundamentally different relationship to both Britain and Europe. To many colonists, the only alternative to membership in the British Empire was a defensive alliance with one of Europe's other imperial powers. Some patriots worried that the American colonies would collapse into an anarchic, disunited state without the Crown connection; others recoiled from a dangerous state of nature in the Atlantic, where small, weak states could not hope to survive without the protection of imperial power.[13] As John Dickinson warned Congress on July 1, 1776, rejecting British protection without a compensating European alliance was tantamount to "brav[ing] the Storm in a Skiff made of Paper."[14] In order to preserve their rights, Americans might well reject future membership in the British Empire; it was inconceivable, however, that they could stay afloat in such rough waters without the patronage of some other European power. In declaring independence without such an alliance, the American Congress and its supporters were compelled to advance a new conception of the Atlantic world, one that could be organized as a system of sovereign and independent states.[15] They did so, moreover, on the assumption that such a system would achieve what the old imperial regime had so obviously failed to achieve, namely, bring lasting peace and prosperity. "What have we to do with setting the world at defiance?" Thomas Paine famously asked in Common Sense: "our plan is commerce, and that well attended to, will secure us the peace and friendship of all Europe; because, it is the interest of all Europe to have America a free port."[16]

Framed in this way, the American Revolution becomes an attempt—even a radical, revolutionary attempt—to bring peace to an inherently unstable world. As David Hendrickson shows, the framers of the Articles of Confederation attributed the chronic state of war in the Atlantic not to the weakness of imperial states like Britain but to the overbearing power of metropolitan authority and institutions. For Americans, Britain now played the role of despotic universal monarch that had once been the part of France's Louis XIV and Philip II of Spain—and against which Britain had historically defined its own empire. Americans believed that constituting the United States as a federation of equal, sovereign states would safeguard it against the principal cause of war in Europe, the quest for preponderant power on the part of any of its constituent sovereigns. The union the revolutionaries envisioned was a radical alternative to the European balance of power, a plan for perpetual peace among the newly constituted American republics. Yet they also recognized that their Congress would have to succeed to many of the Crown's imperial prerogatives in order to guarantee the preservation of the union and to secure American interests in a dangerous and unpredictable Atlantic world.

Even as they resisted the assaults of a supposedly despotic imperial state that meant to return them to colonial submission, revolutionary Americans necessarily became state-builders themselves. Don Higginbotham underscores the connection between war and state formation in early modern Europe; whatever their ideological predilections, Americans could not escape the same imperatives. The need to defend the United States from counter-revolutionary forces set the stage for the Philadelphia Convention's bold effort to establish a strong federal state, a republican empire of liberty. Though the Federalists succeeded in the ratification campaign, dissident Antifederalists and Republicans guaranteed that Treasury Secretary Alexander Hamilton's attempts to transform the United States into a modern, bureaucratic state along European lines would be frustrated. The United States in 1800 may have been a more centralized polity than the revolutionaries of 1776 had hoped for, but it was unlikely to ever become a replica of Britain.

What sort of regime would the Americans establish? Before the framers convened at Philadelphia, the most sustained and creative efforts at constitutional design were focused on the state level. In his influential "Thoughts on Government" (1776), John Adams devoted only a few concluding lines to problems of union among the states: the need for some sort of interstate alliance was self-evident, but the authority of the Continental Congress—the embodiment of that alliance—"should sacredly be confined to . . . war, trade, disputes between Colony and Colony, the Post-Office, and the unappropriated lands of the Crown."[17] The revolutionaries' great challenge, Adams insisted, was to devise constitutions for the states that would guarantee liberty and lay a durable foundation for the superstructure of republican government, including the union of state-republics. For Adams, Richard Ryerson argues, the British Constitution—purified of the corruptions that had destroyed the empire—provided the template for new state charters. Though Adams's efforts to give his state a strong, independent executive with an absolute veto were rebuffed, the 1780 Massachusetts constitutional convention adopted his design for a bicameral legislature, including a senate that would attract—and contain—home-grown aristocrats. Adams's prescriptions would prove influential for constitution-writers in other states and, eventually, for the framers of the federal Constitution.[18]

Adams also recognized the crucial significance of accommodating constitutional regime to social structure, though modern commentators differ markedly on the "relevance" of his insights into political psychology and sociology. Are "aristocratic" impulses "natural" in all polities, even in republics?[19] Divergent local responses to the proposed federal Constitution testify to the prevalence of distinctive political cultures that had emerged in different states and that were codified in their constitutions.[20] Mary Schweitzer shows that voters in the Great Valley, extending through western Pennsylvania and Virginia, rejected or endorsed the Constitution because of their differing experiences with local and provincial government, not because their economic interests or cultural backgrounds differed in any discernibly significant way. Accustomed to more responsive governments on all levels, skeptical Antifederalists in western Pennsylvania wondered how the new system would work for them; their counterparts in Virginia tended toward Federalism, both because they expected less of their political system and because they recognized the importance of a stronger interstate compact for access to markets.

The problem of the "extended republic" was thus not merely one of conceptualizing and implementing an effective division of authority between levels of government. As Schweitzer suggests, the effort to superimpose a more "energetic" federal regime over such a wide variety of state polities made Americans acutely conscious of differences among them even as they struggled for a more perfect union. Few Antifederalists believed that the Articles of Confederation were adequate to the exigencies of a union they professed to cherish, but they had good reason to wonder how well they would fit into a renovated federal system that "consolidated" unprecedented authority in the central government. And Antifederalists were not alone in calculating the costs and benefits of union. Even the most ardent friends of the new system sought to promote the particular interests of their own states and regions.

The dialectic of whole and part, of diversity in union, was central to the business of constructing a viable constitutional order for the United States. This same double consciousness, the coexistence of parochial provincial identities with an all-embracing British imperial identity, had defined the colonists' situation before independence. The great question was whether identification with Britain could be redirected toward "America," and whether an alliance of state-republics could effectively replace, and fulfill the promise of, the imperial connection.[21] Of course, American patriots insisted that their republican empire represented a radical, revolutionary improvement on its corrupt, monarchical predecessor; it was "a new order for the ages." In soberer, less exultant moments, however, they acknowledged the great advantages they had enjoyed under Britain, at least before 1763: protection against external foes (and even, as Adams's catalog of congressional powers suggested, against each other), commercial prosperity, security of property, and the rule of law.

The revolutionaries of 1776 had no intention of sacrificing all those good things. While they drafted new state constitutions and groped toward some sort of postimperial union, Americans insisted that property relations and legal systems in their respective colony-states remained fundamentally undisturbed. "Before the revolution," Jefferson wrote in 1799, "the nation of Virginia had, by the organs they then thought proper to constitute, established a system of laws. . . . When, by the declaration of Independence, they chose to abolish their former organs of declaring their will, the acts of will already formally & constitutionally declared, remained untouched."22 The new states affirmed the continuing authority of colonial statutes, appropriately modified to reflect the new republican dispensation, and the local common law precedents of colonial courts; they formally "received" the English common law that had been in effect when the American colonies were founded. Ellen Pearson's chapter on the American reception of English jurist William Blackstone's *Commentaries on the Laws of England* illuminates this process of preserving legal continuity in the midst of revolutionary change. Significantly, however, Blackstone's legacy was tailored to the particular circumstances of different states, thus reinforcing the distinctions among them that the logic of federalism encouraged. Jefferson's argument for the continuity of the common law in Virginia was an argument against the idea of a *federal* common law that ultimately would have obliterated distinctions among the states.

Americans wanted to enjoy the benefits of union without jeopardizing traditional provincial liberties. The biggest challenge was to reconstruct viable trade relationships in the Atlantic economy that would guarantee the future prosperity of the entire union. Congressmen first sought to negotiate commercial treaties that would give American staple producers and shippers access to lucrative new markets beyond the limits of the old British Navigation system; meanwhile, they reasoned, Britain's self-interest would guarantee the restoration of commercial ties with its former colonies. Just as Americans sought to secure the continuity of legal regimes and property relations when they declared their independence, they expected overseas trade to return to familiar channels after the war. As Paine suggested, the widely diffused benefits of free trade would interest Britain as well as its European rivals in preserving peace in the Atlantic and thus in guaranteeing American independence. Such expectations were both radically progressive and profoundly conservative. In effect, the new nation would revolutionize the Atlantic world—replacing British maritime hegemony with a self-enforcing multilateral free trade system—in order to avoid serious economic dislocation and social disruption in their own small worlds on the Atlantic's western periphery.[23]

The frustrations and failures of revolutionary diplomacy ultimately forced Americans to scrap the Articles of Confederation and draft a new federal Constitution. The mere recognition of American independence did not, by itself, transform the European diplomatic system; in order to negotiate more favorable terms of trade, the separate states therefore would have to forge a much "more perfect union" among themselves and the federal government would have to take on the role of a sovereign power, capable of enforcing its will.[24] Moves toward "consolidation" were always halting and controversial. Prominent Virginians, for instance, strongly favored giving congress sufficient power to negotiate commercial treaties that would open new markets for their tobacco crops, but they were wary of any system that would make them overly dependent on *other* American regions or interests. To an extraordinary extent, Chesapeake tobacco planters struck an effective balance between these conflicting imperatives. Steven Sarson shows that planters in Prince George's County, Maryland, were able to sustain their traditional way of life and social structure through a period of radical, disruptive change in the Atlantic political economy. They were able to do so not only because ties with British merchants and consumers proved so durable but because a responsive federal government protected and promoted their interests. Social and economic continuity in Prince George's County also depended on opportunities for enterprising whites to move freely to more dynamic and productive regions in other parts of the union.

Mobility within the union was matched by immigration from abroad. The social dynamism that was obscured and displaced in Prince George's County was much more conspicuous both in frontier regions and in urban centers like Philadelphia. The influx of new, often Catholic Irish immigrants constituted a fundamental threat to traditional conceptions of Philadelphia's polity, as Maurice Bric shows, a threat that was exacerbated by the revolutionary radicalism of Irish refugees from British anti-Jacobin repression in the 1790s. The new nation could not be insulated from the radical effects of the French Revolution, despite efforts by fearful Federalists to raise the bar to naturalization and expel dangerous aliens.[25] For a commercial people whose livelihood depended on transatlantic ties, isolation was never an option. The very effort to contain the Jacobin threat was itself symptomatic of the centrality of foreign policy issues in domestic politics, particularly in cosmopolitan places like Philadelphia. If the great desideratum of American politics, as set forth in President Washington's Farewell Address, was to "steer clear of permanent alliances, with any portion of the foreign world," the reality of the late 1790s was that Americans could not avoid choosing sides in the great continuing struggle between Revolutionary France and Counter-revolutionary Britain.[26]

Yet the appearance of violent partisan conflict in Philadelphia was as deceptive as the appearance of social peace and stability in the rural Chesapeake. Political mobilization transformed the polity, Bric shows, drawing partisan antagonists—and their ethnic constituencies—into a more dynamic, competitive balance. The idealized notion of a single-interest polity thus gave way to a more pluralistic conception that could accommodate the ethnic and religious diversity that had in fact long characterized Pennsylvania. As the new nation's capital city through most of the 1790s, Philadelphia was also centrally located in the emerging partisan political networks that struggled to build coalitions of diverse interests across the continent. Local political divisions thus reflected party-building efforts within the union as well as the great geopolitical struggles of the Atlantic world. Responding to perceived crises, Americans joined their fellow citizens in voluntary associations, some expressly political, others performing a wide array of civic and social functions in a rapidly expanding public sphere.[27]

The perpetuation of the American union, all patriots agreed, was the absolutely essential condition for reciprocally beneficial associations of all kinds. Yet it was at the level of national politics that Americans became most conscious of fundamental differences that might not be so amenable to fair competition, compromise, or accommodation. The very survival of the union itself, moreover, remained in doubt from 1776 until the Treaty of Ghent in 1814 finally brought peace to the Atlantic system. Throughout this period European observers remained convinced that the union would inevitably collapse. In a classic early prediction, Lord Sheffield assured his readers of the union's imminent demise: "The authority of the Congress can never be maintained over those distant and boundless regions, and her nominal subjects will speedily imitate and multiply the examples of independence."[28] Ratification of the Constitution was supposed to resolve this problem, but Americans themselves soon became acutely conscious of the fragility of the founders' achievement. Beginning with the inauguration of the new government, Melvin Yazawa shows, congressional brinksmen invoked threats of disunion to gain any possible incremental advantage over their foes. Cynical as such tactics might now appear, however, they proceeded from a consciousness of deeper, underlying differences among the states that a stronger union made more salient. Conscious of those differences, congressmen recognized that disunionist threats were not necessarily idle, even when the pretext—the adoption of a novel formula for calculating the distribution of seats in Congress, for example—seemed relatively trivial. Taking each other's threats seriously, they struggled to compromise their differences, knowing compromise would not always be possible.[29]

In 1792, James Madison, one of the leaders of the emerging Republican opposition, argued that a true "consolidation" of interests in the federal republic depended on preserving the federal balance and preventing a dangerous concentration of power in the central government.[30] The most powerful bonds of union were based on consent, not coercion; on proliferating family ties; on spreading commercial and transportation networks; and on the voluntary association of independent, liberty-loving men (and, by the 1820s, women, too) in the churches, civic groups, debating clubs, libraries, fraternities, and other organizations that constituted an expanding public sphere.[31] Marc Harris shows how popular political mobilization in the revolutionary period—the democratic impulses that portended anarchy and disunion for fearful conservatives—was channeled into a vigorous, stable associational culture. Within this new public space, political parties that the founders feared came to play a crucial role in providing the institutional and ideological sinews of an expanding electorate.

The dialectic between union and disunion, between institution-building and the centrifugal social forces unleashed by the Revolution, was no less central to American religious life. The separation of church and state threatened social disorder and moral degeneration to conservatives in states where established churches survived the break with Britain. But, as Robert Calhoon demonstrates, disestablishment ultimately energized disestablished churches as well as dissenting sects in the emerging denominational culture of antebellum America. Freed from state control, churches responded creatively to "market" forces and helped foster a dynamically expansive public sphere. "Primitive" churches, with their radically democratic, antinomian appeals, countered institution-building tendencies, guaranteeing that the emerging denominations would remain responsive to the people's social and spiritual needs. Vigorous competition for new members both exaggerated sectarian differences and made religious controversy more predictable and less dangerous. By offering a model and a framework for popular mobilization, the churches also made a more positive contribution to the new republic's expanding public sphere. For the fiction of "popular sovereignty" to be translated into reality, the new nation had to accommodate and promote the associational impulses that French visitor Alexis de Tocqueville found so remarkable in the 1830s. Religious entrepreneurs played a key role in this "democratization" process.[32]

We opened this introduction by asking when the Revolution began. Several of our contributors invite us to consider the related problem of when (and where) it ended.[33] To American historians, the most important of the Revolution's effects has typically been the contested, complex legacy that it held (and continues to hold) for the internal history of the American nation—what Carl Becker famously called "the struggle over who should rule at home."[34] Considered as an internal struggle, the Revolution's history stretches at least to the eve of the Civil War, and scholars have continued to detect its influence through the democratic upheavals of the twentieth century, notably the civil rights movement of the 1950s and 1960s. Yet the external conflict over home rule was no less transformative, and this was true not only for the subsequent national history of the United States but also for peoples beyond the new nation's borders.

Loyal British subjects who balked at independence and were driven into exile were among the Revolution's most conspicuous victims, fellow subjects and citizens whose suffering the upheaval's internal struggles made external to subsequent chapters of American history. Impervious to patriot appeals, loyal exiles sought the security, opportunity, and British liberties they had enjoyed under imperial rule. As Keith Mason maintains, however, the Loyalists' forced migration also played a key role in the reconstitution of Britain's far-flung empire. The vast transmigration that Mason describes—involving between 60,000 and 100,000 individuals, making it considerably larger than the seventeenth-century migrations to Ireland, Virginia, and New England—ruptured a transatlantic community, in many cases irreparably. Yet as striking as the losses sustained by George III's loyal subjects in the United States were the opportunities most found to start anew elsewhere, demonstrating that Britain remained an empire of liberty, even after the failed attempt to avert American independence. Mason underscores this point by including in his analysis not only England, whose alienated and embittered community of loyal refugees has received the most scholarly attention, but also Canada, the West Indies, and Sierra Leone, where American émigrés quickly resumed the same "pursuits of happiness" that had defined their lives in the colonies that rebelled.[35] The Revolution transformed the Loyalists' lives in countless ways, forcing many to endure dislocation and penury, but it did not require them to surrender the liberty they had claimed as British subjects before 1776.

For those on the margins of the United States—blacks, Indians, French and Spanish creoles—the Revolution precipitated equally far-reaching changes. By defeating what had been the most formidable imperial power in the Atlantic world, Americans implicitly created similar possibilities for others, whether in Upper Canada, Venezuela, or Haiti.[36] One of the most vivid demonstrations of this mimetic liberation was the formation of a common racial identity among both blacks and Indians. As James Sidbury argues, this new consciousness was especially fraught for black authors (and former slaves) like Ottobah Cugoano and Olaudah Equiano. Achieving prominence in the years just after the Revolution, both Cugoano and Equiano mounted damning critiques of the institution that had forced them to endure years of servitude. To stir the sympathies of white readers, however, they had to market both themselves and their "Africanness" in ways uncomfortably reminiscent of the trade in human beings that they claimed to oppose. In an Atlantic world that was starting to be organized as a community of nations, people of color came under intense pressure to think of themselves, not as Fanti and Ibo, but as Africans (or African Americans and Afro-Britons), and to employ such monolithic categories in ways that made sense to metropolitan and creole Europeans. Yet this reconceptualization was never merely a process of non-Europeans adopting labels whites had fabricated for them. In a development whose effects are still felt today, nation-making in the revolutionary Atlantic led directly to race-making, with groups that both Britons and Americans refused to recognize as full citizens appropriating national (or racial) identities for their own liberationist ends.

Nowhere was this relationship between empires, nations, and races more complex than in the Caribbean, where Britain's possessions still included strategically and commercially valuable colonies like Jamaica, Barbados, and Antigua. Economically and geopolitically, these colonies remained closely tied to the thirteen North American colonies that rebelled; however, they were also vitally important parts of the British Empire. As Edward Cox shows in his analysis of developments in the Caribbean in the 1790s, nearly constant military conflict between the principal European imperial powers perpetuated the region's character as a middle ground or "zone of war." Before the Revolution, Britain had been able to meet threats to its interests in the Caribbean by drawing heavily on the resources of North America. Shorn of this connection, West Indian planters were forced to respond to renewed war with revolutionary and Napoleonic France by mobilizing forces from within—including, significantly, military units made up of black freedmen and slaves, who were in turn able to begin making demands against the islands' longtime masters. Although the British Caribbean was spared the internecine racial conflict of Haiti, the geopolitical pressures bred by American independence and war with France made it impossible for white settlers to hold off the inexorable forces of black liberation indefinitely.

The American Revolution's other consequence for the British West Indies, as Trevor Burnard demonstrates, was to force its slaveholding elite to confront mounting abolitionist demands in Britain on its own. Before the Revolution, West Indians seeking to defend their right to traffic in human lives from metropolitan interference had been able to count on the assistance of like-minded colonists in Virginia and South Carolina. By seceding from the British Empire, Americans placed their erstwhile fellow-subjects in a far weaker position, leaving the way clear for British humanitarians to compel Parliament to abolish the slave trade and, ultimately, slavery itself. By the early nineteenth century, the British could once again boast of their empire of liberty, often in ways that trumped similar claims made by the republican empire that had supplanted it on the North American mainland. To substantiate this contentious point, Burnard draws on the experiences not just of the West Indies but of maritime Canada and Australia as well; however, it was in the Caribbean that British humanitarians scored their greatest victories. Although independence was not an option open to the smaller West Indian colonies, white Jamaicans might well have stood a better chance of preserving slavery had they elected to join the United States in 1776. In a centralizing imperial state, slave owners were far more vulnerable to abolitionist sentiment and mobilization than in a loose confederation of sovereign states.[37]

As an international event, the American Revolution thus sparked a series of transformations that were at least as far-reaching as the internal upheavals with which American historians today are most familiar. In the Revolution's wake, Britain continued to play the role of maritime hegemon; however, Britons and Americans alike increasingly thought of the Atlantic world, not as inherently imperial space but as a region that could be organized as a system of independent states, an international regime defined by free trade and the rule of law. As had been true of the pre-revolutionary Atlantic, the world created by the American Revolution remained shot through with contradictions. Among the more glaring was the way the Revolution's language of universal rights called into question the exploitation of blacks and Indians, even as the independence of the United States expanded opportunities for white Americans to continue subordinating the rights of such groups to their own happiness. Yet to acknowledge the ambiguity of the Revolution's international legacy is to admit its fundamental modernity, for in a very real sense it is a legacy with which we still live.

Part I / Reconstituting the Empire

CHAPTER ONE

Fears of War, Fantasies of Peace

British Politics and the Coming of the American Revolution

Eliga H. Gould

In recent years, scholars have devoted considerable attention to the growing consciousness of the English, Scots, and Welsh as a nation forged by nearly constant war with France. Based on a steady diet of warfare abroad and chauvinism at home, the British people developed a sense of unity so pervasive that—in Linda Colley's apt words—it appealed to "all classes" and "both sexes."[1] Little of the fighting in this epic struggle took place on English or (after 1746) British soil. Nonetheless, historians accept that the rivalry sparked by the Glorious Revolution (1689) unleashed a popular *rage militaire* that set the dominant tone in British politics into the nineteenth century, trumping Britain's geographical divisions and playing a crucial role in the nation's final triumph at Waterloo.

One would not want to underestimate the extent of such sentiments, let alone their larger significance, particularly in matters involving war with France. Yet not all Britons embraced the more enthusiastic varieties of patriotism. Despite Britain's notorious anti-Catholicism, both Anglicans and Dissenters occasionally voiced doubts over the morality of the nation's foreign adventures.[2] Another source of unease, especially for the poorest strata of British society, was war's prohibitive cost, whether in the form of economic dislocation, debilitat-ing taxes, or battlefield casualties.[3] Mindful that popular frenzy at home could be as politically disruptive as the hostile activities of external enemies, even Britain's rulers were sometimes reluctant to encourage the more virulent forms of patriotism.[4] Although rarely more than a subtext in the dominant strains of bellicosity, such concerns were never completely absent from public discourse. Indeed, on several occasions—notably in the years before the Peace of Utrecht (1713) and again at the close of the American Revolution—they assumed con-siderable importance, shaping popular opinion, influencing back-bench politi-cians, and dictating the actions of government.

The decade between the end of the Seven Years' War (1756–63) and onset of the American Revolution represented such a moment of political retrench-ment and moral self-scrutiny. Of course, to many Americans (then as now), the defining feature of British politics in the years before the Revolution more closely approximated confidence, even arrogance—what Jack Greene memo-rably called a "posture of hostility" toward any group foolish enough to defy a nation whose fleets and armies had vanquished its foes in every region of the world.[5] For all their cocksure certainty, however, the British saw their actions toward the colonies as fundamentally pacific. Not only did the government's apologists maintain that taxing the Americans was an inherently "moderate" policy—as Lord North assured the House of Commons in early 1775—but the king's ministers drew much of their support from the assumption that strengthening Westminster's imperial authority would bring lasting peace both to North America and, indirectly, to Europe and the rest of the Atlantic world.[6] The global conflict that resulted gave the lie to such notions. Still, Britain's actions throughout the imperial crisis were, at least in part, those of a war-weary nation, one whose leaders depicted their ill-fated colonial policies, not as a prelude to future hostilities, but as the best means for ensuring peace, pros-perity, and repose.

A Mighty Empire at Peace

Superficially, of course, the most conspicuous feature of Britain's mood in 1763 was not exhaustion but exhilaration. Although the war's burdens had been considerable, even ordinary men and women took an inordinate pride in the extent of Britain's triumph, with victories in Europe, West Africa, India, Canada, the Caribbean, and (following Spain's entry) the Philippines. Indeed, during the early 1760s, there were people who favored continuing the war until France and Spain had been stripped of all their colonial possessions. Among this group was John Wilkes, a hitherto obscure colonel in the Buckinghamshire Militia, who predicted in 1761 that Britain already stood to gain from its French conquests and that a "*Spanish* war" would not "impoverish this nation, because it must be a *naval* one; and all the charge of our navy is paid *to ourselves.*"[7] "Will any body then say," asked another writer, "that he wishes for a peace at this time?"[8] "Every conquest opens new views," remarked the future attorney general Sir James Marriott during the war's final year, "and the imagination already grasps the mines of Chile, Peru, and Mexico. What subjects for declamation! Every voice and every pen is employed to increase the national rage of perpetuating war."[9]

Beneath the surface of this "national rage," however, lurked a countervailing set of concerns over the martial fantasies spawned by Britain's success. Despite Marriott's allusion to perpetual war, these fears had a good deal to do with the one-sided terms upon which Britain seemed determined to make peace. In the words of a typically lavish statement, the nation's ultimate goal should be to compel France and Spain to "*sue*" for peace, which would enable the government, "with a feeling of humanity, and a true spirit becoming conquerors," to demand a settlement that would "reimburse our expences, and fix our security for EVER on a firm basis."[10] To many observers, ending the war on such harsh terms seemed certain to produce only resentment and a desire for revenge. "The having all of North-America . . . dazzles the eyes, and blinds the understanding," warned one commentator in 1761.[11] "The utmost rational Aim of our Ambition," concurred Edmund Burke's cousin William, should be "to possess a just Weight, and Consideration in *Europe.*" "The Power of the Nation should be rather respectable than terrible."[12] Some writers even worried that Britain was seeking the kind of hegemony in the Americas that people had long associated with France in Europe. As an observer cautioned during the war's final year:

We have changed Sides with that Power which we formerly opposed, in conjunction with the World; and the Descendant of *Lewis* XIV. may head a grand Alliance, in a Maritime League against the *British* Aspirer to universal Monarchy. The *Spaniard* hath already taken the Alarm, and wages open War against us: The *Dutch* have done enough to demonstrate their Disposition to do more: And *Britain,* the ancient Friend of *Europe,* hath scarcely now an Ally who will be hired to stand her Second in a Contest.[13]

Along with these fears over Britain's soaring ambition in the colonies, there was a widespread sense that the war in Germany, which was ostensibly about maintaining the European balance of power, had degenerated into a conflict Britain was fighting for the sole benefit of its allies, Prussia and Hanover. The latter, of course, was George II's birthplace, which he continued to govern in his capacity as a prince-elector of the Holy Roman Empire. As long as the aging king lived, this disposed many (if not all) Britons to help defend the electorate from a French invasion. However, with the accession in 1760 of George III, the first English-born monarch in over forty years and a prince who shared none of his grandfather's affection for Germany, there was little apparent reason to continue with this assistance. The same perceptions also weakened support for the Prussian alliance, which seemed to have become nothing but a means for subsidizing what one writer called the "insolence and arrogance" of its king, Frederick the Great.[14] "Our continental wars should not be immortal," wrote Benjamin Franklin's friend Israel Mauduit in 1761.[15] In the words of a history often attributed to Edmund Burke, events showed that Britain could gain neither real victory nor lasting peace from a German war, because "we waste our strength only to entangle ourselves further."[16]

Above all, people worried about the war's extraordinary costs. Not only were Britain's annual expenditures throughout the Seven Years' War more than twice that for the War of the Austrian Succession (1740–48), but they promised—in the words of one writer—to "load posterity, and leave immense debts on our poor children."[17] In particular, commentators voiced concerns about the war's long-term economic effects, with the Dean of Gloucester, Josiah Tucker, going so far as to suggest that the government of William Pitt and the Duke of Newcastle had "squandered" the national wealth bequeathed by the pacific ministry of Sir Robert Walpole. "Victory, like Charity," wrote Tucker, "coshereth a Multitude of Sins."[18] Despite the popularity of the war in America, England experienced recurring waves of domestic unrest, including riots over the price of grain (1756), the militia ballot (1757), and taxes on strong beer (1760) and cider (1763).[19] As Samuel Johnson remarked in his essay on the bravery of the English common soldier, "every man that crowds our streets is a man of honour, disdainful of obligation, impatient of reproach, and desirious of extending his reputation."[20] But that did not make the war's burdens any lighter or less real. "Ask the Farmer, the Hopp Planter, the Manufacturer, and Grazier," observed a writer during the war's final year, "and every one will tell you, that in some Cases they have been Sufferers."[21]

Notwithstanding the bellicosity of the popular press, apologists for the Earl of Bute, whose ministry negotiated the Peace of Paris (1763), thus insisted that Britain had compelling reasons to end the war upon terms that were both mild and just. Although Britain gained control of all of North America east of the Mississippi and several islands in the Caribbean, the settlement restored some of the war's most glittering prizes, including the French islands of Martinique and Guadeloupe and the Spanish strongholds of Havana and Manilla, the last of which Britain abandoned without demanding any compensation in return. The treaty also affirmed France's right to fish off the coast of Newfoundland and permitted it to resume trading at selected stations in India. These provisions were hardly enough to mollify France and Spain, but most Britons thought the peace a fair one. In the words of one writer, the settlement demonstrated the king's "Moderation and Christian Equanimity" by disavowing any measure that could "force the Enemy to such Extremities, as might soon have produced a fresh and more desperate War"; according to another, the peace was evidence of Britain's desire "to live in friendship with all mankind."[22] Significantly, the outcry with which news of the treaty was greeted in Parliament and the London press sprang, not from worries that its provisions were overly harsh, but from a sense that the government had made too many concessions in its effort to assuage the pride of France and Spain.

Despite its claims of moderation, of course, Britain still enjoyed a commanding position at the war's conclusion. There was a general hope that Britain's strategic dominance in both Europe and North America would dissuade the Bourbon powers from violating the settlement's terms, whatever desires for revenge they nursed in private. "What nation in Europe would think of commencing war with her?" wrote William Knox of Britain's international stature during the 1760s.[23] As another observer noted, "that nation is best circumstanced, whose internal strength and situation set her most above the reach of injury."[24] In the words of the old opposition Whig William Pulteney, Earl of Bath, Britons had every reason to hope that the nearly constant wars that had beset their nation since the Glorious Revolution were finally at an end:

> Our frontiers [in North America] . . . cannot be invaded by land, but by small parties of American savages whose power can easily be controlled; and if an enemy should threaten to invade our distant territories by sea, our floating fortresses are always ready to carry succours thither, and to retaliate the injuries of the invaders. While we therefore maintain our superiority at sea unrivalled,

our territories in America need not be looked upon as disjoined from Britain, and so long as they continue thus, we need not fear being over-toped [sic] by the great Russian empire, or any other power in Europe.[25]

Britain's actions during the 1760s gave ample evidence of its determination to capitalize on these advantages. These included taking a firm stand against threats like France's encroachments in the Bahamas (1764) and the Falkland Islands imbroglio with Spain (1770).[26] But the clearest indication of the government's priorities was its increased attention to the affairs of empire. Although, in time, Britain's actions would come to appear anything but moderate, statements in Parliament and the press made clear that the Royal Proclamation of 1763, the Sugar Act (1764), and even the American Stamp Act (1765) were all meant to signal a determination to make the recently concluded peace as beneficial and durable as possible. In a clear reference to the Whigs' long-standing preoccupation with Europe, Thomas Whately, Grenville's private secretary, explained that "there have been Ministers ignorant of the Importance of the Colonies; others, have impotently neglected their Concerns; and others again have been diverted by meaner Pursuits." The result had been a steady loss of imperial authority on the part of both the Crown and its colonial agents. By contrast, the policies adopted since the end of the Seven Years' War showed that Britain's "Real and Substantial" interests were "now preferred to every other Consideration."[27] In the concise words of another pamphlet on the new measures, Britons everywhere could rejoice at the government's desire to heal "the wounds of an exhausting war."[28]

To Britons who happened to reside in America, of course, Grenville's reforms were hardly cause for celebration. During the Stamp Act crisis, more than a few warned that Parliament's disregard for the fundamental right of no taxation without representation seemed designed, not to achieve peace, but to turn the recent victory over France into an occasion for transatlantic civil war. "I have been here above sixteen years," wrote an observer of the hostile response in Boston, "and I don't know of one single man but would risque his life and property to serve King George the Third." However, the writer cautioned, "touch our birth-right, and our body politick ... [will] do its utmost to shake it off."[29]

In putting forth such objections, American patriots highlighted the extent to which Bute's and Grenville's reforms reflected metropolitan—as opposed to colonial—perceptions of how Britain's empire ought to work. Where many Britons assumed that maintaining peace required a new measure of imperial centralization, Americans insisted on the need to preserve the empire's character as a looser consortium of partially self-governing provinces.[30] Yet even as they denounced the policies of the Bute and Grenville ministries, neither the Americans nor their metropolitan apologists denied the general rhetorical power of Britain as a mighty empire at peace, one held together by common ties of personal liberty, economic prosperity, and constitutional government. In the words of James Otis, Britain's hegemony in North America had laid the basis for the first benevolent "universal monarchy" in history, one founded on "principles of equity, moderation and justice."[31] "May the interest of *Great-Britain* and her colonies be ever united," concurred Richard Bland of Virginia, adding, "may [the colonists] enjoy the freedom, and other benefits of the *British* constitution, to the latest page in history!"[32] As the colonial patriot and London alderman Arthur Lee wrote in 1774:

> A State of contention between Great Britain and America, is not only disagreeable but dangerous. We have every influence of interest and affection to attach us to each other, and to make us wish to preserve the union indissoluble. The same laws, the same religion, the same constitution, the same feelings, sentiments and habits, are a common blessing and a common cause. We have these general benefits to defend against the rest of the world, which is hostile to all, or the greater part of them.[33]

Although all rejected the validity of Parliament's reforms, the desire to achieve lasting peace—and the belief that Britain's victories in the colonies had made it possible to achieve that goal—resonated as widely in America as it did in Britain.

A Needless Expense?

Where the British and Americans found it nearly impossible to agree was over whether securing this legacy required a standing army in the colonies. As people on both sides of the Atlantic knew, two of the most objectionable of Grenville's reforms, the Stamp Act and the American Mutiny Act (1765), were a direct result of the Crown's decision to leave ten thousand regulars in North America at the end of the Seven Years' War. As was clear from the army's general disposition—Quebec, Fort Niagara, Detroit, and the Floridas all had substantial garrisons—the government intended this force (at least initially) to occupy territory that had only recently been ceded by France and Spain and that in many places, especially the Ohio Valley, was still controlled by Indians hostile to Britain. To many colonists and their British friends, however, this peacetime establishment smacked of the same useless military expenditure that the recent war was supposed to have ended. In the words of the Massachusetts House of Representatives, Americans had always defended themselves, making "a standing army in the colonies a needless expence."[34] As colonial writers occasionally noted, the British had once shared their dislike of professional soldiers—a point John Dickinson underscored in 1774 by quoting a lengthy condemnation of standing armies that the father of General Thomas Gage, commander-in-chief of the British forces in America, had delivered in the House of Lords nearly forty years earlier.[35]

There were good reasons for Americans' confusion. To an earlier generation of writers—especially the Tory and Patriot Whig opponents of Sir Robert Walpole—the British government's ability to wage pointless wars and negotiate useless treaties in Europe depended heavily on the mesmerizing effects of a large standing army, a highly centralized system of excise taxation, and an ever-increasing public debt.[36] Of these, the army was by far the most dangerous.[37] In rhetoric that frequently echoed the British preoccupation with religious enthusiasm and superstition, the Whigs' opponents claimed to be deeply troubled by the regular army's beguiling pageantry, whereby the arcana of splendid uniforms and carefully executed maneuvers blinded the public to the waste of blood and treasure that was the professional soldier's real business.[38] It was no accident that *The Recruiting Officer* (1706)—George Farquar's enormously successful comedy, which reached the height of its popularity on the London stage during the 1750s—opens with Sergeant Kite (whose name denoted both a "high-flying" Tory and a cheat) reassuring the Shropshire crowd that his grenadier's cap, with its miter-like shape and Latin inscription, has "no Conjuration" or "Gunpowder-plot" in it.[39] In fact, the army's critics often seemed to regard the attributes of martial regalia with the same suspicion that most Britons reserved for the baroque trappings of Popery and absolutism. According to William Pulteney, the general practice of maintaining standing armies was a "fashion" that "first began in France."[40] Another observer likened the officers charged with commanding and administering the army to "high Priests and Augurs of State, who are so deeply skilled in Mysteries, as to be able to make great Discoveries both out of the Fights and Flights of Eagles and Vultures, the Cackling of Geese and Hens, the Entrails of sacrificed Calves, and the very Evolutions of the Smoke which Rises from the Altar."[41]

As Britain's wars with France demonstrated, fielding an army was also expensive. In order to pay the king's soldiers, the Treasury had been forced to develop fiscal institutions that enabled it to borrow sums far in excess of the annual revenue.[42] For the Whigs' admirers, the results of this "financial revolution" were often wondrous to behold, bestowing an almost miraculous capacity to wage war while spreading the costs over several generations.[43] As critics never tired of noting, however, the new instruments of credit fed the public appetite for Quixotic foreign adventures, which in turn greatly increased the bill that ordinary men and women would eventually have to pay. In the words of Jonathan Swift, the Whigs' unflagging support for their European allies during the wars against Louis XIV had swollen the public debt into a vast "artificial Structure." Because these funds lacked a "Foundation in the Hearts of the People," successive ministers had come to rely on the support of "Usurers" and "Stockjobbers," who were only too willing to lend whatever sums the government requested.[44] Even someone as suspicious of opposition polemic as the Scottish *literatus* David Hume warned that it was "very tempting" for a minister "to make a great figure" abroad by such destructive means.[45] In short, wrote another observer, the "artificial Wealth" of deficit finance had created "a monstrous expence, by which private men may indeed be gainers, but the Public must suffer deeply, though silently and imperceptibly."[46]

Underlying these fears of martial fantasy and war-induced poverty were apprehensions over the growing coercive power of the British state. Because both the army and the public debt were financed in large part with borrowed funds, there was always a danger (or so opponents claimed) that the general public would be lulled into a false sense of security, impervious to the threat that such institutions posed to their rights and liberties. As the Tories and Patriot Whigs constantly insisted, however, this was only because Britain's rulers had become "more careful"—in Lord Bolingbroke's revealing formulation—not "more honest." To the Tory historian Thomas Carte, the practice of lifetime enlistment turned soldiers in the army's lower ranks into "a sort of Slaves," which in turn "tempted [them] to look with Envy on the Freedom of all about them."[47] The *Craftsman* made the same point, comparing the experience of service in the army to "being chained down, like the Slaves in *America*, to drudge in the same Mine for Life."[48] Soldiers themselves frequently complained of incidents like the Oxford riot of 1716, where crowds threw dirt at the king's troops, broke the windows of their quarters, and called them "Round-Heads."[49] Given the military's unsavory reputation, wrote William

Pulteney in 1742, people were bound to conclude that there was "little Difference between being oppressed by a Standing Army of Natives [and] a Standing Army of Foreigners."[50]

In questioning the government's plans for a standing army in the colonies,
Americans were thus drawing on a legacy with deep roots in British political
culture. It was, however, also a legacy that no longer possessed quite the reso-
nance with the metropolitan public that it once had. Although the British subjects of George III continued to view redcoats and excisemen with suspicion,
such attitudes increasingly reflected unease over the specific purposes to which
Britain's military and fiscal bureaucracies were put, rather than discomfort
with the bureaucracies themselves. Indeed, the end of the Seven Years' War produced a spate of pronouncements on the army as "a school of great and glorious achievements," as the ministerial apologist William Guthrie wrote in
1764.[51] Even the government's opponents claimed to respect the "candour,
publick spirit, and knowlege" of the military establishment.[52] Writers occasionally exclaimed at the way people had been "amazingly" reconciled to "having a far more numerous Body of regular Troops . . . than any true Lover of his
Country in former Times thought could be allowed without endangering the
Constitution."[53] To a broad swath of the British public, however, the army's
new respectability seemed unexceptional. "The Duty of a soldier is honourable
and honest," wrote the author of a military treatise from the late 1750s. "None
are distinguished, none honoured, none recompenced but the man of Worth,
who regulates his Duty by *Religion, Humanity,* and *Justice.*"[54]

Several factors contributed to this change in attitudes, among them the
growing number of landed gentlemen in the army's upper ranks, the effectiveness of professional troops in keeping the domestic peace, and the presence of
current and former officers among the Whigs' opponents in Parliament. More
than anything else, though, the army's new image was the result of two developments, both related to Pitt's prosecution of the Seven Years' War. The first
was the English Militia Act of 1757, which enabled the government to raise
nearly thirty thousand men for home defense between 1759 and 1762. Although
the Whigs' opponents had long envisioned reviving England's moribund
county militia as a way to rid the country of professional soldiers, Pitt and his
allies took care to mute any lingering antipathy toward Britain's "national
troops," insisting that the semiprofessional force would complement the army,
not replace it. Insofar as the old animus against standing armies remained part
of the new measure, it was directed toward the Court Whigs' practice of

deploying European auxiliaries on English soil—what one writer termed "the precarious assistance of foreigners," as opposed to "the natural support" of natives.[55] But the king's ministers ensured that the reformed militia resembled nothing so much as a "second standing army," with rules and regulations that mirrored those of the king's regular forces. In the words of the English jurist Richard Burn, the militia was best seen, not as a repudiation of a professional army, but as the domestic component of a tripartite imperial establishment: "Our navy will preserve our superiority at sea; our army [will] maintain and extend our conquests abroad; and our Militia [will] be sufficient to frustrate any attacks that may be made by invasions or rebellions."[56]

The upshot was a force that appeared to answer a longstanding demand of Walpole's opponents but that also compelled English gentlemen and commoners alike to adopt the practices of an institution many still distrusted. As the destructive militia riots of 1757 demonstrated, the prospect of serving in the new county regiments was not nearly as popular as supporters of the reform claimed.[57] Nor did the militia enjoy the unqualified support of the army—as was evident from incidents like the dispute over the town watch at Stamford, during which a regular officer stabbed a corporal in the Lincolnshire Militia with his "espontoon."[58] Despite such conspicuous problems, however, the three years that the militia spent under canvass, starting in the summer of 1759, gradually fostered greater familiarity with the customs and procedures of the king's regular forces, and with that familiarity came a growing respect. "The more we consider ourselves as a Part of the Army," wrote an officer in the Wiltshire Militia in 1760, "the more Likelihood there is that a Harmony should subsist between us."[59] The author of *The Complete Militia-Man* (1760) made the same point, urging officers in the militia to cultivate the same "coolness, or insensibility of danger" as their compatriots in the army.[60] In the words of George Townshend and William Windham's influential *Plan of Discipline for the Norfolk Militia* (1759), which appeared in at least nine separate American editions between 1768 and 1774, "there are many of our military gentlemen, and some of them of high rank, who study the sublime branches of their profession with genius and application."[61] Such statements belied the animus that many Britons still felt toward professional soldiers. Nonetheless, taken together, the public reception of Pitt's militia signaled a growing sense of the army as an ordinary, if not entirely welcome, feature of British political life.

The other reason for the army's growing acceptability was the role that it played in Britain's victory in North America. Between 1757 and 1761, the size of the combined British and Irish establishment in the colonies rose to more than thirty thousand effectives, eclipsing any previous commitment of regular troops in America and even exceeding the fifteen to twenty thousand provincials that served annually on behalf of the individual colonies.[62] Walpole's opponents had often attributed the use of professional soldiers to Britain's involvement in Europe, occasionally suggesting that a king who concentrated on trade and empire might dispense with such forces altogether. By contrast, sending troops to America showed that the army was good for more than fighting pointless battles on "the plains of Flanders."[63] In a typical rendition, a panegyric to the Earl of Loudoun, who commanded the British forces in America in 1756 and 1757, depicted the imperious Scot's departure for New York as taking him on a daring voyage "Far from the silky Sons of soft Delight, / Where Folly-Fools disseminate; / Far from Debauchery's intemp'rate Night, / And flutt-ring Joys effeminate."[64] General James Wolfe, the slain conqueror of Quebec, was an especially compelling symbol of the army's transformation. "Oh! how glorious, how immortal is the Man, who thus parts with his Life in his Country's Cause!" intoned William Beckford's Tory (and pro-Pitt) journal, *The Monitor*: "A *Marlborough* and an *Eugene* have left us many Examples of *British* Conduct and Valour in time of War; but this one Act of General WOLFE has added more Lustre to the *British* Crown, and done more Service to his Country, than all the Sieges and Battles won by these brave Generals."[65]

If professional soldiers held the key to victory, many Britons assumed they were also essential to guaranteeing a lasting peace. Here, the most striking feature was the army's discipline and professionalism, which critics had long claimed to find so disturbing. In its tribute to Wolfe, the *Annual Register* listed among the general's principal virtues the "unwearied assiduity" with which he studied the "profession of arms" in the peacetime army of George II and the Duke of Cumberland.[66] Similarly, the panegyric on Lord Loudoun's departure for America cast him as an experienced commander whose disciplined example would encourage political unity among colonists weakened by faction, excessive luxury, and dependence on African slavery.[67] Indeed, to many writers, having a large body of regulars in the colonies appeared crucial to the stability of Britain's empire, both during the Seven Years' War and in its aftermath. Benjamin Franklin's proposal that the colonies' peacetime defense be left in the hands of provincial troops elicited several statements to this effect.[68] In the words of one respondent, a permanent establishment would ensure that the defense of Britain's new "frontiers" remained in the hands of "persons of abilities and disinterestedness"; another even suggested that withdrawing the regular army from North America would lay the basis for colonial independence, in fact if not in law.[69] As an anonymous officer explained in one of the few British pamphlets to anticipate the depth of American feelings against the new measures, there were numerous reasons to keep professional troops in the colonies, including the presence of nearly a hundred thousand "Roman Catholicks" in Canada—"enthusiastick, bigotted, and superstitious, in proportion to their Ignorance"; an equal number of Indians, whose "natural Barbarism" had been made worse by "the Horrors of *French* Christianity"; and several million colonists, who (despite occasional suggestions to the contrary) depended on British soldiers "for their Security and Defence."[70]

To some observers, of course, the decision to leave so many soldiers in America indicated that government's intentions were anything but peaceful and that it regarded the Peace of Paris as little more than an "armed truce," as William Pitt (now out of office) assured the House of Commons.[71] In the words of David Hartley's enormously popular pamphlet, *The Budget* (1764), expanding the army only made sense if one considered the peace settlement "hollow and unlikely to be permanent."[72] Yet Hartley did not challenge the general practice of maintaining a standing army, and many other figures—including, significantly, Pitt himself—hoped an enlarged establishment would dissuade France and Spain from avenging their losses.[73] The metropolitan literature of the early 1760s betrayed a discernible sense that having regular soldiers in North America would provide a far more durable peace than provincial troops, who were widely perceived as ill-disciplined, unreliable, and inclined to acts of barbarism. According to one writer, the colonists had "already shewn themselves incompetent, in never producing any one general plan for [their own defense] from the peace of Utrecht to the war of 1756."[74] "In this age," wrote another author, "all the kingdoms in Europe maintain a standing military force"; therefore, in order to ensure that France and Spain respected the recent peace settlement, "America must have a considerable share" of such forces too.[75] There were even colonists—among them James Otis and Daniel Dulany—who conceded the need for regular troops (though not parliamentary taxation).[76] As John Dickinson observed in his *Letters from a Farmer in Pennsylvania* (1768), Britain's military and fiscal policies, despite their pernicious effects, "seemed to have something gentle and kind in [their] intention, and to aim only *at our welfare*."[77] In the words of William Knox, "the colonies would never be permitted to live in peace" unless Britain assumed the chief responsibility for their defense.[78]

By the close of the Seven Years' War, the peacetime maintenance of professional troops had thus come to seem both necessary and normal. With this momentous development came an equally far-reaching shift in attitudes toward the other two attributes of Britain's military-fiscal state: deficit finance and permanent taxation. To the colonists, the insistence on parliamentary taxation without representation seemed like an inexplicable act of madness—what a student essayist at the College of Philadelphia called "a fatal, undescerning [sic] policy."[79] From the standpoint of the metropolitan public, however, the true madness lay in the notion that any part of the British Empire might benefit from the government's protection without paying taxes levied in Parliament to help with the costs. Although Americans contributed to the British revenue through their compliance with the Navigation Acts, many Britons argued that this was, at best, an indirect form of taxation, which fell short of the direct payments that the advent of a standing army had turned into an unavoidable duty for the king's subjects in England, Scotland, and Wales. Furthermore, the massive scale of Britain's debt, over "fifty millions" of which had been spent "to defend America" (according to James Scott, writing as "Anti-Sejanus" in the *London Chronicle*), ensured that ordinary men and women at home would have to assume whatever costs the colonists refused to bear.[80] "Great-Britain is sufficiently exhausted already," declared a typical metropolitan writer during the mid-1760s. "She has spilt plenty of her blood in [the colonies'] cause, she has expended many millions in their service, and has by these means contracted an immense load of debt, of which she is never likely to be eased. Must she then expire under her pressure?"[81]

Although only a rhetorical question, it was a revealing one. Where Americans detected in Grenville's reforms a continuation of the metropolitan penchant for empty gestures and useless expense, the British saw measures that were as necessary as they were just. Indeed, to many Britons, allowing the colonists to have the security of regular troops without paying taxes for their support threatened to turn their overseas empire into a dysfunctional confederation of semi-autonomous states not unlike Poland, the Netherlands, and the Holy Roman Empire. In the revealing words of George Grenville, the nation's North American colonies seemed to think of themselves as "independent communities in alliance with us and only governed by the same Prince as Hanover is."[82] Of course, for a growing number of radicals on both sides of the Atlantic, establishing such a confederation seemed entirely desirable; it would be what the British naval officer John Cartwright called a "perpetual league . . . for the preservation of that warm affection and harmony which ought ever to subsist between a mother-country and her offspring."[83] There was no denying the humanity in this idealized vision. Still, those who doubted the affectionate tendencies of imperial confederations needed to look no further than the ill will spawned by Britain's "perpetual league" with the ruling family's native German electorate. Even more alarming, in many respects, was the conflict-ridden example of Germany. As William Allen reminded English readers in 1774, "the Empire of *Germany*" had been "divided and dismembered" during the seventeenth century along much the same lines as Americans were proposing for the British Empire: "What is now the Consequence? Why, the King of *Prussia*, alone, is not only independent of the imperial Crown, but almost able to give Law to his master!"[84]

If the British Empire were to devolve into such a loose-knit confederation, France and Spain would soon be tempted to avenge their recent losses, and the British people would end up subsidizing the colonists in the same way that they had funded the German allies of George II, as well as their own over-large ambitions. Given this prospect, the nation's only hope for lasting "safety" was to ensure "the union and dependence of the colonies," as Charles Lloyd reminded British readers in 1767.[85]

A War for "Amity and Love"

The idea that the colonial policies of the 1760s and the early 1770s would foster peace turned out to be deeply mistaken, even fantastic. Indeed, the American Revolution ultimately showed just how difficult it was to escape the illusions spawned by imperial greatness. "History proves, that great conquests have always been ruinous to free governments," lamented Alexander Carlyle in 1776. "Was it for us," he asked his congregation at Inveresk, "to extend our dominions from pole to pole, and to all the shores that are washed by the Indian or Atlantic oceans?"[86] Adam Smith was even more pointed, noting in *Wealth of Nations* (1776) that the metropolitan inhabitants of an imperial power like Britain often felt so little inconvenience from foreign wars that they became addicted to "reading in the newspapers the exploits of their own fleets and armies" and dreaded the return of peace.[87] In the words of Richard Price, Britain had squandered "a situation of honour and dignity never before known amongst mankind," all because its rulers—and, by implication, its people—were not content "with a degree of power, sufficient to satisfy any reasonable ambition."[88]

Although the pacific expectations fostered by the Seven Years' War proved illusory, they were not inconsequential. Historians have long recognized the decade before the Revolution as marking the origin of the great humanitarian movements that helped define the subsequent phase of Britain's imperial epoch: abolition, free trade, and the administrative reform of British India. Each of these initiatives sprang from its own sources, yet all partook of a common desire to purge Britain's empire of what Richard Watson, bishop of Landaff, called the use of "unjust force."[89] "He that admits no right but force," wrote Thomas Day in condemning the slave trade, "arms every man against himself, and justifies all excesses."[90] William Bolts used nearly identical terms in his discussion of the administration of justice in Bengal, urging that "despotism and arbitrary violence are not more pernicious to individuals than they are unpropitious to trade."[91] In neither Africa nor Asia did the absence of peace threaten to involve Britain in another European war, as hostilities in North America clearly did. Still, the same pacific hopes that had informed George Grenville's misguided reforms continued to animate imperial policy, even as the full extent of Britain's folly in America became apparent.

But of the various effects produced by Britain's quest for peace, none was more striking—or ironic—than the part it played in fueling the arrogance and sense of superiority that ultimately governed metropolitan views of the American Revolution. Although the North ministry's decision in early 1775 to use force was obviously a hostile act, the government insisted to the very end that it was engaged, not in a war of conquest or ambition, but in a struggle for what the Carlisle Peace Commission called "the blessings of peace" and "domestic security."[92] In the words of East Apthorp, vicar of Croydon, Britain was fighting for the day "when England and her Colonies shall be reunited in the golden chain of amity and love, by an equitable system of government and dependence, of reciprocal commerce, aid, and protection."[93] Such claims were never allowed to go unchallenged, either in Parliament or among the wider public. Nonetheless, the idea that Britain was contending for peace helps explain both why so many men and women supported the decision to commence of hostilities in 1775 and why it took nearly eight years for a majority to change their minds.

CHAPTER TWO

The First Union

Nationalism versus Internationalism in the American Revolution

David C. Hendrickson

This chapter is an inquiry into the nature of the union established in the first years of American independence. That is, of course, an old topic: though over-shadowed, and often made subordinate to, the question of the nature of the "more perfect union" proposed by the Federal Convention in 1787, it is one that has attracted a considerable amount of attention from historians. The result is a "new orthodoxy" regarding the formation of the union, holding that a "national government was in operation before the formation of the states," that the Continental Congress was organized "with the consent of the people acting directly in their primary, sovereign capacity," and that the Union was "spontaneously formed by the people of the United States." The states, according to this view, did not create the Union; instead, "the separate States, possessing a limited or internal sovereignty," were "a creation of the Continental Congress, which preceded them in time and brought them into being."[1] This "nationalist" interpretation is compelling because it provides a pedigree—and explanation—for the new nation's subsequent development. Unfortunately, as I will show, it is mistaken.

My objection to the nationalist theory is not to the conclusion, but rather to the historical premises: as history, it constitutes a vast anachronism in which the needs, language, and aspirations of later periods of American history have been imposed on an earlier epoch. In these accounts, as indeed in most narratives of founding and "national development," there is an inveterate tendency to confuse the acorn with the oak, or to find in 1776 a full-grown sentiment of nationalism that was in fact very long in the making. The new orthodoxy fails to explain the sense of anxiety and peril that accompanied the writing and ratification of the Articles of Confederation, and radically underestimates the enormous difficulties that had to be overcome in making a union of any kind.

It is difficult for contemporary Americans to disassociate a federal system from a strong central government, and the term has almost entirely lost its formerly close association with diplomacy and international order. In 1776, the case was otherwise. A federal tie meant an arrangement distinctly contrary to a centralized national government, and was rather used at the juncture of the worlds of constitutionalism and diplomacy. The federative power, as Locke had defined it, concerned those powers of war and peace, of treaty and alliance that commonwealths needed in their transactions with other states; the formal compacts among equal parties resulting from the exercise of this power—written constitutions, treaties, alliances—were things to which the adjective "federal" might apply.[2] When Adam Smith called for a "federal union" between Britain and America, he meant a relationship founded on equal respect and mutual interest, and by the explicit renunciation by Britain of its authority over the colonies.[3]

At the root of the federal principle, as then conceived, was the idea of a covenant or *foedus* (its etymological root). This and "synonymous ideas of promise, commitment, undertaking, or obligating, vowing and plighting one's word," as S. Rufus Davis has suggested, were joined together with two other things: "the idea of cooperation, reciprocity, mutuality," and "the need for some measure of predictability, expectation, constancy, and reliability in human relations."[4] Today, "internationalism" or "multilateralism" would be the terms used to describe the application of these values to interstate relations. Though those words were unknown to the political vocabulary in 1776 (as, in fact, was "nationalism"), the phenomenon or aspiration they describe was well known. Statesmen who sought to instantiate such values in the world of states spoke instead of the construction of a "federative system" or a "federal union."

Whereas the idea of the nation suggested a certain homogeneity (all Americans were different from Europe in certain basic respects), the idea of the union suggested heterogeneity or the reconciliation of difference. Everyone realized that if they were to have a national character, they had to have the union; the union, in turn, rested on the consent of the states, as the authority of the states rested on the consent of their people. The union was more than a means, but at the same time it had to be a means—that is, an instrument by which states and sections might achieve their goals—if it were to be successful.

While loyalties to particular states, a basic division between the eastern and the southern states, and a felt need of the union as a fundamental necessity were all present at the very outset, the experience of war and revolution, which forced them to work together in all sorts of unprecedented ways, also had vital effects on the way this cluster of identities, loyalties, and interests was understood. It not only forced them—really for the first time—to "think continentally," producing in some the sentiments of nationalism and in most a keen sense of "the safety of the Union" as a fundamental desideratum of policy; it also confirmed the historic sense of particularism founded on loyalty to individual states and produced a much sharper sense of the political meaning of America's regional diversity, in particular a deepened sense of the division between the northern and the southern states.

The Federal Imperative

Federal norms came readily to American revolutionaries because of the American experience in the British Empire. The concluding phase of their constitutional argument, defining the terms of their membership within the empire, bore closely on the opening phase of their attempt to define their relationship among themselves. When the colonies revolted, they did so on the basis of the constitutional claim that their colonial assemblies and Parliament were equal legislative authorities within an empire held together by allegiance to a common king. The colonial case against Great Britain, as Adams later summarized it, was that King and Parliament had torn up "thirteen solemn and sacred Compacts under which a Wilderness has been subdued and cultivated."[5] In the Whig view, the people with whom those sacred compacts had been made remained in existence and were now joining together, through the states of which they were a part, to vindicate the rights that those compacts had recognized. Nor was this position a sudden inspiration. They claimed in 1774 what John Dickinson had claimed for them in 1767: "the same rights, that all free states have, of judging when their privileges are invaded, and of using all prudent measures for preserving them."[6]

That they constituted themselves in 1774 and 1775 as a "Congress" rather than a Parliament was not adventitious. "Congress" was a diplomatic term, signifying an assembly of states or nations, such as Westphalia or Utrecht, in which no state was understood in the law of nations as binding itself by its mere appearance: it would be obligated only to the extent it agreed to be obligated.[7] "We have no coercive or legislative Authority," said Edward Rutledge of South Carolina in the first meeting of the Congress. "Our Constituents are bound only in Honour, to observe our Determinations."[8] Even in diplomatic assemblies, of course, to be a minority may require acquiescence from a practical standpoint, and other states do not need a legislative authority to exert pressure on isolated malcontents. (Commercial boycott and the granting or withholding of recognition are among the instruments they may employ.) Nevertheless, the rule of unanimity does confer a blocking power on recalcitrants, and the delegates to Congress recognized that this was the rule they were obliged to follow. The "great, unwieldy body" of America, in Adams's words, was "like a large fleet sailing under convoy. The fleetest sailors must wait for the dullest and slowest."[9]

In the months leading up to the declaration, the voices urging caution, led by John Dickinson, began insisting that agreement on union was necessary before considering either independence or foreign alliance. Those pushing for an immediate declaration, like Adams, did not deny that "the natural Course and order of things" was to institute new governments in the states, form a union, declare independence, and seek foreign help, with each step in the sequence a plighting of faith vital for the subsequent avowal. They argued, instead, that it was impossible to observe the proper sequence. "We Shall be obliged," Adams told Henry, "to declare ourselves independent States before We confederate, and indeed before all the Colonies have established their Governments."[10]

By assumptions not terribly implausible, it was in fact possible to argue a kind of logical precedence for each of the steps the Whigs wanted to take. Faced with this Gordian knot, Congress boldly cut through it by in effect waiving the question of precedence and agreeing to do all four things together and at once. That was the essential meaning of the triple resolution calling for independence, foreign alliances, and confederation introduced by Richard Henry Lee in early June 1776, followed shortly thereafter (June 12) by the appointment of committees to consider each of these three subjects, and then (on June 15) by the call to the states to new model their governments.

The realization that these things would have to be done together dawned simultaneously in Philadelphia and Williamsburg, and when Adams recalled, late in life, how "thirteen clocks were made to strike together," he doubtless remembered his elation on learning of the coincidence.

> The colonies had grown up under constitutions so different, there was so great a variety of religions, they were composed of so many different nations, their customs, manners, and habits had so little resemblance, and their intercourse had been so rare, and their knowledge of each other so imperfect, that to unite them in the same principles in theory and the same system of action, was certainly a very difficult enterprise. The complete accomplishment of it, in so short a time and by such simple means, was perhaps a singular example in the history of Mankind.[11]

This well describes the kind of unity that Americans possessed in 1776, something very inadequately conveyed by later ideas of "the nation." Their unity expressed itself not in their similarities—they were, on the contrary, profoundly conscious of their differences—but in their commitment to the same principles of government, their common detestation of the British ministry, and their deep-seated fear of the consequences of disunion.

This meeting of the minds led directly to the Declaration of Independence. "When in the course of human events," ran the preamble, "it becomes necessary for one people to dissolve the political bands which have connected them with another, and to assume among the powers of the earth the separate & equal station to which the laws of nature and of nature's God entitle them, a decent respect to the opinions of mankind requires that they should declare the causes which impel them to the separation." After stating those causes in the body of the document, it was declared in the conclusion, in the name of

> the representatives of the United States of America in General Congress assembled, . . . and by the authority of the good people of these colonies . . . that these united colonies are & of right ought to be free & independent states; that they are absolved from all allegiance to the British crown, and that all political connection between them & the state of Great Britain is, & ought to be, totally dissolved; & that as free & independent states they have full power to levy war, conclude peace, contract alliances, establish commerce & do all other acts & things which independent states may of right do.[12]

It seems most improbable that the author of those lines, Thomas Jefferson, intended with this language to constitute such a single body politic; the conclusion seems wholly inconsistent with everything we know about his characteristic mode of constitutional reasoning. It is nevertheless the case that alongside these free and independent states now possessing full and unvarnished sovereignty there was also the claim that Americans constituted, in some sense, a single people. So, too, it was the case that these states were now solemnly pledged to secure their independence in common. Could they now claim in good faith that they were free to go it alone? If not, was their sovereignty not thus sharply qualified at the outset? Whatever the right interpretation is (and what, after all, is an "is"?), it seems clear enough that the delegates in Congress were not then looking to the declaration to discover the proper relationship between the union and the states. It was in the committee on the confederation established for this purpose in June 1776, that congressmen would begin the task of defining the nature and hammering out the terms of their continental connection.

Jefferson would recall, late in life, that the Declaration of Independence was the fundamental act of union of these states.[13] It would probably be more accurate to say that the declaration was the fundamental act that committed Americans to making the union of the states; certainly by itself it could not resolve the ambiguities inherent in both disuniting from Britain and uniting amongst themselves.[14] Because the terms of union had not been reached, July 4, 1776, may perhaps best be regarded not as their day of betrothal but as their night of forbidden passion, a glorious consummation to the warm embraces of the previous two years but an act that fell short of a regular marriage. The final line of the declaration was a pledge that they would see each other through the making of the union and the winning of independence, but it was not an achievement of either. In a technical sense, therefore, they were living in sin. If the fond hope of British strategists was to catch these Americans *in flagrante delicto*—that is, without the union—American Whigs were just as determined to proceed rapidly to the formalization of their vows.

Toward Confederation

Many of the formative acts of "the united States," as this association was often styled in the first years of the war, can be taken as defiant answers to charges leveled against the colonies during the imperial crisis. British and Loyalist writers had predicted that the new republican governments, shorn of the monarchical and aristocratic elements that gave balance to the British constitution, would

end up making citizens less free than subjects.[15] As they drafted their state constitutions, Americans sought to show the contrary. Hostile commentators had
also argued that the former colonies would be incapable of maintaining their
independence and would soon find themselves in the thrall of the French
monarchy.[16] The development of an American foreign policy that sought peace
and commerce with all nations, and entangling alliances with none, was an
answer to that charge. But the charge of charges—the mother of all accusa-
tions—was that the colonies would fall out amongst themselves if independent. If this analysis were sound, there was little likelihood that the American
states could either sustain free governments or maintain an independent foreign policy. Most Britons found the idea of a durable American union very
nearly absurd. Josiah Tucker and Adam Smith prophesied the disunion of the
American states; republicans like Richard Price feared it; the old Whigs urged
it as a complaint against the North ministry; and ministers made it the basis of
their policy. In 1776, as David Ramsay recalled two years later, "Our enemies
seemed confident of the impossibility of our union; our friends doubted it; and
all indifferent persons, who judged of things present, by what has heretofore
happened, considered the expectation thereof as romantic."[17]

Indebtedness to prior experience was manifest in the nature of the union that
emerged from a committee of the Congress in July 1776. Though the Articles of
Confederation were immediately weakened on their submission to Congress,
above all in the loss of the provision that gave Congress the authority to cut off
the extravagant claims of the landed colonies, its basic character changed very
little in the sixteen months that elapsed from the first draft of June 1776 to its
submission to the states in November 1777. As a firm league of friendship into
which the states severally entered, the Articles proposed a division of authority
between Congress and the states that closely resembled the allocation that
Americans had previously seen in the constitution of the British empire. That
mixture of executive, judicial, and "federative" powers, which, in the American
theory, had belonged to king and council, were now basically given to "the
united states in congress assembled"; those powers that belonged to the legislatures of the provincial colonies passed to the newly founded states.[18]

In the traditional theory of the British constitution, the king enjoyed the
powers of war and peace and of making alliances that Locke had identified with
the "federative power." This authority was vested in Congress under the Articles, which excluded the states from everything touching on foreign relations.
By the same token, the arrangement the Americans made among themselves

displayed the same dependence on the provincial legislatures that they thought had characterized the constitution of the British empire. While Congress was to propose, the states were to dispose. They were under both a legal and a moral obligation to fulfill these requests—so long, at least, as others performed their part of the bargain—and in that sense the obligation was weightier than that of the colonial assemblies to the king and his representatives. But if in this respect the Congress under the Articles enjoyed more authority than the king, in other respects it enjoyed less. Unlike king and council, Congress had no general veto power over the acts of provincial institutions. Unlike king and council, it could not sustain any claim to the ungranted lands that lay within the charters of the landed colonies.

Though it is customary to see the Articles as a precursor to the federal Constitution of 1787, and though they did mark out an allocation of authority similar in vital respects to that of 1787, it is misleading to describe "the united states in congress assembled" as a "national government." It had no distinct executive, judicial, or legislative departments, though congressmen would soon enough appreciate the need for them. As a "deliberating Executive assembly," as Thomas Burke precisely described it, Congress had to combine the secrecy of executive deliberation and the courtesies of parliamentary bodies, and this caused much inconvenience and confusion.[19] That it was a committee and not a king, while enjoying kingly responsibilities, gave it a peculiar, anomalous character, especially if seen from the perspective of 1787.[20] Americans, nevertheless, did have a closely held theory as to why it should work. In the decade before independence, the colonists had repeatedly claimed that they were willing to support any fair and reasonable request from the Crown, and had acknowledged the importance of the superintending role that king and council played in settling boundary disputes and in organizing united action. In the American interpretation—and particularly that of Massachusetts and Virginia—colonial troops, raised in this fashion, had played a valuable, even critical, role in the great victory over France in 1763. The American "narrative" of these events, it might be said, was both partial and inflated, but it was theirs, and it was not without supporting evidence: they *had* contributed, Parliament *had* reimbursed them; the war *had* been won. As they formed their new union, the revolutionaries had the opportunity to show that their theory of the imperial constitution had been workable, and that such an association could be run effectively on the basis of the faithful cooperation of the contracting states. They could not make their own union on the principle that such cooperation would not succeed without severely undercutting much of what they had been saying to the British over the past decade.

Historians have often misconstrued what happened to the draft Confederation in its progress through Congress. Most authorities place an altogether implausible emphasis on Thomas Burke's amendment of April 1777, which provided that "Each state retains its sovereignty, freedom, and independence, and every Power, Jurisdiction, and right, which is not by this confederation expressly delegated to the United States, in Congress assembled."[21] The amendment, in fact, was supremely unimportant, and simply re-stated the conventional understanding of the Congress with respect to the sources and limits of congressional authority. That is why it was approved with near unanimity. The amendment did not diverge significantly from Adams's understanding in *Thoughts on Government,* that the authority of the continental councils should be "sacredly confined" to certain objects, for this certainly presumed a whole and entire sovereignty in whatever had not been granted.[22] Burke's emphatic language added nothing of substance to the paragraph (Article II in the Dickinson draft) that had defined the association as a "firm league of friendship" into which the states severally entered. Burke's invocation of the states' sovereignty, freedom, and independence was in no way contrary to the essential character of the "firm league of friendship" as it was understood in public law. This was the language of Burlamaqui, Vattel, Pufendorf, and Montesquieu, who each had written in a similar vein: "A number of sovereign and independent states," as Vattel put it, "may unite to form a perpetual confederation, without individually ceasing to be perfect States. Together they will form a confederate republic. Their joint resolutions will not impair the sovereignty of the individual members, although its exercise may be somewhat restrained by reason of voluntary agreements. The obligation to fulfill agreements one has voluntarily made does not detract from one's liberty and independence."[23]

The formula in Article II did not clear up all confusion about what belonged to Congress and what belonged to the states, and indeed every month seemed to bring a new and unexpected twist on that familiar problem. But Burke's amendment brought no such clarification either. It did not reach those powers that had been granted, and it took an inordinate faith in the force of the word "expressly" to believe that it would confound those who wished to probe the implications of those grants. In fact, supporters of an expanded authority in the Congress would always reason downward from the specific and ample grants of authority allotted to Congress under the Confederation. Burke himself acknowledged the legitimacy of that approach when he wrote that "the United States ought to be as One Sovereign with respect to foreign Powers, in all things that relate to War or where the States have one Common Interest."[24] The obstacle to any effective expansion of congressional power, as subsequent events would show, had nothing to do with Burke's amendment, and everything to do with the provision requiring the unanimous consent of all thirteen states for an amendment to the Articles to take effect. That provision, however, existed in all the drafts of the Confederation from July 1776 to November 1777.

Representation and Union

Neither the absence of a power of taxation over individuals, nor the absence, more generally, of a power of compulsion, nor even its status as a "firm league of friendship," reached the real source of disagreement that the committee report met with on its presentation to Congress. Those disagreements centered instead on the equities of the arrangement as they were to be established in the related provisions for representation, control of the western lands, and the quota of contribution. The first great blows in this controversy were struck in the heated exchanges that occurred in the summer of 1776; the lines of the controversy were identical to those that, a decade later, almost tore apart the Philadelphia Convention. The bitterness of these debates has often led historians to the conclusion that the confederation as proposed had no expounders, only critics. That is not so, however, for the committee draft found an able defender in John Witherspoon of New Jersey.[25]

Witherspoon noted the unanimous opinion that union was an absolute necessity in the achievement of independence; even those "who have expressed their fears or suspicions of the existing confederacy proving abortive, have yet agreed in saying that there must and shall be a confederacy for the purposes of, and till the finishing of this war." Witherspoon did not deny that "from the nature of men, it is to be expected, that a time must come when it will be dissolved and broken in pieces," but hardly accounted that a sufficient reason for not aiming at permanent union. If it were impossible to reach agreement now, "when the danger is yet imminent," it would be madness to suppose it might be done thereafter, when the sense of common danger had slackened.

Witherspoon had no monopoly on the belief that one of the greatest dangers the colonies faced was of "treachery among themselves, augmented by bribery and corruption from our enemies," though he made this danger serve the interests of the smaller states. If the consequence of their independence from Great Britain would be to subject them "to the power of one or more of the strongest or largest of the American states," they had every incentive to withdraw from the confederacy. Would not those states, Witherspoon asked, "prefer putting themselves under the protection of Great Britain, France, or Holland, rather than submit to the tyranny of their neighbors, who were lately their equals?" It was no argument that these "rash engagements" might issue in "their own destruction"; the "mixture of apprehended necessity and real resentment" might nevertheless produce that result. The small states knew that "the subject states of republics, have been of all others the most grievously oppressed." The same arguments "which we have so often used against Great Britain" were equally applicable to the subjection of the small states by the larger.

The peroration of Witherspoon's address affirmed the possibility of "great improvements" in "human knowledge" and "human nature," and placed the founding of the American confederation in a line of progress that began with "the disunited and hostile situation of kingdoms and states" two centuries previously and had led to the firm establishment in Europe of "that enlarged system called the balance of power." The next step, from the balance of power to federal union, had to cover an even lesser distance than that earlier leap; Witherspoon deemed it "not impossible, that in future times all the states on one quarter of the globe, may see it proper by some plan of union, to perpetuate security and peace; and sure I am, a well planned confederacy among the states of America, may hand down the blessings of peace and public order to many generations."

The particular claim that Witherspoon sought to defend—equality of voting by states—was of course bitterly assailed by large state delegates, and particularly those from Pennsylvania. But Witherspoon's opponents joined him in predicting disunion if a rule were adopted contrary to their own sense of equity. Franklin warned that a confederation that did not link representation and taxation could not last.[26] If voting were by numbers, Benjamin Rush insisted, then "we cannot deposit too much of our liberty & safety in the hands of congress. . . . But if we vote by colonies I maintain that we cannot deposit too little in the hands of congress." To its critics, the committee draft introduced into the union the vicious principle of virtual representation they had spent the last decade denouncing. Though Rush spoke eloquently to the idea that "we are now One people—a new nation," he lost out on the bid to define the association as a body politic and to the great corollary claim of proportional representation according to numbers. What he said this association ought to be, and what it was, were vastly different.[27]

The general appreciation that effective representation and power within the union was inextricably linked with the powers that could be safely entrusted to the union subverted any clear alignment of "nationalists" against "federalists" in 1776. A substantial historiography to the contrary notwithstanding, there was no such cohesive alignment.[28] Witherspoon and other landless state delegates who wanted congressional control over the West can scarcely be considered nationalists, and had that claim of congressional power been sustained it would not have meant that their association was an "incorporating" as opposed to a "federal" union. Virginians who argued for representation according to numbers did not believe that they would thereby establish a consolidated government with the power to define or to delimit Virginia's boundaries. The large state delegates who spoke of the principle of nationality, or, like Adams, of melding the colonies into one united mass, did so for the purpose of achieving an equitable representation: they were not looking to calibrate the precise line between the authority of Congress and the states but rather to establish a fair rule for the direction of the partnership.

The most remarkable feature of the great debates over union in the summer of 1776 is that they prefigure a volume of subsequent commentary over the purposes and problematics of American union:

1. The union was seen as a species of international cooperation, its historical significance as a successor to and elaboration on the peace plans that had sought to take the vital and not impossible step from the balance of power to federal union over an area of continental dimensions. Witherspoon said this in 1776; Franklin and Wilson said it in 1787.[29]

2. This aspiration for peace and security over half a continent was stated alongside the recognition that Americans had a serious security problem, one represented by the likely interaction of the ambitions of foreign powers and the internal divisions among the American states. Americans would hear much more of that analysis in coming years.

3. Despite a developing consensus that there was no real alternative to permanent union, we find the repeated prediction that the union will dissolve if made on an unjust basis. Every great question touching representation and burden-sharing was considered in these terms, and there was always a delegate ready to proclaim that a wrong turn on representation, or control of the West, or the

rule for apportioning expenditures among the States would send the confederation over a cliff.

4. There was, finally, the repeated invocation of arguments "so often used against Great Britain," making the American understanding of their rights and grievances under the British Empire—also a "union" in the American estimation—a template by which to assess the wisdom and fairness of their own association. It becomes immediately apparent that any principle of representation or burden-sharing they choose will be found by some group of states to undermine a crucial fount of legitimacy, implicating the union in a violation of the very principles they had taken up arms to oppose.

Sectionalism

In his speech in favor of proportional representation, John Adams had argued that the distinction between large and small states was entirely artificial, and that the real division of the continent was sectional in character. Considering the distance from one another of Virginia, Pennsylvania, and Massachusetts, and considering, too, "their difference of produce, of interests, & of manners," the large states would never have an interest in oppressing the smaller. What was likely to happen (and what largely did happen) was that regional blocs would form, with "Jersey, Delaware & Maryland" generally pursuing the same objects as Pennsylvania, Virginia leading the southern states, and Massachusetts carrying the banner for New England. This analysis—later more famously detailed by various speakers in the Federal Convention of 1787—points to another theme of great importance: from the outset, the union was not simply a confederation of sovereign states, but an alliance of sections.

"One of the happiest days of my life" was how Adams characterized the moment in 1774 when it finally became clear "that America will support the Massachusetts or perish with her."[30] That the southern states, led by Virginia, had come to the aid of New England in its time of need was a fact of great moral and political significance, but the transaction was also fraught with peril. Seeking support from the outside, the New Englanders knew that there was a "strong jealousy" of New England in general and Massachusetts in particular. "Suspicions entertained of designs of independency; an American republic; Presbyterian principles, and twenty other things" were picked up by Adams's sensitive ear, but perhaps the greatest suspicion centered on the possibility of "a New England army under the command of a New England General." This entailed "a Southern party against a Northern" one, stemming from the fears— "some plausible, some whimsical"—that New England would "soon be full of Veteran Soldiers, and at length conceive Designs unfavourable to the other Colonies." Adams cut through these difficulties with his magnanimous, and thoroughly unexpected, resolution that "Congress should adopt the army before Boston, and appoint Colonel Washington commander of it." This bold stroke felled three birds: it allowed Massachusetts to warmly acknowledge the generous assistance of "our sister colony of Virginia, which ranks highest in numbers"; it allayed the jealousies that "an enterprising eastern New England general proving successful, might with his victorious army give the law to the Southern and Western gentry"; and it exerted civilian control over the military, as the Massachusetts Provincial Congress had urged the Continental Congress to do. It was the first great sectional compromise in American history.[31]

Unanimity in council, however, did not translate readily into unity in the camp. Once Washington arrived in Massachusetts to take command, he let loose a steady stream of prejudicial remarks about New Englanders in his private correspondence, finding "an unaccountable kind of stupidity in the lower class of these people which, believe me, prevails but too generally among the officers of the Massachusetts *part* of the army who are *nearly* of the same kidney with the privates!"[32] Adams, whose apparent masterstroke had elevated Washington, learned of these comments and was now driven to ask if "every Man to the Southward of Hudsons River behave like a Hero and every Man to the Northward of it like a Poltroon."[33] The reverse seemed the case to one of Adams's correspondents, who told him of a group of riflemen "from the Southward" who were "as Indifferent men as I ever Served with, their Privates, Mutinous and often Deserting to the Enemy, Unwilling for Duty of any kind, Exceedingly Vicious . . . [but] Truth may not best go from me any further."[34] No, indeed. Washington, stung by the leaks in what he had supposed to be a privileged correspondence with friends in Virginia, reached a similar conclusion, and thereafter studiously avoided such aspersions in his private letters. All could see the merit of Witherspoon's observation that "if local provincial pride and jealousy arise, and you allow yourselves to speak with contempt of the courage, character, manners, or even language of particular places, you are doing a greater injury to the common cause, than you are aware of."[35] Still, it was difficult to keep these things down; the sense of heterogeneity, of regions that differed "as much as several distinct Nations almost," bespoke the plain facts of the situation. From the very beginning it was understood that without consideration and forbearance the divisions among these proto-nations would certainly be fatal.[36]

That sense of fatality was keenly tested during the war. By late 1776 Richard Henry Lee was already being hounded with the accusation in Virginia that he had sold out to New England. Lee responded with a flood of acrimony that laid bare the motives of his policy as well as the nature of the revolutionary coalition. "Our enemies and our friends too, know that America can only be conquered by disunion," Lee wrote. "The former, by unremitting art had endeavoured to incite jealousy and discord between the Southern and Eastern Colonies," and Lee was certain "that had it not been for Virginia and Jersey, with Georgia sometimes, that our Union would eer now have been by this means broken like a Potters vessel dashed against a rock and I heartily wish that this greatest of all political evils may not yet take place before a safe and honorable peace is established." Lee defied "the poisonous tongue of slander to produce a single instance in which I have preferred the interest of New England to that of Virginia. Indeed I am at a Loss to know wherein their interests clash."[37]

Increasingly, however, Virginians did know where their interests clashed with those of Massachusetts. The great collaboration between Virginia and Massachusetts was already on the ropes in 1778, but the bitter debate over foreign policy that erupted in 1779 finished it off as a working coalition.[38] Lee supported New England's interest in the fisheries—were not the southern states equally interested in a strong merchant marine and navy?—but that stance left him isolated in Virginia. Wrote Governor Thomas Jefferson to William Fleming, a delegate in Congress:

> We have lately been extremely disturbed to find a pretty general opinion prevailing that peace and the independence of the thirteen states are now within our power, and that congress have hesitations on the subject, and delay entering on the consideration. It has even been said that their conduct on this head has been so dissatisfactory to the French minister that he thinks of returning to his own country, ostensibly for better health, but in truth through disgust. Such an event would be deplored here as the most dreadful calamity.[39]

Nothing more disgusted the French minister, Gerard, than New England's obstinate attachment to the fishery. Nothing, in turn, disgusted New England more than the disposition in the southern states to view the claim to the fisheries as a "particular" interest bearing only on three states. New Englanders saw grave peril in the willingness of the southern states to place American peace negotiators under the guidance of France. "Before France had given us one encouraging word," Elbridge Gerry told Congress, "the people of New-England had poured out their blood like water in defence of their rights; they had been cheered also by their southern friends, but at first they had stood alone; and by God's blessing they would stand alone again without allies or friends, before they would barter away their rights."[40]

The vital interests of the sections were those that, if bartered away or abandoned, would justify secession from the confederacy. But the southern states also felt a keen sense of vital interest and imperious necessity, particularly in 1779. After the defeat at Saratoga in 1777, the British ministry abandoned its designs on New England, instead concentrating its full might on the conquest of the southern states. The sense of many southerners that they had been left in the lurch by New England felt like an aggression. Christopher Gadsden, then desperately attempting to organize the defense of Charles Town, recalled to Samuel Adams how South Carolina had always been "particularly attentive to the Interest and feelings of America," and how it had, in the Stamp Act crisis of 1765, listened to the call and rushed to the aid "of our Northern Brethren in their Distresses." Without Carolina's support, Gadsden averred, Boston would have been ruined, because without it there would have been no Congress. "Now the Tables are turn'd, and we [are] in far greater Distress than New England ever was. . . . But who feels for us? We seem to be entirely deserted, even the Continental Troops of our Neighbours are retained with the grand army and denied us." Proclaiming himself "an American *at large,* anxiously wishing for the Happiness and confirmed Independency of the Whole, not having, indeed scorning a Thought in Favor of *any one* State to the prejudice of the rest," Gadsden could only conclude that while he had remained the same man, others had changed. Where was the fairness, where the equity, in that? Given New England's apparent readiness "to leave [us] in the Lurch" and British success in recruiting back-country banditti to the counter-revolutionary cause, the southern states were bound to fall, with disastrous consequences for the whole union—including New England.[41] To New Englanders, however, all this came with very ill grace. They could only discern in southern support for the French propositions a dislike of their political principles, and an intention to destroy "their Trade, and consequently their power and Influence. What would more Effectually do that [than] by Ceding all right and Claim to the fishery to get a Peace, rather than see us flourish?"[42]

An American State-System

These sectional divisions point, in turn, to a final theme. Attempts to constitute the American union—to form a compact of sovereign states, and a federative bond among the sections—took place against the avowed recognition that they themselves constituted a state-system. While the Congress, once it was formally constituted as a league of states in 1781, may not formally be best described as a "diplomatic assembly," as John Adams called it in 1787, its deliberations certainly had a diplomatic character.[43] The "difficulty of combining in one general system . . . a continent divided into so many sovereign and independent communities";[44] the rapt attention given to the balance of power among the sections; the emergence of a hazy line of jurisdiction between Congress and the states, inviting protracted conflict; the suspicion that those who spoke of a common cause were always inveterately pursuing their own particular interests—all these characteristics suggest that the American society of states was not far removed from a state of nature. This association of bodies politic aimed, assuredly, at union, but did so in circumstances that seemed forever tending to an actual condition of disunion.

It is in the context of the anxieties of internecine war that we might consider the celebrated question of whether any of the unions formed in the years from 1776 to 1788 allowed for either the nullification of its provisions by one or several of the sister states, or secession from the compact itself.[45] The question also arose even before the Articles had been ratified, and the terms of that initial discussion are revealing. "Some States," as Thomas Burke summarized the constitutional crisis of 1779, "seem not very clear that they are bound by any thing which has hitherto been done, and others Scruple not to declare that if Congress Should, on a Question for agreeing to Terms of peace decide in a manner Contrary to the Sense of those States they will Neither Submit or Confederate."[46] Burke wanted a clear avowal from New England on the latter question—was she in or out of the union?—but as to the former he did not doubt that the states were so bound: "That for every purpose of common defence and common Exertions in the progress of the present War and for the conclusion thereof, the States are unquestionably, united by former acts of the Several States."[47]

Everything to which the states had unanimously bound themselves by that date—the joint winning of their independence, the joint prosecution of the war, the joint payment of the debt—could be considered as falling within the terms of their original compact. A right of sovereignty or of supremacy in Congress over certain objects was readily deducible from these prior commitments.[48] Yet, despite various avowals of an implied right of compulsion in the Congress both before and after 1781, there was a vast gap between the authority Congress might claim in theory and what it could actually exercise in practice. The States might be obligated to the debt contracted in their name, but they could not reach agreement on an equitable way of apportioning the shares, nor on the two most eligible sources of general revenue (imposts and the western lands). The Articles might speak of perpetual union, but many Americans presumed in 1780 and 1781, with Madison, "that the present Union will but little survive the present war."[49] Already observers were estimating as the more likely reality that the "several states would ultimately form several confederations rather than a single nation."[50] The stark contrast between the claimed authority and real power of Congress, and the concomitant and numerous violations by the states of their obligations, could not, moreover, but weaken the practical force of the argument appealing to an implied power of congressional compulsion. Was one obliged to fulfill the terms of a treaty if the other parties to it were not fulfilling theirs? Was this the rule of the law of nature and of nations?

Before and after the ratification of the Articles, Americans found themselves in a most peculiar and indeed strange situation. They had agreed to cooperate, but could not agree on terms seen as equitable. They saw that Congress, to be legitimate, must be representative, but could not agree on what or who it should represent. They had constituted a government whose efficiency would rest on "a disposition of accommodation in the States to each other, and of Congress to all,"[51] but then found themselves ill-disposed to make the necessary accommodations.

"A More Perfect Union"

The title of this chapter asks us to consider whether the first union of the American states was national or international in basic character, and to this we have returned the unconventional answer that it was more international than national. Practical conclusions favorable to the nationalist animus against nullification or secession can certainly be deduced from the history of the times, but we misinterpret the spirit of 1776 if we see the formation of a national government claiming its powers from a sovereign American people. The union was

not built in a day, but was the work of many years; the sentiment of nationality did not spring up in a fortnight, but crept up on Americans unawares, more
a consequence of their mutual entanglement than of the conception they
formed of their relationship at the beginning.[52]

In the beginning, the union proposed itself as an experiment in interstate or
international cooperation, constituted against the background of pervasive
fears that no such thing was possible. It was a compact made between states conscious of their corporate identities, and of sections almost as different as several
distinct nations; theirs was the quintessentially federal act of "coming together
to stay apart." If this outlook is set against the background of the sorry record
of the transactions of neighboring nations, which was little better than that of
perpetual war, the emergence of an association that took perpetual peace among
its members as its fundamental task must be and was seen as describing a generous ideal. In the first instance, the union was a means that the people of each
colony thought vital to their own independence and sovereignty, but from the
beginning it also proposed a great and glorious end. Estimating the value of the
union by the specter of disunion, it is not difficult to see why a "more perfect
union" would in 1787 be thought necessary, nor why men and women would
come to love it even in its imperfections. Such sentiments formed the real *fons
et origo* of an American patriotism, the sentiment of nationality most appropriate for a union that embraced such manifold diversities.

CHAPTER THREE

War and State Formation in Revolutionary America

Don Higginbotham

Without the War of Independence there would have been no American national state in the eighteenth century. This would have been true even if Britain had agreed to grant the American colonies their independence in 1775 or 1776. Without the burden of fighting for their independence from the world's dominant superpower, the American republics might have formed a loose league or confederacy—weaker than the Articles of Confederation—or several regional confederacies. They might instead have gone at each others' throats like the Greek city-states of antiquity. Or some or all of them might have been wooed back into the imperial fold.

As critical as the War of Independence was to the creation of the American nation-state, it led only slowly to the constitutional settlement of 1787 in Philadelphia. And yet historians have all but totally neglected the connection between war and state formation in the creation of the United States. We can best examine war and state formation in America in a comparative context. The origins of the national state have received considerable attention from scholars who have studied the subject elsewhere, particularly in early modern Europe. Most scholars agree that nations are "constructed" or "invented" in response to war or some other crisis or catastrophe in order to impose a sturdy institutional framework over people who may be quite diverse in language, religion, and ethnicity. To be sure, some measure of social homogeneity may speed the political process, but it is not always critical or paramount. Once the political framework is in place, a "people" may overcome—or ignore—some of their cultural differences and create new symbols of their nationhood. The nation as a political fact comes first, reflecting the aspirations of "nationalists" and promoting the emergence of a widely shared national identity.[1]

The "Military Revolution" in early modern Europe provided the crucial impetus for state formation. Recent work by Michael Roberts on Sweden and Geoffrey Parker on Spain shows that the kingdoms or states that antedated this revolution became "modern" to the extent that war increased enormously centralizing tendencies. Numerous wars stemming from dynastic, geographic, and religious factors produced heavy taxes, large armies, technological advances in weapons, and bureaucratic agencies to manage military undertakings. The forms of centralization and bureaucratization remained with the advent of peace.[2] Charles Tilly has employed the findings of the new military history in his studies of state formation, emphasizing the dramatic expansion of these war powers in governments' long-term fiscal and administrative activities.[3] Parker summarizes the dominant historiographical view: "military activity and state formation have always been inextricably linked, and periods of rapid military change have usually coincided with major political innovations."[4]

Are states that emerge in wars—or that are radically transformed by conflicts—necessarily inhospitable to representative institutions and the rule of law, turning instead to military-bureaucratic absolutism? The histories of England and its American colonies suggest that different outcomes are possible. Other factors may be crucial as well, including demands on internal resources, the ability to secure financial support abroad, and success in establishing military alliances. Britain's liberal institutions survived more than a century of wars with more populous France because it possessed vast commercial wealth and was able to exploit valuable continental alliances. After 1660 Britain never faced the threat of a vast standing army because the navy provided a first line of defense. In contrast, France and Brandenburg-Prussia responded to enormous wartime pressures by harnessing the domestic sector and then leaving in place afterward strongly centralized governments.[5]

The Colonial Experience

State formation in America began well before independence. The thirteen colonial polities became more vigorous and self-reliant during a period of institution-building and increasing internal unity in metropolitan society. As Linda Colley demonstrates, the years following the 1707 Act of Union with Scotland saw the expansion of British national feeling among the peoples of England, Wales, and Scotland. At the same time, the island kingdom ended its lengthy period of comparative international isolation during which England had been a minor military power. Its post-1688 imperial wars were fueled by a dynamic and flexible economy that could support the financial and political structures of a fiscal-military state that challenged and eventually dominated European rivals.[6]

Fortunately for the political liberties of Britons on the imperial peripheries, metropolitan authorities were always reluctant to pay for military and civil establishments across the Atlantic. As a result, provincial governments enjoyed an extraordinary degree of internal autonomy. The colonial legislatures were thus able to sink intractable roots. It would have been imprudent to challenge colonial institutional development as long as Britain had its hands full with France and its allies and needed the wartime assistance of its distant overseas dependencies.

Although the lower houses increased their powers dramatically during the imperial wars, those were not the only occasions when the provincial bodies ignored the governors' constituted military authority, to say nothing of their other jurisdiction. The lower houses found chief executives particularly vulnerable because of pressures from England to raise men and money promptly for frontier defense and for expeditions against the French. Provincial lawmakers became imperial policymakers by indicating how monies were to be spent, the number of soldiers to be raised, the period of months they would serve, and where they would be deployed. Sometimes provincial legislators even insisted on their right to appoint commanders of expeditionary forces and to select oversight committees from their own membership. Consequently, colonial legislatures seized greater authority over military affairs than the House of Commons ever acquired in Britain.[7]

An institutional transformation had taken place in provincial political life. Massachusetts brought what William Pencak describes as a structural expansion not unlike the state-building process in Europe.[8] The assemblies, writes

Jack P. Greene, emerged from the pre-1763 era "with an increased awareness of their own importance and a growing consciousness of the implications of their activities."[9]

This state formation, within an imperial framework, was not replicated elsewhere in the eighteenth century. Some peripheral lands and territories had endeavored to preserve ancient privileges by negotiations, even with the monarchs of France and Spain. Yet these units, however much they might retain from a Louis XIV or Phillip II, faced pressure from consolidating ministers like Richelieu in France and Olivares in Spain. Britain's American polities had not so much bargained to retain old rights, long practiced as part of their English heritage, as they had hammered out new ones, based on behaviors and precedents following 1688.[10]

When imperial reform efforts threatened "traditional" rights and more recently won liberties after 1763, provincial legislators exercised their authority by still other creative methods. They had rarely needed appeals to public opinion, but now they encouraged petitions, memorials, pamphlets, broadsides, patriotic meetings, and associations such as "Sons of Liberty."[11] Beginning with the Stamp Act crisis, royal governors retaliated by dissolving legislatures or by failing to call them into session. They could also attach suspending clauses to colonial laws, employing the Crown's relatively infrequently used right of legislative review. But these executives could not do without the assemblies indefinitely—and they paid a steep price when they did so.[12]

Gradually, from the Stamp Act crisis onward, the assemblies and a stream of American essayists moved from denying Parliament any authority to interfere in the internal affairs of the provinces to the position that any laws emanating from the metropolis were acceptable only if they benefited the whole empire. Radicals staked out an even more advanced position, insisting that trade legislation and other external statutes required the explicit consent of individual assembles or of an intercolonial congress. Even before the outbreak of hostilities in 1775, influential writers such as Thomas Jefferson, James Iredell, and James Wilson called for a commonwealth conception of the empire—a "cordial union of many distant people . . . warm in their affection and zealous in their attachment to each other, under the influence of one common sovereign," as Iredell phrased it.[13] It was a concept Britain would finally accept in the twentieth century.[14]

Independence could have come only when it did because so many assemblies had separated themselves from imperial officials. Meeting independently, lower houses announced new elections and renamed themselves provincial congresses or conventions. Militia officers resigned their royal commissions in order to free themselves from interference from the governor (as the assemblies themselves had done) and reconstituted local forces under authority of provincial congresses and conventions. Only highly sophisticated political bodies could have effected this extraordinary transformation.[15] The legislators were aided, declares John Phillip Reid, by the primacy of custom and local law, based on community support, in governing behavior and protecting individual rights. In the 1760s, imperial law grew weaker. Provincial law at legislative and judicial levels maintained its popularity and vigor. British authority proved ineffectual in suppressing the resistance. Governors could not declare martial law without the approval of their councils, and magistrates had to issue written approval for redcoats to be sent against civilians. Virtually every colony functioned as an independent state, in control of its political and military establishment, months before July 1776.[16]

Revolution and Union

The subsequent story of war and state formation for the American nation-state was complicated by the distribution of authority in an evolving federal system. The post-1763 imperial crisis began with the colonies in possession of political and military structures that could be employed creatively. The situation of the colony-states resembled that of the kingdoms of Europe, before the onset of wars initiated the process of state formation. But there was also a highly significant difference: the absence of any kind of intercolonial structure or institution to build on; there was nothing like the Holy Roman Empire, nor even a diet or an ancient council of notables to give Americans focus or direction. British generals and governors, foreign visitors, and prominent colonials all commented on jealousies and rivalries between the provinces. The assemblies lacked a precedent for pulling together on common issues, a serious liability during the imperial wars. Furthermore, the success of the assemblies in gaining the upper hand within their own borders made them less than enthusiastic about sharing their newly won supremacy with an American congress or confederacy.

Only the threats to the assemblies themselves and to the liberty of Anglo-Americans in general can explain their bold steps beginning in 1774. It took the Coercive Acts to bring about the First Continental Congress. It took Britain's military action against Massachusetts to transform the Second Continental Congress into a quasi-central government that would eventually declare American independence. No organic growth of an American nation lay behind these actions, nor can American national*ism* provide the explanation.[17] Concerns for self-preservation can propel people vast distances.

The initial thrust for an intercolonial congress at Philadelphia was, to most of its principal proponents, somewhat conservative: they hoped to head off radicals agitating for instant retaliatory measures, particularly a suspension of trade with Britain. Although its delegates had been given considerable latitude by their respective colonies, the first Continental Congress was never looked upon as a permanent body.[18] Even so, Congress displayed a great deal of unanimity and a toughening stance as the crisis escalated. Delegates denounced Parliament, embraced Massachusetts's Suffolk Resolves, with their threat of military action against Britain, and adopted the Continental Association, thus committing their colonies to an ambitious scheme of economic coercion that would be enforced at the grassroots level. The association was a first, limited step toward American nationhood, for it came to be interpreted as an oath of allegiance to Congress and to extralegal, revolutionary authorities in the colonies.[19]

Congress still hoped for accommodation with Britain, but it continued to have no interest in a constitutional reorganization of the empire that might make it a permanent institution. Its first objective remained gaining repeal of the Coercive Acts and securing redress for other misguided British initiatives since 1763, as set forth in its Declaration of Rights and Grievances.[20] Although they called for another congress the following year if Britain failed to address their concerns, delegates had no plans for future action.

Political moderates such as John Dickinson of Pennsylvania did not see the elections for the Second Continental Congress as dangerously provocative. As the conservative New York City leadership explained, the Second Congress, like its predecessor, sought to keep the lid on anti-British zealots—to focus on negotiating with the mother country and on forestalling violence, not on creating organizations or institutions that could bring about some future union within or without the empire.[21] Virtually all members opposed separation and still sought an imperial settlement. That mindset failed to last. When Congress met in May, fighting had erupted at Lexington and Concord, followed in June by the Battle of Bunker Hill. At the urging of Massachusetts, Congress adopted the New England army besieging Boston and selected one of its own members as its commander, the highly visible Virginian George Washington, whose appointment would help pull the southern provinces into the war effort. At the same time, Congress dispatched its Olive Branch Petition to London, still hoping for reconciliation. The delegates displayed "a Strange Oscilation between Love and Hatred, between War and Peace."[22] Dickinson angrily accused John Adams of opposing a negotiated settlement *within* the English-speaking family. As late as January 1776, James Wilson sought a formal statement from Congress against independence. Yet these reluctant revolutionaries supported Congress's military responses, and they in turn received the support of their more radical colleagues in opposing Samuel Adams and Benjamin Franklin's proposal for some kind of confederation. The appearance of *Common Sense* that January, London's rejection of continued American appeals, and new British hostilities, such as the Prohibitory Act, naval raids on the American coast, employment of mercenaries, and reports of a massive invading force soon to be bound for America, turned the tide in favor of independence. A radical step, with implications for a future American union, the break nonetheless came reluctantly, only after congressional head-counters anticipated a unanimous vote.[23]

The prestige of the Second Continental Congress crested in 1776, only to erode over the next several years. Before severing ties with Britain, Congress had conducted a war for fifteen months and encouraged the colony-states to write new constitutions. The Declaration of Independence came at a critical juncture. Congress needed a legal base for seeking alliances abroad and running a war effort, especially for controlling an army, for "standing armies" always posed a threat to liberty.

Despite compelling incentives, the Revolutionary War did not lead to the immediate formation of an American nation-state. Why was it such a vexed undertaking, whereas the southern revolutionaries of 1860–61 constructed a Confederate nation-state quickly and with a minimum of controversy? Southerners, with a little fine-tuning, kept the predominant features of the federal Constitution. Their concern had not been with that instrument but rather with how it had been interpreted and with what President Abraham Lincoln's Republican Party would do with it. Southerners also had been able to draft their charter before the outbreak of the Civil War at Fort Sumter.[24] The American Congress, on the other hand, had to write and obtain ratification of a constitution in the midst of war. As Richard Henry Lee noted, "the immensity of [that] business" often deflected attention away from their political engineering for weeks on end.[25] Like the Confederates, the revolutionaries of 1776 claimed that they had revered the old institutional framework—in their case, the British constitution. But Congress could not fall back on the British model, for it embraced monarchy and a legislative apparatus based on hereditary social distinctions.

Just as Congress had proceeded at a relatively moderate pace between 1774 and 1776, conscious of the need for consensus, congressmen continued to move cautiously when they confronted the challenge of establishing a constitutional union. Because of the ministry's general policy of "salutary neglect," the British empire before Parliament's disastrous endeavors to transform it after 1763 had been loosely structured and lightly governed. It is therefore hardly surprising that Congress should form a loosely structured confederacy that had more in common with the pre-1763 empire than with the version of federalism that triumphed with ratification of the federal Constitution. Even so, the Articles of Confederation served as a bridge between the old and the new federalism; the union they constituted bore little resemblance to past and present versions of confederated systems in Europe—the Greek city-states, the Swiss Confederation, or the United Provinces of Holland.[26]

At first glance, it seems amazing that Congress, now eager for a confederation with constitutional underpinnings, would take nearly sixteen months to complete its task. (Ten years later, the Constitutional Convention forged an unprecedented and much more muscular federalism in seventeen weeks.) The process of state ratification then dragged out from the fall of 1777 to the spring of 1781. In the meantime, Congress—though still an extralegal body—managed the war and concluded the French alliance. In the short run, a patriotic outpouring, a *"rage militaire,"* muffled provincial jealousies. Patriotic fervor combined with pressing military concerns—particularly the well-founded report in the spring of 1776 of a major British offensive against New York City and the middle colonies—to enable congressmen to obtain "powers in an ad hoc fashion" as they "responded to contingencies."[27] History showed that military despotism loomed as the foremost danger to liberty during revolutions and the formation of new states. But so long as Washington remained alive and served as commander-in-chief of the Continental army, that possibility remained remote. Already, after only a year in his post, Washington's relations with Congress had set precedents for deference and respect for civil control that would be hard for any successor to overturn. He also had increased Congress's standing and prestige with the states by clarifying the chain of authority. All calls for assistance from him must be routed through Congress.[28]

The Confederation that Congress drafted in 1776–77 invested the government of the union with specific responsibilities that would reappear in the federal Constitution: making war and peace, raising an army and navy, concluding treaties, appointing ministers, conducting Indian relations, organizing a postal service, issuing currency, and borrowing money. All of these powers were related more or less directly to defense, security, and the international order, the preeminent concerns of early modern national states everywhere.

The jealousies and rivalries of the Seven Years' War that had led to the failure of Franklin's Plan of Union alerted delegates to the obstacles ahead. Sensitive subjects struck closest to home: how to raise monies without giving Congress the taxing power, how to determine representation in Congress, and how to control the western lands. In their deliberations, delegates deferred to their state legislatures; during the ratification process, the legislatures raised objections and demanded changes. Legislative "egotisms" thus blocked progress. If Parliament in the 1760s and 1770s was reluctant to share powers with colonial assemblies that it had won from the Crown in the seventeenth century, the American state legislatures after 1776 were similarly loath to concede much of *their* jurisdiction to Congress. They had existed too long as corporate entities to contemplate absorption in a wholly new continental state during the Revolution.[29] State-level politicians were willing enough to go along with ad hoc acts of Congress: for instance, when it bestowed temporary dictatorial authority on Washington at several critical junctures, so long as these emergency measures were understood not to entail any formal recognition of Congress's expanded powers. Throughout the war, the absence of historical or theoretical debate about America's first national constitution is striking, especially compared to the lively exchange of ideas about government that characterized both the controversy with Britain prior to independence and the subsequent movement to draft and ratify a new federal Constitution. The possibility of establishing an "extended republic," a crucial theme of political debate in the late 1780s, was also conspicuously missing during the war years.[30]

The question of sovereignty failed to receive careful attention in debates over the Articles, despite its centrality in the imperial crisis and in later controversy over the distribution of authority in the federal republic. Congressman Thomas Burke of North Carolina proposed what became the second of the Articles of Confederation, that "Each state retains its sovereignty, freedom, and independence," in all areas except those "expressly delegated to the United States, in Congress assembled." But Burke's measure elicited little debate and received a nearly unanimous vote.[31] Historians who maintain that sovereignty was truly divisible in the first national constitution would have had trouble convincing George Washington and other leaders who thought in increasingly continental terms as the war wore on. Sovereignty can only be divided if each political component can effectively perform its assigned functions. This was possible in the old empire before 1763 because the metropolitan government had the means to manage the external affairs of the empire: war and peace, foreign affairs, and trade and commerce. Samuel Johnston, North Carolina's most powerful political figure of the era, reminded his states' rights friend Burke that Americans should face the fact that until they won the war and enjoyed opportunity for deeper reflection, all "Leagues, Confederations, and Constitutions are . . . temporary expedients."[32] Gouverneur Morris, a New York delegate, complained that Congress was "inadequate to the Purposes of Execution" for performing the functions assigned it under the Articles.[33]

Morris hit the nail on the head. Because Congress possessed no mechanism for enforcing treaty terms on the states, the effectiveness of agreements with foreign powers always remained doubtful. Because Congress lacked the taxing power and the states contributed such a small percentage of their annual requisition monies, Congressional indebtedness soared; the principal victims being officers and men of the Continental army. Because the states insisted that their Continental soldiers be formed into state regiments and demanded some form of equitable representation among the general officers, Congress's authority to raise an army suffered. Congress also floundered concerning the militia. Although the Articles stipulated that the states "shall always keep up a well regulated and disciplined militia" "and constantly have ready for use" all necessary "arms, ammunition, and camp equipage," Congress had no way of enforcing these provisions or of calling out the state militias. In numerous other instances the states subverted Congressional jurisdiction as prescribed in the Articles of Confederation: creating state navies, sending agents abroad, and failing at times to provide Congress with a quorum so that it could conduct business.

Tensions between the states and federal authorities persisted throughout the Revolutionary conflict. They recalled friction between the colonists and British officials in the Seven Years' War over such issues as raising money, contributing men for the regular army, and employing militia to cooperate with professional troops. British generals had complained of royal governors who were intimidated by their assemblies. Revolutionary generals fumed about state legislatures that prevented their own state governors from moving decisively.

Governor Thomas Jefferson chafed at executive impotence in Virginia. So did James Madison, member of Virginia's Council of State, which had a veto over major gubernatorial decisions.[34] Generals Robert Howe and Benjamin Lincoln, each at one time head of the Southern Department, faced deliberate obstructions from civilian leaders in Georgia and South Carolina.[35] The Confederation seemed to hit rock bottom in the final year of the conflict. Thanks to Washington, the Newburgh Conspiracy aborted when the commander-in-chief put his reputation on the line with disgruntled officers over back pay and other emoluments. Later in the year angry Continental enlisted men surrounded Congress in the Pennsylvania State House. Pennsylvania officials refused to turn out their militia to protect the federal legislators, a painful reminder that the Confederation government had no jurisdiction over the capital city of the United States, a point not forgotten later when the framers provided for a national capital on soil belonging to the nation, not a state. Adding insult to injury, the unhappy Continentals then expressed more confidence in Pennsylvania than in the United States when they asked the state to settle their accounts. Even the treaty of peace, which should have brought rejoicing in Congress, prompted near panic because the lawmakers lacked a quorum to ratify it. The British, as tired of war as the Americans, ignored the technicality. The two sides exchanged ratifications in Paris early in 1784.[36]

Constitutional Reform

Rarely have victors in a major war been so troubled and unclear about their future as were the American Revolutionaries. John Dickinson feared that Americans might become the victims of their own success. What would replace the old British imperial structure, which, for all its inadequacies, had held the colonies together? Like Gouverneur Morris, many congressmen had been pessimistic about the viability of the Articles of Confederation well before that document finally received unanimous state approval. Charles Thompson, who knew Congress better than anybody, serving as its secretary throughout its fifteen-year existence, doubted that the union would long survive the war's end. Between 1780 and 1783, Washington, Colonel Alexander Hamilton, and General Henry Knox all advocated the calling of a convention to examine ways to make Congress more effective and to tighten the union. Washington was recognized as the most persistent and eloquent critic of the American political system, and he never let up until the federal Constitution achieved implementation nearly a decade later.[37] Such sentiments became more evident in Congress during the last three years of the war, though to speak of a "nationalist ascendancy" overstates the numbers and cohesiveness of reform-minded critics. Hamilton, who switched from the army to a seat in the legislative counsels, was one of the most vocal nationalists, whose ranks also included James Madison, Robert Morris and James Wilson of Pennsylvania, ex-General John Sullivan of New Hampshire, Samuel Johnston of North Carolina, and John Mathews of South Carolina.[38] At the state level, too, some legislators advocated more vigorous support of the national war effort and were willing to interpret Congressional power under the Articles more broadly in the postwar years than many of their fellow representatives. Jackson Turner Main shows that these "cosmopolitan" activists generally lived close to coastal areas or on other waterways affected by commerce. By contrast, "localists" who were preoccupied with their state's internal concerns and suspicious of federal encroachments were concentrated in the interior and backcountry of their states and were more likely to have been in the militia than in the Continental army.[39]

As advocates of greater continental cohesion pondered the future, they could acknowledge some achievements beyond independence itself over the past eight-and-a-half years. If their national institutions were disappointingly weak, they had not seen the lengthy struggle tear apart the fabric of society or strain American resources to the breaking point or lead to extreme forms of centralization. The War of Independence did not bring a European-style absolutist state. Substantial amounts of foreign aid in terms of military stores, cash contributions, and loans (from Holland as well as France) and the French military alliance helped keep either extreme possibility, absolutism or anarchy, from occurring.

Postwar America looked to be moving in the opposite direction from even the modest form of centralization authorized by the Articles of Confederation. The several executive departments established by the Confederation Congress seemed to be eroding. The office of Secretary at War, filled by General Benjamin Lincoln during 1781–83, had no occupant from 1783 to 1785. After appointment as Superintendent of Finance in 1781, the energetic and enterprising Robert Morris devised schemes to pay some of the nation's bills, but he resigned in frustration in 1784 over his failure to secure permanent federal revenues; Congress thereafter resumed control of the Confederation's business affairs. The Department of Marine never became operative because Congress failed to form a postwar navy. Although the final administrative unit voted by

Congress, the Department of Foreign Affairs, kept its doors open, its successive secretaries, Robert R. Livingston and John Jay, were thwarted by Congress's impotence in their efforts to negotiate with foreign powers. America had only two permanent ministers in foreign posts, London and Paris, by 1784. In short, the dangerous signs of disintegration in 1783 became even more conspicuous. By that year, the negative results were in on Congress's Impost of 1781, when the states failed to provide the unanimous vote for ratification needed to give the Confederation an independent source of revenue from duties on incoming foreign products. The Impost of 1783, a second attempt, also foundered, even though its time limit of twenty-five years and its provision that duties be collected by state appointees should have made it more palatable to states' rights advocates. Such an income would have made at least a dent in the foreign and domestic debt of the Revolution and would have indirectly provided some resources for a modest peacetime military establishment, which never reached as many as a thousand men after 1783, although the minuscule army had responsibility for controlling the vast American West. Crippled finances also explain why Secretary of Foreign Affairs Jay refused to support the recommendation of Jefferson, then minister to France, that America join an alliance of European nations to protect their Mediterranean trade from the Barbary pirates. To do so, Jay said bluntly, would have required a navy.[40]

Of the variety of other frustrations that plagued the Confederation in the immediate postwar years, two are particularly relevant here, namely, the government's inability to provide either for national security or for internal order. No polity can survive without resolving these fundamental security dilemmas. Wherever sovereignty is supposed to reside, whether with the king-in-Parliament or with the people collectively, who may in turn delegate different functions to governments at the center and the peripheries of the federal republic, it is a meaningless fiction if unwanted foreign troops occupy a nation's soil. America confronted that painful reality when, after the Peace of Paris in 1783, Britain retained its military posts at Detroit, Niagara, Michilimackinac, and elsewhere in the Northwest. The British justified their continued presence as retaliation for Congress's failure to implement peace treaty provisions concerning the Loyalists, although the desire to retain control over the Indians and the fur trade in the region was clearly an important consideration. American diplomats in Paris, conscious of Congress's limited authority over the states, could only promise in the treaty to "earnestly recommend" that the states adhere to provisions on the restitution of Loyalist property. Loyalist issues were, with the exception of debates over paper money and other debtor mat-ters, the most hot button items in domestic politics between 1783 and 1787.[41]

Internal discord also exposed the Confederation's grave inadequacies. When Shays's Rebellion erupted in Massachusetts in 1786, Congress feared that simi-lar debtor-creditor tensions, which existed in every state, might bring further disorder and violence. Congress took modest steps to enlarge its tiny army, but even if these steps had been promptly accomplished (and they were not), most delegates doubted that the federal lawmakers had the authority to use force to restore internal order in the states. When some congressmen argued that the nearness of the federal arsenal at Springfield to the center of rebel strength justified intervention, Secretary at War Knox refused to act in a matter for "the internal government" of Massachusetts.[42]

The Confederation appeared to be unraveling within even as it faced dan-ger abroad. Southern spokesmen denounced Don Diego de Gardoqui and Sec-retary for Foreign Affairs Jay because of their tentative agreement in 1786—never approved by Congress—on the terms of a Spanish-American trade treaty, which would have included relinquishing America's claim to the free navigation of the Mississippi River to the Gulf of Mexico. Some southern-ers and westerners talked of secession. (Disunionist impulses lessened north of the Ohio River with Congress's adoption of the Northwest Ordinance in 1787, providing automatic statehood for transmontane territories once a population reached 60,000.) Secessionist grumbling abounded in the Maine District of Massachusetts. Similar breakaway sounds came from Nantucket. Islanders spoke of cutting their own deal with Britain, which imposed a heavy duty on their whale oil and bone.[43]

Given this decline in the vitality of the union, how do we account for the fact that four years after the Revolutionary War, Americans produced the federal Constitution? If the war had been the glue that brought the colony-states together, however belatedly, into a union that finally became legitimized in 1781 with the ratification of the Articles, what was the cement in 1787? We have no single answer to a conundrum that has long divided and perplexed historians. In 1787 constitutional reformers could call on more than a decade of experi-ence at the state and federal levels; in 1776, by contrast, revolutionaries had no such frame of reference—no point of departure. For all their defects, state and federal charters served as springboards for discussion and analysis. Willi P. Adams argues that the constitutions adopted in Massachusetts in 1780 and New Hampshire in 1784 provided particularly valuable models for the framers of

1787. Peter Onuf shows that the states, although failing to agree on amendments to the Articles, still needed the union, for Congress remained a forum for airing their grievances against one another and a potential source for resolving boundary and other interstate controversies. To Washington and other centralists, the states were culprits. Yet, individually, in the post-1783 years various states, including Virginia, North Carolina, and New Jersey came up with schemes for strengthening the "federal head."[44] But leadership to coordinate and implement reform proposals always seemed lacking.

What made the Constitutional Convention possible was a sense that the federal system required a shot of adrenaline. Future Antifederalists who were knowledgeable about the affairs of the union conceded that point. But they would have denied a crisis existed—not a crisis, at any rate, that was the equivalent of war, the phenomenon that drove nation-state formation from the sixteenth century onward in Europe.[45]

But the crisis analogy to European state formation applies to those public figures who spearheaded the campaign to revise the federal structure in 1786 and 1787. These centralizers occupied major positions in the Revolution outside their own states. They were profoundly distressed by conditions in the country and by the failure in the late summer of 1786 of the Annapolis Convention, with a meager agenda confined to commercial affairs. Events that year aroused them to call for a more broadly conceived convention to meet at Philadelphia the following May. These activists, by virtue of service as army officers, congressman, diplomats, and Confederation officials, had learned to view America continentally. They included not only such well-known figures as Washington, Madison, Hamilton, Jay, Knox, Wilson, Robert Morris, Gouverneur Morris, and James Duane, but almost every general in the Continental army and the great majority of former members of the Continental Congress. (By more than a three-to-one ratio, the signers of the Declaration of Independence and the Articles of Confederation backed the new political system.)[46] To that category must be added Jackson Turner Main's "cosmopolitan" state legislators: 92 percent of their leaders supported the adoption of the federal Constitution.[47]

Reform was in the air. But Washington cautioned that did not mean that the reformers would coalesce on a proper revision of the government or that the public would agree to a fresh approach to federal government.[48] Though constitutional reform was the work of many hands, Washington emerged as the crucial figure. He had consistently criticized the Confederation as inadequate, and almost everyone who shared those views corresponded with him. Washington had expressed a vision of America, strong and united, possessed of a national character, in his "Circular to the States" before resigning his commission as commander-in-chief of the Continental army. Disseminated in newspapers at the time, it now reappeared in gazettes everywhere.[49]

If by deeds and words and by being the most meaningful symbol of unity and nationhood, Washington had laid the groundwork for reform, James Madison became its principal strategist, both in generating momentum in the fall of 1786 and in the spring of 1787 for the convention and later in defense of the Virginia Plan on the floor of the State House in Philadelphia. The Washington–Madison collaboration leaves small doubt that without their respective contributions a constitutional reformation would never have taken place in Philadelphia. One can even question whether the convention ever would have been held. Madison and his Virginia allies, who quickly selected their state delegation, made it known that Washington would attend the Philadelphia gathering as head of the Virginia representatives (before he had agreed to do so!), which prompted the other states to send their own distinguished men to this "assembly of demigods," as Jefferson described it. Madison and his colleagues elected Washington president of the convention; and they had no difficulty getting him to allow the Federalists to use his name during the ratification contest. In fact, Washington took a more active part than he had intended. Antifederalists, reflecting on their eventual defeat, often said he was a major difference, especially in key battleground states such as Virginia, where Antifederalist Monroe said that without Washington the Constitution's opponents would have prevailed.[50]

Although Washington's influence as a general, constitutionalist, and president will always remain somewhat elusive to us, his performance would have seemed explicable to the architects of national states in the two centuries before 1776. Their belief in a great-man theory of history remained alive in the eighteenth century. Voltaire, Rousseau, and Hume attributed state formation largely to the accomplishments of remarkable men. Voltaire agreed with Rousseau's contention in the *Social Contract* that the statesman "is the engineer who invents the machine." Peter Gay observes that, despite the philosophes' cynicism about much in their day, the Enlightenment itself hardly rejected great-man history. Such figures as Peter the Great or Frederick the Great received praise "as the founder of states, the preceptor of his country, and the father of his people."[51] For revolutionary Americans, Washington personified the great-man theory at its best. He had proved that he could be trusted with the power that he had willingly relinquished at the end of the Revolution. Moreover, in 1787 it was well known that he had preached the gospel of American unity to the Congress, the states, and the people since 1775. If we described Washington in European terms, we would call him Washington the Unifier, a role he continued to assume during the ratification contest and during his presidency.[52]

An American Nation-State

The American nation-state that emerged between 1763 and 1787–88 revealed both similarities and dissimilarities with the national polities that appeared in early modern Europe. Those European entities, with the notable exception of Britain, were unitary national states. Britain still adhered to long-held concepts of individual liberties anchored in the common law and the Bill of Rights of 1688–89. And her transatlantic settler societies had a significant degree of de facto internal autonomy. With the adoption of the Constitution of 1787, the American nation-state continued to be federal in nature, as the colonies had been in their relationship with the mother country before the Revolution and as the United States had been under the Articles of Confederation.

But the United States, when the government began to function under President Washington in 1789, displayed an energetic and consolidated form of federalism previously unknown in America. The Constitution mixed national and federal features to create the new federalism.[53] Not only did the Constitution provide, as had the Articles, that the central government could make war and peace, raise an army and navy, conclude treaties, coin money, create a postal service and so on, but it now possessed the crucial power to enforce its authority. The lack of legal ways to compel compliance had been the most signal weakness of the Articles. The term employed by students of state formation for such superintendency is coercion. The Constitution provided multiple means of enforcing obedience. Under certain circumstances, the army could be employed to enforce the laws and to maintain order; and so could the state militias, which could be taken into national service. The Constitution stipulates that the Constitution and "the Laws of the United States . . . shall be the supreme Law of the Land." State officials are also compelled to take an oath to uphold the Constitution. Failure to do so means that federal courts can take action against state-level officeholders. Even Elbridge Gerry, who refused to sign the Constitution, admitted the value of linking "officers of the two Governments" into "the General System."[54]

Because the framers addressed so fully the Articles' deficiencies by providing for both internal and external security and order, Walter Millis calls the Constitution a military and a political document. As Governor Edmund Randolph of Virginia explained, government's first responsibility was to be "a shield against foreign hostility, and a firm resort against domestic commotion." The Constitution proved so successful in these areas that Americans have not added a single amendment concerning war-making and security.[55] For many years, the American centralized state appeared weak by European standards, but by 1800, writes Richard H. Kohn, America had established the military institutions that would remain largely unchanged until the twentieth century. For the people of the West, says Andrew Cayton, "the use of an army" during the Washington administration "became crucial to proving the value of the national government. Nothing else it did was more important in attaching people to the United States." Because of America's "free security" from Europe for nearly a century following the War of 1812, America did not need a sizable military apparatus to counter threats from outside the hemisphere, but the constitutional basis existed in the Constitution should the need arise, which came about only after 1900.[56]

Throughout the course of state formation, America had become a nation without a well-developed sense of nationalism, although leaders with a continental vision such as Washington, Hamilton, and Madison—nationalists by any definition—had created an institutional structure in which nationalism evolved in the nineteenth century. After 1815, the process seems to have quickened. Scholars are not of one mind about this process or all of its ingredients; but some are indisputable: Washington, the Revolution, and the Constitution. Cultural common ground probably came more slowly for Americans, a pattern noted previously for European nation-states. It increased following the War of 1812, when Americans jettisoned the foolish notion that the Federalist and Republican parties were respectively ideological clones of monarchical Britain and revolutionary France. Had the Articles of Confederation continued to operate into the 1790s, confronting internal and external threats stemming from the French Revolution, it is doubtful that the United States would have survived under one flag. The third and final phase of federalism and state formation came just in the nick of time.

CHAPTER FOUR

John Adams, Republican Monarchist

An Inquiry into the Origins of His Constitutional Thought

Richard Alan Ryerson

John Adams appears fixed in American historical memory as the nation's most conservative Revolutionary leader. But what does this image really signify? At no point in his public career was Adams the most conservative figure of his generation on any issue of foreign or domestic policy. In the final run up to Independence he stoutly opposed every Loyalist and timid fence-sitter. In the nineteenth and twentieth centuries his voluminous works, with their many passages defending the traditional social order, had less appeal for defenders of the social order than those of a host of other writers, perhaps because there is so much else in Adams that deplores the power of wealthy elites.

By one measure only has John Adams appeared conservative for a Revolutionary American: the character of his constitutional thought. So striking were his views of organic law that Adams's republican opponents, beginning in 1787, and with increasing fervor, until his involuntary retirement from public office in 1801, and in some cases for years thereafter, accused him of being an aristocrat, an Anglophile, and a monarchist. Some critics added that his long stay in Europe had forever corrupted his republican morals. In his two late, extended writings on government, *A Defence of the Constitutions of Government of the*

United States,[1] and *Discourses on Davila,*[2] they found plenty of ammunition for each of these charges.

In so characterizing John Adams, his critics committed two errors because they were not political theorists but deeply committed political actors. First, the men and—in the case of Mercy Otis Warren—the woman who charged Adams with being a monarchist did not read and consider all of his political writings. Second, they did not imagine that a genuine supporter, indeed a creator, of the Revolution could hold profoundly different assumptions about republican government and society from those embraced by most Americans. In conceding these points to Adams's critics, however, one precipitously comes upon a central problem. If John Adams did hold different beliefs about the nature of government and society from those of his countrymen, how did he acquire such beliefs? The explanation cannot simply reside in his regional environment. His republican quarrels, after all, were not only with Virginians—Jefferson, Madison, and John Taylor of Caroline—but also with Yankees—Samuel Adams, Roger Sherman, and Mrs. Warren. Indeed, in his approach to many constitutional matters John Adams was utterly distinctive.

The Exceptional Founder

To discover the origins of Adams's constitutional thought, it is first necessary to identify his most exceptional ideas. In distinguishing Adams from other American political thinkers of the young republic, however, one must begin by showing how much he was like them. As long as Adams remained a "mainstream" thinker, he largely defined that mainstream. He was one of the first Americans to declare, in a prominent public document, that the only constitutional link between a British North American colony and Great Britain was their common monarch (1773).[3] He was the first American to apply the term "republic" to both the British monarchy and Britain's colonies in North America (1775).[4] When several of those colonies resolved to create governments independent of the British king and nation, it was John Adams who most effectively taught them how to structure their new republics (1776).[5] And it was Adams who, in the Massachusetts Constitution of 1780 (written in 1779), designed the first state constitution that assigned to its major organs of government distinctive powers with distinctive titles and established the strongest American executive to that date, thereby creating a constitutional blueprint that would exert a powerful influence, both in form and substance, upon the drafting of the United States Constitution.[6] Throughout the 1770s, the thought of John Adams was—or appeared to be—the very essence of American constitutional thought.

Like the majority of his countrymen, by 1775–76 John Adams had come to believe that the people were the ultimate foundation of authority in any republic, and further, "that there is no good government but what is Republican."[7] Like many if not most of his countrymen, he sought a government that mixed democratic, aristocratic, and monarchical elements into a finely balanced whole. Like so many patriots, he felt the indispensable need for a two-house legislature, a single executive, and an independent judiciary. And in 1776 it was John Adams who led America's more moderate revolutionaries in favoring a strong executive. These "strong executive" forces, who were perhaps in a minority in the new American states immediately after Independence, were rapidly regaining majority support by 1780.

After 1780, however, as Gordon Wood has memorably argued, Adams appeared to depart from America's constitutional mainstream, most notably by failing to approve or perhaps even comprehend the emerging new understanding of the relationship between a two-house legislature and the people. Both intellectual and constitutional developments in the rapidly evolving states, and then in Philadelphia in 1787, established the core belief that legislative upper houses could express the will and interests of the whole people as effectively as the lower houses that had long been accorded this role.[8] In time, executives too would be seen in this new light, until by the 1820s Andrew Jackson and his supporters would claim that the president was uniquely the voice of all of the American people—a belief that subsequent presidents have been eager to embrace.

To place John Adams's departure from America's constitutional mainstream at about 1780, which was—not coincidentally in the view of Wood and several other scholars—the beginning of his long stay in Europe,[9] and to center his unique political vision in his arrested view of the role of the legislative upper house, however, is to understate the duration, character, and force of his intellectual separation from his peers, a separation that began earlier and grew to include his view of several fundamental concepts of republican government. A brief survey of Adams's essential differences with the majority of America's Revolutionary leaders should suggest the profound gulf between him and his countrymen.

Republican Monarchist

What sets John Adams apart from all other Revolutionary constitutional thinkers is his view of the proper role and essential nature of both the executive and the upper house of the legislature. His insistence upon the creation of strong senates, both to empower and to contain aristocracies, and his belief that aristocracies were coeval with human society and an ineradicable feature of it comprise the better known part of his constitutional argument. Yet his convictions about executive power are more strikingly original, appear earlier in his constitutional thought, and are perhaps even more fundamental to his constitutional vision.

Adams first presented the ideal structure of government in a conventional way for a British North American, by praising the British constitution. Writing as "Clarendon" in the *Boston Gazette* in 1766, he offered this succinct description:

> Were I to define the British constitution, therefore, I would say, it is a limited monarchy, or a mixture of the three forms of government commonly known in the schools, reserving as much of the monarchical splendor, the aristocratical independency, and the democratical freedoms, as necessary, that each of these powers may have a controul both in legislation and execution, over the other two, for the preservation of the subject's liberty.[10]

A striking feature of this passage is its warm affection for every part of the British constitution. But "Clarendon" wrote just as the colonists had effectively nullified the Stamp Act in North America and just before Parliament passed the Declaratory Act, a categorical defense of its supremacy throughout the British empire, as the price of repealing the hated impost. The ensuing seven years of rising tension between the colonial assemblies and Parliament, an escalating conflict that was particularly acute in Massachusetts, did not force Adams to abandon his profound admiration for the British constitution—nothing in his long life would ever do that. But it did permanently alienate him from Parliament and force him to become more creative. If Parliament was not and could never be a sound link between Britain and her colonies, how could the British empire, in which John Adams was still deeply invested, survive?

In January 1773, Adams delivered his first comprehensive answer. Governor Thomas Hutchinson, exasperated by years of feuding with an assembly that refused to acknowledge Parliamentary authority and alarmed by the recent resurgence of resistance to that authority in Boston and other towns, had finally decided to instruct the unruly legislators in the true nature of the constitution that held the British empire together, a constitution that granted the colonies liberties that were less extensive than those enjoyed by Englishmen in the mother country. The leaders of Massachusetts's House of Representatives, determined to counter Hutchinson's address, asked John Adams to advise them in preparing a response and then allowed him to draft the text. Adams, citing a host of seventeenth-century English charters, grants, royal orders, and Parliamentary statutes—and mischaracterizing a few of them—demonstrated that neither the colony's first settlers and their descendants nor the Stuart monarchs had believed that Massachusetts was subject to Parliament, or even to the Crown. Rather, he argued, both in the January "Reply" and in a second answer to Hutchinson's counter-reply in March, that the sole constitutional connection between Massachusetts and Great Britain was through the person of the monarch.[11]

In the eyes of both Parliament and George III, of course, Adams's novel resolution of the imperial crisis was dubious as history and preposterous as theory, but once it had received the legislators' endorsement it was devastating to Governor Hutchinson's rapidly dwindling respect and Parliament's waning authority in Massachusetts. It was also highly appealing to colonial leaders, and within two years, following important variations penned by James Wilson, Thomas Jefferson, and others, it became colonial and congressional orthodoxy.[12]

For Adams himself the replies had broader implications. What he was now describing, while still a limited monarchy, as it had been for "Clarendon" in 1766, was a new and different kind of limited monarchy. By removing both Lords and Commons from the field, Adams had in effect restructured Massachusetts's existing constitution. In his new model the democratic element remained strong, with the popularly elected House still nominating the members of the governor's Council; the aristocratic element, which Adams appeared largely to identify with Parliament itself, nearly disappeared; and the monarch, freed from parliamentary meddling, became stronger than ever because he could deal directly with the popular assembly.

For two years neither Adams nor any other American had a name for his problematic but increasingly popular creation. In 1775, however, writing as "Novanglus" to defend the authority of the Continental Congress and Massachusetts's provincial congress against the Tory essayist "Massachusettensis,"

Adams began to rethink the whole imperial problem. By early March, he was ready to declare that the government he was defending, the only government that could preserve the colonies' liberties within the British empire, was in fact "a republic." Anticipating the astonishment of his readers upon learning that they were living in a republic—an astonishment that he probably still felt himself—he promptly asserted that the highest ancient and modern authorities on government would recognize that "the British constitution is more like a republic than an empire" because it was "*a government of laws, and not of men* . . . in which the king is first magistrate." He then assured his countrymen that "This office being hereditary, and being possessed of such ample and splendid prerogatives, is no objection to the government's being a republic, as long as it is bound by fixed laws, which the people have a voice in making, and a right to defend."[13]

By March 6, 1775, John Adams had become a "republican monarchist." Beginning with his highly popular celebration of the political significance of the settlement of New England in his *Dissertation on the Canon and the Feudal Law* in 1765,[14] and then advancing this still parochial interpretation as the historical basis for Massachusetts's constitutional relationship with Britain in the two replies to Hutchinson in 1773, he finally connected his creation with what he regarded as the main sequence of political theory in Western thought, from the ancients through Machiavelli and Harrington to his own day, and gave it the only name proper to it—a republic.[15] All that John Adams and British North America needed to do in the spring of 1775 was to convince Parliament that it had no business governing America, and to persuade George III to claim his rightful place as America's first magistrate, its republican king.

The colonists' violent opposition to British authority at Lexington and Concord was perhaps not the best means to effect this persuasion, but the historical record suggests no obvious smoother path. And once both king and Parliament had chosen swords over words, John Adams was forced to become creative again. He did not experience any great personal crisis in surrendering his hopes that George III might play the role of America's republican monarch. At the same time, Adams, unlike most American patriots, felt no deep personal animus toward the king. He later remembered that even during his direct involvement in drafting the bill of indictment that became the body of the Declaration of Independence, "I never believed George to be a tyrant in disposition and in nature; I always believed him to be deceived by his courtiers on both sides of the Atlantic, and in his official capacity only, cruel."[16]

Before the final break several of Adams's congressional colleagues, impressed with his years of studying and writing about mixed and republican constitutions, sought out his counsel on creating new independent governments for their home colonies. Deprived of a monarch who would protect them and defend their liberties, these colonies required some manner of effective executive power. Adams's solution, expressed with only minor variations but increasing elaboration in successive letters and then in one of his briefest and most effective pamphlets, was as slight a modification of Massachusetts's own charter government as could meet the challenges of America's new kingless world.

The people, he wrote, should elect an assembly, which in turn would choose a council, either from among its own members or from citizens outside the chamber. Both chambers would then jointly choose a governor. In a letter to Richard Henry Lee, the first of several detailing his ideas, he stated that each institution—assembly, council, and governor—was to be "a distinct and independent branch of the legislature, and have a negative on all laws."[17] In his third letter, to North Carolina congressman John Penn, he was more explicit: "But there ought to be a third Branch of the Legislature: and wherever the Executive Power of the State is placed, there the third Branch of the Legislature ought to be found."[18] In *Thoughts on Government* (April 1776), which grew directly out of these letters, he repeated the point, describing his upper legislative chamber as "a mediator between the two extreme branches of the legislature, that which represents the people and that which is vested with executive power"; and again, the governor "should have a free and independent exercise of his judgment, and be made also an integral part of the legislature." In 1776, Adams believed the governor could play this role only after he had been "stripped of most of those badges of domination called prerogatives."[19] As he had in 1766, however, he insisted that the executive in any sound government must be "an integral part" of the legislature. It was a point to which he would return again and again, each time with greater insistence and broader implications.

In the three years following Independence John Adams wrote little about constitutional questions. He was pleased when most of the states, in some cases explicitly following his advice in *Thoughts on Government*, promptly framed constitutions that provided for a bicameral legislature and a single executive, although their executives were seldom given substantial legislative powers. He was also pleasantly surprised that several southern states, while adopting the balanced bicameral model he had espoused, created more popular governments than he had expected.[20] But virtually all Adams's waking hours were spent first in providing for the Continental Army as head of Congress's Board of War, and then, in France, in bringing system and order to America's three-man commission to the Court of Versailles. In the summer of 1779, however, the unexpected termination of his diplomatic commission allowed him to return home just in time to be chosen a delegate to Massachusetts's constitutional convention. That body appointed him to its drafting committee, and the committee placed him on its only subcommittee, where he found himself, in mid-September, with a rare opportunity, to draft the entire text of a constitution before showing it to anyone.

In the ensuing six weeks John Adams distilled nearly two decades of reading, thinking, and writing about both practical politics and fundamental law into the most carefully crafted and enduring constitution of the Revolutionary era. Because someone, very likely Adams himself, destroyed any and all notes, extracts, and drafts that went into making this superb structure, the exact result of his labors remains slightly obscure. But the earliest surviving plan, entitled *The Report of a Constitution or Form of Government for the Commonwealth of Massachusetts: Agreed upon by the Committee—to be laid before the Convention* (Boston, [Oct.] 1779), gives a fairly accurate idea of what he had achieved.[21]

Following an elegant Preamble and a comprehensive Declaration of Rights, the *Report's* central Frame of Government opens with a classic reformulation of Adams's preferred definition of a republic, the definition he had used in both *Novanglus* and *Thoughts on Government:* "In the government of the Commonwealth of Massachusetts, the legislative, executive, and judicial power, shall be placed in separate departments, to the end that it might be a government of laws and not of men."[22]

Adams then proceeded to describe, in great detail, a senate, a house, and a governor, and for good measure, a governor's council as well. He prominently featured an independent judiciary. But the resulting structure was very different from that in *Thoughts on Government.* In 1776, heavily influenced by the Massachusetts Charter of 1692, the only government that he knew from direct experience, Adams recommended that a popularly elected house choose the council, and that both chambers then select the governor. By 1779, however, no American state, including Massachusetts, would tolerate such indirect elections, and Adams himself had become convinced that popularly elected tripartite, bicameral governments would be secure against the most unruly popular forces. He therefore provided for annual direct elections for members of both the house and senate and for the governor. Still, the members of the governor's Council were to be chosen from those elected to the senate by a joint meeting of the house and senate. And for the powerful governor, Adams required rotation in office. Finally, the *Report* gave the governor "a negative upon all the laws—that he may have power to preserve the independence of the executive and judicial departments."[23]

John Adams's thoughts about executive power passed through several more stages before he departed for his second and longest stay in Europe. In 1766, as "Clarendon"—and apparently from his college years—he favored a "limited monarchy, or a mixture of the three forms of government commonly known in the schools," and placed the British constitution squarely under that heading. In 1773, as the principal, anonymous author of the Massachusetts House of Representatives' two replies to Governor Hutchinson, he advocated a government headed by a king with broad powers, balanced by a popular assembly that also enjoyed broad powers. Neither Adams nor anyone else assigned this government a name, but without Parliament (including the House of Lords), or an independently chosen upper legislative house, it no longer qualified as the sort of mixed government taught in the schools and was in danger of becoming something quite different. In March 1775, as "Novanglus," Adams renamed both the British and the Massachusetts constitution "republics," and properly became a republican monarchist. In April 1776, however, with the impending constitutional demise of George III in America, Adams appeared, in *Thoughts on Government,* to be a fairly straightforward republican.

At this point the evolution of Adams's constitutional thought could have ceased, and many of his countrymen would later wish that it had done so. But John Adams did not stop thinking, and his irrepressible creativity soon led him in a new direction, along some old and recently abandoned paths. In *Thoughts on Government,* at the most conventionally republican phase of his political development, he still recommended that the governor be regarded as the third branch of the legislature, with an absolute veto on all proposed laws. But he gave little thought to the governor's relationship to the people, and he calmly assumed that any republican executive would be "stripped of most of those badges of domination called prerogatives." By October 1779, however, Adams began reaching back to certain executive powers that his fellow patriots had abandoned. His Massachusetts governor, required to possess a freehold worth at least £1,000, would live a very different life from that of the average citizen. He would exercise extensive appointment powers, including some, like the naming of militia officers, that Massachusetts's armed citizens had recently claimed for themselves. And it now became imperative that he be formally designated the third branch of the legislature—the mere possession of an absolute veto would not do.[24] Finally, in his letter to Elbridge Gerry, Adams introduced a new theme in his constitutional thought: the fear of aristocracy.

This concern throws into relief a remarkable feature of John Adams's characterization of the executive, from his earliest provincial writings to his draft of the Massachusetts Constitution. Of all Americans who ardently supported independence from the British Crown, Adams consistently displayed the least fear of executive power, whether in the person of a royal governor, a reigning monarch, or a popularly elected executive. In his view, individual governors and monarchs might (and would) abuse power, either through ignorance and gullibility (his view of George III), or, on occasion, true malevolence. But this did not invalidate the institution of first magistrate, which Adams always believed was indispensable in any orderly government. In the intensity of his commitment to effective executive power he resembled America's Loyalists more than his fellow patriots. The full development of Adams's ideas of executive power, however, could only occur after he began to assess the character of the upper legislative house and the nature of the class upon which it ought to be based.

Fear of Aristocracy

That John Adams, like most other American political writers, paid little attention to the respective characters of upper and lower legislature chambers in the decade before the Revolution is not surprising. Only Connecticut and Rhode Island elected their upper houses outright; Massachusetts chose its council through a unique legislative-appointive process; every other colony had an appointive governor's Council. Moreover, most colonial lower houses were already highly elitist, either in their full composition or in their leadership, and they were becoming more elitist over time.[25]

When the prospect of independence loomed large and Thomas Paine's *Common Sense* espoused a more democratic future for America, John Adams became concerned that new legislative-centered governments would be weak and disorderly, and in *Thoughts on Government* he argued forcefully for the necessity of two-house legislatures, as well as strong executives, to insure constitutional stability. But he showed little interest in the character of the new upper houses, which he believed could be chosen either from among and by the members of the lower houses, or by the citizenry, with equal propriety. In drafting Massachusetts's new constitution in 1779, he began to show an awareness that upper and lower houses might be designed to represent different social classes. This could explain his provision that candidates for the senate must have freehold estates worth £300, while members of the house need have only £100 freeholds.[26] But in 1779 Adams had yet to advocate an aristocratic senate, or even to recognize this possibility explicitly. His lament to Elbridge Gerry that the drafting committee had denied the governor full legislative status, while clearly generated by a fear of those whom he would later describe as aristocrats, did not associate those persons with the senate, but viewed them as operating in the legislature as a whole. Moreover, in 1779 Adams had yet to explore the nature of aristocracies in all societies and governments. This development first appeared during his stay in Europe.

When Adams returned to Europe in the fall of 1779, he shifted his focus from constitution making to diplomacy and devoted nearly all his efforts to that activity, both in France and Holland. He did not cease thinking about constitutions, however, for two reasons. First, he was proud of his draft of the Massachusetts Constitution (the committee's *Report*), which he soon had translated and published in Holland. When the full convention altered his work to produce the finished document he also arranged to have that published, along with other state constitutions, even though he thought it inferior to his original. Second, Adams believed that a crucial function of his role as a diplomat was one of educating Europeans about America. No American achievement was more impressive, to Adams's mind, than its set of strong, balanced constitutions. And so he not only had them published, he summarized, commented upon, and referred to them whenever he thought it might help America's quest for financial, military, and diplomatic support from European powers.[27]

For several years, Adams was too preoccupied with his diplomatic labors to resume his exploration of the forms and purposes of constitutional government. This changed in 1784 when he received a new, less time-consuming diplomatic assignment. For reasons that will probably never be known, Adams turned nearly his full attention to political theory, beginning with a thorough study of Plato.[28] The materials needed to reconstruct his course of reading are lacking, but by October 1786 he had mastered enough ancient, Renaissance, and modern political theory and history to begin his magnum opus, *A Defence of the Constitutions of Government of the United States of America, Against the Attack of M. Turgot, in His Letter to Dr. Price, Dated the Twenty-Second Day of March, 1778,* which he published in three volumes in London in 1787 and 1788.

Adams's immediate motivation for writing this unusual work is not entirely clear. Two essentially unrelated events that some scholars have considered proximate causes, the gradually increasing turmoil that culminated in the Assembly of Notables in France, and Shays's Rebellion in Massachusetts, occurred too late to play this role, although they may have encouraged Adams to persevere through his three volumes.[29] The rise of the Patriot party in the Netherlands is a more plausible initial cause, and Adams perhaps first intended his work as a guide to radical Dutch leaders.[30] The most personal cause, however, is that given in the title itself. This massive work was a defense of America's state constitutions, to which John Adams had contributed so prominently, against the charge by the philosophe Ann Robert Turgot that most American constitutions were defective because they parceled out power among bicameral legislatures and strong executives.

At one level, Adams's *Defence of the Constitutions* was just what it claimed to be, a thorough exploration, through all of recorded history, of the superiority of those political principles that animated America's new governments. Yet this massive work announced Adams's departure from America's constitutional mainstream in two ways. First, he took the three types of government—monarchy, aristocracy, and democracy—which in classical political theory existed either separately, in pure or degenerate form (the latter as tyranny, oligarchy, and mob rule), or as three ideally equal elements in mixed and balanced governments, and introduced each of them as the lead element in each of three types of republics. He then applied these terms to every European country that met his longstanding definition of a republic—a government of laws and not of men. He included small agrarian democratic republics in Italy and Switzerland; moderate-sized commercial aristocratic republics in Switzerland, Italy, and the Netherlands; and just three monarchical republics, of which only two, England (not Great Britain) and Poland, were of any size. Adams did not identify any pure democracies or aristocracies, which he thought could not exist for even a short time. Nor did he consider any pure monarchies, which he regarded (without tactlessly identifying them) as mere tyrannies. Then, after considering the constitutional opinions of a host of ancient and modern philosophers and historians, he applied the same labels to a broad range of ancient republics, large and small.

Having offered a typology of republics, Adams next turned his attention to aristocracy, which he saw as a disruptive middle force in any republic, threatening to both the monarch and the people, whom he saw as natural allies. Because aristocracies were inevitable in all societies, however, they must be included and controlled in any stable republic. In a brief "Recapitulation" of the first volume, he characterized the general relationship of the monarchical, aristocratic, and democratic elements that he found in all republics. His account of monarchy and aristocracy neatly epitomizes the heart of his new political science:

> Among every people, and in every species of republic, we have constantly found *a first magistrate, a head, a chief,* under various denominations. . . . [W]e may fairly conclude that the body politic cannot subsist, any more than the animal body, without a head. . . . [T]herefore . . . the Americans are not justly liable to censure [by Turgot and other unicameral centralizers] for instituting *governors.*
>
> In every form of government we have seen a *senate,* or *little council,* a composition, generally, of those officers of the state who have the most experience and power, and of a few other members selected from the highest ranks and most illustrious reputations. . . . The admission of such senates to a participation of these three kinds of power, has been generally observed to produce in the minds of their members an ardent aristocratical ambition, grasping equally at the prerogatives of the first magistrate, and the privileges of the people, and ending in the nobility of a few families, and a tyrannical oligarchy. But in those states, where the senates have been debarred from all executive power, and confined to the legislative, they have been observed to be firm barriers against the encroachments of the crown, and often great supporters of the liberties of the people. The Americans, then, who have carefully confined their senates to the legislative power, have done wisely in adopting them.[31]

Shortly after the completion of this first volume of the *Defence,* Abigail Adams, writing to introduce the book to her eldest son, worried that her husband, in arguing for a strong executive who would have a direct share in the legislative power, and yet would not share his extensive prerogative powers with any council or senate, would be viewed in America as favoring the "sitting up a King" (that is, thirteen little kings). John, she continued, stoutly denied this, saying that he only wanted to give every state governor "the same Authority which the British King has, under the true British constitution, balancing his power by the two other Branches."[32]

For many Americans in 1787, this would have sounded little different from "sitting up a King." But if his countrymen still had any doubts of Adams's constitutional intentions, he effectively resolved them for at least one American. Writing to Thomas Jefferson in December 1787, to explain both his general approval of and major reservations concerning the new federal Constitution, Adams declared: "You are afraid of the one—I, of the few. We agree perfectly that the many should have a full fair and perfect Representation.—You are Apprehensive of Monarchy; I, of Aristocracy. I would therefore have given more Power to the President and less to the Senate."[33]

Europe and Massachusetts

How was it possible for an American revolutionary to develop this view of executive and legislative power? The answer most commonly given over the last four decades is "Europe." Among America's more conservative patriot leaders, this argument runs, John Adams did not hold unusual opinions about the essential nature and proper role of either executive or legislative authority until he went to Europe and lived for several years among the more aristocratic societies of Paris and London.[34]

This conviction has long appeared plausible for several reasons. First, Adams did not write extensively about aristocracy, the most striking subject of his later political inquiry, before he began publishing his *Defence of the Constitutions of the United States* in 1787, while he was still in London. Second, he did not openly disagree about the meaning of republicanism with any American leader who supported a bicameral legislature before his spirited exchange of letters with Roger Sherman in 1789 and Samuel Adams in 1790, immediately following his return to America. Third, Adams's long service in Europe cut him off from a direct knowledge of some of the most novel and important constitutional developments, both at the state and national levels, that his countrymen would experience during the Revolutionary era. Finally, only two American leaders spent nearly a decade at some of the most opulent and refined courts in Europe. One, Benjamin Franklin, was already seventy upon his arrival, too venerable, perhaps, to be susceptible to pernicious Continental influences. The other, only forty-two at his first arrival, was John Adams.

A study of the whole course of Adams's constitutional writings from the 1760s to the 1790s, however, strongly argues that the two most important changes that occurred in his thought cannot be attributed either to what he observed in Europe or to what he personally experienced in his relations with Europeans. His political mood, previously one of enormous optimism for America's republican experiment, did darken in Europe and retain its new coloration upon his return. This probably owed more to his mounting frustration with a feckless, distracted Congress that failed to support him or appreciate his diplomatic labors than to his well-known disgust with both the French and British courts.[35] But the two most prominent features of his later political writings, his admiration for monarchical power and his concern for controlling aristocratic power in a republic, had deeper, native sources.

This is more readily apparent with respect to monarchy. Of all Adams's major writings, only his *Thoughts on Government,* written in the heady months leading up to Independence, glossed over the question of executive power and assumed no need for any kind of prerogatives. In every other important essay, before or after 1776, he praised constitutional monarchy ("Clarendon," 1766), elevated its role in Massachusetts ("Reply to Hutchinson," 1773), recast it as republican monarchy ("Novanglus," 1775), and finally attempted to create a governor with most of the powers of a constitutional monarch (draft of the Massachusetts Constitution, 1779). Only the last of these occurred after Adams's first, relatively short stay in Europe.

John Adams's growing concern over the power of aristocracy may have owed more to his European experience, but not much more. His first expression of alarm at aristocratic forces, in correspondence following his draft of the Massachusetts Constitution, appeared after his first, shorter European stay, and if any part of his alarm originated there, it must have been in reaction to his shabby treatment at the hands of the (aristocratic) Congress.[36] Thereafter, both American and European historical experience shaped his view of aristocracy.

Yet Adams's contemporary critics and many of his modern interpreters, noting his insistence that aristocracy was an ineradicable element in any society, have stubbornly missed the obvious: John Adams feared aristocracy, even in its more constructive forms, and he was always suspicious that any aristocracy might quickly degenerate into an oligarchy. Thus he admired the British constitution because it controlled aristocracy, however imperfectly, not because it empowered or celebrated it. Conversely, Adams showed little fear of democracy at any time in his life. He did not identify with the common people in the way that Benjamin Franklin and James Wilson did, nor did he ever patronize democratic aspirations and values, as Thomas Jefferson did so brilliantly. But

John Adams deeply respected the democratic element in a sound republic, and he always defended it.

If John Adams's commitment to a strong executive, even to a republican monarch, arose out of his experience, that experience largely occurred before his first departure for Europe in 1778, before even his commitment to the cause of constitutional revolution in 1773. Of the possible origins for his distinctive constitutional beliefs, at least four appear to have played a significant role: his social origins, his particular colony (his "country"), his unusual course of reading, and his profession.

Adams's social background—the first son of a moderately prosperous farmer and respected local officeholder—was common enough among political leaders in late colonial New England. At the intercolonial (congressional) level, however, among those who became the so-called Founding Fathers, Adams's origins were rather exceptional. Most of his colleagues from the middle and southern colonies, and several from New England, were born into more affluent and politically prominent families. A few, notably Benjamin Franklin, were from humbler homes than Adams's, or were, like Alexander Hamilton and James Wilson, immigrants of great talent but modest means. Adams, however, was neither an aristocrat nor quite a common man at birth, but a member of a rural—but not very rural—middle class. Moreover, neither his father's nor his mother's family had moved more than ten miles since emigrating from England in the seventeenth century.

In his marriage John Adams continued to follow this middle path. Washington and Jefferson greatly increased their considerable inherited wealth through marriage; Wilson and Hamilton, with scarcely an inherited penny, married heiresses. But John Adams, like his father before him, probably improved his social standing but not his wealth by marrying a woman whose ancestry was somewhat more distinguished than his, but whose immediate family was of only local prominence. Both the family into which he was born and the family that he established by his marriage were thoroughly respectable, with a few memories of past glory, but without either wealth or fame. Adams was proud of his family and saw its virtues of honesty, piety, hard work, and local public service as those of his colony and his nation, but he never entertained illusions of elevated social status. Until his own rise to professional and then political prominence, his social position was squarely middling. Just one more fact need be noted: Young Adams deeply admired a small number of men, all of whom, except for his father, were Massachusetts lawyers or judges.[37]

The province that John Adams always called home enjoyed a quite distinctive political structure, one that placed it, like Adams in his social origins, in a middle position. In the majority of British North American colonies political power was divided, on paper rather evenly, between a popular assembly and a royal governor who was assisted by a council that he (or his Crown superiors) appointed. In Connecticut and Rhode Island the people chose their assemblies, councils, and governors. Alone among Britain's colonial assemblies, the Massachusetts House of Representatives enjoyed the right to nominate the governor's Council, subject to that royal governor's negative of each nomination.

This unique structure had several important effects. First, unlike some unfortunate royal colonies, Massachusetts did not suffer the indignity of having British-born placemen sitting on its Council. Second, the Council could function effectively as the embodiment of a native aristocracy, albeit one that was intimately tied to the more democratic House. Its anomalous character may also have had a role in shaping John Adams's thoughts on aristocracy and developing his understanding of an upper legislative chamber. Third, as the imperial crisis deepened the Council, despite the governor's negative of several key nominations (including that of John Adams himself), gradually became nearly as radicalized as the House. Parliament finally corrected this anomaly by the Massachusetts Government Act of May 1774, which terminated the right of the House to nominate the Council, but in attempting to execute that statute, Britain effectively lost control of Massachusetts forever. This singular structure of government may help explain John Adams's unusual lack of fear of executive power. Massachusetts's chief executives, whether English- or American-born, were not usually so threatening or so powerful, even on paper, as the royal governors of several other colonies.

There were, of course, hundreds of well-educated, politically active middle-class residents of Massachusetts, and several became Revolutionary leaders without ever developing John Adams's distinctive constitutional ideas. If Adams shared his social and provincial worlds with many other men, however, he developed an intellectual world that was, increasingly, his alone. There is some scholarly recognition that in the fields of law, political theory, and history, John Adams was the most widely read man in late colonial New England, and perhaps in British North America. What is not well understood, however, is the unusual focus of his reading. Where many of his well-read colleagues ended their studies after mastering Locke and Blackstone, gaining a familiarity with a few figures of the Scottish enlightenment, and dipping into a few classical authors, Adams forged on, back to seventeenth- and sixteenth-century English law and political theory, across the Channel to Continental and international law, and finally to a close reading of Roman and Greek political theorists. He alone, among the Founders, eventually displayed a comprehensive knowledge of the political thought of Harrington, Machiavelli, Justinian, Cicero, Polybius, Aristotle, and Plato. Although he was also conversant with a few near contemporary exotics, like Rousseau and Beccaria, Adams's reading was, by the standards of his day, decidedly old fashioned. In his writings Harrington and Machiavelli loom large, and John Locke almost disappears.[38]

Adams's distinctive course of study, so much at odds with that of his contemporaries, helped to shape a mind that found its inspiration and comfort in the world view of the seventeenth-century English Commonwealthman and the sixteenth-century classical republican, in Harrington looking back to Machiavelli, and in Machiavelli looking back to Livy and Polybius.[39] This was not the new political world of ever-shifting interests and factions that Wilson and Madison found so appealing but an older world that focused on a limited set of political institutions—varying from culture to culture largely in their formal titles—that related directly to immutable sociopolitical classes. For Adams democracy was not a process, but a distinct social class, the class into which he had been born. Aristocracy was not so much a legal or traditional established class, although in Europe it usually had that status, as it was an ineradicable mix of talent and ambition, forever operating in every society, that had elevated him and his political colleagues to power and fame. Monarchy, that is, effective executive power exercised by a single individual, whether in absolute or republican, inherited or elected form, was an essential, indestructible requirement of human society.

Adams's middling social origins, modest enough to spur individual ambition and vulnerable enough to warrant protection, may have encouraged him to acquire these views. Massachusetts's provincial constitution, imperfectly tripartite in character, may have impelled him to discover, through years of exacting and quite exceptional study, how it might be perfected. But Adams's social and political context could not, by themselves, have shaped such an unusual reader, thinker, and writer. For this one thing more was needed: the law.

Many leaders of the American Revolution—colonial and state legislators, councilors, senators, and governors, delegates to Congress, and roughly a dozen members of the Constitutional Convention of 1787—were practicing attorneys. Several of these men, however, were part-time lawyers, most commonly lawyer-planters or lawyer-gentlemen. John Adams was not this kind of lawyer. The law was his only profession, his only important source of income before he entered Congress, for years his only object of serious study, his only access to reputation, and his only professional source of identity. John Adams was, if not obsessed with the law, at least extraordinarily committed to it. His commitment was handsomely rewarded. By the early 1770s he appears to have been the most active and widely respected attorney in Massachusetts.[40] He was certainly the most learned.

The law reinforced, amplified, and ratified John Adams's constitutional conservatism and his intellectual daring at every turn. First, as Daniel Coquillette has demonstrated, Adams's hunger for legal distinction drove him to acquire and display a deeper and broader knowledge of the law than any of his contemporaries. His initial efforts gradually earned him the respect he sought, but by 1770 his studies had taken on a life of their own, spurring him to master obscure English common law precedents, Continental civil law, and international law, far beyond the needs of his practice.[41] Yet no matter how seemingly obscure his learning, he made use of it, whether in referring to Count Beccaria in the Boston Massacre trials, to a host of obscure English statutes in his essays on the independence of the judiciary, or to Moore's reports in the Massachusetts House's second reply to Governor Hutchinson.[42] Adams's reputation for great learning had a direct impact on his public career and drew him at least four important assignments: the replies to Governor Hutchinson, *Thoughts on Government*, Congress's Plan of Treaties (the first blueprint for American foreign policy), and the Massachusetts Constitution. His long years of study also insured that as he considered constitutional issues, he would have as his authorities the principal authors of the classical republican tradition, from Plato and Aristotle through Machiavelli and Harrington.

The law had a second effect upon John Adams as well. From 1758 through 1774, Adams's world was not simply his books but Massachusetts's legal profession. The world of the law in the Province of Massachusetts Bay was in many ways a deeply conservative one, teaching a reverence for precedent, for authority, and for one's professional seniors and superiors. John Adams took all of this very seriously. Except for his father, Adams's personal heroes were venerable Massachusetts lawyers or judges—never legislators, ministers, doctors, merchants, or mere gentlemen, no matter how distinguished.[43] It may also be significant that among his heroes, and among his legal contemporaries for whom he felt the greatest affection, several inclined to Loyalism as the imperial crisis deepened: notably, Jeremiah Gridley, Samuel Quincy, Jonathan Sewall, and General Timothy Ruggles. In contrast, of the many provincial leaders who became ardent patriots, John Adams consistently expressed admiration for only one, his cousin Samuel Adams.

A brief study of the Massachusetts legal profession as a whole, on the eve of the American Revolution, has shown how pervasive Loyalism was within its ranks. In a province in which only a small fraction of the population supported the king after 1775, half of all barristers, the distinguished legal cohort to which John Adams belonged, were Loyalists. In John Adams's principal area of practice, Suffolk County (which included Boston), six of the twelve barristers became Loyalist refugees. Of the nine Suffolk County barristers who were under fifty in 1773, only three were Patriots: James Otis, Jr., Robert Treat Paine, and John Adams. The provincial judiciary was even more heavily Loyalist, especially at the top. Of the five judges of the Massachusetts Superior Court on the eve of the Revolution, three became Loyalist refugees, and only one became a Patriot.[44]

No one factor determined that John Adams would become a conservative revolutionary. If the elements of his background and early life course presented here impelled him to favor older constitutional traditions, one could easily turn the whole matter around to show that as a semirural, nominally Calvinist Yankee with no Crown appointment, Adams could only have become an ardent patriot. In a sense, both interpretations are correct. Without being in the least ambivalent about the Revolution, Adams gradually developed a unique constitutional approach that allowed him to retain his affection for Britain's venerable constitution while rejecting what was, in his view, that nation's increasingly corrupt government and society.

The Last Classical Republican

The present chapter has addressed three sets of questions that appear, under various guises, to have long perplexed students of John Adams's political thought. First, was John Adams a monarchist, and if he was, what manner of monarchist was he? Second, was Adams a republican as well as a monarchist, and if he was, what manner of republican was he? Finally, if Adams was a republican monarchist, when and why did he become one?

The evidence presented here argues that John Adams was a monarchist in his thinking about executive power, and a republican in his thinking about the whole structure and purpose of government. Indeed, as J. G. A. Pocock has observed, he was the last major writer of the classical republican tradition.[45] Because his novel and distinctive approach to creating political stability embraced both concepts, it seems fitting to call him by a new name, a "republican monarchist." If this label has any virtue, it is the forthright recognition of the highly unusual character of John Adams's political thought.

John Adams remained a most conservative revolutionary because everything he had ever seen and ever read, indeed, all that he had ever been, taught him that men had an unquenchable lust for power and distinction. Only by organizing themselves into societies that explicitly recognized the different levels of ambition and talent, distinctions that created the many (democracy) and the few (aristocracy), and that acknowledged the need for one powerful figure to balance the whole (monarchy), could they achieve stability. Most Americans wanted a leader with few pretensions and fewer prerogatives, subject to frequent elections. Adams wanted the nation's leader, and every governor, to have both the power and the majesty to impress unruly aristocrats and survive legislative assaults. Whatever worked to this end—elevated titles, copious prerogatives, and for the federal president, infrequent elections—would be all to the good in establishing America's republican monarchs.

CHAPTER FIVE

Revising Custom, Embracing Choice

Early American Legal Scholars and the Republicanization
of the Common Law

Ellen Holmes Pearson

In the mid-1820s, while studying at Henry St. George Tucker's law school in
Winchester, Virginia, Charles James Faulkner penned an essay on the distinc-
tiveness of American law. "The peculiar situation of this country," Faulkner
wrote, "has given a very peculiar cast to our legal institutions." Emigrating
"from a nation whose body of civil regulations had already acquired a perfection & intensity and at a period when the knowledge of human rights & remedies had grown into a science," Virginia's citizens, he announced, left the
mother country, "not as infants without ideas & [not] without a conception of
these rights" that were their inheritance, but with solidly formed beliefs about
their own rights as English people. Although they settled far from their homeland, Virginia colonists never stopped thinking of themselves as Englishmen
who were entitled to the same rights and laws as those who remained in England. "By a kind of fiction," therefore, they "merely extended the bounds of that
Empire where this law was to exercise its full influence & operation."[1]

Faulkner's essay communicated an effective picture of what had once been
Americans' sense of their place in the British empire and the role that the common law played in colonial society. Anglo-American cultural identity, so tied

to custom and an immemorial constitution and law, shaped the formation of colonial British America from the first settlements to the establishment of independent governments and legal systems and beyond. Considering themselves part of an extended British jurisdiction, colonial Americans molded their legal institutions in the image of those of the parent state. The colonies, however, were relatively simple societies that did not require all the trappings of English legal process. Because English law was custom-based and locally variable in nature, each colony formulated customs that were suited to its peculiar social circumstances and, over time, began to harden them into law.[2] Although colonial law, like the colonial settlers, remained British, distance and social circumstances gave colonial law a somewhat different content from that of its English progenitor.

Upon declaring independence from Britain, Americans self-consciously sought to build on these differences. Despite impressive economic growth and increased social sophistication, colonial settlers never felt that they measured up to metropolitan standards.[3] These notions of cultural inferiority did not end with the Revolution, but, from 1776 onward, Americans depicted their experiment in republicanism as the first step in building a society vastly superior to any already in existence, including that of England. They proudly announced to the world that they had removed all of the corrupting, feudal vestiges of the Norman invasion and restored the English common law to its pre-invasion form.[4] Furthermore, because of the decentralized character of American federalism, local versions of common law continued to evolve as each state built its own form of republican government and redefined the common law system to fit new republican parameters. Americans agreed that their legal and constitutional innovations on English common law were among the principal cultural advantages that distinguished their republics from the former parent country.

Even as they proclaimed the superiority of their own law, however, American legal scholars remained indebted to English precedent.[5] The writings of the nation's first law professors and legal scholars reveal a tension between the attempt to distance American common law from that of the English and the desire to identify with purer, pre-feudal versions of English law. In confronting these tensions, the early republic's legal scholars changed the law's very character, redefining concepts of custom, consent, and choice to explain American modifications to English precedent. Along the way, they sculpted a vision of America as a nation of superior laws, a nation that they claimed would realize unsurpassed cultural and social achievements.

Sir William Blackstone and America's Common Law

In the years after they declared independence from England, the leaders of the new polities debated whether they should retain a system of law that was so uniquely English or whether they should scrap the common law for the more orderly and scientific mode of codification, after the fashion of the civil law. English common law was a confusing, unwieldy system, and by the mid-eighteenth century many English judges and lawyers were persuaded that it needed change. Lord Chief Justice William Mansfield led the first wave of reform in England, which included the establishment of a standardized law reporting system and the creation of a commercial law code.[6] Radical English reformists like Jeremy Bentham agitated for a codification of English law, and some Americans agreed that it was time for English—and American—lawyers to reduce their law to a scientific, rational code, styled after the continental Europeans' civil codes.[7]

Ultimately, however, because generations of Englishmen had been "gradually tied up and imbued with the principles"[8] of English law, few Americans could conceive of abandoning English common law in favor of a different system. Their own colonial experiences told Revolutionaries that abandoning or retaining the common law was not necessarily an "all-or-nothing" prospect. Each colony had already molded English law to its own purposes, and the legal systems in place at the outbreak of war with England generally served each state's needs. Framers of the new states' governments eventually concluded that to abrogate their entire legal system and to compose a new code of law after Justinian's example would be too bold a measure and, in the words of Thomas Jefferson, "an arduous undertaking, of vast research, of great consideration and judgment."[9] The exigencies of war and the time constraints involved in creating new governments left no time for such luxuries as compiling fresh codes of law. Perhaps most importantly, despite their animosity toward the English government, American revolutionaries were convinced that the common law system was the best in the world, because it combined "in the most exalted degree the attainment of human rights with the least possible inconvenience & delay."[10] Pennsylvania jurist and law professor James Wilson conceded that the ancient laws and customs of England were "not only good, but the very best."[11] Therefore, instead of replacing them, the revolutionaries chose to retain the common law's fundamental principles, along with the various modifications they had made over the years to fit the needs of their respective colonies. From this template, they could make further changes to fit their newly independent polities.

The decision to retain the common law system was a mixed blessing for America's law practitioners. Their familiarity with and fondness for the common law made them refuse to relinquish their use of it, but they also knew that it was cumbersome and outmoded. At the very least they wanted a more rational, scientific system than the English model provided, and with Sir William Blackstone's *Commentaries on the Laws of England,* Americans thought they might have discovered a temporary alternative to wholesale legal reform.

In his four-volume treatise, Blackstone, the first Vinerian Professor of the common law at Oxford, synthesized the work of generations of judges, legal treatise writers, and political theorists and made their principles accessible even to those not schooled in the law. Arguably, the *Commentaries* was the "most influential systematic statement of the principles of the common law,"[12] and it served as the most popular and most important introduction to the study of the English law written up to that time. For some American students, it was the only major law book they studied before admission to their local bar.

The new nation's legal scholars welcomed Sir William Blackstone's four-volume *Commentaries on the Laws of England* as a temporary text—until an American version appeared. While the *Commentaries* served American law practitioners and scholars as a convenient resource for the study of English law, it could also help Americans define how they were different from the English. The work served as an easy target for criticisms about unrepublican elements within English law and to point out how American lawmakers had improved on the common law to make it fit their societies. American legal scholars had to reconcile the many outmoded monarchical traditions contained in Blackstone's work with the republican missions they wanted to impart to the young men who attended their classes and read their treatises. Legal educators in the new nation felt compelled to supplement the *Commentaries* with explications of their own states' innovations, as well as their own ideas about law in a republic. They combined the disciplines of history, law, and politics in their lectures so that they could articulate to their students the origins and evolution of the common law within their states and their nation.

Students felt Blackstone's presence in the American law classroom from the first day of lecture, as most professors followed the English master's lead and began with his lesson on the municipal law from Volume I of the *Commentaries.* American professors and legal writers also followed Blackstone's practice of dividing the law into *lex scripta* and *lex non scripta,* or written and unwritten law. The English law professor explained that unwritten law included general customs common to the entire country as well as "*particular* customs" and laws valid only in certain localities within the kingdom. In ancient times, according to Blackstone, all laws were "intirely traditional" and transmitted orally. By the eighteenth century one could find these laws in the country's court records, but because of the local nature of these oral traditions, variations in custom still existed from place to place.[13] Written law, on the other hand, consisted of the statutes, acts, and edicts enacted by the king in Parliament. Although statutes were the explicit work of a legislative body rather than the product of ancient custom, Blackstone assured his readers that they were not independent of the common law. Instead, they either upheld a portion of the common law or they remedied a defect within the common law. Therefore, the king in Parliament saw fit to enact a statute to revive certain customs that had fallen into disuse, to fix a flaw in the common law that resulted from change of time and circumstances, or to remedy the "mistakes and unadvised determinations of unlearned judges."[14]

Present-day readers may find it astonishing to learn how small a part statute law played in Revolutionary-era American or English law. Up to and beyond the Civil War, American legislatures passed very few statutes. In the decades before and after the Revolution, Anglo-American legislatures made or modified law only in those rare cases when the construction of a law was not applicable to the circumstances of a government or people, or if a practice had become absurd or outmoded.[15] According to James Wilson, statutes were only a small proportion of Pennsylvania's laws, and they should be "considered as a supplement" to the "most important part of her system of jurisprudence," the common law.[16] American legists generally subscribed to the idea that the less a legislative assembly interfered in the workings of the common law the better. Although statute law was a far smaller proportion of Anglo-American law, Americans still had to grapple, just as they had to do with the common law, with the question of what parts of it were still useful to their new governments and what could be jettisoned in favor of republican innovations.[17]

Custom and America's Right to the Common Law

Much of this unwritten Anglo-American law derived its authority from immemorial usage and long-standing local custom. To overstate the importance of custom to English social and legal cultures is difficult. The idea that the English common law was born out of immemorial custom was deeply ingrained in the English consciousness, and the common law's ability to endure across the ages was a source of great pride for Englishmen. Habitual usage was, to the English mind, the most perfect litmus test of a regulation. If a practice could hold up to years of use without rejection by the governed, it carried great legal authority among the English. Americans shared English pride in their common legal tradition, and they too emphasized the importance of custom, particularly in solidifying and giving strength to a constitution and law seemingly without beginning.[18] The idea of an ancient, unwritten law was so much a part of Anglo-American culture that it was difficult, if not impossible, for many to imagine living without it. In his address to the incoming law students at the College of Pennsylvania in 1824, Philadelphia lawyer and law lecturer Peter DuPonceau called the common law "a metaphysical being" grown out of feudal customs that had gradually "become incorporated and in a manner identified not only with the national jurisprudence, but, under the name of *Constitution*," with America's government. He proudly acknowledged that the common law was America's "national law," stating that the common law was "interwoven with the very idiom" that they spoke, and that it would be impossible for Americans to "learn any other system of laws without learning at the same time another language." Americans could not even discern right or wrong, according to DuPonceau, "but through the medium of the ideas" that they "derived from the common law."[19] DuPonceau's inclusion of elements of the common law within "every civil and political institution, and every thing connected with the government of the country" stretched the common law's arms into the daily lives of every American citizen.[20] The mundane workings of justice in the states also depended on the existence of the common law. One Litchfield, Connecticut Law School student quoted professor James Gould's insistence that "every sovereign state in order to have any national system of jurisprudence must have an unwritten law . . . for the stat[ute] or written law" could not "afford a rule for every action," nor, in Gould's opinion, could any statute "furnish rules sufficient to give notice in one single & the most simple case imaginable." Replacing the common law form with legal codes would, in Gould's opinion, leave no resources with which to fill in the gaps between statutes, and such a lack would cause "Difficulties in infinitum."[21]

Once they had explained to their audience why the Founders decided against scrapping the English common law system in favor of a distinctive

American legal system, legists had to defend this choice against claims that America could not have a true common law of its own. Blackstone defined a valid custom as a practice that was of continuous local usage and in existence so long as to make it impossible to remember its beginning. The practice had to be the object of peaceful acquiescence, and it had to bear the qualities of reason, certainty, and consistency. Above all, it had to be compatible with the common law.[22] To some, the notion of an American common law worked against the fundamental principle of the common law's immemorial status. How, critics asked, could places that had been founded within legal memory possess legal systems that were immemorial? To justify America's right to a common law of its own, legal scholars used a variety of creative arguments primarily based on reinterpretations of Blackstone's list of criteria for a legitimate custom.

According to English legal tradition, for a custom to qualify as immemorial it must have existed before the accession of Richard I. Any custom proven not to exist before that period was not truly custom. Under this definition, of course, there could be no custom in the former colonies because there were no English settlements in those places at the time of Richard I's reign.[23] Litchfield's James Gould dismissed the criterion of "immemorial" existence by responding that England had no exclusive right to immemorialness or to the common law system. Common sense dictated that a common law system was the most practical form for colonial British America and after the Revolution that practical necessity had not changed. He flatly rejected the idea that the American states could have no common law of their own simply because they had no immemorial existence, usage, or custom. This absurd idea, recorded Gould's student Ely Warner, was based on a premise that legists called "*petitio principii*—we cannot because we cannot."[24]

In their lectures Gould and his mentor Tapping Reeve set out to refute the notion that the common law was an exclusive fraternity to which young upstart polities need not apply. They wanted to do away with the idea that a legal system could be secure only if it originated in the mists of time immemorial. To accomplish this objective, Reeve and Gould attempted to dismantle the concept of an immemorial English common law altogether. They argued that if English law really was immemorial, no former British colony could have had a common law of its own but rather was "bound down by the English precedents entirely and indeed to the common Law as it stood before the time of Richard 1st." They called this idea "absurd," because much of the contemporary English common law had, like the American colonies, grown up within the time of legal memory. Law merchant, the law of paraphernalia, and executory devises, for example, all evolved after Richard I had been long dead.[25] Thus, Gould and Reeve asserted that to have valid common law it clearly was not necessary that it should have existed from time immemorial.

Around 1800, upon assuming sole responsibility for the Litchfield school's introductory lecture on the American common law, Gould further advanced Reeve's argument that even English common law was not entirely of time immemorial. He taught his students that the rule making the accession of Richard I the moment that "immemorial time" began had been established only sixty years after Richard's accession. He concluded that because sixty years was sufficient time to establish England's body of fictional, immemorial customs, surely the same amount of time was adequate for the establishment of American legal tradition. A Litchfield student paraphrased Gould's lecture in his notebook, stating that "the notion of immemorial usage" was "a mere *fiction,*" and that "the common law was built up by *Courts of Justice.*"[26] According to Gould, if English law was not truly immemorial, then to require that a distinctive American common law must descend from immemorial usage was "preposterous and absurd."[27]

The College of William and Mary law professor St. George Tucker freely admitted that English jurists' narrow definition of custom excluded his home state of Virginia from the privilege of owning her own set of customs. But he argued that each Englishman who settled in an American colony brought English legal custom with him to the new world. For settlers in need of municipal regulations in their new environment to adopt English law, the system they knew best, was only natural. Not only did English emigrants import the rights and privileges to which they were entitled as Englishmen, but they also brought with them "that portion of the laws of the mother country, which was necessary to the conservation and protection of those rights." He pointed to the charter of 1584 between Queen Elizabeth and Sir Walter Raleigh in which the monarch promised that every English settler on Raleigh's land, along with their heirs, would enjoy "all the privileges of free denizens, or persons native of England."[28] All subsequent Virginia charters, Tucker claimed, contained the same guarantee, thus making it official both that Virginia settlers came to the New World with their status as Englishmen and full protection of the common law intact and that they then retained by compact with the Crown this protection as their birthright.[29]

A second argument against American possession of any form of English common law came from Sir Edward Coke's reports of *Calvin v. Smith* (1608), also known as *Calvin's Case*. This case involved, among other things, the issue of what parts of the empire were entitled to the protection of English law. In his *Commentaries,* Blackstone used the case to argue that, because England gained possession of American colonies by conquest, and English common law had no automatic authority in conquered lands, Americans could not claim common law's authority. Blackstone included a discussion of the case in all editions of his *Commentaries,* but he expanded on his original treatment in the seventh edition, published in 1775, probably in response to colonial leaders' increasingly strident demands for the rights and legal protections of Englishmen. In the later edition he included more direct references to the American colonies' particular situation. He stated that *Calvin's Case* set up two kinds of colonies, those that England claimed through the settlement of a deserted and uncultivated land and those already populated lands that England procured through conquest or treaty. If English citizens populated an uninhabited country, then all applicable English laws then in being transferred to the colony. If, however, English citizens conquered a land that was already populated and possessed of its own laws, the Crown was entitled to make alterations to existing laws. Until the monarch made these modifications, however, the laws of the conquered country remained intact. Blackstone's controversial argument was that the English brought America under their rule by conquest of the indigenous people or by treaties, and that English common law, therefore, had "no allowance or authority" in Anglo-America, "they being no part of the mother country, but distinct (though dependent) dominions."[30]

American legists objected to Blackstone's designation of America as conquered territory. To suggest origin in conquest was to admit that America was, and would always be, under Britain's spell and that only Britain's monarch could bestow upon America the right to use the common law. Even after America's status as an independent nation had been determined through a successful revolution, American legists viewed such conquest theories as another way for England to assert her cultural and political superiority over her former colonies. To maintain their cultural independence, Americans felt compelled to persistently dispute this theory long after the Revolution.

In response to Blackstone's depiction of America as a conquered land, St. George Tucker countered that the only former colonies fitting the description of a conquered land were New York and New Jersey, which the English took from the Dutch by conquest and subsequent treaty in 1667. The other colonies, however, regardless of mode of acquisition—purchase, conquest, or cession— were not settled by conquered people but rather by "the conquerors themselves, or colonists, settling a vacant territory." Blackstone's claims regarding the status of a conquered territory simply did not apply "to any colony, which was settled by English emigrants, after the Indian natives had ceded, or withdrawn themselves from, the territory."[31] James Wilson dismissed Blackstone's reference to *Calvin's Case* by summoning evidence that refuted claims of an English conquest of America. By whom, Wilson asked, was America conquered? By examining the history of colonial settlement, Wilson believed that he could prove that colonists, "permitted and commissioned by the crown, . . . undertook, at their own expense, expeditions to this distant country, took possession of it, planted it, and cultivated it." As Englishmen in their own corner of the king's empire, "they grew and multiplied, and diffused British freedom and British spirit, wherever they came." Were these, Wilson asked, countries of conquest?[32] Tucker and Wilson drew these arguments from English jurists who, by the late seventeenth century, had recognized colonization as a valid mode of acquisition, alongside descent and conquest. The two American jurists confidently asserted that Coke's opinion on *Calvin's Case* did not fit America's colonial situation and thus that the colonists could legitimately claim all rights and protections of English citizenship.[33]

Concepts of Consent and Choice in American Law

It remained important for American legists to communicate to their students that they had fought the Revolution to gain the rights of Englishmen because, once they had made that point, they could begin to show that after independence, they had improved on the rights of Englishmen and had created distinctive and much broader sets of American rights, privileges and protections. Legists' discussions of American improvements on English models served to diminish lingering feelings of cultural dependence on England and to strengthen their arguments that American society was superior to that of England.

As legal scholars described how the framers set up American rights and privileges, they also referred to Blackstone's interpretation of *Calvin's Case* to distinguish between Blackstonian notions of law as command and American conceptions of law founded on popular consent. Blackstone defined municipal law as a command or "rule of action dictated by some superior being." The language of law was one of obligation, "thou shalt, or shalt not" commit a specific act. Consent of the people did not, according to Blackstone, bind the sovereign originator of the command.[34] While American legists agreed with Blackstone that law was a permanent, universal rule of action obligatory upon the whole community, they disagreed with the English jurist as to the legitimate source of the rule. In contrast to the English monarchical government and hierarchical legal system, Americans rested their governments and laws on the foundation of direct popular consent. In the words of Connecticut lawyer and treatise writer Zephaniah Swift, law derived its authority from the "universal and immemorial consent of the people."[35]

The idea of consent was also the basis for their defense of their right to a common law of their own. St. George Tucker built his case for American law founded on consent on Virginia's first charters, issued in the early seventeenth century. He stated that when Virginia's first settlers claimed English common law as their natural and conventional right they "had the authority both of reason and of compact . . . which they had neither forfeited nor waived by emigrating; such emigration being undertaken with the consent and approbation of the parent state."[36] Tucker then turned Blackstone's words of common law and consent to America's favor, quoting from the first volume of the *Commentaries:* "The common law depends upon custom which carries this internal evidence of freedom along with it, that it probably was introduced by the voluntary consent of the people."[37] He emphasized the idea of consent in this passage to suggest that even the venerable Blackstone believed that the authority of the English common law in America did not rest on "the ground of an *express adoption* by the *several colonies only,* but upon . . . the mere implied consent and usage of the first settlers."[38] James Wilson's lectures echoed Tucker's sentiments when he discussed the relationship between custom and consent. The Pennsylvania jurist believed that a long-standing custom carried with it "intrinsick evidence of consent," for long and general custom was founded "on nothing else, but free and voluntary *consent.*" To Wilson, consent-based law of such long-standing authority was "a most secure asylum from the operations of absolute, despotick power."[39]

American legists, however, were not content to rest their adaptations of the common law merely on popular consent. The key to their ability to incorporate English common law into a republican legal system and then to adapt that law to their distinctive republics lay in how they used the concept of choice. Pennsylvania judge and treatise author Hugh Henry Brackenridge, for example, asserted that because they settled the colony as Englishmen, the common law was each Pennsylvanian's birthright. William Penn's charter stipulated that the laws governing his colony would be "by the general course of law in England," until the laws were altered by the Proprietors or the freemen of the province. Brackenridge maintained that the wholesale transfer of law from England to Pennsylvania would have been impractical, because law "founded in the nature of colonization" could not carry with it all the regulations of the mother country, "but such only as have *subjects to attach upon*" and that were "not excluded by the change of situation."[40]

Connecticut jurist Zephaniah Swift used strong language turning on the concept of choice when he asserted that, because Connecticut's first inhabitants "settled this country without the aide of the British crown" and were therefore independent from the beginning, they "were under no obligation to obey the government, or observe the laws of the country, from whence they emigrated." They could have instituted a completely different government and legal system but instead they voluntarily received English laws "by the general consent of the people." After the Revolution the people of Connecticut again faced the choice of abolishing the English legal system or retaining it and again they chose to keep the system, as far as it was "warranted by reason, and conformable to [their] circumstances." Swift pointed out that since the Revolution Connecticut courts still studied English judicial decisions when they deliberated on similar questions. While this practice allowed state courts to incorporate English legal improvements in their own law, Swift was quick to add that these English precedents had "no intrinsic authority" in the American republics.[41]

Tapping Reeve also discussed the importance of choice with regards to which parts of the common law were valid in Connecticut. If the colony's courts or "customs of the people by long establishment" adopted a particular common law practice, or if the assembly voted to make it part of statute law, only then did it become part of the law in Connecticut. Where applicable, Connecticut officials adopted the common law of England, but they also freely rejected those parts of the law that they did not consider applicable to colonial circumstances. Connecticut courts generally considered common and statute law previous to Henry VIII binding, and all decisions in English courts of common law after that time nonbinding, although American jurists still followed English decisions "when consistent with reason & applicable."[42] Strictly speaking, the common law of England had no authority in Connecticut, but judges and lawmakers over the years chose to adopt certain portions as part of their own law. When deliberating over "novel questions," Connecticut courts often resorted to common law answers, as *"prima facie* evidence" of what was right. But at the same time, Connecticut courts were "at liberty to examine and reject" those parts of common law that were not appropriate to their locality's governance.[43]

The "Accommodating Spirit" of the Common Law

James Wilson used Blackstone's theories about the transfer of the common law to Anglo-America to show that custom and choice worked together to make a more fluid system that accommodated changes in society over time. In fact, Wilson saw custom and choice as parts of the same process, for just as rules of common law were introduced by experience and custom, they could also be withdrawn by discontinuance and disuse. The beauty of the English common law system, according to Wilson, was that the common law's "accommodating spirit" offered flexibility and, because the common law contained "the common dictates of nature, refined by wisdom and experience," it weathered centuries of invasion and revolution. Yet the common law always kept "the great ends of liberty . . . constantly in view" and thus, according to Wilson, was the ideal system for adapting itself to America's very distinctive social needs.[44]

Wilson used Blackstone's words to illustrate the common law's character, but he tailored the English professor's views to fit his own purposes. Wilson's rejection of the theory of America as a colony of conquest in favor of a theory of rights by settlement allowed him to argue for Americans' rights to choose which English laws were applicable to their new polities.[45] As the colonists modified their daily lives to fit their new surroundings, Wilson explained, they also changed their customs. Though they preserved the core of the common law while making revisions to their legal systems, colonists chose to streamline their legal practices to match their simple societies' needs. The common law's flexibility made it easily adaptable to the unique socioeconomic situations each colony faced.

Fellow Pennsylvanian Peter DuPonceau echoed Wilson's admiration for the common law's mutability. Because the common law was more *"malleable . . .* than written codes or statutes," it was well disposed toward constant, gradual improvement.[46] He quoted one of Wilson's charges to the grand jury on the common law's openness to refinement, assuring the reader that any new situations gradually helped the common law to attain "higher and higher degrees of perfection."[47] Maryland's David Hoffman effectively captured the common law's flexibility when he wrote that the system had "survived many ages, and many revolutions of manners, and [had] yet been accommodated to them all." This "peculiar" feature allowed the common law to retain "its *form*, while it . . . altered its *spirit*" in order to mold itself to the society in which it functioned.[48]

The common law's mutability gave American legists license to effect improvements they considered necessary to ensure its suitability to republican societies, and men like James Wilson and St. George Tucker claimed that in so doing, Americans had resurrected a purer and more English form of common law than that which England possessed. James Wilson lauded the common law in America as a purer form than that of England, bearing "a stronger and a fairer resemblance to the common law as it was improved under the Saxon, than to that law, as it was disfigured under the Norman government." Wilson examined Blackstone's history of the alterations the Normans made to the common law and then proudly pointed to the feudal elements that Americans had stripped away from English law in order to return to the original. Americans' elimination of feudal vestiges like primogeniture and entail allowed a legal system born in an ancient monarchy to fit their new republican governments.[49]

St. George Tucker welcomed the concept of mutability of the common law in a slightly more reserved fashion than did his counterparts to the north. Tucker was just as proud of American legal innovations as his colleagues, but his writings reflected a concern, shared by his fellow Republicans, that ideas about legal change and choice could be taken too far in the direction of federal uniformity. He used the history of each colony's distinct social, economic, and cultural development to show how these variations affected the evolution and diversity of American legal cultures. One of the central messages in his lectures on the common law's introduction into America was that one could identify no general theory or process by which the colonies adapted English common law. These variations made application of the common law in each colony "as various as their respective soils, climates, and productions." He used Virginia and New England as examples of the diversity of purpose, circumstances, and development among the colonies. Virginia, "the most ancient of the British colonies," had been founded as a cooperative commercial venture between Crown and Proprietor and, according to Tucker, enjoyed a harmonious relationship with Crown officials throughout the colonial period. In Tucker's version of colonial history, Virginia remained staunchly loyal to England "even to the period when the revolution commenced." This loyalty, Tucker claimed, resulted in Virginia's adoption of a greater portion of the common law and statutes of England than perhaps any of the other colonies. On the other hand, the New England colonies "owed their establishment to that spirit of independency" which originated in their leaders' discontent with the established church and the Crown. Because the circumstances of New England's settlement revolved around a desire for religious independence, Tucker insinuated that their propensity toward dissent could extend beyond religion and into government and law as well, making them more likely to improvise rather than adopt English law as extensively as had Virginia.[50]

After his synopsis of how variations of circumstances in each colony's founding and development affected the adaptation of English law in each locality, Tucker then addressed the question of which parts of English law the states abolished or retained upon independence. He stated that because the colonies rejected the sovereignty of the Crown, all laws securing the dependence of the colonies or respecting obedience to the king and his prerogatives were the first to go. The early state legislatures then turned to modifying, abridging, or annulling any laws that addressed issues of kingly office or government. For Tucker, an important consequence of the Revolution was the instant sovereignty of each state upon the declaring of independence from England. "From that moment," Tucker asserted, "there was no common law amongst them but the general law of nations, to which all civilized nations conform." Once each state established its own constitution and laws, separate and independent from all other states and all other nations, there were no laws in one state that were obligatory in another. Thus it followed that, "although it might produce a general conformity in their municipal codes," the adoption of laws "was the separate act of each state." Each state retained the right to make changes or impose limits or restrictions within their own laws without the interference of any other state.[51] After briefly reviewing the contents of each state constitution with regards to adoption of English common law, Tucker concluded that, although the common law had the force of law throughout the Union, each state had independently "modified, limited, restrained, repealed, or annulled" the system to fit its own needs. Moreover, any future amendment, repeal, or annulment of common law would be up to the sole discretion of each polity. Because state legal modifications differed, in Tucker's opinion, it would be "altogether a hopeless attempt, to endeavour to extract from such discordant materials, an uniform system of national jurisprudence."[52]

St. George Tucker, James Wilson, and their colleagues wanted their students to understand that the English common law was unique expressly because societies could adapt it to their own needs and make it into American common law. They appreciated the honored place of immemorial custom within the common law tradition, but they used the cautionary tales of ancient feudal corruptions to teach their students that custom could—and sometimes should—be undone. In the American legal tradition concepts of popular consent and popular choice had overtaken the veneration of custom.

The Written Foundation of American Law

This shift of emphasis from custom to choice gave Americans the ability to create their own separate traditions and customs, not out of the fog of time immemorial, but rather out of the distinctly memorable events of the establishment and development of colonies and the eventual, even more memorable, break with the mother country. While Englishmen expressed pride in the difficulty of tracing the origin of the Old World forms of government, America's identity rested on the notion that all Americans' rights were more secure because the framers had set them upon a written foundation. The post-Revolutionary generation of American jurists derived security from the ability to trace the origins of their system of laws back to a solidly visible foundation based on consent, choice, and new customs tailored to the needs of America's vigorous republican societies. Peter DuPonceau, for example, boasted that American legal and political institutions no longer depended on "uncertain traditions, but on the more solid foundation of written compacts." The common law was an important point of reference for legal questions, but early national jurists began to look to the common law as a means of exercising justice, a system of jurisprudence that rested on the foundation of a written constitution.[53] This tangible source of fundamental law was a novelty to the first generation of U.S. legal scholars, but it would become as much a part of American custom as were their own individual forms of common law.

As the new nation moved beyond its first decades of independence, Americans' emphasis on tangible constitutional foundations spread into the legal realm as well, where a vocal minority continued to raise questions about whether the common law was compatible with their expanding societies, and whether use of the English legal system might be hindering the nation's quest for cultural independence from the parent country. Territorial expansion, commercial success, and a growing body of indigenous precedent that was increasingly accessible through published law reports gave Americans more confidence in their growing independence from England. But for some, a growing body of more accessible American legal precedent still did not provide a suitably separate American legal identity. American lawyers still relied far more on English precedent and treatises than some preferred. Blackstone's *Commentaries* was still the preeminent text with which they learned the fundamentals of common law, and American legists had to rely exclusively on English and continental European treatises for their foundations in the growing field of commercial law. Demands for a distinctive American form of law, combined with a strengthened desire to treat the law as a rational science, provoked more calls for American law texts, treatises, and digests.

Early national legists like Vermont judge and treatise author Nathaniel Chipman acknowledged that Blackstone's *Commentaries* contained considerable useful information that derived from "the democratic part of the British constitution;" but was there no American legist, he asked, who was equal to the task of producing a guide containing the changes Americans had made to accommodate their democratic republics?[54] Some, like Pennsylvania judge Hugh Henry Brackenridge, Connecticut's Tapping Reeve, and Peter DuPonceau of Philadelphia, published works on specific legal topics or local aspects of the law.[55] One of Virginia's most prominent judges and College of William and Mary law professor St. George Tucker came closest to answering the call for an American Blackstone when in 1803 he published his edition of the *Commentaries,* complete with his own appendixes on Virginia and U.S. law.[56] Piece by piece, these legists created a body of indigenous legal literature to help law students and practitioners understand the workings of the law within their polities.

In 1826, New York jurist James Kent produced the comprehensive American law text for which Chipman and other legists yearned. Kent's *Commentaries on American Law* (1826–30) was the most important codification of American legal principles in the first half of the nineteenth century. Although his work did not entirely replace Blackstone on law students' reading lists, it did supplant the English master's work as the preeminent explication of common law principles for American lawyers. He used numerous examples of New York statute and case law, and he extended his work beyond his own state's borders into every other state's law as well. Additionally, he concentrated much energy in highlighting the rapidly growing body of federal judicial decisions from the previous thirty years, making his work the first comprehensive national survey of the major principles and precedents in American law. This digest would, in Kent's opinion, make the laws more manageable by "retaining what [was] applicable . . . and rejecting every thing that [was] obsolete and inapplicable" to American institutions.[57] In effect, Kent advocated a scientific approach that simplified the law while maintaining a flexible common law foundation.

Kent took great pains to distinguish *American* common law from *English* common law. One of the ways in which he set American common law apart was in his interpretation of the place of custom in American law. By the time Kent published his *Commentaries* it was a foregone conclusion that in America, immemorial custom was not the preeminent protector of common law rights. Earlier treatise writers had already untied American common law from English law's feudal origins by removing the necessity for an immemorial common law and by freeing America from outmoded conquest theories. Following their lead, Kent built a new premise derived from the universal source of "natural justice" to justify common law principles. The essence of Kent's argument was that if a practice met with universal consent and application, then that universality was "pretty good evidence" that the rule or obligation had "its foundation in natural law."[58] This justification of America's common law practices through natural law application of universality and natural justice was far more compatible with American notions of social equality and equal access to the law than were English notions of an immemorial common law.

For Kent, America's freedom to move away from England's immemorial common law allowed its polities to experiment with laws that would provide the appropriate measure of universal acceptance and natural justice for their own individual needs. Kent believed that if the law was a science, then legal scholars were obliged to investigate principles from all available legal sources and then choose and apply those principles that were most appropriate to their needs, regardless of origin. In Kent's opinion, this mixing of legal traditions and ideas was also an ideal way to create a distinctly American blending of the common law.

Early national legal scholars' works were part of the move toward a more scientific study and application of the law as well as the building of distinctive American identities. In different combinations, these legists answered the needs of their legal communities by interpreting the American common law as a unique creation of their American culture as well as part of the identities of the individual polities that comprised the nation. As they measured their polities' legal, constitutional, and cultural progress against Blackstone's descriptions of English common law, America's legists identified some of the central features that made American law different from—and, in their opinions, superior to—that of Britain. The uniqueness of the American legal culture was a product of republican ideas about consent and choice. Legal scholars did not try to deny their common law's English heritage; rather they took pride in the retention of the "republican parts" of that heritage while at the same time celebrating the republican innovations within their laws and constitutions.

While some American legists still anxiously warned that continued reliance on English legal principles and forms was destroying America's ability to formulate its own independent identity, most American legal scholars did not share this anxiety about the remaining continuities between English and American common law. In fact, legists agreed with Peter DuPonceau that taking the common law out of American law would have been like taking the English language away from Americans.[59] Their response to lingering doubts about cultural dependence was to negotiate a system of laws that, to American legal scholars, combined the purest forms of English legal heritage with their own innovations to create a superior common law system that became an integral part of their American identities.

Part II / Society, Politics, and Culture in the New Nation

CHAPTER SIX

The Ratification Paradox in the Great Valley of the Appalachians

Mary M. Schweitzer

The Great Valley of the Appalachians cuts a seven-hundred-mile-long swath of arable land through the mountains from Albany, New York, to Salem, North Carolina, creating the largest conduit for internal migration in eighteenth-century British North America. Entering the third generation of settlement by 1787, the Great Valley can best be understood not as the frontier West, but as a separate region unto itself: America's first "Midwest." Showing little regard for the five state borders the Great Valley crossed, settlers traversed the region freely as an immense undivided whole. New Englanders and New Yorkers traveled alongside Ulster Scots and Germans, Pennsylvanians and Virginians. Farmers whose first language was German lived next to English-speakers; the same church building where Presbyterians worshiped in the morning served a Lutheran or Dutch Reformed congregation in the afternoon. The region supported a rapidly developing economy based on small, family-run farms; local small-scale artisan production; small mills and foundries; crossroads taverns and churches; a history of trade and communication with and through Philadelphia; and a number of small but growing commercial towns. Throughout the Great Valley, farmers shared not only the same tolerant blend of ethnicities, religions, and nationalities, but often even the same extended families.[1]

Homogenous in its heterogeneity, the Great Valley could have produced a unified response to major political events or divided internally along social lines that cut through the entire geographic region. Instead, when presented with perhaps the most important political decision of their time, the question of whether to ratify the new federal Constitution of the United States in 1787, the Great Valley split in half into a pro-Constitution South and an anti-Constitution North. The sudden appearance of a "North" and a "South," where no distinction had heretofore been present, is best exemplified by the vehemence with which Pennsylvania's central valley residents rallied to form the strongest Antifederalist coalition of the ratification process, while the Shenandoah Valley of Virginia voted unanimously Federalist.[2]

How could a region populated by people linked in so many different ways have emerged from the Revolution so divided by North and South? The answer lies in the political cultures that emerged during two decades of war and Confederation. Local institutions, family, and community answered most political needs before the Revolution. After 1775, however, the governmental structures of the individual state Commonwealths dominated political life. Direct participation in Revolutionary committees and the militia convinced residents in central Pennsylvania that the continuation of a prosperous way of life depended on retaining control over political institutions large and small. The war taught Shenandoah residents different lessons. The structure of Revolutionary government in Virginia reinforced the slaveholding elite's control over the principal decision-making mechanisms. Shenandoah farmers seemed content with a practical division of labor in which the nuisance of governing was allocated to the wealthy. As long as the patrician politicians who served the Shenandoah supported the Constitution, the document would face little local opposition.

The Revolutionary process that promoted union among Americans from different provincial political cultures had the opposite effect in America's first Midwest. Had the Great Valley not been divided by arbitrary boundaries set in the seventeenth century by distant governors, the outcome of the next century of politics might have been quite different. But the Great Valley, previously seamless in culture, economics, and society, split in half. Lands west of Pennsylvania became the "Midwest," those west of Virginia and the Carolinas were drawn into the "South." North-south migration was abandoned for migration east-west, and the future of the new nation was forever altered.

Deferential Politics in Virginia

By the 1700s, the government of Virginia was dominated by an elite whose continued prosperity depended upon the ownership and distribution of land and slaves. The powerful planters of Virginia's Tidewater had over a hundred years in which to cultivate a pattern of deferential politics among their constituents. Virginia's governing elite successfully expanded that political system westward to newly opened areas, including the Shenandoah. Though the Revolutionary crisis forced the elite to make rhetorical and even philosophical concessions to the common folk, it successfully held on to power. Social and political conflict was much more conspicuous in Pennsylvania throughout the Revolutionary period. The Revolution brought the proliferation of elected governing committees and widespread participation in Pennsylvania's uniquely democratic militia, solidifying the active relationship that already had developed between local yeomanry and government. At the end of the 1700s, Pennsylvania's culture leaned heavily toward the participatory, while Virginia's was far more deferential.[3]

Local government in Virginia centered on three institutions: the parish vestry, the county court, and the local militia. The county court controlled land distribution and disputes over debts. The parish vestry was charged with tax collection, poor relief, and the enforcement of morality. Finally, all residents were required to serve in the militia. The vestry, county court, and militia were controlled through self-perpetuating elite bodies of local gentry with ties to the east. Although the governor made the appointments, the usual procedure was for him to accept the recommendation of those currently serving. The same members of the local gentry often held positions in all three institutions simultaneously. The county court effectively appointed candidates to lesser offices, such as sheriff and surveyor. Common landowners elected members to the House of Burgesses, but the system of voice voting precluded much disagreement with powerful members of the local elite. Officeholders throughout the colonial period in Virginia were of higher social rank and economic standing than their constituents. Provincial offices were open only to those of the highest social standing.[4]

The source of the unique powers of the Virginia local gentry lay in the economic and social structure of Tidewater planter life. Ambitious Virginians desiring to increase their wealth could do so mainly by controlling larger and larger amounts of land. This in turn required government cooperation.

County courts also served as an effective buffer against possible attempts by metropolitan authorities to interfere with the status quo, and it guaranteed that the institution of slavery remained protected. Young Washington was deeply involved in the Shenandoah and Augusta County as a surveyor and militia leader because his uncle was grooming him for a place in politics and land acquisition. From the end of the 1600s, wealthy tidewater planters thus secured control of both local and provincial government.[5]

As the colony spread westward, the gentry was quick to establish its system of governmental control in the newly settled areas. Unlike other colonial governments, Virginia encouraged the early establishment of western counties and the development of local ties with Williamsburg. In the Shenandoah, the tripartite system of local government—vestry, court, and militia—helped build a local elite indebted to and firmly linked with the families of eastern land speculators. Justices in the Shenandoah owned less wealth than those in the tidewater, but still ranked in the highest wealth categories in their own region.[6]

The eastern gentry overlooked ethnic and religious differences in the effort to quickly establish a local elite in the Shenandoah. German-American John Peter Muhlenberg, son of the well-known Pennsylvania Lutheran minister Henry Melchior Muhlenberg, was recruited to be a pastor in the Anglican Church to bring his fellow countrymen into the parish system—apparently with his father's blessing. The Hite and Bowman families, who made their fortunes through land development and iron production in both states, assimilated quickly into the local Virginia gentry and established ties with the east through church membership, marriage, and education.[7]

Presbyterians and Ulster Scots also found places in Virginia government. By law, membership in the Anglican Church was a prerequisite for government participation in Virginia. With an interest in encouraging settlement of the entire Virginia frontier (including parts that later became western Pennsylvania and Kentucky), the Virginia government ignored Presbyterian incursions into Anglican government. Presbyterians served on the Augusta County Anglican parish vestry, and several Presbyterians rose to prominence in valley politics while remaining active in their dissident religion.[8]

Local Democracy in Pennsylvania

The political culture of Pennsylvania developed along different lines than that of Virginia. Pennsylvania was founded on the basis of a political ideology that prohibited the language, if not the actual practice, of deferential politics. The egalitarian precepts of the Society of Friends did not necessarily lead to an egalitarian social structure, and the provincial government was as vulnerable to capture by elites as Virginia's. Nevertheless, the government was characterized by a remarkably participatory culture when compared with those of its neighbors.[9]

William Penn intended to manage Pennsylvania as a giant "manor," with land sales contingent upon residents having to pay annual "quitrents." For most of the colonial period, however, efforts to collect quitrents met with little success, and farmers behaved as if they owned their land in fee simple. The Penn family also owned large blocks of land outright, but their agents had their hands full trying to keep squatters from settling there. The land office was in disarray. Court justices sometimes found themselves ruling on cases involving their own neighbors versus a stranger from abroad. Consequently, courts tried to settle disputes over land ownership by granting farms to the family that had lived on and developed them. The prospective landholder with title from England would then be persuaded to settle upon an alternate piece of ground. The only significant tenancy occurred in six northern townships owned by the West New Jersey Society and three Chester County townships owned by the New London Company. Tenants were able to develop sizable farms on a long-term, informal basis, with rights to all improvements and negotiable leaseholds. They were counted in the tax records as freeholders, and they could vote. The arrangement more closely resembles the practice of owning urban land and charging "ground rent" than anything associated with tenancy today.[10]

Unlike tobacco, wheat farming never lent itself to large-scale landownership. The most efficient way to run a wheat farm was to operate it as a family business. Indentured servants could be brought into the family for periods of time, and during harvest season young people picked up extra income hiring themselves out from farm to farm. But a successful wheat farm required diversification and flexibility. Many farmers practiced a trade on the side; all farmers produced goods other than wheat for sale.[11]

Ambitious local entrepreneurs in Pennsylvania had numerous outlets beyond agriculture. Because the international tobacco market was centered in London, Virginia never developed a major trading port. In contrast, the expanding trade in foodstuffs to the West Indies, and eventually to southern Europe, required decision making at a port on the American side of the Atlantic. Philadelphia grew rapidly as an information-gathering center for merchants involved in the wheat trade; in 1790 it was the largest city in the new United States. Through most of the colonial period, the interests of the small farmer never collided with those of the merchants in Philadelphia; policies that increased prices for Pennsylvania flour abroad or aided the growth of local trade were popular with both groups.[12]

Elite Pennsylvanians, unlike their Virginia counterparts, had no need to invest time and effort in local and provincial government, unless they were personally so inclined. Merchant families in Philadelphia apprenticed young heirs to their own or other merchant houses, or sent them to cultivate face-to-face relationships in the West Indies and the major trading cities involved in the intercoastal trade. Intermarriage among merchant families in different cities led to an urban culture more familiar with the Atlantic World than their own backcountry.[13]

Both land development and local government thus remained largely in the hands of local residents through Pennsylvania's colonial period. Pennsylvania residents avoided provincial taxes until the onset of the Seven Years' War. Great Valley residents in Pennsylvania simultaneously benefited and suffered from the relative inattention they received from Philadelphia. On the one hand, local matters, including land distribution, were left almost totally to local discretion. On the other, the legislature delayed so long in establishing new counties that the residents of central Pennsylvania found themselves badly underrepresented through the entire colonial period. The counties themselves covered extensive territories with rapidly growing populations. Citizens of central Pennsylvania had more opportunities to elect their government officials than settlers in the Shenandoah, but on the county and provincial level they had far fewer representatives proportional to territory and population.[14]

Provincial legislators in Pennsylvania were elected annually by secret ballot. Representatives tended to come from the upper strata of society, but they were not as a group noticeably wealthier than many of their neighbors. The counties themselves were each governed by three commissioners, elected by secret ballot, who served rotating three-year appointments. The structure was highly democratic, but the size of the counties resulted in underrepresentation on the county as well as the provincial level. During the colonial period county justices were appointed in Pennsylvania, as they were in Virginia. There were, of course, no Anglican parish vestries in Pennsylvania. Tax collection was performed by tax assessors and collectors who were elected by their neighbors. The sheriff was appointed from the two candidates who had received the highest vote in an election. A prospective sheriff who could not get elected could not get appointed. Generally the position fell to the candidate with the highest number of votes.[15]

Township government more closely resembled the level of representation in the east, because western townships were similar in size to their eastern counterparts. Tax assessors and supervisors of the highways (who assigned road-work duty) were elected, the overseers of the poor appointed. Pennsylvania townships held meetings to appoint officials as they did in New England, though perhaps not so formally. As in the case of county positions, there was frequent rotation in local office. Overall, central Pennsylvanians had many opportunities to participate in government before the Revolution. There were at least five elections to attend scattered throughout the year. Even if the county and provincial elections poorly represented the population, the election itself served as an occasion for people to gather and discuss candidates or issues.[16]

Despite more opportunities for political participation in colonial Pennsylvania, the everyday lives of farmers in central Pennsylvania and the Shenandoah before 1775 differed little. Both concerned themselves mainly with informal networks based on church, family, the local tavern, and the occasional extralegal association. Over the next decade, Revolutionary participation would dramatically expand both the opportunities and requirements for local citizens in Pennsylvania to become involved on all levels of government. Opportunities for local participation increased with the restructuring of government. At the same time, circumstances pulled the residents of Pennsylvania's central valleys into issues of provincial and eventually national concern.

Revolution-making in Virginia

The period of the Revolution brought surprisingly little change to the system of gentry control in Virginia. The total number of officeholders increased, but county courts remained firmly entrenched as the central distribution point of power. The proliferation of Revolutionary committees in 1775 and 1776 posed a temporary threat to the stability of the region. Violent behavior against Scottish tobacco factors spread fear among plantation owners. Faced with rent strikes in the Northern Neck and on the Eastern Shore, the Virginia legislature quickly regained control from the committees, declared independence, and crafted a new government similar in structure to that which had effectively controlled Virginia for over a century. On the local level, the power of the vestry waned, but that of the county courts and the militia increased with independence. Local elites retained firm control over these institutions.[17]

For most residents of the Shenandoah Valley, participation in the Revolution took the form of membership in the militia. Military rank and social status remained highly correlated. County court justices and field officers were selected from the core of large property owners. As before, the same people often held both positions, but now they also directed the courts martial in Virginia, a powerful position through the Revolutionary War. The structure of the militia in Virginia reinforced the leadership role of the gentry. To the extent that officers actively participated in battle with their men, deferential ties that bound local gentry to local electorate grew even stronger.[18]

Through the colonial period, all that had been asked of the elite in Virginia was a certain level of charm, the appearance of a lifestyle that was morally above reproach, pageantry at court and in church, and the free dispensation of liquor at election time. The local populace usually cooperated, but their motives were undoubtedly mixed. Constituents could have been indifferent to the issues at hand, or may have felt there were no other choices. Independence had little effect on the power of the governing elite, but it did change the parameters of interaction between the elite and their constituents.[19]

The war required much more in the way of sacrifice from local residents than had ever been asked of them before. Unreliable currency, high taxes, and, most of all, frequent military conscription were not immediately or passively accepted by all Virginia citizens. Despite these strains on the relationship between the elite and their constituents, outright rebellion or even political confrontation remained rare through the Revolutionary period. Local Welsh and German religious leaders in the mountainous west and southern Shenandoah opposed the Revolutionary government, convinced that it was dominated by land speculators and profiteers. Recruitment for the militia prompted dissent as Virginia pushed its boundaries into Kentucky and southwestern Pennsylvania. Local citizens increasingly proved reluctant to continue to leave their homes and families for distant fighting. The only serious case of organized resistance came in the spring of 1781, when draft riots broke out in Augusta and Rockbridge counties in the southern Shenandoah. The local gentry successfully intervened, persuading the rioters to cooperate with the war effort and in return protecting them from prosecution by the state.[20]

Local protests against state policy in the Shenandoah usually took the form of passive rather than active organized resistance. The local citizenry discovered that if large numbers simply refused to pay their taxes, or to march off to war, the state government was incapable of retaliating. The local Virginia elite responded to this effective veto power by changing the way they approached their constituents, persuading a recalcitrant population to cooperate by speaking to local issues and concerns. Historians note in this change of language and intent a softening of the institution of deferential politics and a movement toward the party politics of the nineteenth century. More may have been required of the Virginia elite to sustain their leadership role; nevertheless, the distribution of power according to wealth did not change significantly. The court system remained in place after the war, the elite firmly entrenched. Local citizens may have had their petitions and their passive veto, but they never achieved real decision-making power in the Virginia system.[21]

During most of the period of the Revolution and the Confederation, the Shenandoah did not vote as a unit. The two northern counties often voted with the Northern Neck and the four southern counties voted with Virginia's Southside or the mountainous west. The Shenandoah's representatives finally united to vote for separation of church and state and payment of British debts.[22]

The positions valley residents took regarding paper currency had little to do with agrarian indebtedness. As in other states, the valuation of debts and property over time had been left in total disarray by years of Revolutionary inflation followed by equally rapid peacetime deflation. Virginia responded to the ensuing financial chaos by forgiving some debts and indexing others, a rational effort to honor the real, rather than nominal, value of inter-temporal financial transactions (a policy that might have averted Shays's Rebellion had Massachusetts adopted it). Winchester merchants resisted having to accept Virginia currency at face value, but only because it was nearly useless for paying off suppliers in Pennsylvania. Had Virginia currency been the only alternative to specie, this could have been a divisive issue, but Pennsylvania currency sufficed for a local money supply.[23]

George Washington's developmental agenda coincided well with the goals of Shenandoah's trading towns. At the Mount Vernon Conference of 1785, Maryland and Virginia agreed to set their currencies at par and to remove trade barriers between the two states. Washington was also negotiating with Maryland and Pennsylvania for permission to dredge the Potomac and dig a canal, hoping to divert some of the Ohio trade into Virginia. Washington's efforts to create an international port at Alexandria by opening more trade routes would be a great boon to the valley's economy. In contrast, the legislature enacted restrictive mercantilist remedies to "encourage" the growth of Alexandria and other port cities. Virginia even taxed "foreign" ships in port, defined as those built outside the state—including ships built in other states in the union. The Confederation had grown so weak that Congress could only scold Virginia for its behavior. The issue reached the Shenandoah when the legislature chose to levy tariffs on all British imports, whether brought by sea or over land. Tax collectors soon found their task greatly simplified if they charged inland importers for all goods brought in from Philadelphia, no matter where they had originated. Shenandoah residents were thus given an incentive to favor Washington's nationalist vision over their own state's restrictive policies.[24]

The Shenandoah's history of ambivalent positions on the issues that had divided Virginians in the 1780s left observers unsure as to which way the region would vote on the Constitution. The northern Shenandoah had strong ties with central Pennsylvania. The Winchester *Virginia Gazette* provided residents of the north Shenandoah access to Antifederalist polemics through 1788. Winchester Federalists briefly ran their own competing newspaper in 1788, after accusing the *Gazette* of Antifederalist bias. Both newspapers managed to reprint virtually all of the important writings of the Antifederalists. The absence of significant Antifederalist opposition in the northern Shenandoah cannot be attributed to ignorance.[25]

Virginia's rituals of deferential politics strongly favored Federalists in the northern Shenandoah. Washington had once represented Frederick County in the Virginia House. The first meeting in Winchester to elect representatives to the Virginia state legislature and discuss the Constitution was held on a muster day, after two regiments of the militia had drilled. Militiamen were no doubt reminded of their relationship with the local elite, and of their loyalty to Washington. The popularity in Winchester of Washington's developmental policies also affected the vote. Nationhood would put an end to the protectionist war between Pennsylvania and Virginia and could only enhance Winchester's role as entrepôt to the West. To no one's surprise, the northern Shenandoah's votes fell firmly on the Federalist side.[26]

Federalists worried more about how the southern Shenandoah would fall. The largest concentrations of Ulster Scots and Presbyterians lived in the southern part of the valley, and Presbyterians in general were believed to be mobilizing against the Constitution. William Graham, president of Washington

Academy in Lexington, began to make preparations to fight the Constitution at the grass-roots level. "The Foederal Constitution has made its appearance here," he wrote Presbyterian planter Zachariah Johnston on November 3, 1787. "I think a vigorous opposition will be necess[ary] if we mean to claim the Privilege or even Name of freeman any longer." [27]

Graham was defeated in his bid for election to the ratifying convention, but Johnston won. Graham's letter fell on deaf ears, because Johnston was already in favor of ratification. In the end, the main obstacle to passage of the Constitution in the Virginia Convention was the absence of a Bill of Rights. Johnston had led the successful charge to disestablish the Anglican Church in Virginia. It was thus significant that he chose the last day for his only formal speech, supporting ratification with the assertion that the Constitution did not abrogate natural rights (though he did note sadly that it failed to end slavery). The Shenandoah then voted unanimously 12–0 against Patrick Henry's resolution to adopt a Bill of Rights before ratification, which lost by only eight votes. The Shenandoah delegates remained unanimous as the convention then voted 89–79 to ratify the Constitution, with the written understanding that basic rights of citizens, including those of a free press and freedom of religion, were not abrogated by the document. The Shenandoah had made the difference.[28]

As long as freedom of religion remained protected, few Shenandoah residents had any reason to find the Constitution personally threatening. A stronger federal government represented the logical extension of the existing political system in Virginia, a system in which nonlocal issues were decided elsewhere by others. When the ratifying convention met, Shenandoah's representatives voted unanimously in favor of the Constitution. Residents of Winchester responded to news of ratification with three days of celebration from June 30 through July 2, including a bonfire, an infantry parade, and a procession of occupations. Staunton, in the southern portion of the Shenandoah, where opposition to the Constitution had been predicted, held a celebration in honor of ratification on July 5. If anyone objected to ratification, or such public Federalist displays, they left no record of their dissent.[29]

In Virginia, the Revolution solidified the ties between local residents and local gentry, on the one hand, and local gentry and eastern leaders, on the other. By contrast, the Revolutionary experience in Pennsylvania intensified a political climate where leadership derived from an open willingness to defy the eastern elite.

Revolution-making in Pennsylvania

Backcountry Pennsylvanians were first drawn into provincial politics by the absence of any militia, which left them undefended on the state's exposed borders with the Iroquois and their tributaries. The government of Pennsylvania, long dominated by pacifist Quakers, had adopted the policy of containing settlement within the negotiated borders of the state. Eastern politicians believed that the Iroquois and their allies posed no threat to legitimately settled regions, and suspected that the impulsive settlers had caused their own problems by expanding settlement illegally to the north and west. The crisis was exacerbated by the refusal of other states to recognize the legitimacy of boundaries achieved by treaty with the Iroquois. By mid-century, Virginia had claimed a large chunk of southwestern Pennsylvania as part of Augusta County in Virginia, and the Ohio Company of Virginia was already selling land there. Connecticut followed suit a generation later and annexed a portion of northeast Pennsylvania to Fairfield County in Connecticut. Central Pennsylvanians saw no reason to obey settlement restraints ordered in distant Philadelphia when other states ignored them. Even in advance of the Virginia and Connecticut encroachments, some Pennsylvania residents had crossed the Juniata River boundary and created what they called "Free Trade" settlements, self-governed and self-defended. These exposed settlements became full-fledged battlegrounds after the eruption of war between France and Great Britain in the 1750s (known in Europe as the Seven Years' War, in America as the French and Indian War). When the Pennsylvania legislature refused to respond to the threat posed by the commencement of hostilities, the underrepresented state of the central valley residents in their provincial government was brought home sharply.[30]

After the Seven Years' War, Pontiac's War brought more disruption to the Great Valley. Fearful of continued attacks by hostile nations, a group of Paxton men determined to rid Pennsylvania of all native Americans marched on a small group of "Christianized Indians" who had taken refuge in the small town of Conestoga. The mob found no warriors: only old men, women, and children. They murdered them nevertheless in what became known as the Conestoga Massacre. The Paxton Boys, as they came to be called, then marched on the legislature to demand that more attention be paid to their defense. They found little sympathy in Philadelphia for their cause; to the contrary, they were lucky they were not prosecuted for the murders. Pontiac's War ended, but hostility between central Pennsylvania and the Philadelphia leadership remained.[31]

The nascent military organization in central Pennsylvani; opposition to, rather than support of, the provincial governn olutionary period approached, the same militia and leadershi strongly committed to the simultaneous removal of British p sylvania's distant government. When Pennsylvania's government refused to support the Declaration of Independence in 1776, it seemed to central Pennsylvanians that they had lost all moral authority to rule.

Southeast Pennsylvania, including Philadelphia, had for decades successfully dealt with unwelcome interference from London by simply ignoring it. They paid off customs inspectors to continue illicit trade with the French, printed paper currency against explicit instructions from the Penn family, and, despite the express prohibition of mercantilist legislation, permitted a flourishing backcountry manufacturing sector in hats, cloth, and iron products.[32]

The reluctance of Pennsylvania's legislative leadership to support the Declaration of Independence stemmed less from the state's pacifist heritage than from a genuine sense that, once again, open defiance might not be the most intelligent choice. They had completely misread the strength of the growing anti-British movement in Philadelphia as well as the backcountry, and soon found themselves isolated and impotent. The extralegal Revolutionary committees created to implement the anti-British boycott of 1774 became the de facto government of Pennsylvania.[33]

The Revolutionary militia had an even broader impact on the relationship between the Pennsylvania citizenry and their government. Militia service was a relatively new experience in Philadelphia and the eastern counties. In central Pennsylvania, however, the militia was already in existence, and already accustomed to running military matters themselves. Cumberland County not only responded quickly to the call for militia brigades, but also voted £27,000 for purposes of defense. Because of the influence of the central counties, the Revolutionary militia was built from the ground up, with the rank and file electing all officers. The legislature would eventually assert its prerogative to appoint officers at the top, but Pennsylvania's rank and file continued to elect 85 percent of their commanding officers until the end of the war in 1783.[34]

In the spring of 1776, the Continental Congress recommended the writing of new state constitutions to replace the existing royal charters. Pennsylvania's Revolutionary committees and militia moved quickly to hold elections for a constitutional convention to write a new document for Pennsylvania. "Let no man represent you . . . who would be disposed to form any rank above that of eeman," wrote Philadelphian James Cannon in a broadside distributed to the militia throughout the state. The principles of egalitarianism united valley Revolutionaries with mechanics in Philadelphia; the result was a constitution they strongly felt was their own.[35]

Nothing could be further from deferential politics than the sentiments expressed by the authors of Pennsylvania's Constitution of 1776. Convention delegates were already working from the most radical of the colonial charters, Penn's Charter of Privileges of 1701. Both Penn's charter and the new constitution included a declaration of rights. Most real power in Pennsylvania had been lodged in the single-chambered legislature through the colonial period. In Pennsylvania, there would be no upper class "Council" or "Senate" to buffer the public from enactment of legislation. The new constitution did not deviate from Pennsylvania precedent, providing only for a popularly elected house. A governing committee would perform the tasks of the executive. The legislature would continue to be elected on an annual basis, but the franchise was explicitly broadened to include all male taxpayers over twenty-one, plus the nontaxpaying adult sons of freeholders.[36]

The new government created more counties, leading to a proportional increase in representation from central and western Pennsylvania in the legislature. During the war, and for several years after, the eastern counties lost representation with the revocation of Quakers' voting rights because their religious views on pacifism precluded military participation. Though still a minority presence, central Pennsylvania now played a major role in state government.[37]

The Revolution also brought a significant increase in individual participation in local government for central Pennsylvanians. More counties meant more county officials. Local justices, once appointed, were now to be elected by their constituents. A new provision required at least one justice be elected from each township, resulting in a significant decentralization of the office. The rest of the local offices, all elective, were left unchanged. Revolutionary committees and militia officeholding offered yet more opportunities for local leadership. Pennsylvania's extralegal committees brought approximately one thousand rural citizens into government between May of 1774 and June of 1776. Political decision making—and political debate—were unavoidable on a very local level within Pennsylvania during the years of the war and the Confederation.[38]

The most divisive issue in Pennsylvania during the Confederation period became the state constitution of 1776. Those who supported the state constitution called themselves Constitutionalists; their opponents adopted the name

Republicans. Pennsylvania Constitutionalists believed the state should retain sovereignty over significant powers such as land distribution, money creation, and trade. They also took pride in the degree of participatory democracy they had achieved in their own government. Conversely, Pennsylvania Republicans were only too aware of the dangers of tyranny by the majority, whether directed against Quakers in the form of treble taxation, "Christianized Indians" in Conestoga, or the Bank of North America in Philadelphia. To convince fellow Pennsylvanians that the government needed a new system, Pennsylvania Republicans had to develop persuasive arguments explaining how to structure a balanced government in a society that admitted to no natural social divisions. They first found success not in Pennsylvania, but in the Constitutional Convention of 1787. The new federal Constitution represented a clear victory over the political principles underlying Pennsylvania's constitution of 1776.[39]

Within the state, Pennsylvania Republicans took a number of positions in direct opposition to central Pennsylvania Constitutionalists. James Wilson, Tench Coxe, and Robert Morris, all major stockholders in the private Bank of North America, attempted to scuttle the state's sixty-year-old land bank and state-issued paper money. The new private bank would serve the requirements of Philadelphia merchants for short-run financing, but could not answer farmers' needs for long-run mortgages or for local circulating currency.[40]

The same group was also heavily involved in land speculation in the vast region suddenly freed up for European-American settlement by the conquest of the Iroquois Confederation during the Revolution. Central Pennsylvanians wanted this land opened to immediate development by individual farmers, historically the common practice in Pennsylvania. The new landjobbers proved either incompetent or simply too slow to satisfy would-be farmers, overpricing the land and failing to take into account the availability of land in the Ohio Valley and New York State. Once again, Pennsylvania farmers saw themselves denied nearby farmland for their children by outsiders who used their power to prevent active development.[41]

Strong philosophical differences would have led the residents of central Pennsylvania to oppose any document written by Pennsylvania Republicans. They were acutely conscious of the potential danger of losing control over economic policy to a group with such clearly opposing concerns. The desperation with which they fought the new federal Constitution came not from localism but from a deeply entrenched conviction that the men who wrote this document planned to use it to further their own agendas. Their fear of underrepresentation in a distant government had a basis in recent history. Their concern over the number of appointed rather than elected positions in the new federal government reflected their experiences with the Philadelphia elite. The ideological arguments that would form the basis of the Antifederalist response were the products of a long period of political activity that had left citizens of central Pennsylvania convinced of the critical importance of their direct participation in the formation of government policy. The prospect of a strong, distant, national government was daunting enough. Far worse, this new government had been designed by men who had, as Pennsylvanians, attacked the very policies that they believed made Pennsylvania prosperous for everyone.

The first attempt by Pennsylvania westerners to prevent the ratification of the new federal Constitution came in a much-criticized, hurried effort to keep the assembly from calling for a ratifying convention in the fall of 1787. Central and western representatives refused to attend the final days of the 1787 session in an effort to force the issue to be tabled until the spring by preventing a quorum. A crowd dragged enough of them back into the state house to make a vote possible. Pennsylvania would have an early ratifying convention in November 1787, not two months after the completion of the Constitution. At the convention, the most vocal Antifederalists represented central Pennsylvania and the West: William Findley, from Westmoreland County near Pittsburgh; John Smiley, from Fayette; and Robert Whitehill, from Cumberland. To their disappointment, they lost the votes of Philadelphia's mechanics, their allies through most of the Confederation period. Pennsylvania became the second state to ratify the federal Constitution. The Antifederalist battle would have to be fought elsewhere.[42]

The defiant Pennsylvania Antifederalists published the "Address and reasons of Dissent of the Minority of the Convention of Pennsylvania to their Constituents," the first of many major Antifederalist pamphlets to emerge from Pennsylvania. Every member of the ratifying convention from central Pennsylvania signed the "Dissent." The authors of the "Dissent" argued that a Bill of Rights was imperative, pointing to the role of the declaration of rights in Pennsylvania's original charters. Minority representatives were also concerned that the document gave too much power to Congress; that life appointments to the judiciary would create a dangerous aristocracy; and that there would be too few representatives for the size of the population. The end result, they argued, would be bribery, despotism, and the creation of a powerful national elite.[43]

While Pennsylvania's Antifederalist literature circulated in the states that had yet to hold their conventions, opposition to the federal Constitution boiled over in the central valleys. In December 1787, a celebration by Federalists in Carlisle in honor of Pennsylvania's ratification of the Constitution was broken up by Antifederalist rioters. The next day, Thomas McKean and local son James Wilson were burned in effigy. Twenty-one rioters were arrested, including John Jordan, presiding judge of the Cumberland County Court of Common Pleas. On February 25, 1788, seven of these refused bail and were imprisoned. The alarm went out to the surrounding countryside. Between five hundred and two thousand militiamen arrived from Cumberland, Dauphin, and York counties, stopping just outside of Carlisle. The militia companies then sent representatives into town to negotiate for the release of the prisoners. Militia representatives conferred with both Federalist and Antifederalist residents of Carlisle; it was agreed that all charges would be dropped, and the jailed rioters would be released. Compromise achieved, the militiamen entered Carlisle and celebrated for a day.[44]

By February locals had begun to convene committees of correspondence for this new emergency. "The people here in [Cumberland] County and Franklin County are forming Societys for the purpose of opposing this detastable Fedrall conspiracy," wrote William Petrikin in February 1788. Six thousand residents of Northampton, Dauphin, Bedford, Franklin, Cumberland, and Westmoreland counties signed petitions requesting the Pennsylvania Assembly rescind their ratification of the Constitution and call for a new convention to be held in the summer of 1788. After news of formal ratification by the requisite nine states reached the backcountry, Pennsylvania's Antifederalists kept their convention date, but used it instead to nominate candidates for Congress.[45]

Fears of central Pennsylvanians regarding the loss of power to a strong federal government proved prescient. The direst predictions of Pennsylvania Antifederalists seemed to be fulfilled when Congress imposed a tax on stills, effectively slapping a tariff on the main export of western farmers. Distilling corn greatly diminished transportation costs; while technically the whiskey was produced for "domestic" consumption, in reality it was as much a staple export in the West as tobacco and flour were in the East. The region was beginning to experience a liquidity crisis brought on by the retirement of Pennsylvania paper currency to conform to the new federal Constitution. For seventy-three years, Pennsylvania currency had been the standard of account not only in the state, but throughout the Great Valley. This was no time for farmers to pay a new tax, particularly one requiring specie (gold or silver coin). It was precisely the type of imposition on small western farmers that had caused Shays's Rebellion in Massachusetts eight years earlier, and western farmers responded as they had in the past.[46]

The Whiskey Rebellion of 1794 spread through the backcountry from Vermont to North Carolina, but Washington targeted western Pennsylvania to make his stand—perhaps because it was close, perhaps because of the strong Antifederalist legacy, and perhaps because he owned a great deal of real estate in the area. Militia in the central counties tried to obstruct the march west, but they stood down when faced with 15,000 militia from four states. Washington's show of military strength demonstrated harshly the dimensions of the new national political culture: the government of Pennsylvania would have negotiated, but the Federalist administration would not. Valley residents found consolation in Democratic-Republican Clubs, and the state's electoral college members, chosen by popular election in each district, voted fourteen to one for Jefferson in 1796.[47]

North Valley Pennsylvanians and Federalists clashed again in Fries' Rebellion in 1798, when German-Americans protested another new federal tax as well as the method of collection. Protesters soon found themselves direct targets of the Alien and Sedition Acts. Roughly forty of them were sent to prison, and three were condemned to death (though all were pardoned). Because the legislature was divided, Jefferson received the votes of only eight of Pennsylvania's fifteen electors in the presidential election of 1800. Federalists moved quickly to block popular participation in the election after voter turnout doubled to elect Democrat Republican Thomas McKean governor in 1799. Historians continue to debate whether Jefferson's election in 1800 amounted to a "revolution," but for residents of the Great Valley in Pennsylvania, it was certainly a relief. Regressive taxation policies were over, the Alien and Sedition Acts repealed or permitted to lapse and, at least in their lifetimes, they would not again see federal soldiers march into their state to enforce the law.[48]

Antifederalists' resistance in Pennsylvania eventually bore fruit. Their pamphlets, widely circulated, paved the way for the compromise by which Federalists finally agreed to add a Bill of Rights to the Constitution as the first ten amendments. The small farmers of Pennsylvania had to accept the loss of traditional methods of resistance, such as expelling tax collectors or temporarily shutting down local courts, but they would not relinquish their rights to self-governance. Through active political participation in a national opposition coalition, they finally regained the powers they thought they had lost to the federal Constitution.

Conclusion

The history of politics in Virginia and Pennsylvania, combined with the twenty-year experience of revolutionary change in both states, left farmers with vastly different expectations toward political institutions and possibilities. Pennsylvania farmers were part of an unusually participatory government structure that increasingly pulled them into larger and larger jurisdictions. In Virginia, however, participation remained highly local and informal for small farmers, and most state institutions were controlled by a local or distant elite. While it is difficult at times to tell whether Virginians were satisfied with this arrangement or simply apathetic, the contrast to their Pennsylvania counterparts is clear. Small farmers in Pennsylvania expected to be part of whatever government had ultimate control over their region; Virginians did not. Pennsylvanians had developed extensive locally controlled political organizations that could be used to articulate and organize protest; Virginians had not. In Pennsylvania, ratification of the Constitution engendered serious debate over which form of government would leave local Pennsylvanians in the most control over political decisions that would affect their lives. In Virginia, ratification was perceived rather as a problem best left to the professional politicians.

Central Pennsylvanians viewed the Constitution from the perspective of small independent householders and members of local community institutions who had long felt threatened by the extensive developmental designs of the Philadelphia upper class. But the political culture that had developed in Pennsylvania proved equally important in determining their response to the Constitution. Active participation in militia leadership, in Revolutionary committees, and in local government had taught them organizational skills with which to translate their concerns about the Constitution into overt political action. They had both the desire and the tools to oppose the Constitution.

There is little evidence to clarify the lack of opposition to the Constitution in the Shenandoah. Once Virginia politicians made it clear they would support an amendment guaranteeing religious freedom, few residents seemed to care much about the details of the document. Shenandoah residents evidenced little interest in the structure of the new government or ideological issues surrounding representation. Active participation in government is costly; it requires time away from other activities. Why should busy farmers have taken the time to become deeply involved with government if there seemed to be no point to it? It is not that the farmers of the Shenandoah lacked conceptions of their role with regard to government. Rather, their own political culture rested on a division of labor that spared them any need to worry about issues of larger import.[49]

American society by 1787 encompassed remarkable diversity. Multiple social and economic factors operated simultaneously in a number of different socioeconomic environments. These environments were changing, but not all at the same time, in the same way, or at the same rate. A number of quite distinct political cultures had arisen within the several jurisdictions that comprised British America. The several constitutions of fourteen state governments (including Vermont) were not merely pieces of paper; they represented fourteen different sets of institutions, conventions, and conceptualizations. Political culture within each of these states could be quite diverse as well. If the multiple social and economic environments are combined with the multiple political environments, the result is not one or two but *numerous* possibilities with which to explain the connection between socioeconomic reality and political possibility.

In the case of the Great Valley of the Appalachians, two quite distinct ideologies clearly emerged among people of virtually identical socioeconomic interest. When faced with the prospect of a new federal Constitution, the farmers of central Pennsylvania thought they were making one kind of a choice; the farmers of the Shenandoah thought they were making a different choice altogether. The motivation for that choice may well have been based upon a set of personal or community goals strongly influenced by social and economic factors. But the choice that ratification presented also depended upon their perceptions of the impact government institutions—and their own actions—might have on those goals. History had taught each of them quite different lessons as to what that relationship was.

There was no single "yeoman ideology," static over the course of a century, against which historians can measure the impact of nation-making or of industrialization. To the contrary, the political world of yeoman farmers contained numerous possible combinations of issues, ideas, and experience. The resulting ideologies converged on some issues, diverged on others. And they changed over time.

The ratification process represented the product of years of ideological formation within the various environments of America, but it was also a major contributor to those ideologies. The shared memory of participating in the Antifederalist activities of 1787 and 1788, and of constructing a Republican consensus through the 1790s, would further differentiate the expectations of small farmers in Pennsylvania from those of small farmers in Virginia.

In the east the Revolution transformed New Yorkers, Pennsylvanians, and Virginians into Americans. It had the opposite effect on the Great Valley, as North Valley settlers became Pennsylvanians, and South Valley settlers became Virginians. The shift in migration patterns after 1790 would have a major impact on the continued development of separate ideologies, but it was perhaps equally a response to it. The increasing importance of slavery in the economic life of the South would reinforce and deepen the basic differences in political ideology with the North. Migration patterns shifted quickly from north-south to east-west. When the frontier moved to the Mississippi, the new lands would be split in public perception into the northern "Midwest" and the "New South," on opposite sides of the Ohio.[50]

Before the Revolution, a small crossroads town was founded at the edge of the Cumberland Valley in Pennsylvania to take advantage of the thriving trade route from the southern branch of the Great Valley to and through Philadelphia. The founders' hopes for a great trading city were dashed when the valley split in half politically and culturally. Within a few decades, the placement of railroads would be critical to the development of a national commercial network. An obvious path would have followed the Great Wagon Road into the Great Valley of the Appalachians, connecting Philadelphia with Frederick, Staunton, and Roanoke in Virginia and Salem in North Carolina. That railroad was not built. Instead, at great cost, railroads were built westward across the mountains. The Shenandoah would not be connected to central Pennsylvania by rail until the 1870s. The region stagnated, particularly from Virginia south.[51]

Between 1774 and 1789, the promise of a single unified prosperous region in the Great Valley of the Appalachians had become the reality of an irreparable breach. Shepherdstown, Sharpsburg, Hagerstown, Chambersburg, Winchester, and Martinsburg—trading towns along the Great Wagon Road—finally achieved significance. Seventy-five summers after the Constitutional Convention met in Philadelphia, South and North reunited in a small town founded with high expectations in 1760, but their purpose was not mutual prosperity. The year was 1863. The name of the town was Gettysburg.

CHAPTER SEVEN

Similarities and Continuities

Free Society in the Tobacco South before and
after the American Revolution

Steven Sarson

On September 6, 1823, Guy Vermillion, "aged seventy two," attended Maryland's
First Judicial District Court (encompassing Charles, Prince George's, and St.
Mary's counties on the state's lower western shore) to claim a war pension. A veteran of Patrick Henry's Virginia regiment and "the battles of White Plain, Tren-
ton, Brandy Wine," at Germantown "he was wounded in the Thum & was obliged
to be amputated." The court awarded an unspecified sum because Vermillion was
"in such indigent circumstances as to be unable to support himself without the
assistance of his country."[1] Leading Chesapeake historians have shown how ordinary people like Guy Vermillion shaped the American Revolution by rebelling
against domestic economic, social, and political inequalities as well as imperial
inequities. Resulting social upheaval pressured elites into declaring Independence and yielding to a more egalitarian society and politics after Independence.[2]
Yet the long-term fate of Vermillion casts doubt on these interpretations.

From the 1750s, much of the Chesapeake switched to wheat cultivation, but
Vermillion's southwest Maryland remained within the tobacco-slave-planta-
tion economy that remained and began to spread into Kentucky and Tennessee. Probate and plantation records prove the continued importance of

tobacco and, while the enslaved proportion of the Maryland population fell from almost one-third to less than one-fourth between 1790 and 1830, in Prince George's County it rose from 52 percent to 56 percent.[3]

This chapter uses censuses, tax lists, wills, inventories, court records, and plantation letters to explore post-Revolution Chesapeake economic structure and social relations. It links an analysis of Prince George's County to similar scholarship on other Chesapeake districts and on Kentucky and Tennessee, and relates its findings to scholarship on the colonial Chesapeake. This long-term perspective uncovers more similarities and continuities than differences and transformations between pre- and post-Revolutionary tobacco society, bearing out Jack P. Greene's skepticism about the transforming effects of the American Revolution.[4]

The growing social differentiation of the colonial period continued after Independence. Planters and larger yeomen prospered while landlessness extended to three-quarters of free householders by 1820. Rather than reversing or even attenuating these century-old tendencies, the Revolution reinforced them by opening up new lands for the recreation of tobacco society beyond the Allegheny Mountains. Yet, following the upheavals of the Revolutionary years (that were perhaps contingent on wartime disruptions), there was little social conflict. Contention was confined to the economic competitiveness endemic in a materialistic, individualistic, market society. Ideological consensus among whites founded on possessive individualism was reinforced by widespread slaveownership. Indeed, with more slaveholders than landowners, the early national tobacco South was more a slave society than a yeoman one.

Large Planters

In 1800, Prince George's County, Maryland, had 15 large planters with 2,000 acres of land or more (acreages capable of supporting the labor of 50 slaves or more in tobacco agriculture) in a population of 1,712 free householders. There were also 54 smaller planters with 800 acres or more (requiring 20 slaves or more for optimal tobacco production) and 123 large yeomen with 280 to 800 acres (requiring at least 7 laborers). Distinctly less affluent were the 287 small yeomen with fewer than 280 acres but at least the 40-acre minimum for tobacco production, though 45 smallholders with fewer than 40 acres, probably part- or full-time artisans, prospered modestly.[5] After these 524 landowners, less than a third of the county's free householders, were 1,188 tenants and wage laborers, most of whom were permanently landless. Finally, Prince George's 12,191 slaves far outnumbered its 8,984 free people.

Prince George's 15 largest planters, less than one percent of free householders, owned 15 percent of taxable wealth in 1800, including under 12 percent of the slaves, but almost 23 percent of the value of land. Their numbers rose to 17 by 1810, then fell to 12 by 1820, yet by 1820 they held over 18 percent of taxable wealth, 14 percent of slaves, and still 23 percent of realty (Tables 7.1, 7.2, 7.4, 7.5).[6] A few large planters experienced economic difficulties. Edward Henry Calvert, Prince George's richest householder in 1800, owed his brother, George, $84,800 in 1826 and later lost much of his property.[7] Some whose fortunes declined, however, were merely practicing premortal bequest.[8] Generally, large planters were highly successful entrepreneurs.

Land constituted over half of large planters' taxable wealth in Prince George's County in 1800, slaves over one-quarter, and tobacco agriculture was planters' principal pursuit. In 1803, the Calverts of Riversdale cultivated 51 hogsheads of tobacco, worth "more than $4,500 . . . enough to live splendidly," according to Rosalie Calvert. Two years later, they made "between 60 and 70 hogsheads."[9] Throughout a decade of trade embargoes and war from 1807, they "continued to grow [tobacco] each year" at Riversdale, diversifying at their Buck Lodge plantation, making a gross profit of around $85,000 from 410 hogsheads exported in 1816.[10] They also "sold 39 hogsheads" locally "at $13 and $15 [a hundredweight]," and "turned down $16 [a hundredweight] for our last year's crop," expecting prices to rise to $20.[11] Planters also made a "safe and extremely profitable speculation [buying tobacco] from small farmers."[12]

Prince George's large planters' agricultural land was worth considerably more per acre than that of yeomen, though less than that of smaller planters (Table 7.5). These high land values were attributable both to planters' purchasing power, and to careful land management, especially balancing labor and land use. Large planters held one full slave worker per 113 to 115 acres in 1800 and 1810, 1 per 86 in 1820. These ratios meant too few slaves to optimize tobacco cultivation, but allowed flexibility without leaving slaves underemployed (Tables 7.3 and 7.4).[13] Large planters hired slaves and at least eight of Prince George's 15 largest planters leased out land. Planters worried that tenants would exhaust soil, sell timber, default on rents, sell leases illegally, and abscond. Yet leasing was worthwhile; planters expected annual returns of over 5 percent on land value, and minimized risks by limiting use of labor, land, and other resources, and by requiring fertilization, crop rotation, and improvements to property.[14]

Diversification also enhanced large planters' wealth, preserved soil, and avoided excessive dependence on exports. George Calvert's 1838 inventory recorded 116 barrels and 143 bushels of corn, unspecified quantities of oats, rye, hay, straw, and animal fodder, 25 horses, 74 head of cattle, 91 sheep, 62 swine, and 3,138 pounds of bacon.[15] Rosalie Calvert ran a dairy and made cheap and long-lasting "cloth for the negroes."[16] The Calverts ran two sawmills on their plantations, leased another near Bladensburg, and leased a granary in the town.[17] Ten of Prince George's 15 large planters owned taxable built improvements, indicating extra-agricultural enterprise.

As in colonial times, planters supplemented agricultural incomes with legal and political offices, financial dealing, manufacturing, and land speculation. Practicing law was not only directly remunerative but also useful for protecting property interests in this litigious society. The latter consideration explains the importance of legal training to colonial Maryland planters, including the Carrolls, whose Catholicism precluded them from public service. After Independence, the Carrolls turned to politics and law with the same enthusiasm as their Protestant neighbors.[18] George Calvert combined public service with private profiteering. In 1813, the Maryland Assembly appointed him one of 12 supervisors of the Baltimore–Washington Turnpike, its shareholders made him their president, and he held shares worth $10,000; a one-tenth stake promising 10.5 percent annual returns.[19] Financial dealing included extending credit. Charles Carroll of Annapolis had loans of £41,000 ($109,470), at 6 percent interest or more, outstanding in 1776, and his son, Charles of Carrollton, continued lending afterwards. The Carrolls were among several planter investors in the Baltimore Iron Works, and the growth of Baltimore, Richmond, and Washington provided opportunities to expand the manufacturing pursuits they had developed before the Revolution.[20] George Calvert was director of the Bank of Washington and of a Georgetown manufacturing company, and he and Rosalie dealt extensively in stocks and bonds.[21] Land speculation expanded with trans-Appalachian migration after Independence. Out-of-state banks, creditors, and speculators owned over a third of Kentucky realty as late as 1820.[22]

Early national planters demonstrated the same aggressive materialism as their colonial forebears. Rosalie Calvert reported more than once on purchasing tobacco and other goods "from people who had the sheriff at their heels."[23] She also used insider information to buy undervalued and then sell overvalued Bank of Washington shares. "Being a director," she related in 1817, "my husband knew that there was a surplus of $80,000, which was to be divided among the shareholders this summer" and would reap 20 percent returns rather than the usual 6, adding "(but this is just between us)."[24] In 1819, she sold these shares at "nine to ten percent above par."[25]

The Calverts had no civic-republican concerns about the common good. They opposed the Baltimore–Washington Turnpike running through Riversdale in 1807, despite acknowledging its public utility. "If they would make it on the other side of the Eastern Branch," Rosalie wrote, "it would be a great benefit for us, giving us an excellent road to Washington and Baltimore which would greatly diminish the distance."[26] The benefits would have accrued to all, but Rosalie thought of the Calverts only. The road eventually cut across a corner of Riversdale, but only under George's supervision and after he secured shares in it. Certainly, for some planters other things mattered besides money. Samuel Snowden, Prince George's third largest landowner in 1800, with 5,703½ acres, was one of many who sacrificed much for others' benefit, manumitting his 71 slaves in 1781. Many served on public institutions overseeing building and maintenance of roads and bridges, poor relief, and administration of justice. Nevertheless, Snowden and others continued to prosper using tenants and wage laborers, roads and bridges aided commerce, alms did not change the socioeconomic order, and magistrates upheld that order.[27] The Calverts were more purely self-interested than most, but they were not fundamentally different.

Like their colonial forebears, early national planters translated wealth into gentility. Large planters held almost one-fifth of Prince George's County's taxable gold and silver plate in 1800 (Table 7.6). George Calvert's inventory recorded household items worth $4,372.56½, including 78 wine glasses, 23 cut-glass tumblers, 14 cut-glass dishes, a 157-piece china dinner set, a chandelier, 372 ounces of silver, an "Open Carriage & harness," and "Chariot with harness for 4 horses."[28] Some refinements had economic utility. The Calverts preferred solid silver to plate because "when the fashion changes or it is damaged in some way, you lose the entire value whereas silver always retains its value," and when "everything is so unsettled . . . it seems desirable to have a certain amount in silver" as movable valuables.[29] The Calverts' Riversdale lake "gives a very beautiful effect and furnishes us at the same time with fish and ice for our icehouse."[30] Their brick outbuildings meant lower maintenance costs and better protected implements, crops, livestock, and laborers.[31] Also, refinement was essential for maintaining Calvert ties with Gabriel Duvall, Comptroller General of Maryland's Treasury, Albert Gallatin, U.S. Treasury Secretary, President and First Lady James and Eliza Monroe, and "other high government officials" and foreign dignitaries.[32]

The Revolution did not eliminate status assertion any more than it diminished wealth distinction. Even in the time of "Mr. Jefferson and his Democratic party who want to introduce a system of equality and economy . . . to please the populace," some planters continued asserting hierarchical ideals through conspicuous consumption. Mansion building continued after Independence. Riversdale was completed in 1804. Constructed from 170,000 bricks, with a two-story central segment, frontal portico, and east and west wings, and surrounded by gardens, it advertised wealth and authority.[33] The Calverts traveled in "very fine equipage," "painted purple" with "Venetian shutters," "a *passé* in the English style," "servant in livery *à l'Anglaise*," and "four beautiful brown horses."[34] As Rosalie wrote in 1806, "Mr. Calvert has become completely European, they give him all sorts of names, such as 'My Lord' and 'Aristocrat.'" She also noted that "one must differentiate oneself a little from the mob in order to be respected by them."[35]

Smaller Planters

Smaller planters shared the economic pursuits of large planters and aspired to live in similar style. Prince George's 54 smaller planters with over 800 acres, 3.2 percent of householders, owned 28 percent of taxable wealth in 1800, near a quarter in subsequent years, though by then they comprised almost 3 percent of householders. They also held over a quarter of the slaves in 1800, falling toward a fifth, and over a third of real estate, again falling slightly. Land constituted over two-fifths of their wealth in 1800, slaves more than a third. Like larger planters, their main pursuit was tobacco cultivation. Smaller planters' land was the most valuable in the county. Their labor-land ratios were between 1:55 and 1:65; closer to the optimum for tobacco cultivation but still allowing flexibility. At least 15 smaller planters rented land to tenants between 1798 and 1800, and some hired slave and wage labor. Thirty owned taxable built improvements in 1800, indicating diversification. Some later lost land and seem to have moved into lower landholding groups over the years, but, again, these were usually older people ensuring their offsprings' inheritances.

Reverend Clement Brooke owned 1,045¼ acres of land and 58 slaves in 1800.[36] Like larger planters, he assiduously cultivated wealth and gentility.

His plantation contained nine tobacco houses, a meat house, two cow houses "with eight foot sheds," milk, lumber, and carriage houses, and tenant and slave accommodation.[37] His 1801 inventory included 40,000 pounds of tobacco, 260 barrels of maize, 20,000 pounds of hay, "A Quantity of Corn fodder," "5 pounds Cotton in Seed," 10 horses, 47 sheep, 72 swine, 6 beehives, "3 old Cyder Mills press and trough," "3 handmills," a millstone, "Shoe Makers tools," "Carpenters & Cooper tools," and many other minor implements. He too was a principal in the Baltimore Iron Company. He also possessed a library worth $200, mahogany, cherry, and walnut furniture, "6 feather Beds," "13 Rose Blankets," clothes worth $100, and 56 items of gold and silver dinnerware, and jewelry.[38] Planters like Brooke held two-fifths of Prince George's County taxable plate in 1800.

Large Yeomen

Large yeomen with at least 280 but fewer than 800 acres of land numbered 123 in Prince George's County in 1800, forming 7 percent of householders. They made similar economic and lifestyle choices to those of planters. They owned 23 percent of total taxable wealth, and similar proportions of realty and slaves. In 1800, 94 percent owned slaves. Their rural land was worth 11 percent less per average acre than planters,' but with labor-land ratios under 1:50 this was probably due to purchasing cheaper land rather than soil exhaustion. They practiced tobacco-based but diverse agriculture. Up to half owned taxable improvements. Eleven large yeomen became planters by 1810 or 1820. Five others became small yeomen and four fell into landlessness, but 62 remained large yeomen. Overall, large yeomen's prosperity increased. By 1810 they numbered 147, or 9 percent of householders, falling slightly by 1820. Still, they held almost 30 percent of total taxable wealth in 1810, over 30 percent in 1820, and over 30 percent of land and slaves in both years. Large yeomen increasingly emulated planter gentility; their holdings of gold and silver plate almost doubled between 1800 and 1820, and their share of it grew from 15 percent to over a third.[39]

Smaller Yeomen

Superficially, Prince George's small yeomanry appears much like the large. Numbering 287 in 1800, they formed 17 percent of householders and owned roughly commensurate proportions of county wealth. Almost 72 percent owned slaves. They practiced tobacco-staple agriculture supplemented with other activities. George Magruder's 231-acre farm contained a tobacco house, meat house, and lumber house.[40] His 1800 inventory included three slaves, seventeen swine, seven head of cattle, five sheep, three horses, two beehives, "Spun Cotton and Cotton in Seed," unspecified quantities of meat and corn, and a loom and "Linen Wheel" with accessories.[41]

The small yeomanry was highly differentiated, however. Some owners of 40 to 280 acres were not actually working farmers. Richard Tasker Lowndes owned $3,849.23 in total taxable property in 1800, including 130 acres of land, a half-lot Bladensburg, nine slaves, and 364 ounces of plate.[42] Lowndes, a regular on Prince George's court benches and close friend of the Calverts, belonged to the local elite.[43] John R. Magruder, Jr., clerk of Prince George's Levy Court, owned 100 acres of land, 20 slaves, 18 ounces of plate, and total wealth of $1,422.79, and stood to inherit from his father's 2,350 acres of land, 52 slaves, 153 ounces of plate, and total wealth of $7,382.04.[44] Also, 23 became large yeomen and one a planter by 1810, eight more became large yeomen and one of those who had already done so became a planter by 1820.

Many small yeomen, however, were poor. Colonial Chesapeake historians argue that the yeoman-farmer era ended in the late seventeenth century.[45] The group's decline continued into the early nineteenth century. In Prince George's County their numbers fell from 287 in 1800 to 193 in 1820; from near 17 percent of householders to 11 percent. Simultaneously, their share of wealth fell from near 20 percent to a little over 10. Of 287 small yeomen in 1800, 158 owned less than the $708.51 county mean of total taxable wealth. Poorest in the group, Ann Adams, owned 50 acres of land, worth $46.16, and no other taxable property.[46] Even the apparent sufficiency of some middling small yeomen was deceptive. George Magruder's taxable property amounted to $595.25. In addition to the aforementioned farming and other goods, he owned three beds and bedsteads, various chairs, tables, crockery, cutlery, other wooden, earthen, and pewter kitchenware, two desks (one "old"), "1 old Looking Glass," and "Old Books" worth a dollar: ample basic essentials, if nothing genteel.[47] Yet the Magruders endured hardship. The tobacco house was where "the old couple retire in bad weather[,] their dwelling house being neither wind tight nor water tight."[48] Creditors sold $448.35 of George's personalty at auction after his death to cover debts, and his widow, Sarah, had to sell additional land so she could retain the rest.[49]

Between 1800 and 1820 35 small yeomen became landless and nine became smallholders. The true figures may be higher, for these statistics do not include those who might have lost land and left the county or died after 1800 but before either 1810 or 1820. Small yeomen's agricultural land was around 30 percent less valuable overall than that of planters, possibly partly because of soil exhaustion. Small yeomen's labor-land ratios ranged between 1:32 and 1:33, below the 1:40 maximum for tobacco cultivation. Also, few owned taxable improvements, implying that a high proportion of their slaves worked the land. Some may have leased land, hired out surplus slaves, or grown less tobacco, to avoid soil exhaustion. Nevertheless, small yeomen's lower land values certainly meant poorer crop yields.

Planters exploited smaller farmers' unwillingness or inability to store tobacco for long periods or afford the risks of transportation. Rosalie Calvert bought tobacco "from the small farmers" "for $4 and $3—even for $2.50 a hundred[weight]," and sold it for "$12 a hundred net, after all expenses, etc.," netting profits of 480 percent.[50]

Moreover, planters tried to buy some small yeomen's farms, though they sometimes encountered determined opposition. Margaret Adams owned 102 acres, 20 slaves, and $1,983.06 in total wealth in 1800, though because "the soil is too worn out and poor to continue cultivating it" the Calverts planned to "cover it with fruit trees" after buying it.[51] In November 1804 a financially troubled Adams deeded her land to Benjamin Armitage of New York for a dollar, leasing it back "for her natural life" for "One Cent Current Money" per annum, retaining the right to sell provided she reimbursed Armitage. Next month she deeded her slaves to Prince Georgian planter Benjamin Lowndes on the same terms.[52] Adams thus retained some economic freedom, but lost full ownership of her property, and her children, if she had any, lost their inheritance.

"Peggy Adams' small plantation . . . ," Rosalie wrote in 1806, "is going to be sold shortly. . . . [W]e ought to buy it because it is completely surrounded by our land. Besides, it is a continual source of problems from the cattle and negroes of its tenants, which frequently cause us a great deal of damage."[53] Yet Rosalie Calvert later wrote that "there is no dealing with that ill-natured shrew. I had a four-page letter from her the other day complaining to me that Mr. Calvert had offered her too low a price, and would you believe that he offered her $16 cash an acre—which is much more than any other land in the neighborhood."[54] The Calverts finally bought the land for $1,000 from Armitage in April 1814, after the tenacious Peggy Adams died.[55]

Although there were individual conflicts of interest, there was no concerted or ideologically based resistance to planters by yeomen. Evidence about small yeomen's ideological dispositions is sparse, but Sarah Magruder's and Peggy Adams's tenacity suggests that they shared planters' possessive mentality. Also, far from collectively resisting planters, Adams made economic alliances with a distant merchant and a local planter. What small yeomen certainly shared with planters was material interest in enslavement. Large majorities of small yeomen held slaves, and slaves formed over a third of small yeomen's wealth in 1800 (declining thereafter because assessors raised the taxable value of land). They held nearly 20 percent of Prince Georgian bondspeople, declining to 13 percent as the group shrank in size, and owned seven slaves each on average. Nonslaveholding small yeomen, some historians' quintessential virtuous republicans, formed a tiny minority in the tobacco belt. In Prince George's, they numbered 81 in 1800 and 65 in 1820, between 5 and 4 percent of householders. Thus, in the early national as well as colonial Chesapeake, slavery helped hold together an increasingly unequal free society through economic interest, disciplinary imperatives, and the illusional equality provided by racial supremacy.[56]

Smallholders

Smallholders with fewer than the forty requisite acres for tobacco production formed a small minority of Prince Georgians but held property roughly commensurate with their numbers in 1800. Like small yeomen, smallholders varied in prosperity and occupation. A few were wealthy owners of townhouses and some were small farmers, but most were probably artisans. Throughout the first two decades of the nineteenth century about half of Prince George's smallholders held town lots, and they held about half the town land in the county. A growing number also owned taxable improvements, and the high value of their rural land suggests the presence of nontaxable improvements. About half of smallholders held slaves, indicating abundant business. The economic viability of small-scale artisanship is apparent in the rising number of smallholders, to 64 in 1810, 68 in 1820, or around 4 percent of householders, and in their slightly rising share of county wealth. Also, smallholders were more upwardly mobile and less downwardly mobile than small yeomen. Of 23 survivors to 1810, four became small yeomen, two became large yeomen and one a planter. One more became a small yeoman in 1820.[57] Only two became landless in these decades.

The Landless

Landowners, however, formed a minority of free householders in the tobacco South. Prince George's landless numbered 1,188 in 1800, 1,333 in 1820, or 70 and 75 percent of householders. These figures demonstrate continued growth of Chesapeake landlessness from 30 percent of householders in 1660 to less than 50 percent by 1760. The landless, like the landed, varied in wealth, occupation, and status. In 1800, 406 landless householders were taxable; possessing nearly 13 percent of total taxable wealth. One owned over $5,000, two more over $2,500, and 45 others more than the $708.51 county mean. Some were effectively landowners. Mary Wootton, with over $5,000 in personalty, controlled 1,500 acres of land ascribed to "Turner Wootton heirs." Clement Hill, Jr., owned $1,316.31, and probably used land in a part of the county where he lived and where his father owned 3,000 acres but no personalty.[58]

In 1800, 239 nonlandowners, more than one in five, were slaveholders. Mary Wootton held 61 bondspeople, and Clement Hill, Jr., was among 9 with 20 or more. Sixty-four nonlandowners held 5 to 19 slaves. Of 250 small-scale owners of one to four slaves, 145, over two-thirds, were landless. Altogether, over a third of Prince Georgian slaveholders in 1800 were nonlandowners. The landless held 1,320 bondspeople; over 17 percent of the slaves. With 652 slaveholders to 524 landowners, more free Prince Georgians had a stake in slavery than in landed independence. Indeed, landless slaveholders' stake in slave society was greater than that of planters, as slaves represented their only capital.

Nevertheless, 1,140 landless householders owned less than Prince George's mean wealth, including 782 with no taxable wealth. James Hinton was one of Prince George's poorest taxpayers in 1800, with just $80.10 in "other" property to his name. His estate, inventoried in 1801 at $234.93 (auctioned for $289.57), comprised three horses, five head of cattle, three hogs, 43 barrels of corn, a peck of beans, "1 Small Grind Stone," "1 Spinning Wheel," "1 pair Brass Candle Sticks" and another odd one, two tables and chairs, three beds, a quilt, a blanket, and 21 other basic household items.[59] Priscilla Howington, among the county's large minority of nontaxables, died around the same time. Her inventory, worth just $42.54, comprised "one Old horse," "One Cow and Calf," "three piges," 21 ounces of "Old Pewter," "one Old Table," "One Old Cupbord," "two Old Beds and Bedsteades," "two old pots and [an] oven," "Old Lumber," and "Nine pounds of old iron and Skillet."[60] Nontaxables numbered 1,006 in 1820, becoming a 56 percent majority of Prince George's householders.

Some people lacked even the basics for subsistence. Prince George's County Levy Court annually allocated $500 to $1,500 for an almshouse and paid $10 to $20 to wealthy patrons for maintaining outpensioners. Also, in 1803, the court paid Alexander Mitchell $12.25 for "nursing and burying" Martin Murphy, "a poor travelling Man," and in 1805 paid Joseph Schofield $8 for "making a coffin" and "digging [a] Grave" for James Fletcher, "a Mulatto Man . . . found dead on the public road." In the early 1800s, there were few outpensioners, although by 1830 the number reached 57, and included Giles and Patsy Ann Vermillion, who apparently inherited Guy's poverty.[61] An 1817 wheat crop failure, following a decade of embargoes and war, created sufficient grounds for Maryland's legislature to pass an act "for the temporary relief of the Poor." Prince George's Levy Court subsequently distributed $3,140 among 217 people deemed "such objects of distress as to require immediate relief."[62]

In the early colonial Chesapeake, freed indentured servants commonly purchased land after accumulating capital from renting. Mobility declined from the late seventeenth century, however, and immobility was common after Independence.[63] Fewer than one in four of the landless who remained in Prince George's County obtained land over the course of a decade, fewer than one in three over two decades. These figures account only for those who remained in the county, some of whom expected to gain by doing so, while the poorest Prince Georgians migrated more often. Poor migrants' prospects were meagre, for landlessness was common and increasing in neighboring St. Mary's County: 65 percent in 1800 and 75 percent in 1840. Over 70 percent of southern Maryland migrants went to Kentucky, but even there landlessness stood at 65 percent in 1792, falling to 52 percent by 1802, but rising again from 1806 when the state government abandoned installment payments.[64]

Tenants

Surviving parts of the federal direct tax of 1798 for Prince George's County identify 183 tenant farmers, 29 tenant artisans, 29 overseers, and 166 others without specified occupations (probably wage workers). If some of the 166 listed without occupation were tenants and others alternated between wage labor and tenancy, then a large majority leased land. The tenantry included some who were quite wealthy and who chose leasing over landownership. Also, as a fifth of the landless were slaveholders, perhaps a third of tenants owned slaves. Tenants were undoubtedly better able than most wage earners to use slaves, and tenements meant bondspeople could cultivate their own food. Few colonial tenants owned slaves or indentured servants, and this new group of wealthier slaveholding tenants rose in the 1770s and 1780s.[65]

Nevertheless, as tenancy evolved from the eighteenth century, it gradually favored landlords more and leaseholders less. Early colonial landlords sometimes offered tenants incentives of low rents (sometimes waived for several years), long leases (although short leases often reflected tenants' ability to buy land), equity and alienation rights in leaseholds, and considerable latitude in leasehold use.[66] Rents increased over time, though. Early national sharecroppers paid thirds and halves of much of their produce, although most tenants paid fixed tobacco rents of between a quarter and a third of their crops. Landlords required payment in high quality tobacco certified at warehouses, and tenants had to make extensive improvements to leaseholds without equity. Early national tenants could rarely sell or sublet tenancies, and leaseholds usually lasted less than a decade anyway. Landlords often directed tenants on what crops to grow, limited tobacco cultivation and labor use, required crop rotation, and restricted timber exploitation.[67]

There was frequent conflict between landlords and tenants, especially, as Charles Carroll of Carrollton found, when tenants in situ refused to accept landlords changing lease terms. George Washington tried to circumvent tenants resisting rent rises by instructing his agent to "set aside every old lease where the covenants, with respect to orchards and buildings, are not complied with—if there is reason to suppose the lotts will let for more than their present rate." Nevertheless, Washington returned to Mount Vernon in 1783 to find that many of his tenants had illicitly sold their leaseholds and "disappeared into the Western country" owing him rent and other obligations. Rosalie Calvert complained that "the tenant ruins your land, never fertilizing it, and cuts your woods without the slightest regard—if he does not take it to market!"[68] Yet the concerted resistance manifest in Virginia and Maryland tobacco cutting riots in the early eighteenth century was absent after Independence. The collective action against Charles Carroll, confined to one plantation and landlord, was not an uprising of the tenantry against the landlord class. Tenants confronted landlords individually in disputes over where their own property rights began and those of their landlords ended, and illicitly selling leaseholds and timber, and absconding with unlawful gains and unpaid rents, suggests that tenants shared planters' materialistic imperatives.[69] Tenants also shared with landlords a slave-based interest in maintaining the social order.

Wage Workers

Although landlords maintained inspection rights, tenants could defend their interests to some degree because they were not subject to constant oversight: an important distinction between tenants and wage laborers. Different kinds of wage workers had different levels of autonomy, however, and overseers had more than most. Even so, overseers were frequently fired. "We discharged [our overseer Watson] at the end of the year for being good-for-nothing," Rosalie Calvert wrote in 1805, "and hired another man who quickly turned out to be a worse and the biggest rascal. We dismissed him at mid-year and rehired Barett, who is a good, honest man."[70] Two months later, her husband was "busy dismissing all his overseers in order to take on new ones who will, I trust, be better than the one at Mount Albion. He let six to eight hogsheads of tobacco be ruined in two days."[71]

As with tenants, planters encumbered overseers with restrictive contracts. Stephen Lee was Mary Pottenger's overseer from January 1803 through December 1806 for "annually seventy five pounds Current Money and one dollar for every thousand weight of Tobacco, that he should carry to Market." If single, he would "live in the family of the said Mary" without payment in kind. If married, he could

> keep two Cows on the plantation to be fed and treated as the said Mary's Cattle, and also two horses, one to be fed and treated as the said Mary's carriage horses are, the other to be fed only on hay and no corn to be allowed, . . . two hogs and . . . raise chickens and ducks, and should be furnished with four hundred pounds of Pork, by the said Mary and corn for the use of his family.[72]

Also, Lee could not "use the Negroes or horses of the said Mary on his private business without" her permission. Pottenger thus protected her own property even while enumerating Lee's entitlements. This protectiveness extended to controlling Lee's family's size and its comforts. If married, his household

> shall not consist of more than four persons, to wit himself and Wife, his child and one Servant only, [and] the said Stephen shall not make use of more fire Wood, than is absolutely necessary for his family, and . . . shall not on any Pretence feed the Horses of any of his Visitors with the Corn, or providers of the said Mary. And . . . the said Stephen shall not keep more than one fire for the use of his family.

Lee's contract was annually renewable. By this common arrangement employers could annually replace employees even without terms being broken. Annual contracts gave short-term protection to overseers too, although George Calvert fired an overseer "mid-year" at least once.[73] Overseers could sue employers for breach of contract, though only following loss of livelihood and after much trouble and expense. Nevertheless, in 1810 Lee sued Pottenger for £500 unpaid wages and expenses, and £300 damages (in current money). He won at least a partial victory, for he assigned £135–13–5 "obtained by me, in Prince George's Court against MP" to William M. Lansdale.

Rosalie Calvert was happier with her domestic wage workers than with any other "servants" (a generic she used for overseers, slaves, and free household employees).[74] Of a "white children's nurse who also sews very well," she wrote in 1804,

> I pay her high wages—five dollars a month—but she is worth it. Never have I seen such patience and good humor about everything. I don't have the least trouble with the children now—she even makes their clothes with very little help from me. . . . Kitty . . . is my chambermaid and an excellent one. She is quite skilful and even puts my hair in curl-papers every night.[75]

It seems unlikely that the unnamed nurse really loved the Calvert children "as if they were her own," or considered $5 a month for her long hours especially generous. Kitty, too, may have been less contented than Rosalie realized. Yet, free domestics were certainly easier to manage than enslaved ones. Mrs. Calvert wrote of the "the torment" of several running battles with household slaves in her early years at Riversdale, although she gradually gained greater control via punitive removal to the fields, sale, and careful selection.[76] Free domestics, working alongside slaves undoubtedly felt relatively fortunate, but their apparent tractability may have been a consequence of constant supervision. "Most of the day is spent continually trotting from one end of the house to the other," Rosalie Calvert once wrote, "in the morning giving directions about what has to be done and then after dinner seeing that my instructions have been carried out."[77] Also, tenants and overseers could probably find new livings relatively easily, while female domestics may have had more difficulty securing new employment.

Indentured Servants

Indentured servitude still existed in early nineteenth-century Maryland, a century after its eclipse by slavery as the dominant mode of labor.[78] In March

1819, Rosalie Calvert wrote that "[I] recently discharged my German gardener, whom we bought along with his wife off a ship. He knew nothing at all and couldn't tell a carrot from a turnip." Yet she had earlier described him as "knowledgable," and even after dismissing him admitted that "he was very industrious and did more work in a day than three or four of our negroes." He was probably less a poor gardener, then, than a victim of his employer's excessive expectations and caprice.[79]

Conclusion

Neo-progressive Chesapeake historians have argued convincingly that Maryland and Virginia elites declared independence partly in response to popular pressure. Doing so allowed them to trade with France and thereby alleviate commodity shortages that were causing unrest and to install new governments that could control that unrest and curb the democratic tendencies it encouraged.[80] Even after Independence, popular pressure forced further concessions. Though both states' 1776 constitutions retained property restrictions for voting and office-holding (eliminated in Maryland in 1801 and 1809), politicians were more sensitive to poorer constituents. Both states made their tax laws more progressive, Virginia courts refused to prosecute debtors throughout the Revolutionary war, and the Maryland legislature allowed debtors to pay creditors in depreciated paper money from October 1777 to November 1780. Maryland signer of the Declaration of Independence Charles Carroll of Carrollton called this tender law the "price of revolution," explaining to his enraged father, a quarter of whose fortune resided in loans, that "no revolution can happen in a state without revolutions or mutations of private property."[81]

Yet revolutions of private property were ultimately minimal. The early national tobacco South was dominated by a planter elite, with smaller planters, large yeomen, and some others sharing in its prosperity. Some smaller yeomen struggled economically, and the large majority of free people were landless tenants and wage workers. A few of the landless were wealthy, others were prosperous enough to own slaves and other personalty, but many were poor and some occasionally required charity.

Social relations among free people were not deferential; poorer people defended their rights and interests as their colonial counterparts had done. Yet they acted in the same possessive-individualistic manner as planters. Furthermore, most small yeomen and a substantial minority of the landless were slaveholders. Even nonslaveholders either aspired to slaveownership, subscribed to a racial ideology that obscured or undermined potential class antagonism, or recognized that the disciplinary imperatives of enslavement made conflict among whites too dangerous. Slavery remained as much a part of the fabric of white society in the tobacco South after the Revolution as it had been before.

Certainly, the American Revolution produced significant political change, religious freedom, and manumission for many slaves. Yet it did not alter the fundamental structure of economy and society in the Chesapeake. In many ways, Maryland and Virginia looked much the same in the early nineteenth century as they did in the middle of the eighteenth. If Chesapeake society changed significantly, it grew more unequal because of processes traceable to the late seventeenth century, not more equal due to Revolutionary transformations. Indeed, the Revolution gave the socioeconomic order of the tobacco South a new lease of life. As Ronald Hoffman and Woody Holton show, the elimination of the Proclamation Line of 1763, a direct effect of Independence, allowed Chesapeake planters to realize their speculations in western lands.[82] It also allowed the replication of tobacco society in Kentucky and Tennessee.

APPENDIX

Tables 7.1–7.6 follow on pages 153–158.

Table 7.1. *Landowning and Nonlandowning Groups as Proportions of Household Heads, 1800–1820*

Landed Group	Acres	No. in 1800	% of Householders	No. in 1810	% of Householders	No. in 1820	% of Householders
Large Planters	2000+	15	0.9	17	1.0	12	0.7
Planters	800–1999	54	3.1	43	2.7	48	2.7
Large Yeomen	280–799	123	7.2	147	9.1	141	7.8
Small Yeomen	40–279	287	16.8	260	16.0	193	10.8
Smallholders	<40	45	2.6	64	4.0	68	3.8
Subtotal	—	524	30.6	531	32.8	462	25.8
Propertied Landless	0	406	23.7	429	26.5	327	18.2
Unpropertied	0	782	45.7	660	40.7	1006	56.0
Subtotal	—	1188	69.4	1089	67.2	1333	74.2
Total	—	1712	100	1620	100	1795	100

Table 7.2. *Distribution of Total Taxable Wealth among Landowning and Nonlandowning Groups, 1800–1820*

Landed Group	1800			1810			1820		
	Total	Mean	%	Total	Mean	%	Total	Mean	%
Large Planters	180,574.65	12,038.31	14.9	319,370.80	18,786.53	19.5	294,284.79	24,523.73	18.2
Planters	341,789.31	6,329.42	28.2	394,066.47	9,164.33	24.1	425,014.31	8,854.46	26.3
Large Yeomen	277,011.81	2,252.14	22.8	485,771.17	3,304.56	29.7	505,326.63	3,583.88	31.3
Small Yeomen	231,290.18	805.89	19.1	263,534.62	1,013.60	16.1	209,914.90	1,087.64	13.0
Smallholders	26,882.11	597.39	2.2	40,556.53	633.71	2.5	45,492.90	669.01	2.8
Propertied Landless	155,407.74	382.77	12.8	133,543.10	311.28	8.1	136,566.00	417.63	8.4
Total	1,212,955.80	708.51	100	1,636,842.69	1,010.40	100	1,616,599.53	900.61	100

Table 7.3. *Frequency of Slaveownership among Landowning Groups*

Landed Group	1800		1810		1820	
	Total No.	No./% Owners	Total No.	No./% Owners	Total No.	No./% Owners
Large Planters	15	14/93.3	17	17/100	12	12/100
Planters	54	52/96.3	43	38/88.4	48	44/91.7
Large Yeomen	123	116/94.3	147	125/85.0	141	130/92.2
Small Yeomen	287	206/71.8	260	173/66.5	193	128/66.3
Smallholders	45	25/55.6	64	31/48.4	68	35/51.5
Landless	1,188	239/20.1	1,089	205/18.8	1,333	190/14.3
Total	1,712	652/38.1	1,620	589/36.4	1,795	539/30.0

Table 7.4. Distribution of Slaves among Landowning Groups

Landed Group	1800			1810			1820		
	No.	Mean	%	No.	Mean	%	No.	Mean	%
Large Planters	886	63	11.4	814	48	12.1	911	76	13.8
Planters	2,038	39	26.4	1,401	37	20.7	1,501	34	22.8
Large Yeomen	1,861	16	24.1	2,119	17	31.3	2,083	16	31.6
Small Yeomen	1,497	7	19.4	1,204	7	17.8	892	7	13.5
Smallholders	124	5	1.6	169	6	2.5	143	4	2.2
Landless	1,320	6	17.1	1,054	5	15.6	1,059	6	16.1
Total	7,726	12	100	6,761	12	100	6,589	12	100

Table 7.5. Total Real Estate Values among Landowning Groups (Rural and Town Land, plus Built Improvements)

Landed Group	1800			1810			1820		
	Value	Mean	%	Value	Mean	%	Value	Mean	%
Large Planters	94,943.64	6,329.58	22.9	232,619.46	13,683.51	24.7	202,028.79	16,835.73	22.8
Planters	143,081.00	2,649.66	34.5	261,010.43	6,070.01	27.8	270,766.31	5,640.96	30.6
Large Yeomen	96,563.00	785.07	23.2	292,953.86	1,992.88	31.2	286,414.63	2,031.31	32.3
Small Yeomen	69,280.41	241.37	16.7	131,934.86	507.44	14.0	103,639.40	536.99	1.7
Smallholders	11,173.03	248.29	2.7	21,331.31	333.31	2.3	23,364.40	343.59	2.6
Total	415,041.08	792.05	100	939,849.92	1,770.46	100	886,213.53	1,918.21	100

Table 7.6. Distribution of Plate (in Weight) among Landowning Groups

Landed Group	1800			1810			1820		
	Ounces	Mean	%	Ounces	Mean	%	Ounces	Mean	%
Large Planters	1,964.65	130.98	18.3	1,093.25	64.31	13.8	1,975.0	164.58	18.3
Planters	4,238.65	78.49	39.5	2,572.30	59.82	32.4	3,293.0	68.60	30.5
Large Yeomen	1,857.50	15.10	17.3	1,924.75	13.09	24.2	3,628.5	25.73	33.6
Small Yeomen	1,065.87	3.71	9.9	1,467.00	5.64	18.5	649.0	3.36	6.0
Smallholders	240.00	5.33	2.2	168.00	2.63	2.1	446.0	6.56	4.1
Landless	1,372.60	1.16	12.8	717.50	0.66	9.0	806.5	0.61	7.5
Total	10,739.27	6.27	100	7,942.80	4.90	100	10,798.0	6.02	100

The Irish Immigrant and the Broadening of the Polity in Philadelphia, 1790–1800

Maurice J. Bric

The "new Irish" immigrants who poured into Philadelphia after 1783 were more substantial, self-assured, discriminating, and politically experienced than their pre-Revolutionary cousins. If only because of this, their presence posed a challenge to the established elites at a time when America was still being invigorated by the "transforming hand" and "loosening force" of the American Revolution. In particular, the new Irish threatened two groups: the "older Irish elites" who dominated Philadelphia's Irish community and the Pennsylvania politicians who, in the late 1780s, helped found the Federalist Party on both the state and national level. In meeting this threat, the "older Irish" and Federalist leaders had two choices. They could try to absorb those "new Irish" leaders who had emerged during and after the Revolution or, as an alternative, refuse to be so accommodating. If they pursued the first path, the "awakened democracy" that swept both Ireland and the United States during the 1780s and 1790s might be contained and, at least, the outlines of a deferential polity retained. If they followed the second, however, those who were economically, ethnically, or socially "outside" would have to invent their own networks and structures in order to make their presence felt in the new republic.[1]

In Philadelphia, the debate on these choices actively involved the Irish community. Indeed, it shaped the development of the city's political and ethnocultural organizations and clubs in such a way that some simply associated "how violently we are stimulated to action by party spirit" with Irish immigrants. From this, it was a short step to suggest that the "new Irish" threatened the social and political consolidation of the new nation and as a result, could never become "useful citizens." Against this background, I want to examine the role of the Irish in broadening the Philadelphia polity after independence and, in particular, to discuss the related debates on definition, as they moved toward the restrictive *formulae* of the 1790s.

Ethnicity and Nationality

By the middle of the seventeenth century, the English in Ireland had abandoned the notion that plantation could be, in the words of Sir John Davies, a "mixed" experiment, where the colonizer and the colonized could "grow up together in one nation." The Penal Laws[2] later elaborated on these ideas in both Ireland and America. These laws also initiated the "age of ascendancy" in which the religious, political, and cultural characteristics of the earliest phases of the First British Empire reinforced the idea that society had but one "morally superior" interest group that could legitimately claim to represent the welfare of society as a whole. This idea continued as an article of political faith in America until the 1790s. In Pennsylvania, even after the dominant Quakers lost their numerical majority in the state legislature, the idea that the "interest of [their] one part of society . . . [was] the object of the whole polity," remained as central to the political culture of the late-eighteenth century as it had been to that of the earlier colony.[3]

This collective ideal was also reflected in a desire to promote of a harmonious and integrated community and an aversion to ethnic peculiarity. Immigrants were thus deemed to have a civic obligation to ensure that they could, and would, accommodate themselves to the conventions of their new home or, as John Adams put it in 1780, to "*our* language, *our* laws, customs, and . . . [the] humours of *our* people," and "love this country [America] much better than that wherein he or his [immigrant's] forefathers were born." Homogeneity was equated with harmony and, as Washington wrote in the first draft of his speech to Congress on December 9, 1796, "to render the people of this country as homogenous as possible, must tend as much as any other circumstance, to the permanency of their union and prosperity." Thus, it was symbolic that while Congress accepted du Simitière's motto, *E Pluribus Unum*, for the Great Seal of the United States, it rejected his original design, which included the national symbols of Ireland, the Germanies, and France. Such considerations reflected the uncertainties that surrounded the identity of the new republic and the fears that internal dissensions, whether domestic or imported, might upset its consolidation. As Adams was to put it in 1798, it was only when one had "no attachments or exclusive friendship for any foreign nation [that] you possess the genuine character of true Americans."[4]

In the Constitutional Convention, such concerns had been central to the various discussions on naturalization, citizenship and accessibility to office. For example, during the debates on whether to require four, seven, or even fourteen years residence for Senators, it was suggested that foreign-born legislators would need time to develop the necessary "local knowledge" to free themselves from their "foreign attachments" before they could become effective representatives. These reservations were partly answered by acknowledging that those who were "not native of this country, had acquired great credit during the revolution." As Benjamin Franklin later observed, "when foreigners, after looking about for some other country in which they can obtain more happiness, give a preference to ours, it is a proof of attachment which ought to excite our confidence and affection."[5] The corollary, however, was that the politically experienced Irish immigrants of the 1780s and 1790s should continue to respect the harmony of the single-interest polity. Thus, as the Founding Fathers discussed the role of the foreign-born in the political institutions and conventions of both the new states and the federal republic, there were ethnic resonances to their debates on how to accommodate newly emerging interests within the existing structures of the public sphere. The ethnocultural character and language of these discussions also challenged the Irish networks of contemporary Philadelphia to balance their own natural "national reflections" with what one commentator termed in 1787, the "establishment of . . . the national character of America."[6]

Irish Jeffersonians

Prior to 1790, the principal Irish network in Philadelphia was the Society of the Friendly Sons of St. Patrick. It had been founded in 1771 and consisted of men of substance who were in the main merchants or professionals. Their elitism was also reflected in a variety of other associations with one another through business, family, or other relationships as well as through the execution of the wills, or the wardenship of the children of deceased members. It was also underlined by the high costs of membership as well as by the fact that many of the Friendly Sons were members of other elite societies. Like the four other "national societies"[7] that existed in the city, it was both a mutual assistance society and a network to support "deserving" and unfortunate immigrants. These activities were seen by the members as a mark of "all [the] civilized nations" that had settled in America. However, although they believed that when in distress, people would naturally turn to "those who were originally from the same Country," and that the same feeling, "the Love of the native Soil," would encourage benevolence from those who were able to give it, the five "national societies" had ambivalent feelings about national attachments per se. Thus, as John Alexander has suggested, societies such as the Friendly Sons were far from being simply altruistic. Instead, they saw themselves as part of a wider "ascendancy" whose benevolent activities would encourage poor immigrants to be deferential to themselves, thus ensuring that in an era of change, they would behave in a "proper way." Moreover, their kind of immigrant-aid would protect their newly won incorporation into Philadelphia society from destitute cousins who might otherwise revive or enhance prejudices that the Friendly Sons wanted left behind in the Old World.[8]

After 1791, the Hibernian Society for the Protection of Irish Emigrants (incorporated as the Hibernian Society in 1792) was less reticent about its particular ethnocultural character. Although it grew out of the Friendly Sons, the society had a bigger program to assess and apply immigrant assistance, to process introductions for newly arrived immigrants, and "to prevent and punish [the] imposition and oppression of emigrants by owners, masters, or freighters of vessels." As a result, as Irish immigrants sailed into the Philadelphia of the 1790s, the Hibernians offered a wide range of services, and to larger numbers than the Friendly Sons had done. Thus, the society embodied a new type of immigrant-aid society that would also become increasingly ethnocentric and was under the control of different leaders from those of the Friendly Sons. There was only a 20 percent overlap in the membership of the two societies. Moreover, the Hibernians were less elite and, as William Martin suggested in June 1790, "all degrees of Persons might have the liberty of subscribing" to the society.[9]

The new culture of the Hibernian Society was also reflected in the more assertive and public ways it celebrated St. Patrick's Day and by the more ethnocentric toasts that were offered on that day. In 1793, for example, not only was the Irish aspect of Anglo-American Patriotism recalled in a more self-confident manner but the activities of the radical Society of United Irishmen were also saluted. Six years later, six of the seventeen toasts recalled the activities and personalities of the United Irishmen "and the army of martyrs to Irish liberty." More fundamentally, however, the Hibernians also rejected the older notion that involvement in politics showed the "highest ingratitude to the country in which we receive our bread."[10] In a sense, this suggests that older organizations such as the Friendly Sons had failed to control and lead the "new immigrants" of post-Revolutionary Philadelphia. Accordingly, both inside and outside the city's Irish community, strategies of accommodating "new" and "old" would become more difficult during the 1790s.

Whether "old" or "new," "national" or not, the history of Philadelphia's Irish networks cannot be considered apart from the shifting sands of contemporary political organization. Prior to 1790, most accepted that the city's politics had been driven by factional associations based on friendships, family, or common interest. The colony's established leaders had not seen any contradiction between these arrangements and the preservation of the organic polity, although after the Revolution, their successors recognized that this kind of political culture could be preserved only by incorporating new "clients" within the system. In this, they were also greatly influenced by the "anti-party" views of Washington and Adams. As a result, many of the factions that had evolved from previous decades were rearranged under the leaders of the new state, as "many revolutionists," in the words of William Maclay, "wished for the loaves and fishes of government" now that the "diadem and sceptre" had been transferred from London to Philadelphia. Therefore, while one should not lump all elections prior to 1794 into one, a case could be made to present them in the words that Adams used to describe the elections of 1792: as between "clashing grandees." In 1794, however, Philadelphia's contested Congressional election dented the traditional political organization of the city when, "to the astonishment of all parties," John Swanwick defeated the Federalist incumbent and leading member of the Friendly Sons, Thomas Fitzsimons.[11]

This election established what were to become the *loci* of Jeffersonian strength in the Philadelphia area: the Irish neighborhoods of the Northern and Southern Liberties and within the city, Philadelphia County, and the peripheral wards of North and South Mulberry. The election was also significant in a number of other ways. Fitzsimons was deemed to be a member of the so-called aristocratic junto that ran Philadelphia; Swanwick was not. Swanwick was a new type of leader who looked to the marginalized wards that eventually elected him. Many of the established elite worried about Swanwick's departures from the traditional "mode of electioneering," according to which "the friends of the candidates were satisfied to use their influence *in private* amongst their own particular friends" while evincing "a becoming respect for public opinion." "It is not in a croud," warned one observer, "that the small voice of reason is held." Such sentiments betrayed "genteel hypocrisy," Swanwick retorted.[12]

Swanwick's electoral "croud" included Irish immigrants who had come from a country that since the 1760s had been in a state of either smothered or actual rebellion. The election provided them with a litany of anti-British and anti-establishment catchwords that facilitated both "the political phenomenon of factions emerging as parties" and the re-invention of their own ethnicity in America. Swanwick's call for tough measures against Britain contributed to his victory over Fitzsimons, but it also helped to revive anti-Britishness as a more powerful language of ethnocultural as well as political identification.[13] The dual importance of this language became even more obvious during the debates on Jay's treaty (1795–96), when Jeffersonians suggested that both the American and European Irish were, in every way, in a common cause against "drawing too near and cordially to England." Thus, it was reported in August 1795 that "the Aristocrats" in Philadelphia, "recollecting that Irishmen were the principal hands in fighting the battles that made America once free, seem[ed] very uneasy at their flocking out in such numbers latterly." Moreover, Philadelphia's "new Irish" community was throwing up assertive leaders such as Blair McClenachan to organize the three major public protests that were made against the treaty during July 1795.[14]

On each occasion, there was a marked Irish presence, especially on July 25. At this meeting, the "complexion" of the audience was underlined when McClenachan introduced the United Irish leader, Archibald Hamilton Rowan, whom he described as having just arrived to "take refuge amongst us, from the despotism of his native country." By then, Rowan had built up a powerful reputation and there were "thousands of kindly souls who sympathize[d] in [his] sufferings." His warmly received proposal "that every good citizen . . . [should] kick this damned treaty to Hell" was often subsequently cited as a milestone in the interaction between Irish immigrants and the development of Jeffersonian Republicanism in Philadelphia. Indeed, it was partly on the strength of organizing the anti-Jay protests that McClenachan himself was elected to

Congress in 1796, defeating the incumbent, Frederick Muhlenberg, who had earlier given the casting vote in favor of the treaty. What Charles Lee had earlier termed not a "Monarchy, Aristocracy nor Democracy . . . [but] rather a Mac-O'-cracy," was beginning to make a political impact within the developing Jeffersonian coalition.[15]

Federalist Reaction

In 1787, Mathew Carey[16] had been told that because of the turmoil in contemporary Ireland, Irish immigrants "seem[ed] to understand better, and to join more heartily in, the true principles and support our democratical Governments, than any other European people." Federalists regarded such comments as both arrogant and "un-American." However, they also used them to express their reservations about not only the "new men" of political influence but also the general direction of contemporary political and social change. It was in this vein that William Cobbett[17] traduced Swanwick's involvement with Philadelphia's Irish community and issued what was to be a repeated warning to "any meddling foreigner who should dare to interfere in our [American] politics." Thus, the *Gazette of the United States* asked on March 28, 1796, "Are you *Patriots* because you have nothing American about you? because most of you are aliens by birth, [and] enemies to America in principle?"[18] Such ethnic stereotyping served to undermine the role of the foreign-born in the political process. The American Society of United Irishmen, headquartered in Philadelphia, was the focus of much of this criticism during the second half of the 1790s.

The Irish parent of this society had been founded in Belfast in October 1791 and developed a radical political agenda that foreshadowed its later role in Philadelphia. First, it sought to encourage "a free form of government, and uncontrolled opinion on all subjects" and second, to promote a more radical presence on the traditional and somewhat aristocratic leadership of the Reform Movement. Finally, it combined its agitation for political reform with support for many of the ongoing agrarian protests against tithes and rents.[19] After the society was proscribed in 1794, some of its leaders emigrated to Philadelphia, "less immigrant than exiles." As Wolfe Tone remarked shortly after his arrival in America in 1795, "the moment I landed, I was free to follow any plan which might suggest itself to me, for the emancipation of my [own] country."[20]

For Tone, America was just another place where republicanism and the "progress of liberty" might be promoted for the benefit of the local polity and "the whole world" alike. It was precisely because of the society's interaction with domestic politics, its all-embracing policies, and its international links, especially with France, that the United Irishmen became a formidable addition to the landscape of both Philadelphia's politics and the Irish community. Moreover, its dynamic leaders would place their experience and reputations at the disposal of the broadening Jeffersonian movement. These radicals "were held in the utmost detestation by every one," Cobbett asserted, "except by a few of Jefferson's party."[21]

The Delaware Valley was the most active theater the American Society of United Irishmen before 1800. In 1798, an overall "Directory" connected "the exertions of . . . individuals . . . in different parts of the United States acting under one . . . superintending guidance" which was supposed to be "now sitting in Philadelphia." With as many as 1,500 members, the society in the greater Philadelphia area had to abandon its usual meeting place at the African School. While Federalists took fright at such reports, they were more unnerved by the suggestion that these "disaffected Irishmen" were ready "to aid the French, if occasion should serve, against the Government of the United States." Accordingly, the term "United Irishman" began to evolve in Federalist parlance as a shorthand for disloyalty, violence, rebellion, and agitated political behavior. According to the *Gazette of the United States,* "the hordes of United Irishmen in America" who had fled to America in the wake of the failed Irish rebellions of 1796 and 1798 were "animated by the same infamous principles, and actuated by that same thirst for blood and plunder, which had reduced France to a vast human slaughter-house." "Can any one be silly enough," an incredulous Cobbett asked, "to suppose that the [United Irish] conspiracy had only Ireland in view?"[22]

In particular, Cobbett used the appearance of these émigrés to taunt Carey and other Irish leaders about their present loyalties and what he presented as their past careers of violence and rebellion. Carey did not respond immediately. Instead, he waited until the "reports of [the] plots, combinations, and conspiracies, of the United Irishmen" published during the heady days of late 1798 and 1799 made it unavoidable. Thus, when John Ward Fenno, editor of the Federalist-oriented *Gazette of the United States,* published a list of seventeen named United Irish leaders in December 1798, Carey regarded it as an "unprovoked and very unjustifiable attack" on the integrity of Philadelphia's Irish immigrants. In Carey's opinion, the loyalty of this community to the United States had not only been proven during the American Revolution but was beyond question in a country that had rescued these immigrants from "the galling and degrading slavery" of the Old World.[23]

Such observations were being made as political and social protest intensified in contemporary Ireland. In Philadelphia, St. Patrick's Day was being marked by a number of new groups apart from the Friendly Sons and the Hibernian Society that presented their communities in a sharper way, especially during 1797, 1798, and 1799. In 1799, while the Friendly Sons offered toasts that were cautious and traditional, the eighteen that were agreed to at a "festive meeting" saluted, among others, the United Irishmen, the "Hibernian Directory," and the "Army of Ireland." Traditional toasts were also offered, including one to St. Patrick, but even to this the group added that "Our island wants again to be purged of wolves and reptiles!"[24]

At another celebration, "agonizing reflections" were made on the "bondage" of Ireland and, in a theme that would become common within the Irish nationalist movements of the nineteenth century, audiences were told not to be afraid to remember this. As one speaker put it in 1799, the trials of our fellow Irishmen "will give a new *edge* to our revenge—a new *spring* to our love of country. . . . It ought to make us cling more closely to the sacred principle of our association."[25] Inevitably, some critics linked such sentiments to the supposedly disruptive presence of the other United Irishmen who had emigrated to America after the rebellions of 1796 and 1798. Their presence became particularly conspicuous when many Americans became convinced that "the United States must fight for its existence against revolutionary France." Thus, the secretary of state, Timothy Pickering, together with U.S. district judge Richard Peters and William Rawle and Richard Harrison, the district attorneys of Pennsylvania and New York, two states with liberal immigration policies, resolved that they would closely watch "internal Foes, who are plotting Mischief," especially United Irishmen. In August 1798, Pickering admitted that he still had no indictable evidence against America's United Irishmen but he assured Peters that "'something' would turn up" and that he would not fail "to avail of it." This only compounded fears among Jeffersonian Republicans that evidence would be concocted against the United Irishmen and that informers would "be well taken care of."[26]

The development of the "Jacobin phrenzy" was also influenced by the energetic debate, in both America and Britain, as to whether the "state prisoners"[27] should be allowed to emigrate to America. The American minister in London,

Rufus King, maintained his own network of correspondents in Ireland, through whom he followed the development of the rebellion, and from whom he concluded that an "intimate connection subsist[s] between the Chiefs of the Malcontents and the Directory." King did not merely consign this information to the diplomatic bag. He had long held the view that much of what he saw as the political "troubles" of contemporary America had derived from "lower class" Irish immigrants who had been "organized for mischievous purposes." He regarded the United Irishmen, in particular, as being "utterly inconsistent with any practicable or settled form of Government" and accordingly, went to great lengths to use both his private reports and his diplomatic status to have the "state prisoners" denied entry to America. His reasoning was succinctly put as follows to Pickering on June 14, 1798: "In case the [Irish] rebellion is suppressed . . . thousands of fugitive Irish will seek asylum in our country. Their principles and habits would be pernicious to the order and industry of our people, and I cannot persuade myself that the malcontents of any character or country will ever become useful citizens of ours."[28]

King also urged the administration to deport foreign-born radicals who were already in America and to tighten the immigration process in general. In February 1798, Charles Nisbet wrote from Philadelphia that "We are in danger of an Inundation of Irish Rebels among us. . . . Nothing can hinder them from transporting themselves hither in private ships, while there is no law here to forbid their Reception, & while we are so ready to make them Citizens & Patriots as soon as they are among us."[29]

Patriotism and Pluralism: The Elections of 1797–1798

The debate on the United Irishmen was not just about the status of a radical political and ethnocultural network. It also challenged whether political pluralism could be accommodated in a country whose "true and permanent interest" had been defined in Washington's Farewell Address (1796) as being "without regard to local considerations, to individuals, to parties, or to nations." During 1797 and 1798, however, the polarization of public opinion was unavoidable as Republicans used dinners, orations, and addresses to keep anti-British feeling high. Moreover, many Federalists regarded the United Irishmen as decisive to the electoral success of Jeffersonian Republicanism in Philadelphia. In January 1799, a correspondent to the *Gazette of the United States* even alleged that in a recent election, judges had "suffer[ed] several to vote . . . who were neither Americans nor citizens." The implication was that if the foreign-born were material to a Republican victory, they were, ipso facto, dishonorable, of questionable judgment, and, therefore, of questionable status in the new republic. What nudged such attitudes to a head was the history of Philadelphia's elections to the state senate in October 1797 and, after it was contested, in February 1798.[30] These contests pitted Israel Israel against the Federalist Benjamin Morgan and were as significant for broadening the Philadelphia polity as that of John Swanwick had been for denting the "old junto" three years earlier. However, what makes them of particular interest was that the stereotyping of Irishmen and United Irishmen was put to effective use by both Federalists and Republicans.

The state senatorial district included the city and county of Philadelphia as well as Delaware County. Israel was a tavern keeper and well-known supporter of immigrant causes, and, as such, he personified all that Federalists considered to be undesirable in a public representative. His philanthropic exertions during the yellow fever outbreaks, when he had "risk[ed] his health in relieving the sufferings of his indigent fellow citizens," gave his platform a popular edge, and, as the campaign unfolded, Israel was presented as the candidate of those who were too poor to leave the city during these scares. However, one Federalist correspondent turned this altruism into something more sordid and suggested that he had used his position on the relief committee as "the means of procuring him many votes." In the event, Israel overcame such charges and "disorganizer [and] bloody Jacobin" though he was deemed to be, he was returned as state senator by a margin of 309 votes.[31]

The returns show that while Morgan was strongest in the more established city wards, Israel had drawn his principal support from the outlying parts of the district associated with Irish immigrants and the poor. In the Northern Liberties and Southwark for example, Israel enjoyed respective margins of 678 to 144, and 498 to 75, over Morgan. Federalists linked these majorities to the malevolent influence of recent Irish arrivals on the electoral process. They also argued that these immigrants were hot-headed, politically immature, and unused to exercising the vote, and, as such, they could not but abuse electoral procedures. Accordingly, Israel's election was challenged and investigated by a senate subcommittee at the very time when Pickering was also reviewing the existing naturalization laws.[32]

The hearings on Israel's election took place on January 22, 1798. Morgan alleged that "the necessary qualifications" of voters had not been checked and that therefore, "*American* interests [had been] neglected—and the *American* character . . . degraded."[33] Israel never directly addressed such arguments. Instead, his counsel praised Israel's character and reputation and rejected the charge that, by championing the right of everybody to participate in the political process, such a man could "contaminate" American politics. This was not enough to carry his case. The investigative committee decided that proof of citizenship had not been presented according to the law and "that a greater number of persons who are not entitled to vote for members of the legislature, have been admitted to vote for Senator . . . in the district of Southwark, than the difference in number between Mr. Israel and the person next highest in the vote." On February 7, 1798, Israel's election was invalidated and a special election was called for the following February 22—Washington's birthday.[34]

During January and February 1798, a number of partisan meetings were held to prepare for this second election. Many of the themes of the first outing were replayed, especially those that highlighted the influence of Irish-born voters. According to one report, Israel's earlier election had been facilitated by "procuring hordes of United Irishmen, to be admitted to the rights of citizenship, in order to influence the election." Such views were part of a much older debate and implied that only those who had been born in America could have a "manifest and permanent interest in its welfare, [and thus] possess the right of suffrage." Thus, the *Gazette of the United States* asked whether "every man whose private interests have brought him here, or whose public *crimes* have driven him from his own country, shall the moment he touches the soil of America possess the power of legislating the rights of property, of personal liberty, and personal security." By association, all Irish immigrants were dubious potential citizens and could never become "truly American":

Believe one whose country is America, that these various tricks will not avail you toward forming a character which you were never intended for. . . . The American disposition delights in uprightness, and every specious of ingeniousness; the outcast Irishman in injustice and every species of low deception. The American uses every effort to promote the welfare of his country, and especially to support the laws and constituted authorities; the abandoned Irishman's chief pride, is to destroy his country's decreed rights, to trample down her laws, and overturn her legal power—ferocious by nature, licentious by inclination; no laws divine or human, will deter the one, or restrain the other—Lay these characteristics seriously to heart; they are such as experience will confirm; and say whether you think it possible you [Irish] can become an American, by the practice of those arts which now hail you chief of a faction.[35]

Against this background, this state election raised "questions of great magnitude." Citizens were urged to recognize this by actually voting and to determine "whether you are . . . friends of *good order and regular government,* or whether you will be likely to prefer the yoke of foreign power to the weight and care attendant upon self government." It was also announced that electoral supervisors would ask electors, first, if they were native to Pennsylvania or had ever sworn allegiance to "any foreign power"; second, if they were citizens (that is, whether they had sworn the required oaths) or were legally naturalized; and, third, if, having lived in Pennsylvania for at least two years, they had paid the required county or state taxes. However, these questions were as contentious in February 1798 as they had been the previous October and the chief justice, the Jeffersonian Thomas McKean, felt obliged to dispute their validity in a broadside that was circulated on the day before the election. In the event, the questions were asked. The election was held and Israel lost by a margin of 357 votes.[36]

Aliens and Sedition

The result did not settle the controversies that had overshadowed the two contests and, in particular, the Federalist campaign to secure public representation from "foreign influence." As might be expected, Republicans had made every effort to prove the bona fides of Philadelphia's Irish-born voters, especially because many of the broader insecurities about the direction of political development had been focused on that constituency. With Morgan's election, however, Philadelphia's Federalists scored an important success in their efforts to curb the role of immigrants in city politics. Their reaction was twofold. The first was reflected in a celebration of Morgan's victory that took place on April 21, 1798, when "the company" was "sheltered" not by "the tricolored emblem of gallic perfidy, but the banner of freedom, the eagle of the United States." During the following months, the Federalists all but appropriated the flag of the United States as a political prop. Of more direct importance, however, was that they also pressed for a new set of legal definitions on citizenship and on what was vaguely described as "sedition."[37] What followed was a program that targeted United Irishmen in particular and the Irish in general under a set of alien and revised naturalization laws. The objective was no different than it had been earlier in the decade: to secure the single interest polity and, on a more immediate level, to disable the emerging Republican coalition. As such, the debates on the naturalization and alien bills of 1797–98 would not be dull.

As Philadelphia's Federalists reacted to their electoral jousts with the city's Jeffersonians, they bemoaned "the Irish way" of doing things and "the facility with which foreigners acquire the full and perfect right to citizenship." In May 1798, congressman John Allen (F., Connecticut) asserted that "the vast number of naturalizations which lately took place in this city [Philadelphia] to support a particular party in a particular election" had been central to the Israel–Morgan contest. From this, it was a short step to suggest that the political stability of the Union was under threat and that, as Fisher Ames (F., Massachusetts) stated in December 1798, the *salus reipublicae* "plainly requires the power of expelling or refusing admission to aliens."[38]

During 1797 and 1798, Ames took a leading part in the debate on revising the naturalization acts. He also sponsored a tax of $20 on certificates of naturalization, although his colleague David Brooks (F., New York) admitted that this was designed "to cut off an increasingly important source of Republican strength" as well as to regulate the flow of immigrants into the country. On the other side of the aisle, John Swanwick (R., Pennsylvania) argued that the proposed tax was politically motivated. He also suggested that $20 was "too considerable a sum for this purpose," that it would hit the "poor emigrant," and that his Philadelphia constituents would "not be happy" if he supported either the principle or the detail of the tax. In any case, Swanwick and most of his Republican colleagues would oppose any moves that would prevent "a great part of the people of our country" from becoming fully active in American life. This was especially so if the administration linked financial worth to citizenship and, by extension, tarnished the image of America as an asylum for the poor and downtrodden of the Old World. Thus, Matthew Lyon (R., Vermont) likened the suggested tax to "a treaty offensive and defensive, with the Monarch of Britain, to prevent his subjects from leaving him and coming hither."[39]

In addition to the recommended tax, Harrison Gray Otis (F., Massachusetts) and Robert Goodloe Harper (F., South Carolina) also wanted at least a ten-year stay of naturalization. These proposals gave both men another opportunity to expatiate on the dangerous influence of the "wild Irish" on contemporary American society. Indeed, it was during the debate on naturalization that Otis made one of the more controversial speeches of the period:

"I do not wish to invite hordes of wild Irishmen, nor the turbulent and disorderly of all parts of the world, to come here with a view to disturb our tranquillity, after having succeeded in the overthrow of their own Governments." Thus, Harper asserted that passage of the bill would enable the United States to "recover from the mistake [it] . . . fell into when it first began to form its constitutions, of admitting foreigners to citizenship . . . [a] mistake . . . productive of very great evils to this country."[40]

Such arguments that partisan controversy since the adoption of the U.S. Constitution had been spearheaded by immigrants were as old as they were familiar. Thus, Harper had also argued that "strangers . . . however acceptable they may be in other respects, could not have the same views and attachments with native citizens." The chairman of the House investigative committee, Samuel Sewall (F., Massachusetts) also repeated a tried theme, that given the "present distracted state of the country from whence they have emigrated," Irish immigrants could not be expected to support the government in their new home. James Bayard (F., Delaware) added that from his observations of those who had arrived since 1796, there was ample evidence for Sewall's view. Thus, several speakers suggested that the bill should be made retroactive because "many Jacobins and vagabonds [had] come into the United States during the last two years, as may come for ten years hence." In the event, the proposal was defeated, largely as a result of the efforts of Albert Gallatin (R., Pennsylvania), and the tax limited to $5. However, the revised naturalization act, as it was signed by Adams on June 18, 1798, did increase the period of naturalization from five to fourteen years.[41]

During the spring and summer of 1798, as America drifted toward war with France, the debates on the Alien and Sedition Acts developed these and other themes even further. These acts defined how foreign-born citizens, or potential citizens, should behave in the new host culture. As paranoia about the fifth-column activities of internal "agents" revived, Federalists were determined "to restrain the evil" and insisted, for example, that "suspect" immigrants could be justly imprisoned or expelled, if their native country went to war with America. The broad implication of this policy was that certain aliens could never be fully Americanized and that, therefore, a kind of two-tier system of citizenship was desirable.

Because the Alien Enemies Act, as it came to be called, introduced the concept of what Robert Williams (R., North Carolina) termed "expulsion on suspicion," the debate on the measure was long and complicated. While the act was still in committee, Congress received the XYZ dispatches on June 18, 1798, and immediately reacted by passing a more repressive, if "temporary," Alien Friends Act. This had originated in the Senate two months earlier, when James Hillhouse (F., Connecticut) had asked that all non-naturalized aliens who were "dangerous" to the country's "peace and safety" should be expelled and that those allowed to remain should be registered by permit. Because Hillhouse's bill had already been read and amended by June 1798 and because the Alien Enemies Act was still in committee when the dispatches were published, the Senate bill was swiftly adopted by both houses and signed by the president on June 25 for an initial period of two years.[42]

This act enabled the president to deport any alien whom he deemed to be dangerous to the peace and safety of the union, or whom he suspected (with or without evidence) to be "in treasonable or secret machinations against the government." It also tightened the procedures of immigration by obliging ship captains to give detailed reports to the office of the secretary of state, of the numbers, origin, and description of aliens brought into the country. Given such sweeping powers, as well as its "temporary" nature, Gallatin overcame objections to move the Alien Enemies Act out of committee, noting that "if this bill is not passed, the President of the United States will have the power of removing from the country all those aliens whom he may think it necessary and proper to be removed, whether they are alien friends or alien enemies." On June 26, 1798, the Alien Enemies Act was finally taken and passed by the House. On July 3, it was passed by the Senate and signed by the president three days later. As finally approved, the act provided that resident aliens of a country with which the United States was in a state of "declared war" became ipso facto "alien enemies" and so could be "apprehended, restrained, secured and removed, as alien enemies" by presidential proclamation.[43]

Together with the Sedition Act adopted in July, the two alien and naturalization acts occasioned fierce debate. Critics considered all three to constitute an excessive interference with the personal liberty of the citizen and perhaps more advisedly, by two later historians, as *Freedom's Fetters* and *A Crisis in Freedom*. The three acts evoked the expected emotive reaction among immigrants and active Republicans and, during the year after their enactment, these interests made their objective known. Not unexpectedly, Jefferson-oriented newspapers and publicists attacked these laws and the associated debates in terms that were, at times, highly emotive. What became known as Otis's "wild Irish" speech was particularly offensive, not just because it castigated the role of the

Irish in the achievement and consolidation of American independence but because it was deemed to indulge "rancorous prejudices" that stretched back to the Tudor conquest of Ireland in the sixteenth century. On September 13, 1797, the *Time-Piece* recalled these ingrained views: "The word 'wild,' it ought not to be necessary to tell you, sir, was a term of reproach bestowed on Ireland by Englishmen because of their impatience of bondage, her violent and bloody struggles for freedom . . . it answers to the word rebel among you. . . . How ridiculous to call that nation [Ireland] which is as high advanced in improvements as any nation in Europe."[44]

While Republicans attacked the laws, the *Aurora* noted that "every man ought to state his opinion respecting [the alien acts], whether his opinion be true or false." The resulting petitions stressed that public servants should be "amenable" to the citizen and, as a result, that government policy had a superior arbiter who could, *pace* the stress that some placed on "natural leadership," assess and recall that policy. The first formal opportunity to do so came in December 1798, when George Logan defeated Frederick A. Muhlenberg, the former speaker of the U.S. House of Representatives. During the campaign, Logan had sought to galvanize Republican strength by criticizing the alien acts and by defending the loyalty and integrity of the immigrant from recent attacks. However, a more important opportunity came when the "natives of Ireland in the United States" petitioned Congress in the so-called Plea of Erin.[45]

The plea repeated that Irish immigrants were refugees from the "horrid outrages and murders . . . [of] a savage British soldiery" and had come to America to enjoy the blessings of the American constitution. The alien and naturalization acts were thus represented as breaking faith with "guiltless immigrants" who shared the same constitutional rights as native-born Americans to personal liberty, "tranquillity, and safety." While the "plea" expanded on this and other legal points, it also suggested that the act "may have" partly resulted from "unjust impressions, concerning the Irish residents in the United States, and the Irish in general." This was all the more galling for the petitioners in view of the fact that "the *blood* of the Irish [had] flowed in your service here, as if it were *their own*, and that they [had] *faithfully* acted in your highest public trusts . . . of the Irish residents in the United States, a greater *proportion* partook of the hazards of the field, and of the duties of your independent republican councils, than of the Americans."

Most telling, however, was the plea's reference to the relative positions of America in 1775 and Ireland in 1798, of which, more than most others, John

Adams was the symbolic link: "The case is rendered deeply impressive by the certain truth, that the president of 1798, was a member of the committee of congress of 1775, who deliberately prepared, and reported the touching address to Ireland, which openly excited them to approve, to assist, and to imitate the American struggle." Therefore, whether in vindication of its role as an open "asylum," or in gratitude for the role of the Irish during the Revolutionary war, or in recognition of a kindred political struggle, Congress should "Suffer us to enjoy among you, the peace, liberty and safety, which our gallant countrymen have helped to establish, till gracious Heaven, by dispensing to Ireland the same blessings, shall grant the remainder of our mutual prayers."[46]

As Congress had earmarked Monday, February 10, 1799, to hear objections to the act, a meeting was held at St. Mary's church the previous day to approve an appropriate memorial. A riot ensued, resulting in the arrest of a number of suspected "United Irishmen." Alexander James Dallas, who had earlier presented Israel's case to the Pennsylvania senate, acted as their attorney. There are two points in his defense that are worthy of mention here. First, he rejected the charge that the defendants had disrespected the church and drew on the evidence of the church's curate, Father Carr, to point out that in contemporary Ireland, petitions were "frequently" endorsed "after retiring from church." Moreover, one of his other witnesses, who himself had immigrated in 1797, stated that "a number" of the congregation would sign only if the memorial was brought to church. As such, it was wrong to suggest that the accused were immoral or blasphemous simply because they had met after mass. From this, Dallas made a more telling point when he argued that aliens had a right to expect that Americans should respect "the habits and customs they [the Irish] brought with them from abroad." In other words, in a truly pluralist republic, those who immigrated into America should not be obliged to ditch the ethnocultural baggage of the Old World. Federalists had always been uncomfortable with this view of American society and, as the trial showed, this was still the case in 1799.[47]

Dallas also asked Americans not to believe that his clients were part of a "dark conspiracy formed to overthrow not alone the constitution but to subvert the very principle of our form of government." However, the prosecution counsel, Joseph Hopkinson, a prominent Federalist and author of the well-known nationalist anthem, "Hail Columbia," made exactly such a charge: "these Irishmen are Jacobins, and of course, they will sign nothing but a Jacobinical address . . . an involution of ideas [has] connected Irishmen and Jacobinism." Moreover, he also argued that in any event, aliens have no right whatsoever to petition, or to interfere in any respect with the government of this country; as the right of voting in elections is confirmed to our citizens, the right of petitioning is also . . . it appears that a majority of the persons assembled to sign and procure signatures on this occasion are not citizens of the United States . . . the greatest evils this country has ever endured, have arisen from the ready admission of foreigners to a participation in the government and internal arrangements of the country . . . [an open door] to the oppressed of all countries . . . had the Americans been left to themselves, we should not this day have been divided and rent into parties.

These speculations, as well as the view that the trial had been "engendered in a spirit of disappointed faction," again suggest a Federalist strategy to discredit Jefferson's ethnocultural supporters.[48]

The castigation of the United Irishmen and, before that, of the emerging political role of the "new Irish" leaders in general, had already highlighted these points earlier in the decade. Moreover, the political activities of Philadelphia's Irish immigrants had also established that community as a focus for a debate that revealed more general insecurities about the direction of the new republic than rehearsed Old-World stereotypes and images per se. However, the city's "new Irish" had wanted to advance republicanism in Ireland as well as in America and, as such, they became heroes of both the "new Irish" and the "new politics." It was these challenges to *both* the political and social economy of Federalist America that made them the focus of such unease and suspicion. They became a measure of defining America by focusing on what was "un-American." As a result, these "new" leaders and, in particular, the United Irishmen, are marked on all the milestones of the decade, from those of pivotal elections to the debates and legislation on political access and activity. On the broader level, they also challenged the institutions of the new republic and through this, the debate on the re-invention of America after 1783.

CHAPTER NINE

Dionysian Rhetoric and Apollonian Solutions

The Politics of Union and Disunion in the Age of Federalism

Melvin Yazawa

"Tranquillity is the old man's milk," Thomas Jefferson wrote in the summer of 1797, but he found none in the business of politics because "passions are too high at present, to be cooled." Unlike the past, when "gentlemen" could differ on the issues but continue to "speak to each other," the current assemblage of political "bulls & bears" had created an atmosphere in which "men who have been intimate all their lives, cross the streets to avoid meeting, & turn their heads another way, lest they should be obliged to touch their hats." Jefferson's description of the "roar & tumult" of politics in the 1790s might serve as an epigraph to prevailing histories of the Federalist era. Since the 1950s, historians have adopted Marshall Smelser's characterization of the period as an "Age of Passion." Contrary to the "way the tale is usually told," Smelser argued in a seminal series of articles, public life in the 1790s was governed by "hate, anger, and fear" rather than "statesmanlike decorum and a reliance on logic."[1]

The problem with this conventional interpretation is not that it misrepresents the passions of the period, for it does not. "Verbal blows" that rival the "ripest vituperation" ever recorded in American history, as Smelser has it, accompanied every major confrontation. The Federalist era was, as John R.

Howe, Jr., observes, "characterized by heated exaggeration and haunted by conspiratorial fantasy. Events were viewed in apocalyptic terms with the very survival of republican liberty riding in the balance." All of this is accurate enough, to be sure, but unsatisfactory because incomplete. The Federalist period was more than an Age of Passion. Smelser himself warned that "this view must not be stretched beyond proportion." He would not dismiss the "good sense and realism of the founding generation," claiming instead only to be organizing his story "differently by writing it as 'emotional history.'"[2]

This chapter seeks to explain the apparent incongruity implicit in Smelser's "emotional history." Richard Hofstadter first took notice of this problem more than thirty years ago. In *The Idea of a Party System*, Hofstadter writes that in the 1790s "something in the character of the American system was at work to unleash violent language but to inhibit violent solutions." Focusing specifically on Federalist acquiescence in Jefferson's election to the presidency in 1800, he elaborates further: "Somehow we must find a way to explain the rapid shift from the Dionysian rhetoric of American politics during the impassioned years from 1795 to 1799 to the Apollonian political solution of 1800–1801." And Hofstadter ventures a tentative answer to this puzzle: Federalists accommodated the Republican victory because they retained control of their own affairs in New England, were hopeful that the public would soon grow weary of Republican misrule and swing back in their direction, felt morally and constitutionally obligated to accept defeat fairly administered, gained some measure of satisfaction from Jefferson's strategy of conciliation, were spared the worst effects of Anglophobia by a lull in European wars, succumbed to the dictates of practical judgment rather than the excesses of propaganda, and perhaps most significantly were by temperament opposed to "extreme or violent measures."[3]

Hofstadter's explanation for Federalist acquiescence is suggestive, but the seemingly paradoxical blend of Dionysian rhetoric and Apollonian solutions was not characteristic of the Federalists alone, nor was it confined to the late 1790s. It was instead, as James M. Banner, Jr., has argued, more generally descriptive of the politics of the "entire half-century after 1765": the "frenzied political climate before 1776 recurred in the 1790s and continued unabated after 1800."[4]

This "continuity of attitude and action" for the period stretching from the Stamp Act crisis to the Hartford Convention is at the core of the "something in the character of the American system" that Hofstadter said was the key to understanding the Federalist era. Americans throughout this half-century were preoccupied with the problem of forging and maintaining a union of colonies and then states, first in order to resist imperial policies, then to win their independence in a protracted war, next to stabilize the confederation through constitutional reform, and finally to realize the promise of the Revolution by securing the republic against all enemies foreign and domestic.[5]

The union Americans managed to forge, however, was always fragile. Centrifugal forces generated by local and sectional jealousies were constantly at work threatening to pull it apart. Even during the War of Independence, with the British army on American soil and national survival in jeopardy, regional animosities were never completely submerged. That the union endured under these circumstances was due largely to the fact that the alternative, disunion, was unacceptable to the vast majority of the people. This was obviously the case for the period before 1783, but was equally true for the decades that followed.

Alexander Hamilton presented the most cogent summary of the progression to which Washington alluded. In *Federalist* Nos. 6 through 9, Hamilton discussed the dangers "which will in all probability flow from dissensions between the States themselves" upon the dissolution of the union. Past grievances, disputed territorial claims, commercial rivalries, the public debt, and other sources of conflict too numerous to name would be reinvigorated by the disintegration into separate confederacies. Hamilton described a recurring pattern of escalation in which competition gave way to discord, which, in turn, led to infractions, then to reprisals, and finally to appeals to the "sword." And after the first appeal to the sword, no state could possibly resist popular demands for the establishment of a standing army to repel or deter anticipated invasions by rapacious neighbors. "To be more safe," the people "become willing to run the risk of being less free." Unfortunately, the necessity of standing armies "enhances the importance of the soldier, and proportionately degrades the condition of the citizen," encouraging the people to consider the "soldiery not only as their protectors but as their . . . masters." The descent from disunion to militarism and despotism, Hamilton concluded, was logically "drawn from the natural and necessary progress of human affairs."[6]

Regardless of the imposition or abuse under which they suffered, complainants anticipated even greater evils if their quarrels led to the formation of competing confederations. Had Americans—"scattered over a large extent of country," as John Marsh described them in 1784, and "living under different governments—entertaining strong local prejudices—having various and opposite interests"—been able to overcome their reciprocal distrust, the fear of disunion might have dissipated. But they were ideologically predisposed to be suspicious and, as John M. Murrin has observed, they "discovered that they really did not like each other very much." Ironically, it was precisely because mutual distrust proved to be so pervasive and persistent that most Americans could not envision separate confederacies coexisting in peace and thus felt compelled to work within the existing union.[7]

The Age of Passion was therefore also an age of calculation. As each new controversy accentuated the differences among the constituent parts of the extended republic and gave rise to rhetoric marked by the "ripest vituperation," it also highlighted the fragility of the union and thereby persuaded the opposing sides, as Jefferson remarked in 1798, "to push [only] as far as events will render prudent." This combination of passion and prudence is best seen in two critical contests of the 1790s. The first is the apportionment controversy of 1791–92, which is largely overlooked by historians of the Federalist era but which commanded the attention of the members of the Second Congress for over five months and affected the way in which state and sectional interests were perceived for the remainder of the decade. The second centers on the Virginia and Kentucky Resolutions, which, though well known, are too often interpreted in anticipation of what was made of them in the antebellum period. The crucial question here is whether the actions taken by Madison and Jefferson in 1798–99 constitute a dramatic reversal of the "prudent" strategy they had pursued earlier in the decade. Had they lost their fear of disunion?[8]

Apportionment Controversy

The apportionment controversy began in late October 1791 as an attempt to satisfy a constitutionally mandated requirement. Article I of the Constitution stipulates that an "actual enumeration" of the people be taken within three years of the first meeting of Congress and that the number of representatives in the House be adjusted thereafter so as not to exceed the sum of one representative for every 30,000 people. The first federal census was completed in 1790, and the Second Congress addressed the problem by apportioning seats as a matter of routine business. On October 31 John Laurance of New York moved that "till the time of the next enumeration, the number of Representatives shall be one to every thirty thousand inhabitants." The proposal was not unexpected, but few could have anticipated what followed. Before it was finally resolved, state and sectional interests had become more sharply defined than ever before, and the burdens of union measured with a precision impossible earlier.[9]

The ratio specified in the Laurance motion meant that House membership would increase from its current 67 to 112. And during the first two weeks of debate most exchanges focused on the adequacy of representation issue. Was the Laurance number sufficiently large to reflect the varied interests of the people, but not so large as to be unwieldy? As the debate gathered momentum, however, this question gave way to more pressing concerns. After all, as Delaware's John Vining observed, it was scarcely possible to believe that the "Liberties of America" rested on the difference between one representative per 30,000 persons and one per 40,000. And yet, "I feel myself more interested in the question than I ever was in any one I have had to decide on," declared John Page of Virginia. Others shared his sense of the momentousness of the decision they were about to make. But what had "occasioned the debate to travel so widely," Vining wondered.[10]

The answer to Vining's query is to be found in the position taken by the North Carolina delegation. Early in the debate Hugh Williamson spoke against the motion and mentioned almost in passing that he hoped that "such a ratio should be adopted as would leave the fewest fractions." A week later, John Steele repeated the recommendation of a ratio that "will leave the fewest fractions." What Williamson and Steele were referring to was the fraction of a state's population left over after the application of the ratio contained in the Laurance motion. In the case of North Carolina, with a representable population of 353,522 (total number of whites plus three-fifths of the slave population), applying the 1/30,000 ratio would entitle the state to eleven representatives but leave a hefty remainder of 23,522 persons theoretically unrepresented. By contrast, Virginia's representable population was 630,559; under the same formula, the state would be entitled to twenty-one representatives and be left with a minuscule surplus of only 522 persons. At this stage of the controversy, no one else mentioned leftover "fractions," but every representative was aware of the problem, and all—save the South Carolinians, whose census returns had not yet been fully tabulated—had probably computed the impact of the recommended ratios on their respective states.[11]

On November 15, by a vote of thirty-five to twenty-three, the House passed the Laurance motion. It was forced to reconsider the apportionment bill, however, after the Senate rejected it on December 8, with Vice President John Adams casting the deciding vote. The Senate's motive in returning the House bill and recommending instead a 1/33,000 ratio was to "reduce the fractions which would result from the ratio proposed by the House." What William

Findley had earlier dismissed as "one of the lesser matters pertaining to the subject" now became explosive.[12]

From the outset, opponents of the Laurance motion had a clear advantage when discussion focused on the uneven impact of the 1/30,000 ratio on individual states. Was it fair for Delaware to be allowed only one representative and Rhode Island two, when the eligible population of the former was approximately 55,540 and the latter 68,446? Supporters of the motion, however, responded to this equity argument by invoking the language of the Constitution. Article I states that the "number of Representatives shall not exceed one for every thirty thousand"; the House therefore could not constitutionally allocate representatives to a constituent base below 30,000, regardless of the size of the "unrepresented" fraction in Delaware or elsewhere. Egbert Benson from New York was the first to suggest otherwise. The constitutional restriction set forth in Article I had been misunderstood all along, Benson argued, especially by those who continued to support the Laurance bill. (Benson was one of the fourteen congressmen who eventually switched sides on the issue.) Properly interpreted, the clause in question required Congress to apply the agreed-upon ratio to the "whole number of people" in the United States in order to determine the total number of representatives to be seated in the House. From that aggregate number, as the Constitution specifies, "Representatives . . . shall be apportioned among the several States."[13]

Fisher Ames of Massachusetts developed the full implications of Benson's constitutional construction. In a lengthy speech on December 19, a day devoted almost entirely to settling the apportionment issue, Ames sought to demonstrate that the House bill was a "bad one." Virginians might disagree with this assessment, but that was because the bill favored Virginia. By applying the 1/30,000 ratio to state populations individually, "thirty thousand in Virginia shall have as much power as near sixty thousand in Delaware and several other States." Would anyone dare to argue that such a distribution was just? No, responded New Jersey's Jonathan Dayton, even some members of the Virginia delegation "admitted the inequalities complained of"; however, they "boldly claimed and exacted those advantages as a right" under Article I of the Constitution. Ames challenged this constitutional argument by appropriating Benson's idea. "The whole number of Representatives being first fixed," the Constitution then "directs that Representatives shall be apportioned among the several States according to their respective numbers." By applying the 1/30,000 ratio to the population of the United States as determined by the federal census,

Ames calculated that the total number of representatives was constitutionally capped at 113. "These are to be apportioned to each State according to its numbers," he explained. What part of this total belongs to Virginia? "The answer is easily found." Because Virginia's population "after deducting two-fifths for the slaves" was 630,559, or the equivalent of 17 percent of the national population, it was entitled to 17 percent of the nation's 113 representatives, or nineteen. The current House bill, however, gave Virginia twenty-one representatives. "Who will say that the words or meaning of the Constitution are pursued?"[14]

Ames proceeded to apply the 1/30,000 ratio to each state's population, which accounted for 106 representatives, and then allocated the remaining seven to those states with the largest leftover fractions, Vermont, New Hampshire, Massachusetts, Connecticut, New Jersey, Delaware, and North Carolina. Under his system, Ames insisted, the "error of inequality" so conspicuous in the House bill was greatly alleviated.[15]

It was an ingenious argument that "was never thought of till lately," grumbled Virginia's John Page. To supporters of the original bill, it was also an infuriating argument, in no small part because it was tantalizingly credible. Even Washington, who eventually vetoed an amended bill incorporating Ames's idea, had to admit that the disputed clause in the Constitution "would bear the construction which the bill put." But above all, Madison lamented, it was a divisive argument, inflaming as it did local "feelings, passions, and prejudices." John Laurance had introduced his motion without having "so much as made a single calculation." Colleagues less scrupulous and less disinterested than he, however, had managed to foul the issue and to make the calculation of fractions the "very essence of the Opposition."[16]

What disturbed Madison most about the debate begun on December 19, what "he had heard with pain," were the increasingly unrestrained appeals to sectional biases. Two years earlier, in the midst of the dispute over an impost bill whose impact would be felt "differently in different States," Madison had been pleased to report that the "interests and ideas of the Northern and Southern States have been less adverse than was predicted by the opponents . . . of the new Government." The proceedings of Congress then, he told Jefferson, were "marked with great moderation and liberality." But no longer. In the current controversy, the "most important points are embarrassed" because the "Northern and Southern interests are held up." Despite his plea for a return to "utmost coolness," Madison said, the debate had "swelled to an immoderate extent" and "every idea of liberality . . . is banished."[17]

The demise of liberality was deplorable but perhaps unavoidable once latent suspicions and interests were aroused. William Smith of South Carolina, who first voted against the original House bill and then was outspoken in "changing his vote," credited his conversion to the "locality and fractions that had been introduced into the debate." Smith's reference to "locality and fractions" could not have escaped the notice of other participants in the apportionment controversy. If, as Madison pointed out, "fractions will exist . . . on every possible plan," then the only difference among the various proposals in contention must be the sizes of the fractions they generated and their particular location. Maryland's William Vans Murray dismissed the Senate's 1/33,000 ratio as "but a commutation of the evil of fractions from one State to another." Abraham Venable, Madison's colleague from Virginia, responded to the Senate's amended 1792 plan, which was an updated version of Ames's December 1791 proposal, by calculating "various particulars to show" that in "transferring the fractions from one State to another" it was unfair to the South.[18]

What had begun as an attempt to shed new light on a delicate subject developed into a full-scale sectional contest. Laurance, whose motion had started it all, was "sorry" that the discussion had "dwindled into a debate on fractions, and on the interests of the Northern and Southern parts of the Union." But the "extreme anxiety" that afflicted Theodore Sedgwick was probably the dominant emotion in the House after sectional interests came to the fore. The source of this anxiety is not hard to find. In opposing any alteration of the House bill, William Branch Giles "averted to the restive spirit in some of the States." Some of the actions of Congress, he warned, were "so disliked, that the people in those States wished themselves separated from the Government." More specifically, Giles mentioned that his Virginia constituents were so committed to the ratio set in the House bill that "he really feared the discontents" among them would escalate "to an alarming degree, should the amendment of the Senate be agreed to." Jonathan Dayton countered that the distribution of representatives in the House bill was so unfair, his home state of New Jersey, for example, had a whopping leftover fraction of 0.99, that if its proponents were determined to reject any and all amendments, then an "absolute separation" of the states might be the only alternative left. This was the "danger" Sedgwick had in mind when he cautioned House members against a "pertinacious adherence to a measure so productive of . . . jealousy." It was the same danger that left Madison hoping in the face of "predictions or threats thrown out in the course of the debate, that no mutilation of the Union would take place."[19]

A comparison of the House votes taken on November 15 and December 19, the former in favor of the Laurance motion and the latter in opposition to the Senate's proposed amendment, confirms the impression that sectional identities were sharpened by the apportionment question. The margin of victory shrank from twelve votes to six in the span of a month, but more important was the altered composition of the opposing sides. To be sure, most of those who had supported the Laurance motion voted against the Senate's amendment, and vice versa. But fourteen representatives, nearly one-fourth of those who voted one way on November 15, had changed their minds by December 19, and had done so on a strictly sectional basis. Thereafter the sectional nature of the competing sides on the apportionment issue solidified. Southern congressmen continued to insist on some version of the 1/30,000 ratio applied to the states individually, while their Northern counterparts refused to yield on the issue of leftover fractions.[20]

The vote on the final bill, taken by the Senate in February and the House in March 1792, manifested the same sectional division. The "vote for and against the bill was perfectly geographical, a Northern agt. a Southern vote," Washington noted as he pondered whether to veto the measure because it relied on aggregate population figures in determining total House membership and dealt with leftover fractions in the manner first suggested by Ames. When the president consulted with cabinet members to help him decide which course of action to take, he found that they too were divided along sectional lines. Alexander Hamilton and Henry Knox urged him to sign the bill, while Jefferson and Edmund Randolph advised him to veto the proposed legislation. Later Washington asked Randolph to meet with Madison and Jefferson. If the three of them "concurred in opinion that he should negative the bill," they were to "draw the instrument for him to sign." But even after, perhaps especially after, his veto message had been drafted, Washington remained uneasy. Persuaded that the bill was unconstitutional because it gave to eight states "more than one [representative] for every thirty thousand," he was apprehensive lest his veto be misconstrued to mean he was "taking side with a Southern party." The "public mind" was already so "dissatisfied" that he wished not to contribute further to its agitation. In private, Washington "expressed his fear that there would ere long be a separation of the union." Convinced of what he must do, but mindful of the "delicacy" of the situation, Washington hesitated, asking for confirmation one last time as he walked Randolph to the door, "as if he still wished to get off."[21]

Washington's veto of the apportionment bill on April 5, 1792, the first use of the executive veto under the Constitution, initiated the last and predictably anticlimactic phase of the controversy. Unable to muster a simple majority, let alone the two-thirds vote needed to override the veto, the House quickly proceeded to alter its bill. With the sole exception of Giles of Virginia, no one spoke for more than a few minutes. And even Giles, who probably rambled on for about an hour covering old ground "in favor of the ratio one to thirty thousand," was not oblivious to the fact he was "trespassing upon the patience" of "gentlemen probably fatigued with the discussion." The House barely waited for Giles to finish before voting on April 9 to adopt a much-anticipated motion for apportioning representatives "at a ratio of one for every thirty-three thousand persons, in the respective States." The new bill was identical to the one the Senate had presented to the House, and the House by a sectional vote had rejected the previous December. A comparison of this first vote with the votes cast on April 9, 1792, reveals only one significant difference—Robert Barnwell, Daniel Huger, and William Smith of South Carolina dropped their earlier opposition to the Senate's ratio. Their reversal was crucial to the new bill's four-vote margin of victory, but only because South Carolina was the sole exception to the dominant pattern of sectional voting. Virginia, North Carolina, Maryland, and Georgia did not deviate from their earlier, unanimous opposition to the 1/33,000 ratio. Connecticut, Rhode Island, New Hampshire, Vermont, and New Jersey remained equally unanimous in their support of the ratio. What Theodore Sedgwick said after the December vote still held, the "opposition of interests between the Northern and Southern States" continued to be "felt in the discussion of every important question which had come under the consideration of the Legislature."[22]

Calculating the Union's Value

Sectional tensions apparent before the eruption of the apportionment controversy were raised to new heights in 1791. Population totals supplied by the 1790 census invited numerical comparisons and enabled opposing interests North and South to bolster their arguments with seemingly irrefutable mathematical evidence. The relative merits of competing plans were appraised with an exactness hitherto unknown, as advantages and disadvantages were measured in tenths. A few, like Vining of Delaware, felt somewhat inadequate in the face of such precision, being "not so old or experienced in calculations as some," but ventured to offer the results of their computations just the same. Not surprisingly, intersectional cooperation, what Madison saw as a "favorable symptom" in 1789, was lost amid the commotion over fractions.[23]

The apportionment controversy also became inextricably linked to disgruntlement over Hamilton's fiscal programs. Attempts to undermine the Constitution and to saddle the federal government with a public debt "greater than we can possibly pay," Jefferson feared, indicated that would-be monarchists were plotting the overthrow of the republic. A favorable settlement of the apportionment question supplied the "only hope for safety" against such schemes. Thus, although the final settlement fell short of his expectations, Jefferson was encouraged because "obvious encroachments . . . on the plain meaning of the constitution" had been thwarted, leftover fractions disregarded, a "*common ratio, or divisor* . . . applied to the numbers of each state," and total membership increased from 67 to 105. At the very least, the "numerous representation which is to come forward the ensuing year" might allow good republicans to overwhelm the "corrupt squadron" currently in control of the House.[24]

But nothing was certain. It was conceivable that the "great mass" of new members would share the "same principles with the present" House majority. If this proved to be the case, the prospect of disunion loomed large. Jefferson confessed that the idea made him "tremble," he could "scarcely contemplate a more incalculable evil than the breaking of the union into two or more parts," but the "division of sentiment and interest happens unfortunately to be so geographical" that such thoughts were impossible to ignore. Consequently, he pleaded with Washington, who seemed determined to retire from public service at the end of his first term as president, to postpone his decision until the composition of the next "one or two sessions" of Congress were known. "If the first corrective of a numerous representation should fail in its effect, your presence will give time for trying others not inconsistent with the union and peace of the states." Only "your being at the helm," Jefferson wrote, will deter the sections from lapsing into "violence or secession." All else failing, "North and South will hang together, if they have you to hang on."[25]

Madison was similarly convinced by the end of the apportionment controversy that Washington's continuance in office might be essential to the preservation of the union. Given the "aspect which things had been latterly assuming," Washington's "retiring at the present juncture might have effects that ought not to be hazarded." When the president responded that "he could

not believe or conceive himself any wise necessary to the successful administration of the Government," Madison respectfully disagreed. "It was well
known," he said, that Washington's "services had been in a manner essential,"
especially with regard to his "uniting all parties under a Govt. which had
excited such violent controversies & divisions." Besides, under the "present
unsettled conditions," he had no obvious successor. Jefferson's "extreme repug-
nance to public life" and the "prejudices in the Northern States" removed him
from serious consideration. And Adams was disqualified because of "his late
conduct on the representation bill." Madison simply could not overlook
Adams's role in the apportionment controversy, and neither could his Southern colleagues. The vice president had broken the deadlock in the Senate by
casting his deciding vote against the original House bill. Upon first hearing of
the bill's rejection, William Smith of South Carolina complained that the will
of the House and half the Senate had been overturned "by the vote of a single
member . . . the Vice President." As the controversy dragged on and sectional
divisions came to the forefront, initial disapproval turned into a "settled dislike" of Adams, "particularly in the Southern States."[26]

In beseeching Washington to make "one more sacrifice . . . to the desires &
interests of your country," Madison was hopeful that the "dangerous influence"
of men like Adams, whose "conduct on the representation bill" betrayed his
preference for "monarchical principles," would be reduced to insignificance
"before another term of four years should run out." Jefferson likewise predicted
that Washington's presence coupled with an "enlarged representation" would
bring about the demise of the "Monarchical federalists" before the "completion
of the second period of four years." Such hopes would not be realized. If anything, the sequence of events culminating in Jay's Treaty indicated that the "faction of Monocrats" remained firmly in control of national politics during
Washington's second term. That Washington had a hand in perpetuating this
sad state of affairs only deepened the dismay of the Virginians. Two years after
Washington's retirement, Jefferson explained that the "irresistible influence
and popularity of General Washington played off by the cunning of Hamilton"
had resulted in the continuation of the "anti-republicans" in power.[27]

As Jefferson wrote these lines in early June 1798, the public was "still in a
state of astonishment" over the XYZ affair, two "detestable" alien bills were
pending before Congress, President Adams was hinting that the "spirit of
libelling and sedition shall be controlled by an execution of laws," and street
brawls were breaking out in the nation's capital between gangs of young men

wearing the "Black (or English) cockade" and those sporting the "tricolored (or French) cockade." But Jefferson refused to entertain any notion of a "scission of the Union." He rejected John Taylor's suggestion that the time had come "to estimate the separate mass of Virginia and North Carolina, with a view to their separate existence." The rule of the New Englanders, oppressive though it may be, was only a "temporary superiority." On the other hand, he asked rhetorically, "if to rid ourselves of the present rule . . . we break the Union, will the evil stop there?" Human nature being as it is, "an association of men who will not quarrel with one another is a thing which never yet existed." Even if the union were reduced to Virginia and North Carolina, "conflict will be established between the representatives of these two States, and they will end by breaking into their simple units." Once the forces of disunion were set in motion, who could foretell "where they would end?" Confronted with a stark choice between the "reign of witches" and the "evils of a scission," Jefferson much preferred the former.[28]

Jefferson's choice was conditioned by two factors, both of which were at least partly influenced by the apportionment controversy. First, the self-interested calculations undertaken by each state during the debates underscored Jefferson's sense of the fragility of the union. The bill Congress forwarded to the president in March 1792 was bound to have a "very pernicious" effect on the union because it took the "fractions of some states to supply the deficiency of others." It took Georgia's leftover four-tenths, for example, and combined it with New Hampshire's seven-tenths, which "makes the people of Georgia the instrument of giving a member to N. Hampshire." In so doing, the bill violated the "plain meaning of the constitution" and failed to dispense an "equal measure of justice to all" of the states. To make matters worse, sponsors of the bill had overwhelmingly rejected an amendment that would have codified the procedure of allocating the "residuary representatives" to those states with the "greatest fractions." It was conceivable, therefore, that "it may be found the next time more convenient to distribute them" in accordance with another criterion, perhaps "*among the smaller states* [or] . . . *among the larger states*" or, indeed, according to any "crotchet which ingenuity may invent, and the combinations of the day give strength to carry." The result would be a mad "scramble, or a vendue, for the surplus members." Supporters of the bill were engaging in a "hazardous game" that threatened the "bond of union." Jefferson's understanding of the centrifugal forces jeopardizing *any* union thus led him to oppose Taylor's suggestion of creating a "residuary confederacy."[29]

Second, the bill Washington signed into law in April 1792 avoided what Jefferson saw as arbitrary dispensations and established a rule consonant with the Constitution, allotting one representative per 33,000 constituents in each state separately considered. The strength of numbers, however configured, worked to the advantage of the Southern states, he assured Taylor. Massachusetts and Connecticut, even in combination with "their natural friends, the three other eastern States," were "circumscribed within such narrow limits . . . that their numbers will ever be the minority." This meant that time was on their side as well. "We must have patience," Jefferson advised as he opposed policies he believed incurred the "horrors of war, and long oppressions of enormous public debt," because the operation of "time alone would bring round an order of things more correspondent to the sentiments of our constituents." Others shared Jefferson's conviction that geography and population trends favored the South, and therefore that the center of political power would over time move from north to south. Because the "rule of representation in Congress is to vary with the number of inhabitants," as David Ramsay had reminded South Carolinians in 1788, "our influence in the general government will be constantly increasing." Ramsay confidently predicted that "in fifty years, it is probable that the Southern States will have a great ascendancy over the Eastern."[30]

Principles of 1798

Within a week of his letter to Taylor advising "a little patience," Jefferson learned that the Committee on Defense and Commerce had "brought into the lower house a sedition bill." Coupled with the Alien Bills, these legislative initiatives flew "so palpably in the teeth of the constitution as to shew they mean to pay no respect to it," he concluded. Nevertheless, led by a House majority Jefferson thought "bold enough to do anything," Congress approved and the president signed the Alien and Sedition Bills into law in June and July 1798. In the ensuing months, Jefferson and Madison consulted with one another and coordinated their public responses to the offending legislation. The results of their work are justly famous. The relevant question here is whether Jefferson and Madison had come to conclude that the "reign of witches" was now too oppressive to be borne. Contrary to the advice Jefferson had given Taylor some five months earlier, were the Virginia and Kentucky Resolutions promoting the "evils of a scission"? The Connecticut legislature certainly believed that Jefferson was appealing to sentiments "hostile to the existence of our national

Union" and calculated to promote "discord and anarchy" among the states. And nearly all of the other state legislatures responding to the resolutions decried their "dangerous tendency" to disrupt the union. To argue that Jefferson, let alone Madison, underwent a fundamental transformation during these few months, however, is to misunderstand the larger context of the Virginia and Kentucky Resolutions.[31]

The resolutions may have been "forward-looking" in their defense of civil liberties, as Adrienne Koch has argued, but their language and logic harked back to the Revolutionary past. In late August 1798, after learning that some congressmen had accused him of being "nightly closeted" with suspected enemies of the nation, Jefferson could no longer hold to his decision "not to suffer calumny to disturb [his] tranquillity." "I know my own principles to be pure," he wrote angrily to Samuel Smith of Maryland. "They are the same I have acted on from the year 1775 to this day." This sense of continuity and consistency of principles is embedded in the Kentucky Resolutions, which Jefferson began to compose shortly after his letter to Smith. His declaration that "confidence is everywhere the parent of despotism: free government is founded in jealousy and not in confidence," which forms the major premise of the climactic Ninth Resolution, was understood by the Revolutionary generation without further elaboration. The patriots of '75 accepted as axiomatic the assertion that the price of liberty was eternal vigilance against the inevitable encroachments of power. In 1798 Jefferson depicted the Alien Act, Alien Enemies Act, and Sedition Act as latter-day counterparts of the Stamp Act, Declaratory Act, Townshend Acts, and Coercive Acts of the 1760s and 1770s. To anyone familiar with the earlier crisis, the progression from one to the next was predictable: "the friendless alien has . . . been selected as the safest subject of a first experiment, but the citizen will soon follow, or rather has already followed." Left unchecked, "these and successive acts of the same character" will lead to the "absolute dominion of one man." The colonists in 1775 were forced to engage in bloodshed and to move finally toward separating themselves from the British empire. Jefferson's hope in the Kentucky Resolutions was that Americans would manage to avoid a similar escalation "into revolution and blood" by taking preemptive action, that is, by arresting abuses of power "on the threshold."[32]

This appeal to the principles of '75 is the defining characteristic of Jefferson's famous August 23, 1799, letter to Madison, which Koch describes as "one of the most extreme statements that he ever made." Disappointed by the tenor and scope of the replies several states had made to the Virginia and

Kentucky Resolutions, Jefferson was "entering the fray with last-stand ammunition; he was now prepared to consider a doctrine that would contain the direct threat of disunion!" But Koch's attention is perhaps too quickly drawn to the phrase "sever ourselves from that union we so much value." In its entirety, the letter elaborates the policy of "passive firmness" that Jefferson had recommended to Madison earlier in the year and that Madison later incorporated into his lengthy Report on the Resolutions. Jefferson had not abandoned the politics of patience. "We are willing to view with indulgence" the errors of the federal government, "to wait with patience till those passions and delusions shall have passed," and "not . . . to make every measure of error or wrong a cause of scission," Jefferson wrote in the passage immediately preceding his reference to disunion. He thus reaffirmed Virginia's "warm attachment to the union" and reiterated his belief that the "good sense of the American people" would guarantee our "liberty, safety, and happiness." However, "were we to be disappointed in this," we are "determined . . . to sever ourselves." Jefferson's dependent clause establishes the crucial context for what Koch labels his "fateful remark." He was calling on the American people to act "before it shall be too late"; if they failed to do so, if they proved no longer to be attached to the principles of '75, if the remaining alternatives were finally reduced to enslavement or disunion, then and only then would he condone the latter. In short, Jefferson maintained the position he had staked out in the Kentucky Resolutions.[33]

A backward-looking defense of liberty is perhaps even more descriptive of Madison's thinking during this period. Nowhere is this better illustrated than in the Report on the Resolutions, which he wrote in late 1799 after reviewing the "replies of the other States, and the sophistries from other quarters." Responding specifically to the charge that the Virginia Resolutions undermined the bond of union by rendering the federal government "hateful to the people," Madison invited his audience to make a "fair comparison of the political doctrines . . . at the present day with those which characterized the epoch of our Revolution." He was confident that such a comparison with the principles of '75 would reveal that his call for the states to "interpose" themselves against abuses of power was nothing more than a "vigilant discharge of an important duty." Madison was careful in clarifying the conditions under which interposition might be justified. It must not be undertaken "in a hasty manner or on doubtful and inferior occasions," he cautioned. The abuse of power that might trigger an interposition must not be "of a light and transient nature";

rather it "must be both wilful and material," and its impact "deeply" felt, "essentially affecting the vital principles" of the entire political system. The "parties to the constitutional compact" must approach the decision on interposition somewhat reluctantly, knowing they acted as a tribunal of "last resort."[34]

Madison situated his doctrine of interposition squarely within the mainstream of the eighteenth-century radical Whig tradition of resistance. He qualified its implementation in the manner stipulated by the Whig concept of a "just" revolution: long train of abuses, malicious intent, wholesale suffering, and last resort. He couched his arguments in the language of the Independence movement: "light and transient" causes, "recurrence to fundamental principles," "deliberate exercise of dangerous powers," "first symptoms of usurpation," "vigilance," and "design." And he equated the actions of the president and Congress in the 1790s with the actions of the king and Parliament in the 1760s and 1770s: creating bloated bureaucracies with hordes of placemen dependent on the "patronage of the Executive," enlarging the "sphere of discretion allotted to the Executive," and extending the power of the federal government "to all cases of the 'general welfare'—that is to say, *to all cases whatever.*"[35]

Madison's criticism of the uses to which the "general welfare" clause of the Constitution had been put was an obvious reference to the Declaratory Act of 1766. To ensure that no one missed the allusion, he returned to the same theme later in his Report. Parliament had once claimed the "power to make laws . . . *in all cases whatsoever*" only to discover that it could "make laws . . . *in no cases whatsoever.*" But unlike Taylor, Madison was not suggesting that it might be wise to calculate the "separate existence" of a "residuary confederacy." On the contrary, he hoped that timely action would "hasten an oblivion of every circumstance which might be construed into a diminution of mutual respect, confidence, and affection among the members of the Union." Thus the "painful remarks" about disunion contained in the replies of some of the states missed the point of the Virginia Resolutions, as did private commentaries that focused on the disastrous effects of a separation into rival confederacies. In *Plain Truth,* Henry Lee summed up the consequences of "dismemberment": "heavy taxes, accumulated debts, standing armies, and loss of liberty." But Madison knew this already, and had said essentially the same thing more than a dozen years earlier in the Virginia House of Delegates. For Madison, as it was for Jefferson, disunion remained an "incalculable evil," and the resolutions were intended to obviate the need finally to choose between the evils of oppression and the evils of secession.[36]

Agreement between the supporters and opponents of the Virginia and Kentucky Resolutions on the value of the union was fundamental. George Nicholas and his anonymous critic could agree on little else, but both disowned the idea of disunion and described its consequences in nearly identical terms: "ruin and destruction," "anarchy, confusion, and ruin," "calamities," "discord and civil war." Nicholas, who defended the Kentucky Resolutions and whose views were known to Jefferson and Madison, considered the dissolution of the union to be so fraught with "attendant dangers" that no one "in his senses" could possibly "wish to see such an attempt made." And, indeed, Nicholas said, he had never heard disunion mentioned in a positive vein in either "public declarations" or "private" conversations. Charges to the contrary were therefore unsupported by the facts and could only be "proceeding from malice." Nicholas was himself personally offended by the falsehoods: "I have been uniformly and warmly, a friend to the union of America," and as a veteran of the War of Independence, "I have proved my attachments . . . as well by my actions as my words."[37]

To the anonymous "Inhabitant of the North-Western Territory," however, the resolutions were "inconsistent with the union" and conducive to its "destruction." As for Nicholas, the "Inhabitant" concluded, "he *was* a warm friend to the union" and he "was among the first of his countrymen to take up arms" in defense of independence. "But what were his opinions or his actions *then* is of no consequence, if his opinions and actions *now* are opposite." If the "opinions he now holds and propagates with zeal lead to the dissolution of the union," Nicholas will not fare well in the annals of history; "he will not stand acquitted at the bar of reason [or] . . . at the bar of his country."[38]

Paradoxically, the controversy over Virginia and Kentucky Resolutions may have served as a "unifying element" in the early republic because it kept the attention of the contending parties focused on the fragility of the union and the costs of disunion. As long as both sides could agree that, as Nicholas put it, there were no anticipated advantages "sufficient to compensate us for the ruin and destruction which would certainly be brought upon our country and posterity" in the wake of the dissolution of the union, they were content to follow Jefferson's advice and not "push the matter to extremities."[39]

Apollonian Solutions

The age of Federalism was an "Age of Passion," as Smelser argued, and the leading figures of the period may have been governed by "fear and hate," but they were most passionate when the union was imperiled by partisan and sectional contests, and they feared disunion more than they hated one another. This was the "something in the character of the American system . . . at work to unleash violent language but to inhibit violent solutions." The impassioned rhetoric of the principals functioned as a kind of early warning system. Worked to perfection in any given crisis, it was supposed to rally the people to initiate appropriate remedial measures before it was too late. If it failed, if these appeals did not result in the introduction of necessary correctives in a timely manner, then the system would deteriorate beyond repair, and the sovereign people would be left with no choice other than to destroy the union and hazard the consequences. The relationship between the Dionysian rhetoric and Apollonian solutions of the period was therefore complementary rather than contradictory. Violent language preempted the need to resort to violent solutions. This uneasy combination could work, however, only as long as adversaries continued to believe that disunion led inevitably to anarchy and despotism. "If to rid ourselves of the present rule . . . we break the Union, will the evil stop there?" Jefferson had asked in 1798. Increasingly after 1830 Jefferson's successors answered, Yes.[40]

CHAPTER TEN

Civil Society in Post-Revolutionary America

Marc Harris

In the very northern reaches of New Hampshire beyond the Connecticut River's upper lakes, townsmen convened in July 1832, to vote on a temporary constitution and government for the small triangle of land known as the Indian Stream settlement. Their modest, pragmatic intention was simply to allow life to go on under some color of law until the United States and Great Britain could decide exactly where the international boundary between New Hampshire and Lower Canada lay. Recent events had made the border problematic, and to meet this uncertainty the regular 1832 town meeting directed a committee to draft a constitution. The committee labored to prepare its plan of government from March into early July, when notices of a ratification meeting were publicly posted, there being no newspaper. Townsmen approved the document by an overwhelming margin of 56 to 3 and promptly organized their new government, fully acknowledging that it would last only until the two countries resolved the boundary controversy. Residents of Indian Stream thus—apparently—had simply extended their normal legal procedures in response to a completely freakish situation, innovatively adapting their town meeting to meld the powers of constitutional and ratification conventions together with those of the ad hoc public mass meetings that had become so prevalent around the country.[1]

The case is, however, more complicated. Indian Stream had never held legal town meetings, because it had never been a town. Since at least 1822 townspeople had met early every March, as did their counterparts in legally established New Hampshire towns, to elect local officials, levy taxes, and discuss local issues, and residents acknowledged that they belonged administratively to Coos County. Because their town was not incorporated, however, their "town meeting" could be considered riotous, or even, in the most Draconian view, treasonous assembly. "Real authority was lacking," the region's historian has written: "the men could vote this or that but then had to rely on voluntary goodwill or a little pressure from leading citizens to enforce their vote." In effect, the "town meeting" always already had been an amalgam of mass meeting and voluntary association. However dubious its legality, the Indian Stream meeting embodied a popular representative proceeding whose legitimacy—not entirely acceded to by all settlers in the area—rested on a combination of adherence to a set of recognized and expected procedures and some degree of recognition of that legitimacy by townspeople.[2]

In this way, the Indian Stream "town meeting" exemplifies many important features of the kind of civil society Americans created and inhabited during the seventy-five-year period following the Revolution. By "civil society" I mean that pattern of group interactions among individuals that was neither solely governmental nor solely personal or economic, but concerned the articulation and achievement of goals that groups of citizens might define and pursue.[3] That pattern was representational in nature rather than merely instrumental, and groups that made effective use of representational civil space through mass meetings, voluntary associations, and parades and other displays, staked their claims to legitimacy by adhering to regular procedures. Groups that did not follow these procedures forfeited their claim to community representation.[4]

The Indian Stream ratification meeting illustrates some central elements of civic procedure in the early republic. Public advance notice alerted interested parties to the meeting's subject, place (the local schoolhouse, a central public location), and time, and, though our historian does not explicitly say so, it was in all likelihood open to any interested party. The meeting itself proceeded in an orderly fashion by electing a moderator and following an agreed parliamentary procedure, with time for debate and several adjournments and a roll call vote of attendees.[5] Except for the roll call, procedures like these were routinely followed by countless ad hoc meetings on public issues. Events were typically announced by publication of a meeting notice, usually in a local newspaper, as an open-ended invitation. Prior notice shielded organizers and association officers from legal harm and, by alerting the community to a meeting's purpose, also gave interested parties a chance to contribute to the result in whatever way they thought appropriate. Meetings typically began with election of officers to preside and keep records; if, as was frequently the case, the purpose of a meeting was to produce resolutions, the body elected a committee to write and present drafts which the meeting then voted on. A meeting report was subsequently published in the local press and communicated to other newspapers as resolutions of "the citizens of" the vicinity; such a report, for example, presented resolutions passed "at a meeting of the citizens of Cleveland on Dec. 4 [1835] on the subject of a railroad from Warren to Cleveland."[6]

Voluntary associations, too, began life with public meetings of this sort, conducted in a similar fashion and reported in a similar way. Responding to public notices, prospective members met in a public venue and, if not outnumbered by opponents, ran the meeting according to similar parliamentary procedures. One vital step was electing a committee to write a constitution which all present were invited to ratify and sign. Often the core group of organizers had already met and prepared a draft constitution, perhaps borrowed from an outside source. Subsequent meetings were announced by public notice and open to any interested parties, who could then join the group by signing the constitution. Meeting reports paralleled those for mass meetings, as in the case of a temperance society in Ravenna, Ohio, whose journal reported that "According to public notice, the citizens of Ravenna convened . . . and . . . resolved, that the constitution of the Society be read, after which the audience were invited to become members."[7] Societies intended to hold property or conduct business required a further step, obtaining a corporate charter to endow them with legal personality and perpetual succession. This required legislative action, for which public mass meetings and their resolutions could demonstrate local support.[8] Reports of mass meetings and association meetings appear to have regularly claimed representational status for their localities.

Association and Representation

Popular organization during the crisis years leading up to the Declaration of Independence took almost exactly this form, and was explicitly representational.

Regular town meetings in New England became forums of debate and then, after the Massachusetts Government Act, illegal popular assemblies that claimed to speak for the towns. In colonies that lacked a legal or customary meeting tradition, county or district mass meetings spoke for localities and supported convention governments built upon local representation.[9]

But this strong parallel, together with the important role played in colonial society by voluntary associations from the mid-eighteenth century onward, should not be taken to imply either direct transmission or equivalence. At least four significant differences separated practices in the two eras.

First, colonial voluntary associations developed as part of a print- and manuscript-oriented, and transatlantic republic of letters, and their importance depended mostly on connection with that larger world rather than with a specific locale. When the ambitious young Benjamin Franklin sought to get ahead in life, he joined forces with other young men to learn the manners of the imperial metropolis, which might earn him a reputation and a patron; when he sought to confirm his elevated status, he became a Freemason and thereby entered into the farthest-flung sodality in the Western world. Later, as a newspaperman, printer, and almanac author he put himself at the center of the new didactic project of diffusing information about great matters of state, commerce, and public affairs outward to a developing citizenry while also teaching them the polite behavior appropriate among equals. Gathering self-selected members of that citizenry on a notionally equal basis into self-ordering groups was an important departure in the eighteenth century, and such groups played a vital role as mediators bringing in the wider world.[10]

In contrast, associations in nineteenth-century America functioned less to represent the larger world to provincial outposts of empire than to represent localities to local people and to a larger world. Hence, even though interested local figures formed the Ravenna Temperance Society largely in response to urgings from the American Temperance Society and the examples of other towns, the society's journal and published reports reflected only local activities. Because editors borrowed freely from other papers, these accounts might also appear in neighboring—and, occasionally, more distant—communities.[11]

Second, the periods differed in the balance between written and oral representations and performative modes. Until the imperial crisis, colonial societies, particularly in the South, were still characterized by face-to-face relationships in which personal status and speech reinforced each other; even in the North, public speaking occasions and settings were orchestrated to reinforce hierarchy.[12]

New religious movements formed an important exception, but the ferocity of battles fought by established clergy to marginalize them underlines the importance of controlling access to speaking venues. Voluntary associations modeled a new mode of speech, polite conversation among equals, but practiced it mostly in conversational circles; the mode itself was most often taught in print, as in *The Spectator*, where Franklin learned it, though he applied its irenic virtues in more public circles as well. Like others, however, he applied the precepts of polite conversation most assiduously in print, reinforcing its nature as a close-coupled form of interchange suited to small groups or between writer and reader. During and after the Revolution a wider range of people could gain access to public speaking venues, but through the 1790s, particularly in New England, rights to the speaking platform remained hotly contested.[13]

In the 1820s, the young Abraham Lincoln needed to learn a very different balance of performative skills. Writing mattered relatively little; speaking, on the other hand, was vital, and speech directed to persuading and entertaining largely self-selected group audiences mattered most. Young men learned persuasive skills by observing orators at small-town and village lyceums and studying attorneys as they attempted to persuade juries and courtroom audiences in every county seat; they practiced and honed their skills in young men's debating societies, and saw effective public speakers carry or disrupt public meetings in courthouse squares and inspire and entertain crowds at political rallies. Lincoln was enthralled by trials he sought out when he was nineteen, in 1828, and he joined a local debating society to develop the persuasive skills that would win cases, win elections, and thereby win patronage and recognition.[14] Newspapers, found by this time in towns of almost any size, reinforced the primary representational status of these civic events by carrying notices of meetings and reports of resolutions. Though they carried general and commercial news and entertainment along with political controversy, the papers' former didactic role was largely taken over by special-interest journals.

Third, nineteenth-century practices were oriented to winning over audiences whose members had chosen to be there. Even if predisposed toward a speaker, they expected to be persuaded; on occasion they might be openly hostile and disruptive. Eighteenth-century practices, on the other hand, counterposed different kinds of small-group or one-on-one modes of address, the courtly mode suited to patron-client relations and the polite mode suited to conversation among equals who chose to meet as a group. Compared to the nineteenth century, when occasions for speechifying were almost uncountable, public speaking occasions were few, and their orchestration reflected hierarchies of social, religious, and intellectual order. (Tavern culture and other potentially independent loci of opinion-formation, though important, legally existed only on official sufferance.)[15] Nineteenth-century audiences were drawn from a more self-consciously mobile populace and could choose from a much wider array of public events. With alternative sources of credit, they could afford to be more judgmental about speakers.

Fourth, mass meetings, voluntary associations, parades, and the public formation of associations in the nineteenth century stood in a more ambiguous relation to government because of their representational nature. The local meetings and ad hoc committee and convention governments of the Revolutionary crisis based their legitimacy on a right of collective self-defense and self-government in the absence of any other effective authority. These ad hoc institutions remedied a temporary defect and would be superseded by settled, constitutional governments. But in the nineteenth century, when Americans tirelessly defended and justified their republican governments before the world, the very opposite was the case. As they multiplied civil-society institutions in the 1820s, they made their governments even more representative through constitutional amendments and by developing a system of organized political parties on the borderline between civil space and government. And as Alexis de Tocqueville pointed out in a famous observation, voluntary societies performed things that looked remarkably like what governments could and should do: "The Americans make associations to give entertainments, to found seminaries, to build inns, to construct churches, to diffuse books, to send missionaries to the antipodes; in this manner they found hospitals, prisons, and schools. . . . Wherever at the head of some new undertaking you see the government in France, or a man of rank in England, in the United States you will be sure to find an association."[16]

Major public projects, as well as more limited and ephemeral initiatives, formed the objects of voluntary corporate action in the civil sphere. If we also include mass meetings and other civil-society institutions, private self-selected groups addressed a vast array of public functions. Often they did so in cooperation with governments; mass meetings, for example, were held to support the grant of a corporate charter, often with the participation of office-holders. This pattern represents not a clear line between state and society, nor even a "state" in the modern sense, but a blurring that makes distinctions between the two extremely difficult to discern, beyond respecting what was purely and formally governmental. I would further contend that the close procedural parallels between the ubiquitous convention system of writing constitutions—a very common activity in the states from 1776 through the early nineteenth century—and the forms of group action in civil society indicate that Americans of this period were attempting to actualize civil society as the broader category, one whose rules operated as a meta-constitutional order within which citizens organized themselves for the purposes they deemed necessary.[17]

As the nineteenth-century pattern emerged, the sphere of civil society in the United States became very extensive. Civil-society institutions and practices were performed by groups that were self-selecting but open to the general public, that created organizations and events by mutual agreement, that followed orderly public procedures, and that claimed to be representative. The representational and public character of these associations creates an ambiguity for modern observers about their relationship to government. They closely paralleled institutions and practices of the immediate pre-independence crisis, but did not develop directly out of them. Rather, they emerged out of nearly a quarter-century of argument about the kinds of representation Americans should enjoy and expect, and about the effects of allowing different kinds of representational institutions to take root in a common-law-based society. Once the limits and parameters of associational practices became clear, they could flourish.

Republican Constitutions and Civil Society

The Revolution professedly made the collective people sovereign, but it did not settle how the public will should be institutionalized nor which representations of that will carried greatest weight. Two related axes of argument emerged over these issues, whose resolutions helped undergird early republican civil society. One axis concerned the legislatures: did these representative bodies truly embody the peoples' sovereignty, or were they properly restrained by other representations of that sovereignty? The other axis concerned the legitimacy of extralegislative representative institutions in themselves. The resolution of controversies over both questions ultimately worked against exclusive legislative embodiment of popular will and in favor of expanded civil-society institutions.

Such an outcome could not have been easily predicted, particularly where legislative authority was concerned. Many Americans, including Samuel Adams in the middle 1780s and the Federalists later, supported the idea that state and federal legislatures should exercise the same plenary kinds of authority that Parliament claimed. Colonial assemblies had staked out a widening purview equivalent to that of Parliament for decades before independence, and injuries to the rights and privileges of these bodies figured very largely in colonial protests through the whole period of imperial crisis.[18] The new states remained common-law jurisdictions and retained common-law modes of thought, and independence left the way clear for legislatures to assume the kind of authority exercised by Parliament in Britain.

In their exercise of plenary power, however, conventions were seen as extraordinary institutions designed to meet a crisis in legitimate authority. In most states they were also recognized as constitutionally deficient bodies, lacking both upper house and executive. And they did not in fact govern alone in most states; drawing their authority from town meetings and county committees and conventions, or some combination of local representative and executive bodies, they governed through a similar network of locally based committees of safety and inspection. All these institutions together comprised the people's collective response to the deficit of royal and proprietary government, on the model of Britain's Convention Parliament of 1688–89. Convention government was exigent but not normal, by definition, and too long a period of convention government might jeopardize the stability of civil life and the security of property. Accordingly, most states replaced conventions as soon as possible by some form of regular government.[19]

In all states except Connecticut and Rhode Island, new governments were authorized by written constitutions intended to define and limit their powers. Fixing a frame of government in writing would, citizens hoped, prevent the disorders that had afflicted the British constitutional system and led Americans to revolt. As Thomas Paine wrote in 1791, "A constitution is not a thing in name only, but in fact . . . wherever it cannot be produced in a visible form, there is none. A constitution is a thing *antecedent* to a government. . . . It is the body of elements . . . by which it shall be bound."[20] William Manning, a Jeffersonian farmer from Massachusetts, warned in 1798 that "in free Governments the most sacred regard must be paid to the Constitutions established by the peopel to gard their Rights. No law aught or can be made or constructed conterary to the true meening thereof."[21] Reducing constitutions to paper, people hoped, would prevent the fuzziness and the executive and parliamentary overreaching that Britain's unstable combination of customary practice and statute law had allowed.

Though Connecticut and Rhode Island lacked real written constitutions well into the nineteenth century, Revolutionary-era governments generally acknowledged the idea of limited government in principle. But their very mode of writing and adopting constitutions implied that legislatures could actually exercise a much wider set of powers than Paine or Manning envisioned. At least ten early state constitutions were written by governing conventions or by the first legislatures elected after conventions adjourned.[22] Only those of New Hampshire and Massachusetts went through an explicit and separate process of approval by the popular voice. The rest, passed and promulgated along with ordinary legislation (albeit in some cases passed again after consultation with the public), lacked an explicit and separate imprimatur of the sovereign people. Legislators who believed that assemblies embodied the popular will could act as if constitutional provisions were theirs to alter.

Traditional habits of thought could also lead in this direction. No matter how committed they were to the principle of written constitutions, Anglo-Americans had grown up in a world in which every act of legislation, every executive practice, virtually anything to do with government, could have constitutional significance. This view derived from the basic common-law understanding that accepted practice took on the force of law, a notion rooted in the idea that all levels of law institutionalized the custom of the community.[23] For the Revolutionary generation, it was not entirely clear where written constitutions fit in practice: for some, such constitutions might set ultimate limits on governments and their component parts because they independently embodied the collective sovereign will; for others, constitutions might serve as guides for the true representative embodiment, the legislature; and for still others, such documents might be subject to even more fundamental law, either laws of nature or customary social practices.

Two court cases of the 1790s underline both the persistence of older habits of thought among legislators, with their tendency to see assemblies as sole representatives of the public will, and the contemporary importance of custom in establishing constitutionality. The first, in Virginia, shows that adopting a written constitution did not resolve all questions about the extent of legislative authority. The legislature and judiciary of Virginia struggled for years over lawmakers' attempts to legislate new duties on judges and expand their responsibilities, even though they had been defined in the state's constitution. In 1793, final disposition of an ongoing case gave the District Court of Dumfries a chance to lecture the assembly about its true position in a constitutional order.[24] In their major holding, all the judges agreed on the superiority of Virginia's written constitution and denied the assembly's claim that it could act as it saw needful. The legislature, they concluded, was bound by the people's sovereign will as expressed in the constitution.

In reaching that position, however, judges developed two different explanations of how the sovereign people had in fact expressed its will. Judge Nelson acknowledged that the state's convention had been a legislative body and that it had produced a constitution in the same way that it produced ordinary laws. However, he argued, its status as an emergency convention gave it extraordinarily wide-ranging powers not vested in ordinary legislatures "to consult in general for the public good." Its acts of a fundamental nature differed inherently from alterable or temporary ones, a distinction signaled by use of the word "constitution" rather than the usual "ordinance," and signifying "that this [constitution] should be of higher authority than those [ordinances]." But the real ratification lay in the fact that Virginia's people had lived for nearly two decades under this governing document: acceptance gave it the force of fundamental law. Spencer Roane's opinion followed a similar line.[25]

St. George Tucker offered a different and, it might be thought, more modern justification of the constitution's authority over the legislature. The convention that produced Virginia's governing document, he wrote, was nothing like a normal assembly, not even the rump of a legislature; it was "in effect, the people themselves, assembled by their delegates, to whom the care of the commonwealth was especially, as well as unboundedly confided."[26] Though the convention ignored royal authority, it never openly denied that authority until it constituted a regular government. Thus, by Tucker's account, the people acting in convention, not a mere legislature, had seamlessly transferred authority from the Crown to themselves, and no subsequent legislature could alter constitutional provisions. The constitution was an independent representation of the sovereign people.

James Henry, a proponent of Nelson's more traditional usage-based reasoning, showed some appreciation of the background to legislators' actions. He reminded lawmakers that old habits of mind might, after all, die hard even in a new dispensation: "Under the former government . . . We were taught that Parliament was omnipotent, and their powers beyond control; now this proposition, in our constitution, is limited, and certain rights are reserved . . . if this were always kept in mind, it might free the mind from a good deal of embarrassment in discussing several questions where the duty, and the power of the legislature is considered."[27] In Henry's view, the legislature's attempt to change the court system without amending the constitution signified its succumbing to a received habit of legislative supremacy. But there was now no warrant to justify a legislature in challenging the written embodiment of the popular will.

A few years later the federal Supreme Court decided a Connecticut case that further underlines both the institutionalizing of constitutions as superior representations of the people's sovereignty and the persistence of common-law constitutional principles by which custom and usage served to institutionalize popular will.[28] In 1795 the Connecticut legislature passed a bill to override a probate court judgment, and at the re-hearing a new judgment found against one Calder's claim to inherit some property. Calder contended that the Connecticut legislature had passed an ex post facto law, contrary to the Constitution's explicit prohibition. The Supreme Court rejected this claim in 1798, while at the same time strongly asserting that legislatures were indeed bound by constitutional limits and courts duty-bound to enforce those limits. Justices Chase and Iredell disagreed exactly where the lines were and whether constitutions might be subject to higher-law limitations, but both agreed that constitutions governed legislatures and pointed this out in no uncertain terms.

Chase granted a wide presumption of legitimacy to state governments' actions, on the one hand, but regarded natural law as an implicit element of any constitution: regardless of written provisions, no legislature could pass laws contrary to "general principles of law and freedom," and he would strike down laws that offended against natural law, though only "in a very clear case." Iredell, on the other hand, would hold legislatures to the letter of their constitutions but would not invoke natural law or other supervening criteria. Courts could not void laws conforming to state constitutions on natural-law grounds, because "the ideas of natural justice are regulated by no fixed standard."[29] Disagreeing whether constitutions were supreme in themselves, the justices nevertheless agreed that these embodiments of the sovereign people's will bound legislatures.

Affirming this principle, the justices also affirmed the centrality of usage in constitutional practice. In setting aside a judicial decree, Connecticut's legislature had apparently violated separation of powers principles. However, Justice Paterson noted, the legislature, under its still-authoritative colonial charter, had always acted in some manner as a court. "This usage," he concluded, "makes up part of the Constitution of Connecticut, and we are bound to consider it as such, unless it be inconsistent with the Constitution of the United

States." Connecticut, therefore, could see its legislature meddle with court verdicts, but only because it had always done so and was not restrained by a written constitution from continuing the practice.[30]

The common thread in all these positions, that constitutions limited legislative discretion, was a vital principle that could counter the assemblies' tendency to extend their authority. By upholding this principle, jurists asserted that American legislatures were not the sole active embodiment or representation of the people's sovereignty but could be checked by a separate and equally active embodiment of that authority, the constitution. Other important questions remained open: the existence of supervening authority such as natural law, the precise way popular authority had replaced royal authority, and, most importantly, the degree to which customary usage and general acceptance might still be seen to represent the popular will.

Popular Sovereignty

The constitutional status of extralegislative popular political mobilization was a leading source of controversy in post-Revolutionary America. The issue was joined most conspicuously in the 1790s when Jeffersonians and pro-administration forces took each other on, but Samuel Adams had laid out the terms of the argument in 1784. After a long and laborious process of drafting, comment, revision, and town meeting ratification, Massachusetts adopted its new instrument of government in 1780. Economic troubles soon brought on unrest among farmers, however, and in addition to vociferously petitioning the legislature as individuals, farmers began organizing county conventions similar to those which had organized the Patriot resistance to Governor Hutchinson and General Gage. These irregular bodies aimed to speak collectively for their counties and remonstrate with the legislature in Boston. But they proposed to assume more authority than Adams, with his considerable experience in irregular popular organization, was willing to concede. "Popular Committees and County Conventions are not only useless but dangerous," he wrote his cousin John in April 1784. However useful they may have been in resisting British despotism, the establishment of duly constituted and legitimate government rendered them obsolete.[31]

Adams's rejection of extralegislative action for political ends did not contradict popular sovereignty, but instead reflected his understanding of that principle. In a later exchange with John Adams he expostulated against his cousin's characterization of republican government as reserving "'an essential *share* in the sovereignty'" to the people. On the contrary, theirs is the whole sovereignty:

> The constitutions of the American States reserve to the people the exercise of the rights of sovereignty, by the annual or biennial elections of their governors, senators, and representatives; and by empowering their own representatives to impeach the greatest officers of the state before the senators, who are also chosen by themselves . . . [the people] delegate the powers of government to particular persons, who, after short intervals, resign their powers to the people, and they will reëlect them, or appoint others, as they think fit.

The power of a sovereign was the power to appoint, refuse, or remove representatives and officers of government; popular sovereignty vested that power in the people at large, without altering the authority of officeholders and representatives.[32]

There was, of course, an alternative view. Revolutionary leaders like Adams had maintained during the crisis years that "popular committees and county conventions" more accurately represented the people than had duly constituted government, and a wide range of such extralegislative institutions and practices coordinated the Revolutionary effort, debated measures, and enforced loyalty. "The people" formed themselves into, and acted through, multiple bodies, often self-selecting in their membership and meeting as exigencies required, alongside and in coordination with the new governments as they were established. These were often understood as "natural" representations or bodies of that collective people whose sovereignty had been asserted in the Declaration of Independence and on which the new governments were constituted; the government of Massachusetts, in fact, had professedly been constituted as a "voluntary association" through acts performed in popular assemblies "by which the whole people covenants with each citizen, and each citizen with the whole people."[33] With written and customary constitutions coming to be seen as distinct representations of popular sovereignty additional to legislatures, was it necessary to conclude that popular representation should be confined to paper, precedent, and assembly only? Was not a continuing system of multiple representations possible?

On the federal level, as Suzette Hemberger has recently shown, this polarity between proponents of single and multiple representation was at the heart of disputes between Federalists and Jeffersonians over the Whiskey Rebellion. Pro-administration figures argued that there could be no legitimate organized expression of political opinion outside of Congress now that the Constitution actualized popular sovereignty; individual petitioners could protest injuries, but there was no place for the political clubs or county meetings in western Pennsylvania that pretended to speak for aggrieved residents, but actually instead threatened the country's stability. This was one meaning of Federalist attacks on "self-created societies." The anti-tax movement, on the other hand, followed Revolution-era precedents (even pledging loyalty to the federal government, as the Continental Congress had to the Crown), and its proceedings had been orderly; they had in fact followed the kinds of orderly procedures later used by civil-society institutions. Attacking these instruments of opposition much as Adams had attacked popular meetings in Massachusetts a decade earlier, Congressman Fisher Ames asserted that they "have arrogantly pretended sometimes to be the people, and sometimes the guardians, the champions of the people. They affect to feel more zeal for a popular Government, and to enforce more respect for Republican principles, than the real Representatives are admitted to entertain."[34]

Ames's strictures pointed to a central problem inherent in attempts at multiple representations—which one *really* speaks for the collective people?—but his position ultimately proved self-defeating. Throughout the crises of the 1790s, the administration regarded all attempts to organize extralegislative opposition to government measures as efforts to destroy the constitutional order: the people had exercised their sovereign authority once and for all when they ratified the federal Constitution. Federalists' reaction implicitly acknowledged the continuing force of custom, but their zeal to suppress popular political action and prevent its institutionalization ultimately jeopardized political stability. Had they finally succeeded in this campaign, legitimate discussion of public issues—a viable public sphere—would have become impossible.

In practice, Federalists maintained that they had no quarrel with legitimate groups and energetically used street theater themselves.[35] But in principle, their position might be taken to mean that any self-created or self-selected gathering, if not approved by authorities, could be suppressed as a threat to constitutional stability. Such gatherings had been commonplace in ports and tidewater areas beginning in the mid-eighteenth century in the form of literary societies, Masonic lodges, and benevolent associations and in less formally organized discussions at coffee houses and taverns. Such groups played direct roles in the Revolutionary crisis, and the openness that allowed them to flourish gave Patriots crucial experience in forming the self-selecting groups that constituted the institutional infrastructure of resistance and revolution. Their presence also helped Patriots define their constitutional liberties and what would later be understood as the public sphere. For this very reason groups of this kind ultimately could not be considered nonpolitical or outside the range of official approval; similar groups in Britain had always existed in a state of constitutional ambiguity, and in the 1790s Pitt's ministry not only kept them under surveillance and suppressed and broke up large numbers of popular associations, but also supported and promoted Loyalist groups.[36] The Federalist position, though based in a version of popular rather than royal sovereignty, did not seem markedly different in application.[37]

For this reason the Jeffersonians' vigorous defense of extraparliamentary organization prepared the ground for the enormous efflorescence of associational life of all kinds in the early nineteenth century.[38] In the meantime people had continued and extended the pattern begun in colonial days of organizing for other than political purposes. Charity was particularly important: societies and institutions had been organized in Boston early in the eighteenth century and appeared in Philadelphia by mid-century, while at least four seaports had sailors'-relief societies by 1770.[39] A principal form of colonial-era association, also largely confined to major ports or long-settled areas until shortly before the Revolution, was Freemasonry. The prevalent early variety, which reinforced hierarchy and imperial ties, gave way to a more egalitarian variety that spread rapidly with the Continental Army and into small towns and villages in the 1790s and early 1800s. By the early 1790s contemporaries remarked on Americans' pervasive associational impulses, and after about 1812 voluntary associations seemed in many respects the preferred American way to approach problems. An important milestone had been reached when, at least as early as 1803, the conservative evangelical Lyman Beecher endorsed and urged on his fellows the "voluntary principle," an invitation they energetically took up, indicating acceptance of the practice across the social spectrum. By 1836 voluntary societies and events were characteristic enough to inspire Tocqueville's famous commentary. Associationism and assembly had become most important customary practices of the American public, exercised in many dimensions.[40]

Associating Openly

The relatively stable system of multiple representation of the early republic and Jacksonian period could be achieved only after experience helped define the parameters of legitimate access to civil space. One key Federalist objection to "self-created societies" was that they could foment factious conspiracies against the common good by encouraging irresponsible individuals to act in secret. The careful secrecy insisted on by many societies, especially the Freemasons and the Cincinnati, seemed to give point to such fears; in the 1790s the Federalist Timothy Dwight excoriated the Illuminati as a world conspiracy, and, most famously, conspiracy theorists targeted Masonry itself in the mid-1820s. Suspicion of conspiracy was (and arguably has remained) endemic in American public culture, and associationism, otherwise so logical an outgrowth of the struggles over political representation, could not take hold without allaying such fears. Dwight's objections to the Illuminati also reflect a related danger sensed by contemporaries, that of mob rule and disorder: a wholesale turn to ad hoc associations and meetings could create such confusion about the public's will, and so much potential for riot, that civic life would become impossible. This was a plausible scenario for the nation's future in the 1790s, when Philadelphia and other American cities were riven by partisan mob violence.[41]

An important step toward answering the problem of secret conspiracy, and thus legitimizing organized associations and, by implication, mass public meetings, was reaching a consensus that groups needed to act openly to be legitimate. Public reaction to the Society of the Cincinnati in the middle 1780s helped develop that consensus. In part a mutual-aid society for ex-Continental Army officers, the society was also intended by Henry Knox to organize these officers' influence across state lines and thus maintain order in the Confederation. With a hereditary membership, a selected corps of coopted civilians, and its own treasury, the society was to meet and correspond systematically and secretly about public affairs. Detractors mounted a pamphlet war of unmitigated ferocity against virtually every aspect of Knox's plan, known or suspected, and struck a deep chord with the public. After stiff resistance, the Cincinnati in effect voted to become only a benevolent mutual-aid society.

Controversy over the Cincinnati helped build agreement that self-constituted groups should be subject to public scrutiny, particularly if they worked toward political goals; they should also make membership more open and inclusive, eschewing ascriptive criteria that smacked of "aristocracy." The need for open meetings was not immediately accepted, but came to seem more desirable as violence between party mobs increased in the 1790s and early 1800s: partisan violence was partly blamed on secrecy and intrigue. By the late 1820s, Anti-Masonry's strength revealed just how strongly the general public feared secrecy. Standards of openness eventually came to include the practices discussed earlier: published meeting announcements, stating time, place, and purpose; open attendance (in most cases); open membership (though often explicitly limited by gender or age); and published reports of resolutions or meetings.[42]

Federalist-era party violence also helped spark a turn toward orderly use of civic space as a criterion of legitimacy. Such violence, as Paul Gilje has pointed out, little resembled the orderly crowds of the Revolutionary era that turned out in order to enforce community norms in well-ordered representations of a community's sense of right. Rather, these mobs were rival gangs, facing off against each other and intimidating party enemies and sometimes sparking full-fledged riots. New York suffered several party riots in the 1780s and 1790s and again on the eve of the War of 1812. Baltimore hosted perhaps the most notorious of these riots in the summer of 1812, when a Republican mob stormed a Federalist editor's establishment and later rampaged through the city jail, where the Federalists had agreed to be taken for their own safety, and mercilessly beat their helpless quarry. By this time, Gilje recounts, leaders had come to regard crowds not as "the people out of doors" enforcing communal moral codes but rather as symptoms of dangerous divisions that threatened civic order. Orderly procedure in meetings, assemblies, parades, and other public events became important signs of adherence to ordered republican liberty. Ethnic riots and class-based violence in New York during the 1820s and 1830s further underlined the importance of the kind of orderly procedures that Revolutionary crowds had followed, especially for the respectable sort who dominated the city's economy and political sphere.[43]

Organized mobbing continued, of course, especially around slavery and abolition, but it had a different character than the partisan mobs. Anti-abolitionist mobbing peaked in the middle 1830s and continued sporadically to the eve of the Civil War. Both Leonard Richards and David Grimsted assert that the mobs were led or strongly influenced by respectable men. Grimsted further notes that, with few exceptions, these mobs caused very little actual destruction or physical harm. They were organized by Democratic partisans less to intimidate abolitionist speakers and potential converts—organizers were well aware that reports of mob-thrown rotten eggs actually "hatched abolitionists"—than to demonstrate solidarity with southern Democrats, who would read newspaper accounts of the mobbings. In other words, then, the mobs aimed to prevent abolitionist meetings from putting communities on record, unopposed, as favoring abolition. Similarly, opponents of the prospective temperance society in Ravenna packed its initial organizational meeting to prevent the town from going on record as favoring temperance.[44]

In this way, nineteenth-century mobbing, far from representing the whole community, recognized and credited the representational nature of mass meetings and the organization of voluntary associations such as anti-slavery societies, when reported in the press. There would be no other reason to create a contradictory story. Anti-abolition mobs could only serve the instrumental political purposes that Grimsted suggests *because* public reports of the actions of groups in the community were understood to represent that community. A report of a meeting unaccompanied by signs of active opposition indicated that the rest of the community at least acquiesced in the organizers' purpose. A similar report, accompanied by report of an opposing mob, denied a clear community voice on the subject and undercut any representational claim in the organizers' report. No longer acting as the body of the people, Jacksonian mobs could prevent others from doing so.

Anti-abolitionist leaders themselves operated within this same representational framework. When James G. Birney decided to set up an abolitionist newspaper near Cincinnati early in 1836, local Democratic party leaders at first suggested mobbing the press. Instead, they decided on a well-attended mass meeting that featured not only the city's leading citizens and Democratic party grandees, one of whom delivered a fiery racist speech, but also Birney himself. Grimsted describes the meeting's tone as "genteel" and concludes that its resolutions were as "toothless" as those adopted at dozens of pro-Southern meetings held the previous summer throughout the North. But such resolutions made a powerful point: when anti-abolitionist leaders in Cincinnati opted for a meeting rather than a mob, they staked out the high ground, representing their position as that of the whole community. By indicating disruptive disagreement, mobs could signal not only divided opinion but outright disorder within a community, while an open public meeting could hardly be seen as anything other than the free expression of the community's will. And the openness of respectable public meetings might help insure that they actually did reflect the public mind. At an 1835 anti-abolitionist meeting in Lowell, Massachusetts, "opponents took over . . . and offered resolves opposing [servile] insurrection but equally condemning slavery and Southern demands."[45] Adhering to openness and orderly procedures—properly claiming the representational civil space—did not always yield what organizers intended.

Revolution in Rhode Island

The authority of access to such a civil space, and the close nature of its relationship to governments and constitutions, was apparent in Rhode Island in the 1830s and early 1840s. At that late date the state still operated under a slightly modified version of its royal charter of 1663. It had been one of the two self-governing corporate colonies, and because a repudiation of royal authority had no immediate practical effect, its form of government remained unchanged. By the 1830s, however, Rhode Island was no longer a society of farmers and a few seaport merchants; it had become a complex industrializing and commercial state with growing numbers of artisans and professionals. But unlike other states where the franchise had been extended widely, Rhode Island government remained in the hands of a very small group of landholders with no interest in widening the suffrage or re-apportioning the legislature. Artisans began a reform movement in the 1830s, holding mass meetings whose petitions the legislature ignored; shortly afterward, a more moderate effort to amend the constitution also misfired.[46]

In 1840 reformers decided to act through a new voluntary society, the Rhode Island Suffrage Association, which initially proceeded through the usual steps of a petition to the legislature and a mass meeting. But in the summer of 1841 the Association decided to call its own constitutional convention, asserting that "The people—the 'numerical force'—have but to proclaim their will, to resume their original powers, and assert their original rights."[47] The Association set its own franchise qualifications for election to its constitutional convention, which proposed a new governing document, the People's Constitution. Voters subsequently ratified it at elections conducted by the Association. Each voting unit in the state held an apparently orderly public meeting, with each meeting choosing a moderator and clerks. In the meantime, the existing legislature called a convention of its own on a different franchise, which proposed only slight modifications that were ultimately rejected. The sitting government ignored the popular convention movement until after the Association's ratification vote. Then, as the date neared for election of officers under the People's Constitution, Rhode Island's charter government outlawed the pending election. The governor also appealed to President John Tyler, who finally agreed that federal authorities would defend the existing government against any "domestic insurrection." The reform election proceeded, the new legislature met in Providence and passed some laws, and the new governor, Thomas Dorr, delivered his inaugural address. But the movement collapsed following an attempt to seize the state arsenal, as the charter government, reluctantly backed by Tyler, arrested many of the movement's leaders. Some contemporary observers believed that the new government would have succeeded in establishing itself if the federal government had not been prompted by party-political considerations to intervene.[48]

Extant and duly constituted governments had earlier been successfully replaced by new governments instituted in parallel, notably in Pennsylvania in 1776 and at the national level in 1788–89. What is most noteworthy here is the use of the civil space, following entirely normal procedures, to create and attempt to put into effect a new political constitution. Reformers acted on the basis that popular sovereignty inhered in all their actions. They considered the right of assembly and the orderly use of civil-society institutions sufficient warrant for creating and adopting new governing institutions.

Reconstituting Civil Society

The Dorrite episode illustrates one reason why the order of civil society that crystallized around 1812 ultimately broke up about mid-century. It could no longer withstand the increasing centrifugal tendencies in American public life. Political uses of civil space, such as the South Carolina Nullification Convention in 1832 and the Southern States Convention of 1850, and increased politicization of that space brought on by the deepening sectional crisis—Oregon meetings and Texas meetings in towns all over the country, for example—threatened to undermine political stability completely. In a broader sense, this order was rooted in an increasingly unrealistic view of communities as largely independent and self-ordering entities. By the 1840s and 1850s, American society was becoming much more deeply and complexly interdependent over a much wider area: in local communities, many more interests were at work—and in conflict—as a result of these changes. Physical interconnection, thanks to canals, railroads, and telegraph lines, also meant that events outside any one community almost immediately affected local residents, further tending to divide communities and draw attention outward. All of these factors made it increasingly difficult for particular communities to sustain multiple representations that had constituted their civic identities, and made those representations less important. As it became clear that a choice had to be made between Union and locally based representations of the public will, the latter yielded, at least in the northern states. The distinctive civil society of the early republic would be superseded by new forms and new spaces.

CHAPTER ELEVEN

Religion, Moderation, and Regime-Building in Post-Revolutionary America

Robert M. Calhoon

An Implicit Bargain?

Was there an implicit bargain between government and religion in the early republic? In exchange for religious liberty and toleration, did Protestant churches agree to inculcate social discipline and moral virtue?[1] These questions troubled the post-Revolutionary republic—and they trouble the nation still. The Protestant denominations created during the 1780s to inculcate order, discipline, and orthodoxy among Presbyterians, Episcopalians, Methodists, and Congregationalists respectively also sought to foster what men of the cloth called "national prosperity,"[2] the morality and humility to ennoble and sanctify the possibly evanescent economic and social prosperity even of a productive, egalitarian, and democratic society. In his Farewell Address, George Washington concurred: "religion and morality" were "indispensable supports" and "great pillars of human happiness, . . . the firmest props of the duties of men and citizens," and part of the "fabric" of common citizenship.[3] This reciprocal blending of civic ideology and religious piety presupposed that the initiative in this enterprise lay with public officials and that churches were interest groups that governments needed to placate. *Denominational Christianity was the determined effort by churches with mature transatlantic identities—literally churches with names (denominations)—to create an American Zion, a spiritual soul within the body politic.*

Not all churches and believers accepted relegation to the status of interest groups nor conceded the initiative to government. The stronger and more ancient the historical consciousness of a church, the less enamored it was with eighteenth-century republican statecraft and the more it looked to the primitive church of the apostolic age for first principles of citizenship and moral obligation. *Primitive Christianity was the belief that God should be worshiped not in Americanized versions of European communions (the denominational churches) but rather in authentic recreations of the early church.*

Primitive churches should not be confused with sects nor the denominational-primitive alignment with Ernst Troeltsch's "church-sect" typology.[4] Instead, denominationalism and primitivism should be understood as ecclesiologies, that is, as theologies of the nature of the church. Ecclesiology is more than the study of the structure of the church; it comprehends structure by examining the way doctrine is embedded within religious mystery to define "holy," "catholic," and "apostolic" forms of Christian community.[5]

The presence of two dissimilar ecclesiologies—one operating powerfully at the center of political culture and the other functioning opportunistically on the periphery—had important implications for American constitutionalism. No one understood this better than Benjamin Franklin, John Adams, and Thomas Jefferson. These prominent deists functioned as brokers between politicized, modernizing churches (responding to governmental encouragement) and apolitical primitive ones (bristling at overtures from the state). They conceded what Jefferson called the "necessity of a superintending power to maintain the universe on its course"[6] but doubted whether religion could, or should, go beyond offering practical advice about morality and ethics. Like the leaders of newly formed denominations, rationalists expected churches to play constructive roles in nation-building; like most Christian primitives, they were hypercritical of ecclesiastical institutions.

Denominational and primitive ecclesiologies moderated both religious strife and political conflict. These theories of religious tradition and affiliation complicated the historical consciousness of the new nation and posed novel questions about obligation and social virtue. Denominationalists were good instrumentalists eager to turn biblical teachings and theological maxims into practical lessons of statecraft, but primitivists, deeply apolitical, refused to play that game. To get a grip on the slippery questions of how piety and power should function in a republic, some of the most thoughtful early American statesmen, including James Madison, James Wilson, Joseph Story, John Quincy Adams, and, eventually, Abraham Lincoln, listened attentively to primitive religious discourse *and,* at the same time, factored denominational organizational expertise into their political calculations in search of common ground between divergent elements in American political discourse.

Denominational Christianity and Regime-building

Three major projects fostered the religious nurture of republican government. The first, and most notable, denominational project for sacralizing politics in Revolutionary America was the transformation of the College of New Jersey at Princeton from a New Side, revivalist Presbyterian college into an outpost of the Christian enlightenment. Within republican political institutions, John Witherspoon detected an appetite for the language, skills, history, and philosophy of statecraft. His contribution to regime-building was his recognition of that vacuum and his determination, as an educator and moralist, to fill it. An eclectic rather than a systematic intellect, Witherspoon unified American Presbyterians by taking a series of separate positions—each eminently defensible—without concern for logical consistency. He embraced the same moral philosophy of Francis Hutcheson that he had ridiculed in Scotland in 1758 as a "pliant and fashionable scheme of religion, a fine theory of virtue and morality."[7]

Believing that social virtue was a learned behavior, inculcated better by persuasion than pronouncement, Witherspoon taught his moral philosophy students that tests of nerve and will within republican government itself would guarantee that checks and balances would function to preserve virtue and expose vice. "Every good form of government must be complex," he posited, "so that one principle may check the other. . . . It is folly to expect that a state should be upheld by integrity of all who have a share in managing it. They must be so balanced that when one draws to his own interest or inclination, there may be some over poise upon the whole."[8] James Madison heard that lecture in 1772 and sixteen years later incorporated the concept into Federalist 51: "the great security of government . . . consists of giving to those who administer each department the necessary constitutional means, and personal motives, to resist the encroachments of others."[9]

The task of systematizing Witherspoon's eclectic mix of Whig politics, Calvinist theology, and moral philosophy fell to his successor as president of

Princeton, Samuel Stanhope Smith. During his first decade at Princeton, Smith wrote what was to be for a generation the leading American book on race. Refuting the notion that races had different origins, he marshaled evidence from the Book of Genesis and from enlightenment science to prove that there was a single human race and that physical differences were the product of "climate," the "state of society," and "habits of living." Smith thus asserted that the moral sense was common to all humanity and that revealed religion could function through either divine revelation or through a divinely ordained system of moral perception.[10] As Mark A. Noll observes, *An Essay on the Causes and Variety of Complexion and Figure in the Human Species* "exemplified the finest scientific procedures," "vindicated a philosophy of common sense," "defended Christianity," and "made possible the construction of rational liberty."[11] Making science, the moral sense, Christianity, and human liberty a coherent whole constituted the Presbyterian contribution to regime-building and the training of future statesmen and citizens during the first generation of the new republic. Ambitious and fashionable, this synthesis disintegrated within a generation.

As a denominational project for sanctifying the early republic, the political philosophy of the Standing Order (Congregationalist) clergy and laity in Massachusetts and Connecticut was fully as energetic as the Princeton curriculum. Standing Order social doctrine held that political and social freedom was attainable only through the "maintenance of fixed relationships among men" inculcated by "habits of subordination."[12] What Jonathan Sassi calls "the public Christianity" of the New England clergy was a vigorous and systematic program nurturing habits of subordination within a network of local social connectivity.[13]

The great educational motif of the Standing Order project was Augustinian: the expectation of two kingdoms, one huddled protectively in the shadow of sin and other arising hopefully in the discipline of piety. This vision, Lester H. Cohen argues persuasively, was "peculiarly modern." As articulated by Yale President Theodore Dwight, the civic credo of New England Calvinism was grounded on two assumptions, first, that human choices were "historically efficacious" in that people could be held responsible for their choices and, second, that people lived out their faith in the "face of indeterminacy." Dwight's recounting of New England's religious history highlighted successive cycles of declension into carnality followed by fresh dispensations of divine grace and societal healing. What was *indeterminate* was whether the cycle would continue.[14]

Shays's Rebellion turned on the social stability and instability of Standing Order churches. Although the uprising traditionally appeared to have been an assault against constituted authority, John L. Brooke has demonstrated that the Shaysites, far from being primitive rebels, were in reality regulators of social conflict in the eighteenth-century meaning of the term. "Responsibility for raising the rebellion lay with men of local standing in orthodox communities: innholders, militia captains, deacons, and selectmen." Understood as part of an economically stressed community, "the Regulation was an effort to stabilize a society disordered by economic upheaval in the larger world" of post-Revolutionary politics and public policy. Brooke divides western Massachusetts into "militia towns," "regulator towns," and "conflicted towns." Towns where social leadership supported the Shaysites were twice as likely to have vacant pulpits as those mobilized to put down the uprising—a strong indication that, in the absence of clerical leadership to mediate debtor-creditor disputes, Standing Order laymen filled this social vacuum.[15]

Two decades later, Congregationalists protective of social harmony were defecting to the ranks of Jeffersonian Republicanism while Calvinists, who attributed harmony to the workings of Providence, faced a serious challenge from Unitarians who substituted human ethical responsibility for faithful reliance on divine protection. Many Standing Order clergy adapted their providential message to these changed circumstances. The Reverend John Elliott, in an 1810 Connecticut election sermon *The Gracious Presence of God: The Highest Felicity and Security of Any People,* posited a five-point test of New England's providential destiny. The first two parts were familiar and traditional—Godly civil rulers and ministers as sent by "the invisible hand" of providence—but the remaining evidences of a regional divine presence (religious revival, missionary spirit, and "a spirit of love, unity, and peace"), Sassi observes, "marked a clear break within the ranks of the Standing Order's public Christianity." Providential deliverance now depended on the social construction of the Kingdom of God through advocacy, benevolent reform, and displays of civic piety.[16]

In 1805, as New England was beginning to emerge from apparent deistic apostasy, Dwight received a letter from John Taylor of Caroline, the Virginia agrarian and republican theorist—fully Dwight's equal as an acerbic polemicist—who was looking for a college for his son to attend. "Permit me to say," Dwight archly informed Taylor, "that I do not think it would forward your design to send your son to this college." Almost all of the Virginians who had enrolled at Yale during Dwight's tenure "despised and hated our manners, morals, and religion." They were irreligious and contemptuous of Yankee piety, and, worse yet, they were lazy. "Your children," Dwight lectured Taylor, "would regard their New England companions as plodding drudges, destitute of talents as well as property. They would esteem New England life as slavery, unreasonable and useless." Agreeing "that it would be extremely injudicious to send my son in search of instruction to one who believes him to be a wretch, destitute of morals, industry, or religion," Taylor angrily countered Dwight's slurs on Virginia. The charge of irreligion was the easiest to refute. Whereas the established Congregational Church in Connecticut fostered an "ambitious and rapacious" clergy, Taylor countered, "our religious sects [in Virginia] mingle and worship in harmony, and the state abounds with Christian ministers whose religion is not banished by intermeddling with civil government."[17]

Virginia's post-Revolutionary settlement of church-state relations, in which Taylor took such pride, was a third—and far and away the most successful—effort to make religion and politics mutually supportive structures of republican government. In November 1776, the Virginia Convention had come close to disestablishing the Anglican Church, leaving only its property intact and providing for compulsory payment of arrears in clerical salaries. On the question of whether there should be a "general [i.e., mandatory] assessment . . . for the support and maintenance of . . . ministers and teachers of the gospel," the Convention—in Jefferson's absence—had stipulated "that so important a subject" should not be "prejudged."[18] That language left the door open for general assessment bills that would have paid ministerial salaries for all Protestant churches. Though never enacted, the distinctively Anglican language of the 1778 assessment bill—lifted from the 1778 South Carolina Constitution—revealed what the 1784 bill discreetly veiled: to qualify as Christian, churches had to teach, as a primary requirement for public funding, that people will face rewards and punishments in a future life. Patrick Henry's anxieties about Virginia's ability to instill public virtue led him to support the 1784 assessment bill, which required all taxpayers either to contribute to the support of churches of their choice or to pay into a common fund to be distributed to all Christian churches in the commonwealth. When Henry was elevated to the governorship in 1785, removing his legendary eloquence from the debate, James Madison challenged the people and churches of Virginia to petition the General Assembly to reject assessment and acknowledge that religion lay beyond the jurisdiction of the state.

Jefferson's eloquence and Madison's resourcefulness imparted direction and substance to regime-building, because they were complementary efforts to make religion a benign rather than a corrosive political force. The language of the Virginia Statute brilliantly highlighted some of Jefferson's thoughts about religion and the state while obscuring others. The General Assembly issued it in 1786, as Statute #82 of the revised laws of Virginia. Jefferson opened the statute with what J. G. A. Pocock[19] calls "a fundamental premise": that the opinions and belief of men depend not on their own will but follow involuntarily … evidence proposed to their own minds."[20] Everything else in the statute was an exposition of legal, moral, religious, and ethical implications of that premise: that no citizen could be compelled to support financially any religious activity contrary to his conscience, that legally obligatory financial support for religion debased the very religious institutions they were intended to support, and that coercive government support of religion contradicted the first principles of Christianity. What was revolutionary here, Pocock emphasized, was Jefferson's equating religious "beliefs" with "opinions" produced in the mind on the basis of "evidence."[21]

Jefferson was fully aware that religion transcended rationality. The writings of Joseph Priestley converted Jefferson not just to Deism, which he had already acquired from classical sources and French enlightenment writers, but also to Unitarianism. "I am a Christian," Jefferson explained, "in the only sense he [Jesus] wished anyone to be; sincerely attached to his doctrines in preference to all others; ascribing to him every human excellence; & believing he never claimed any other."[22] Priestley's and Jefferson's Unitarianism was not the rationalized Puritanism of the New England Unitarians. Instead, the two men regarded Unitarianism as a form of primitive Christianity from the first and second centuries when myriad forms of Christianity co-mingled in the ancient world and when heresies and orthodoxies battled freely for dominance.

In this sense, Jefferson was drawn more to primitive than to denominational Christianity. Priestley rejected both Trinitarianism and Arianism—that is, both the divinity of Jesus and also the Arian belief that Jesus was a subordinate but still pre-existent deity—because both Christologies detracted from the full humanity of Jesus. For Priestley, Christ's humanity dictated the religious life of the early church: weekly worship through songs, hymns, teaching, and, the supreme didactic moment, the Lord's Supper. While the Anglican establishment was Priestley's bête noire and dissenting churches were, in his view, sources of pernicious superstition, he admired Roman Catholicism for basing doctrine and practice on both scripture and tradition. Although Priestley and Jefferson may not have believed in life after death, they did believe in the resurrection of Jesus, based on the eyewitness testimony of the gospels and in the promise that the dead would be raised at the last judgment. Though vigilantly protective of his religious privacy, Jefferson appears to have internalized and affirmed the corpus of Priestley's beliefs.[23] "Jefferson," Thomas Buckley concludes, "enunciated a civic faith related to and dependent on a transcendent God that most Americans understood and accepted."[24]

If Jefferson considered Unitarian Christianity and Christian moralism foundations of the republic, Madison found the assessment controversy a bracing test of the Commonwealth's capacity to incorporate into public policy contending passions and conflicting interests of the people. Just as in his subsequent career as a principled moderate during the ratification of the federal Constitution, in 1785–86 Madison placed himself between two contending forces and sought to persuade partisans that their purposes could be secured by seeking common ground with their adversaries. He took advantage of the fact that, in 1785, the General Assembly had before it six bills on religion, all part of a much larger revision and codification of Virginia's statute law in response to American independence. Only two of these bills were in direct conflict: Jefferson's 1777 Statute on Religious Liberty and the 1784 bill drafted by pro-assessment legislators for "Establishing a Provision for Teachers of the Christian Religion."[25]

Fearing that, in a head-to-head contest, the 1784 bill would prevail, Madison allowed the other religious measures under consideration to advance toward enactment as a kind of buffer between the libertarian goals of Jefferson's Statute and the broadly appealing provisions of assessment.[26] Madison voted for a bill to incorporate the Episcopal Church, though he had reservations about the measure, because he realized that defeat of that bill, or even a bitter struggle over its enactment, would increase Episcopal "eagerness" for "the much greater evil" of assessment as a solution for that church's financial problems.[27] In return for his support of incorporation, eight Episcopal delegates joined Madison on Christmas Eve 1784 in voting to postpone final action on assessment until the following November. And on the 23rd or 24th of December, Madison played the part of a "forensic" legislator—a role he usually disdained—speaking twice on the danger that, through religious assessment, the state could contaminate spirituality among its citizens. Revealing his intellect and emotional intensity, he argued that the issue in the assessment debate was not whether religion was beneficial to society but whether the "establishment" of Christian teaching by the state (something very close to establishment of religion itself) would both violate human freedom and actually damage religion.

Reduced to written prose at the urgent request of George Nicholas and his brother, Wilson Cary Nicholas, and published as *A Memorial and Remonstrance against Religious Assessments*, Madison's formulation was a model petition to the legislature. Circulated widely in Presbyterian and Baptist counties in the summer of 1785, Madison's treatise inspired more than ninety anti-assessment petitions, signed by more than eleven thousand citizens. Madison diagnosed the pernicious tendencies of civil regulation of religion. Assessment should be rejected "because the bill implies that the civil magistrate is a competent judge of religious truth, or that he may employ religion as an engine of civil policy; the first is an arrogant pretension, . . . the second, an unhallowed perversion of the means of salvation."[28]

In his assistance to the brothers Nicholas, Madison fashioned a primitive Christian solution to a denomination problem. Applying the "Render unto Caesar" principle to republican citizenship, Madison shielded denomination churches from the temptation to function as interest groups. In much the same way, the Congregational laity in Shaysite towns in Massachusetts (as we have seen) invested the moral authority of the Standing Order in social justice and public order—exactly the role religious hierarchy was intended to play in the early church.[29]

The Virginia debate over religious assessment echoed what J. C. D. Clark has called "the long eighteenth-century" discussion of church and state in England, which began in 1660 and would continue until 1832.[30] The most distinct echo of that debate was Madison's borrowing of two axioms from Locke's *Letter on Toleration:* first, "homage" to God" preceded "in order and degree of obligation the claims of civil government" and, second, that when a person enters into political compact, he "must always do it with a reservation of his duty to the universal sovereign."[31] The toleration that Locke justified was not simply a liberty of individual conscience but also, and more significantly, it was Locke's theological contention that, by making man a social creature, God "requires him to follow those rules which conduce to the preserving of society."[32]

Locke understood the contested nature of the middle ground between Anglican defense of religious uniformity and dissenters' determination to control their own worship. Because Charles II had granted religious toleration in 1661 as a royal indulgence—which James II had endorsed in 1685 before he impatiently sought to bend the Church of England to his will and which was then emphatically reinstated by William and Mary in the Revolution settlement of 1689—the concept of indulgent toleration took on a life of its own during the late seventeenth and early eighteenth centuries. By the 1750s, indulgent toleration defined Great Britain as a coherent national state.[33]

Although indulgent toleration offended Baptist ecclesiology (which held that indulgence in spiritual matters was the prerogative of God alone), the religious settlement of 1786–87 owed much to the British model. In England, neither high church Anglicans nor dissenters got everything they wanted from the Toleration Act of 1689, but both discovered that they got what they needed: a very widespread uniformity of Anglican worship and parish life and exemption of dissenters from overt persecution. In Virginia, the Revolution effectively ended sporadic jailing and whipping of sectarian preachers,[34] and by the mid-1780s it became commonplace to think of Episcopal, Presbyterian, Baptist, and Methodist church bodies not just as denominational organizations but also as worshiping communities with interests that should be acknowledged and protected by government.[35] By making the denominational churches into major players in the Virginia religious settlement while at the same time addressing Baptist, Quaker, and Mennonite fears[36] that the state would contaminate their spiritual communalism, Madison moderated religious and social conflict.

Jefferson's primitive Christology, Madison's appreciation of primitive ecclesiology, and both men's Lockean and British enlightenment embrace of Locke on toleration gave the Virginia religious settlement its breadth of appeal and stabilizing strength.

Primitive Christianity as a Cautionary Tale

In the summer of 1777, George Kriebel, a member of the German pietist sect, the Schwenkfelders, astounded the Berks County court, in Pennsylvania. He explained that his son could not perform militia service without violating his pacifist conscience—a claim the court might have understood—and then he announced provocatively that Schwenkfelders would not swear allegiance to the Revolutionary regime in Pennsylvania because the war with Britain was not yet over and, consequently, God had not yet revealed which side in the conflict He had chosen to reward with victory.[37]

That the court convicted and fined the Kriebels, father and son, damaged but did not obliterate that enclave of security that their consciences and conscientious civic behavior created. While Kriebel addressed the court, the enclave existed; in the court record, a remnant of it remained. Primitive Christian enclaves were integral components of the republican political order.

Everything they did at variance with the dominant ideology and local norms of political and social subservience was therefore political in nature. Sometimes the primitives challenged denominational churches, but typically their religious witness brought them into conflict with republican political institutions and social practices. Denominational churches and republican political institutions therefore had to deal with enclaves; enclaves, in turn, proved to be indigestible social fragments, and this indigestibility was their political strength.[38] If celebratory nationalism nourished regime-building, the cautionary language of primitive Christianity about the limits of republican authority on the fringes of the social and political order, conversely, more subtly disciplined and moderated the regime-building project.

Primitive Christian religious experience altered the social basis of republican citizenship in numerous small, limited, but telling ways. Revivals in northern New England and in Kentucky began the process. On these outer fringes of republican society, groups of converts experienced an ecstatic state of spiritual communitas that transformed their political consciousness. Itinerant Universalist preacher Caleb Rich targeted the membership of a flourishing Separate Baptist church in Richmond, New Hampshire, in the late 1770s with his revivalist preaching of universal salvation in opposition to Separate Baptist belief in predestination and the division of humankind into the few who were saved and the many who were damned. (Separate Baptists in New England were, to be sure, more primitive than denominational, but their Calvinism and, in northern New England, their central place in town life made them conscious protectors of the region's theological orthodoxy.) Rich's pronouncement of "universal salvation," therefore, "excited [in them] horror mingled with disgust and was denounced as the most dangerous heresy ever propagated." But far from marginalizing Rich and his converts, that aversion and fear of contamination bonded them into a new community. Rich's method of teaching scripture produced a polity in which each member "read or prayed or sung or spoke as the Spirit directed, and all were edified." The evangelical community was self-actualizing, and its granting of edification of "all" was the radical promise of popular religion.[39]

In the years leading up to the great Cane Ridge revival in Kentucky in 1802, Presbyterian clergyman James McGready watched as bonding among small groups of revival converts inverted local social hierarchies: "numerous instances we have of those who, four or five years ago, were drunkards, dancers, Sabbath breakers, Deists, &c. &c. who are now humble, praying, sober, temperate Christians."[40] McGready's terminology was crucial; public inebriation, social dancing, Sabbath revelry, and deism were all displays of superiority (masculine, social, or intellectual) that evangelical conversion rebuked and disciplined.

The "national-minded" Virginia gentlemen[41] who transported republicanism and Protestantism to Kentucky in the 1790s built a political regime and religious culture around a framework of masculine superiority, discipline, and sobriety.[42] When the great revival came at Cane Ridge, groups of converts simultaneously fell to the ground in what must have appeared, to elite Virginia settlers, an exhibition of religious immoderation and political anarchy. Though an ancient way of exhibiting submission, even the Kentucky Presbyterian ministers leading the revivals—themselves veterans of the Hampden Sydney revival in Virginia of 1787—had never seen anything like it and feared they were losing control of the situation.

Instead of dismissing falling, jerking, and gyrations as deviant behavior, the Presbyterian clergy watched the phenomenon to see where it led. The sight of a thousand people "tossed to and fro, like the tumultuous waves of the sea, or swept down like the trees of a forest under the blast of a wild tornado" or like the waving of "a field of grain before the wind" signaled permanent shift in social structure. "The falling of the multitudes," these ministers noted, "happened under the singing of Watt's *Psalms and Hymns* more frequently than under the preaching of the word."[43] And the Isaac Watts hymn, "Character of a Citizen of Zion," described the spontaneous communitas of the revivals and proclaimed its ethical and egalitarian character: "He speaks the meaning of his heart / Nor slanders with his Tongue / Will scarce believe an ill report / Nor do his neighbors wrong / The wealthy sinner he contemns / Loves all who fear the Lord / And though to his own hurt he swears / Still performs his word / His hands disdain the golden bribe / And never gripe the poor / This man shall dwell with God on earth / And find his heaven secure."[44] Bands of revival converts, bound together by shared conversion experiences, emerged throughout the country and constituted a new form of voluntarist association in the republic. Resisting absorption into a homogeneous citizenry, the people learned the moral and ethical requirements of citizenship in face-to-face encounters that lessened the power of elites, increased the self-confidence of ordinary folk, and thereby moderated conflict between the many and the few.[45]

Primitive Christian churches and local social networks moderated political and religious conflict in several ways. They guarded the moral boundaries of the spiritual community, mediated between institutions and individuals, provided a place of shelter and fragile security, and merged works and grace—healing the soul. *Community, self-worth, spiritual wholeness,* and *shelter*—this agenda was the primitive Christian reaction to the genteel, organizing, institutionalizing requirements of republican regime building.[46] Enacted in piecemeal encounters on the fringes of polite society, that agenda took much longer to pursue than did denominational regime-building. Eventually, in small and subtle ways, primitive ecclesiology affected and altered the allocation of political and social authority.

Primitive Christian *community* moderated the political system by introducing an ancient set of historical precedents into a political culture that acknowledged the legitimacy of custom. "Certain it is," declared the authors of "the great Virginia petition" of 1785, "that the blessed author of the Christian religion . . . supported and maintained his Gospel in the world for several hundred years without the aid of civil power." The Baptist petitioners rued the day "when Constantine . . . first established Christianity by human laws"—ending persecution, to be sure, but exposing the Church to the ravages of "error, superstition, and immorality."[47] The Baptists knew that the lives of socially marginal believers had historically been blighted by persecutors and churchmen who connived with the powers that be to intermingle ecclesiastical and political authority.

Affirming the *self-worth* of the oppressed, primitive churches modified the very nature of citizenship. As slaveholding and cotton production increased among upcountry farmers in South Carolina between the 1780s and 1820s, churches both maintained social hierarchy and offered sanctuary to the socially marginal. Baptist disciplinary practices, though male dominated, sometimes took the side of abused women against their husbands and ordinary folk against their social betters. The evangelical ideal was the well-ordered family, and churches moved against drunkenness and spousal abuse when those sins threatened the well-being of family members and the stability of neighborhood society.[48] While the abuse of slaves usually lay outside the purview of church discipline, white Methodists in the South managed to instill into slave-holding church members a profound moral ambivalence. Daniel Grant, a Georgia Methodist in the 1790s, tried to examine his own slaveholding from what he had been taught to understand as God's perspective. His own motives, he acknowledged to himself, were selfish if understandable: "ease & self-interest & grandeur of life & the [apprehensive] thoughts that my postirety [sic] may labor hard for a living and perhaps not be so much thought of in the world if they did not have slaves." Yet when he realized that "the eyes of the law" and the attitudes of his neighbors regarded slaves as "no more than . . . dumb beasts, it fills my mind the horror and detestation." Mediating between Grant's conscience and his self-interest was his Methodist duty to strive for "deadness to the world" and to emulate Christ who "despised the great and gay things of the world."[49]

Proclamation of the *wholeness* of life—the radical inversion of hierarchy in which the last shall be first—was a foundation of African American spiritual enclaves that were resistant to white authority and that moderated slaveholder hegemony. Just how this resistance functioned was revealed by Charles Colcock Jones, the Georgia planter and Presbyterian minister who, as a student at Princeton Theological Seminary, had first experienced a divine call to combat the evils of slavery. As part of his denominationally grounded mission to the slaves, Jones instructed missionaries that "strictest order should be preserved at all religious meetings of the Negroes. No audible expressions of feeling should be allowed. . . . Tunes should . . . be plain and awakening. One great advantage in teaching them good psalms and hymns is that they are thereby induced to lay aside the extravagant and nonsensical chants and catches and hallelujah songs of their own composing."[50] Jones had been listening carefully to black worship for years before he wrote that instruction, and in this passage he inadvertently caught the essence of syncretic African-Christian religious experience.[51] Disparaging but also precise and observant, Jones's cautionary language about "groanings, cries, and noises, . . . chants, catches, and hallelujah cries" presented the aural and musical structure, and suggested the theology, of African American Christianity.[52]

That religious life was also a fragile *shelter* against the intrusion of law, authority, and hegemony into slave quarter spiritual fellowship. Around the edges of shelter, the authority of the dominant society could be challenged, and in small ways, moderated and modified. "Master John, I want permation [sic] of you pleas to speak a few words," a slave preacher wrote to his own former owner and Presbyterian pastor, the Reverend John Fort, in Robeson County, North Carolina, in 1821: "I want you to tell me the rezon you allwaze preach [facing] the white folks and keep your back to us. . . . Is it because these give you the money? . . . Money appears to be the object. We are carid [carried] to market and sold to the highest bidder. Never once [did you] inquire whether you sold a heathon or a Christian. . . . I understand the white people are praying for more religion in the world. Oh, may our case not be forgotten in the prairs of the sincear." The writer of this letter, who signed it simply, "Your Sir-vent, Sir," assured Fort that he was not angry or judgmental and hoped that "you will not think me too bold." Because he could read and write, he felt a responsibility to speak from his own religious community to Fort's white brethren—to be read in their "church, if you think proper."[53] The fact that these concerns were committed to paper, that they had percolated through the slave quarter of a North Carolina plantation for several years, that the letter itself was preserved in a plantation family archive indicate the small, subtle, ambiguous ways in which primitive Christianity fostered slave literacy and inverted power relationships.

Shelter, or sanctuary, was an issue of power for pious Methodist women who affirmed John Wesley's primitive Christian spirituality and understood his moderate style of church politics. Educated Methodist women, living comfort-ably in homes provided for them by husbands, fathers, even adult sons under-stood the captivity that gender roles imposed upon them and were sophisticated political moderates out of social necessity and attracted to prim-itive Christianity by its experiential character. If a slave's handwritten mani-festo had only a limited impact, the printed word was a more potent weapon in the hands of the politically marginal. Beginning in the 1830s, newspapers and magazine edited by women asserted the competence of women to shape pub-lic discourse. Female editors like Frances M. Bumpass felt a call to use the reli-gious press as a vehicle for education and empowerment of female and, for that matter, male readers as well. She was the widow of a Greensboro, North Car-olina, Methodist minister, Sidney Bumpass, who had founded, and on his deathbed in 1851, bequeathed to her, a religious newspaper, *The Weekly Message.* She published it for twenty years. Though thoroughly middle class and, when cornered, paternalistically pro-slavery, Bumpass was also a Wesleyan sentimen-talist who challenged herself and her readers to take charge of their own lives and education. Inspired by Phoebe Palmer's doctrine of holiness, Bumpass helped return a portion of Southern Methodism to its primitive origins as a religion of the heart, a succor to the poor and outcast, a herald of a new mil-lennium, and of a church in which women enjoyed, if not institutional author-ity, something more potent: their own spiritual insight and responsibility for the souls of family members and neighbors.

The Weekly Message—carrying on its masthead an engraving of a dove, sym-bol of the Holy Spirit as a feminine force—became, for its editor, contributors, and readers, a sanctuary. "As we become attuned to a paper," wrote Tryphena

Mock, a regular contributor, explaining the aura surrounding the publication, "as we drink the spirit and moral tone which it breathes, so we become united to all its readers. We feel, . . . as if with them, we formed a great congregation looking up weekly to the same source for an intellectual and moral feast."[54]

The most mature program for societal transformation under primitive Christian auspices, and the most recognizably moderate in its political rhetoric, occurred in confessional churches. Confessional churches—so called because they adhered to Reformation-era confessions of faith, the Westminster Confession for English and Scottish Calvinists, the Augsburg Confession for Lutherans, the Heidelberg Catechism for German Calvinists, and the Thirty-Nine Articles for the Episcopal Church—were also primitive in that they regarded their confessional documents as authoritative interpretations of the early church and because they called themselves "primitive." Confessional laity may not have been socially marginal, but, in an aggressively denominational and Americanized religious culture, they were culturally marginal.[55]

As textualists, confessional Christians were sensitive to the ways in which state and national constitutions might augment, but also undermine, their own historic ecclesiological doctrines. Confessional Christianity confirmed what republican legislators and jurists in the 1770s and 1780s only vaguely sensed: that religion and government could interact functionally because they had been doing so ever since the Council of Nicea in 325. That sixteen-century span of history, the confessional churches taught, impinged on the present because political abuses within the church and religious mischief by the state had become a reservoir of cautionary wisdom, because theology treated human freedom and dignity as treasures of western civilization, and finally because secular concepts of liberty and civic order were rooted in Christian as well as classical writings about power and authority.[56]

As catechists who believed that texts, properly taught, could transform human character, confessionalists gloried in pedagogy and regarded controversy over religious education as politics in its purest form. David Henkel, the confessionalist Lutheran in Rowan County, North Carolina, led an exodus of his family and supporters from the North Carolina Synod in 1820 to create the Tennessee Evangelical Lutheran Church,[57] which, for the next 102 years, maintained fidelity to Lutheran confessional documents and upheld the magisterium, or teaching authority of the church.[58] Henkel's pamphlet, *Carolinian Herald of Liberty, Religious and Political* (1821) employed classical republican theory, with all of its Machiavellian pessimism, to argue why the absorption of

North Carolina and Virginia Lutherans into an American-style denominational church body, centered in Pennsylvania and New York, was an assault on
the liberty, not just of confessional Lutherans, but of all citizens: "O Americans! ... Liberty can only be enjoyed by a wise and virtuous people, but dupes
and asses cannot live without tyrannical masters. ... Truth, justice, and mercy"
were at stake.

Truth, for Henkel, was the real presence of Christ in the Eucharist; justice,
the accountability of the ordained to God alone; and mercy, the specific act of
participating in the death and resurrection through baptism and communion.
An American Lutheran denominational church competing with other Protestant denominations, Henkel predicted, would jettison its Catholic heritage and
retain only its celebration of Luther as a man of the Bible and foe of papal
authority. To relegate Luther to the status of a mere Protestant reformer,
Henkel argued, or to dilute the Catholic, evangelical drama of Eucharistic, confessional liturgy, Henkel declared, was both blasphemy and an assault on the
public good.[59] Henkel's bête noire, the former Moravian, Gottlieb Shober,
demanded to know how pious Lutherans could *not* interfere: "Have you not
heard him preach that whosoever is baptised and partakes of the Lord's Supper is safe and that those who insist on further repentance and conversion are
enthusiasts and bigots?"[60] Shober had seized the moderate high ground and
had successfully painted Henkel and his Tennessee Synod followers as immoderate troublemakers. But over the next century Henkel's successors in the Tennessee Synod, operating largely in Virginia and the Carolinas, used historic
confessionalism to mediate tensions within society. In 1822 the Synod urged the
North Carolina legislature to seek a practical way of abolishing slavery, "a great
evil in our land," and, by the Progressive era, Tennessee Synod clergy and laity
formed the vanguard of the social reform movement in Catawba County,
North Carolina.[61]

John Henry Hobart, Episcopal Bishop of New York, likewise a confessional
churchman who identified with the early church, understood that the authority to teach derived from ancient principles rather than contemporary culture.
In 1809, he instructed confirmands to consider questions of ecclesiology: "Am
I a member of the church of Christ, ... the channel of his *covenanted* mercies
to a fallen world? ... Do I keep my due submission to the ministrations of this
church of its priesthood, deriving their authority by regular transmission
through Jesus Christ?"[62] In this didactic way, Hobart laid the foundations of
the high church Episcopal tradition in the United States. That tradition held

that only a church drawing its authority from ancient sources could mediate contemporary human disputes. One of Hobart's students, Levi Silliman Ives, Bishop of North Carolina from 1830 to 1852, created, in 1846, a classical mission school at Valle Crucis, in the North Carolina mountains. A convert to the Anglo-Catholic Oxford Movement, Ives sought in 1849 "to quiet . . . some minds" in his diocese by assuring his critics that nothing was practiced or taught at the Mission School "which is not in accordance with the principles and usages of our branch of the Holy Catholic Church contained in the Book of Common Prayers"—language that quieted none of his critics and fore-warned his flight to Rome and conversion to Roman Catholicism in 1852.[63]

More successful in moderating religious and political passions was Bishop Charles P. McIlvain of Ohio, an evangelical, low church Episcopal leader who learned how to make common cause with his high church, confessional critics. McIlvain defended "episcopal and liturgical . . . institutions" because they were "so *evangelical,* so *comprehensive,* so *catholic,* and so *moderate* [that] they are the only ones that bid fair to stand unmitigated" by rancor, division, and political passions in Jacksonian America. In juxtaposing "catholic" and "evangeli-cal," McIlvain acknowledged that high church and evangelical were permanent poles of the Episcopal Church in America and that both were indispensable antidotes to American individualism and sectarianism. His terms, "compre-hensive" and "moderate" stipulated that Anglican religious history took prece-dence over American denominational history. The purpose of the Elizabethan settlement of 1559 (the political foundation of the Anglican Church and the Tudor monarchy), McIlvain implied, was to hold society together by *compre-hending* each of its religious and social elements. The humanist ideals shared by Renaissance Protestants and Catholics alike, McIlvain contended, were a moderate formula for religious and political peace.[64]

A stunning instance of primitive confessional Christianity confronting constitutional government occurred in up-country South Carolina, where Associate Reformed Presbyterians (ARP) settled in the 1820s. Standing aloof from the Presbyterian Church in the United States (PCUS), known in South Carolina as "General Assembly" Presbyterians, the ARP insisted on the unac-companied singing of Psalms and daily devotional services in which each member of the household, including slaves, shared in reading aloud from the Bible. The ARP declared that these practices were biblically mandated, not by isolated proof-text scriptural passages, but by the totality of biblical teaching about worship.[65]

When the South Carolina legislature in 1834, in a post-Nullification crack-down on racial and political moderation, outlawed teaching slaves to read, up-country ARP churches were in crisis because obeying that state law meant violating the dictates of scripture.[66] Just how deeply the law of slavery in South Carolina intruded into the life of the ARP enclave in South Carolina became manifest sixteen years later, in 1850, when George, a slave belonging the Dr. Robert Grier, the president of the ARP's Erskine College and Seminary in the town of Due West, told other slaves what he had learned in family devotions in the Grier household: that the debate over California statehood and fugitive slave law was a portent that God was about act to abolish slavery. George's abolitionist "preaching" was overheard by the owner of those listening slaves, Lemuel Reid, a prominent PCUS layman. The ensuing community uproar[67] demonstrated how primitive Christianity—a church founded not on republican foundations but on Ulster Calvinist adherence of the Westminister Confession—could substitute confessional historical consciousness for Anglo-American constitutionalism and thereby defy the South Carolina regime under which Scottish Calvinist traditionalists and their slaves lived.

Conclusion

Primitive Christianity inculcated in its adherents appreciation for ancient notions of moral and spiritual authority, and, in so doing, primitive church-men and women in the early republic challenged the dominant culture. In contrast, denominational Christianity predisposed Americans to regard constitutional government as the work of statesmen and statesmanship as the desirable product of Protestant civic education. Primitive Christianity warned other Americans that their regime might well be an aggregation of religious and social enclaves held together by nothing more than divine whimsy.

How did advocates of these two ecclesiologies understand the premise with which this chapter began: that, in the beginning, there was an implicit bargain between religion and the early republic? The denominational leaders and statesmen of the early republic believed as a matter of prudence that civic discourse and enlightenment history were necessary tools for separating, without entirely divorcing, religion from government. Primitive Christians never accepted that kind of statecraft. These more principled moderates sought to mediate between the political needs of a developing nation and the uncompromising demands of biblical morality. Accordingly, they were quite prepared to consider the possibility of a bargain between religion and the republic. But if such a compact existed, primitive Christians felt certain, it was an implicit act of divine providence, hidden from view by the mystery of creation, and to be disclosed to the American people by dire misfortunes.[68]

Functioning in that creative tension, the intermingling of denominational and primitive Christianity within one polity was an integral part of what Jack P. Greene has called a "fortuitous convergence" of "culture" and "contingency" in the post-Revolutionary Atlantic world.[69]

Part III / The American Revolution and the Atlantic World

The American Loyalist Diaspora and the Reconfiguration of the British Atlantic World

Keith Mason

The American Revolution triggered a kaleidoscopic redistribution of Loyalist exiles across the British Atlantic world. Yet this migration's significance has traditionally been downplayed, both by American historians intent on analyzing the birth of the new republic and by students of British imperialism concerned primarily with charting the "swing to the east."[1] Even in recent works by Stephen Conway, Eliga H. Gould, and Andrew O'Shaughnessy that otherwise perceptively deploy a broader Atlantic perspective toward the American crisis, the Loyalist migrants remain ghostly, marginal figures despite their suggestive position at the interface of the late eighteenth-century American and British experiences.[2] Outside Canada, their designated place in the historiography is akin to that of the Jacobites: a people whose story merits inclusion in the larger narrative but who are usually represented as having little impact on the course of Anglo-American history.

This chapter's principal objective is to challenge that orthodoxy. If scale bears any correspondence to significance, there can be no doubting the Loyalist outpouring's importance. In a ten-year period from 1774 to 1784, thousands fled the rebel colonies to seek refuge beyond the borders of the embryonic

United States. The precise number is difficult to determine because of the migration's duration and segmented character. Most scholars' calculations range from sixty to one hundred thousand.[3] As with the parallel debate over the size of the original Loyalist population, the estimates depend on how scholars address elusive but critical questions concerning motivation and definition.[4] But even accepting a conservative figure, this migration was still comparable in scale to other major early modern British population movements. It was larger than the exoduses westward that established the Chesapeake and New England colonies during the early seventeenth century; it was equivalent to the flow of settlers from England and Scotland to the Irish plantations.[5] By exploring the magnitude, character, and meaning of the Loyalist migration at both macro- and microcosmic levels, this chapter highlights the critical role this movement of peoples played in the post-Revolutionary reconfiguration of the British Atlantic.

An Atlantic Diaspora

The Loyalist migration, like the eighteenth-century Scottish or nineteenth-century Irish diasporas, was a genuinely Atlantic phenomenon. The exiles moved in complex patterns around the ocean littoral. Their destinations included Britain, its remaining possessions on the North American mainland, the British Caribbean, Central America, and West Africa. Because of their visibility, historians have conventionally paid most attention to the approximately seven thousand Loyalist refugees who arrived in Britain, mainly London, in the first instance.[6] They included many elite members of the pre-war colonial political and religious establishment, but also encompassed large numbers of the Crown's ordinary supporters—farmers, artisans, urban labourers, free blacks—who fled during the American Revolution. Most, sometimes uneasily, made their new home in the metropolis. For others, it proved to be a stepping-stone on a journey in quest of opportunities elsewhere within the empire.

Despite the primacy accorded it, this eastward movement was not the largest branch of the Loyalist outflow. The vast majority of migrants resettled in other parts of the British Atlantic world. The most sizable cohort ended up in the upper reaches of North America where it played a significant role in establishing British Canada's identity as the new American republic's main continental rival. Approximately forty thousand exiles were evacuated to the Maritime Provinces, mostly following the British departure from New York in 1783.[7]

Here, the arrival of some fifteen thousand refugees on the St. John River paved the way for the creation of the new province of New Brunswick. Like the British exiles, not all of these migrants stayed at their initial destination. Most notably, many of Nova Scotia's ex-slaves later moved to West Africa during the early 1790s where they participated in the development of the coastal colony of Sierra Leone.[8]

Although fewer Loyalists arrived elsewhere in North America, their impact was profound. The island of St. John, for example, received only 550 exiles, but this still represented a major injection to an existing population of under five hundred families. The Loyalist presence in Quebec was much stronger. Almost seven thousand came to the Province, approximately five hundred to the bay of Chaleurs or Gaspe, some to Sorel, and the vast majority further west along the upper St. Lawrence. Some six thousand ultimately established their homes there and went on to play a leading role in consolidating the British presence around the Great Lakes frontier region.[9]

On the southern perimeter of British America, East and West Florida, especially the garrison towns of St. Augustine and Pensacola, proved another magnet for Loyalist refugees. In particular, these provinces attracted planters from the Carolinas and Georgia, along with their slaves. A trickle out of those states began in late 1775 and the flow accelerated as the war progressed. Possibly as many as seven thousand refugees entered East Florida in 1778 alone.[10] A second wave then reached the province after the evacuations of Savannah and Charleston in 1782. Around five thousand whites along with just over eight thousand black slaves arrived during this period.[11] The imperial government's decision to cede East Florida to Spain then triggered another out-migration, propelling nearly ten thousand exiles around the Atlantic world. Their ultimate destinations included Nova Scotia, various parts of the Caribbean—including Jamaica, the Bahamas, Bermuda, Dominica, and Grenada—and Britain itself. Among other significant effects, these journeys consolidated the interconnections between the remaining regions of British America.[12]

Even more significant than its scale, range, and multidirectional nature was the Loyalist outflow's underlying character. It was also, in essence, a diaspora. By that I mean a migration under traumatic circumstances that produced both dispersal and cohesion.[13] Loyalist exiles, as has been seen, scattered to several destinations across the Atlantic world. They were a diverse group in terms of rank, socioeconomic standing, ethnic composition, and racial background, ranging from colonial officeholders to fugitive blacks. They constituted, in

John McLeod's phrase, "composite communities."[14] The motives animating their loyalty to the British cause also varied considerably, from the protection of privilege to the acquisition of freedom. Yet dispersal and diversity did not nullify either the impact of the Loyalist migration or the refugees' sense of identity. "All diasporas are differentiated, heterogeneous, contested spaces," Avtar Brah maintains, "even as they are implicated in the construction of a common 'we.'"[15]

Strong countervailing forces gave the Loyalists a shared history that persisted into the nineteenth century. First, and most fundamentally, there was their displacement during the American Revolution. Having prompted their migration in the first place, the war experience continued to provide them with a distinct political signifier. Second, with the exception of those who remained permanently in the metropolis, they assumed a shared status as settlers. The migrants all confronted the same problems of re-establishing themselves in an unfamiliar environment, adjusting to new conditions, and adapting their inherited social values and structures accordingly. Third, there were enduring kinship, social, and economic ties among diaspora members that opened and consolidated channels of communication between otherwise far-flung Loyalist communities. Fourth, there was the actual experience of exile and their resulting liminal status. Like others in the Atlantic basin, they found themselves caught between worlds and suspended between the past and the present. Under these circumstances, as Paul Gilroy points out in *The Black Atlantic,* "routes" often became more important than "roots."[16] Finally, regardless of their precise background and status, they shared a perception that they had suffered from persecution and discrimination. This feeling persisted during their exile within the British empire and, for example, influenced both white and black Loyalist attitudes toward the compensation, pension, and land grant arrangements that the imperial government offered.

Viewed as a diaspora, the Loyalist migration ultimately helped reconfigure the British Atlantic world in several interrelated ways. First, and most obviously, there was its geographic and demographic impact. The empire's physical axes shifted as the exiles dispersed to several destinations in their efforts to get re-established. Loyalist migrants extended imperial boundaries as they occupied areas of the British Atlantic where settlement colonies either had been weak or had not taken hold before the 1770s. Often, as in Upper Canada, this was a direct result of government policy. The ministry anticipated that these new frontier communities would, as Lord North claimed, "serve as a barrier ... against any incursions from the inhabitants of those Colonies that had revolted from their Allegiance."[17] But, these Creole settlers were not simply instruments of an expansive, aggressive imperial state. As well as harboring their own economic ambitions, they were determined, as had been their predecessors who left the British Isles for New England and Virginia, to retain as much of their English heritage as possible, including libertarian concepts like the rule of law and representative government. Hence Loyalist migrants helped impart long-established colonial imperatives and structures to new regions, perpetuating the same notions of liberty and English identity brought westward by those who had originally settled the provinces that became the United States.[18]

In a British Atlantic characterized by ongoing processes of fragmentation and consolidation, the Loyalist migration also acted as a strong integrative force.[19] As they moved from settlement to settlement, the exiles maintained their family and kin connections, affirming the social bonds that helped tie the post-Revolutionary empire together. In addition, émigré merchants in pursuit of profit proceeded to carve out niches for themselves in both recently acquired and long-established colonies. As these refugees exploited their own, sometimes extensive commercial networks, new trading and personal connections were established between the inhabitants of otherwise far-flung imperial outposts. The Loyalist outflow finally helped define the British Atlantic's relations with its neighbors, most notably the United States and Spanish America, and extended British informal influence beyond its political perimeters. Some migrant kin groups, after all, continued to span both the empire and the republic, acting as a conduit between those two now-distinct entities. Meanwhile, former Loyalist merchants operating in the southeastern Caribbean became actively involved in commerce with the Spanish mainland. These connections on the margins of empire show how mobile groups like the Tory exiles could exploit the porousness of geopolitical borders during an era of imperial reconfiguration.

Secondly, an important perceptual shift accompanied the Loyalist outflow. As has been noted, by no means all the exiles were white, English, and Protestant. Instead, they were a heterogeneous band that, in William H. Nelson's phrase, encompassed "conscious minorities."[20] Among the Loyalists there were Lowland and Highland Scots, Scotch-Irish, Germans, Dutch, and Native Americans of all ranks, as well as adherents of various religious denominations. There was also a sizable black slave and ex-slave contingent. Not all these groups fled the colonies in proportion to their strength in North America. Nevertheless, their dramatic departure still drove the British authorities to a fresh appreciation of the empire's diverse, multiracial character. Though this process had been underway since the Seven Years' War, the Anglophone nature of the thirteen colonies had earlier concealed its full extent. Now, following the American Revolution, those predominantly British and Protestant possessions lay outside the imperial fold, while the heterogeneous Loyalist émigrés remained within. The Atlantic world they helped shape therefore took on, in Eliga Gould's phrase, "a different complexion."[21] Perhaps the most striking demonstration of this transformation lay in the support given to the establishment of a predominantly nonwhite, settlement colony on the African coast in Sierra Leone.

The Loyalist exodus influenced imperial policy as well as perception. Some scholars argue that the American crisis precipitated a shift toward authoritarianism on the part of British officials. According to Christopher Bayly, this was characterized by political centralization at Whitehall, viceregal autocracy in the colonies, aristocratic military government, and a growing emphasis on racial hierarchy and subordination.[22] Certainly elements of this drift toward "proconsular despotism" can be discerned especially in Asia, but it is misleading to think that it was the dominant motif across the empire. In the case of North America, where the most profound imperial restructuring in the late eighteenth-century British Atlantic took place, the Constitutional Act of 1791 incorporated the royalist and paternalistic principles of patronage powers for the executive, appointed Councils, and the endowment of the Anglican Church in Upper Canada in a way that suggested that the British authorities had indeed learned some conservative lessons from the American Revolution.[23] At the same time, however, there was a recognition that attention had to be paid to the settlers' wishes to order to insulate them from the contagion of liberty potentially emanating from the United States. The right of Parliament to tax the colonies for revenue was not revived and legislative assemblies, though circumscribed, still enjoyed some autonomy. With their commitment to principles of self-government, Loyalist migrants would not have had it otherwise. Indeed, some, like William Smith, even contemplated a quasifederal structure for the British empire within which the colonies retained clearly defined rights and powers.[24] Partly because of Loyalist aspirations, goals, and pressure, any authoritarian or reactionary thrust to colonial policy in the 1780s and early 1790s was of necessity muted. Britain, as a result, did not become the "counter-Revolutionary hegemon" that some scholars claim.[25]

Finally, the Loyalist presence within the empire contributed to a refashioning of the imperial self-image in the era following the American Revolution. At least as far as the metropolitan establishment was concerned, the way in which the nation sought to defend Loyalist interests in the Treaty of Paris, received the exiles, provided them assistance via pension provision and compensation, and promoted opportunities for resettlement offered clear proof of the British empire's inherent liberality, humanitarianism, and civility. Although conscious of the competing demands of fiscal prudence and "economical reform," a generous, responsible nation recognized and assumed this imperial burden with good grace. As John Eardley-Wilmot, one of the claims commissioners, reflected in 1815: "However . . . we may deplore the causes, the progress, and the issue of the Contest [i.e., the War of Independence]—its retrospect will afford some consolation to every lover of his Country to reflect, that, among the many other Gracious acts of the present Reign, the Remuneration of these Loyal and meritorious Sufferers will be commemorated as a distinguished Testimony of public Beneficence and public Faith."[26]

This self-image of the empire as enlightened, benign, and ultimately patrician is perhaps best captured in Benjamin West's famous allegorical painting, *Reception of the American Loyalists by Great Britain in 1783* (see Fig. 12.1). West depicts religion and justice extending the mantle of Britannia as she herself is holding out her arm and shield to receive the refugees. Under the shield is the Crown of Great Britain, surrounded by a cluster of Loyalists. At the head of the delegation stand various prominent individuals representing the law, the church, and the government. Behind them, however, are arrayed a more eclectic group that encompasses grateful widows, Native Americans, and freed slaves, all with their arms outstretched in supplication and acknowledgment. They are also about to be welcomed into the imperial fold. This well-crafted, idealized image composed by George III's history-painter portrays exactly how the British establishment wanted to view both the Loyalists and the diverse, reconfigured empire that had come into being at the conclusion of the War of Independence. Not very subtly it also hints at a contrast with the alleged vindictiveness, instability, and racial exclusiveness of the newborn republican United States.[27]

Four Exiles

Capturing the meaning of this Loyalist exodus from its participants' perspective is a difficult task. As Robin Cohen has pointed out, diasporas are

Figure 12.1. "Reception of the American Loyalists by Great Britain in the Year 1783," by Benjamin West. Courtesy Yale Center for British Art, Paul Mellon Collection.

invariably complex phenomena and can assume different degrees of signifi-cance for those displaced.[28] However, by concentrating on the microhistories of four specific individuals and their families—Thomas Hutchinson, James Parker, Samuel Williams, and Thomas Peters—at least some of the migration's essential characteristics can be discerned. Hutchinson, the governor of Mas-sachusetts during the early 1770s, epitomizes the archetypal Tory official attracted to the metropolis during the conflict's early stages. His priority was the maintenance of a high public profile in order to influence the controversy over the imperial-colonial relationship. Ultimately, however, he failed in his objectives. As a result, somewhat ironically given his standing, the exiled Hutchinson exemplifies the *victim* strand within the Loyalist diaspora.

The other cases all highlight variants of the settler impulse that predomi-nated after 1783. A Scottish immigrant and Virginia merchant, James Parker experienced revolution and war first-hand before returning to Britain at the conflict's conclusion. Turning his back on public affairs, his principal goal

became restoring his family's battered fortunes by exploiting his predominantly Scottish transatlantic commercial connections to establish his two sons
within the British empire. Parker, then, demonstrates the importance of the
trade diasporas operating within the Loyalist migration. A planter from North
Carolina, Samuel Williams did not have Parker's advantages. Though less well
documented, his relations' dispersal highlights the opportunities as well as the
restrictions confronting poorer Tories forced to relocate within the British
empire. Their story draws attention to the diaspora's *imperial* dimension.
Finally, Thomas Peters provides a glimpse into the black Loyalists' journey.
Having gained his freedom during the war, Peters then played a leading role in
Nova Scotia's refugee communities and in the subsequent migration to Sierra
Leone. His principal concern throughout seems to have been to safeguard his
precarious liberty through official recognition of his status and the acquisition
of land. Beyond that his experience reveals the way in which the Loyalist migra-
tion acted as a transatlantic *multicultural* diaspora.

First of all, the story of Governor Thomas Hutchinson of Massachusetts
dramatizes the plight of privileged office-holding exiles drawn to the metropolis. Figuring prominently in conventional histories, these are individuals whom
one would anticipate playing a key role in the diaspora, arguing aggressively for
the Loyalist cause and possibly exerting genuine influence over imperial affairs.
Certainly the British authorities initially feted Hutchinson when he first
arrived in London in June 1774. He met the secretary of state, Lord Dartmouth,
and even had an audience with George III who questioned him about the
unrest in the colonies. Further consultations followed with other ministers or
prominent politicians, including Lord North. During these discussions,
Hutchinson urged moderation and accommodation. Still seeing American
resistance as the product of radical agitation, he remained committed to effecting a reconciliation between the imperial government and the colonies that
would mean his eventual return to Massachusetts.[29]

Feeling at ease in London, Hutchinson took heart from British official-
dom's apparent responsiveness. "My reception here," he claimed, "exceeded
everything I could imagine."[30] Flattered by the attention he was receiving,
Hutchinson contemplated joining an English establishment that seemed so
open to him. "I am sometimes tempted," he wrote, "to endeavour to forget that
I am an American, and to turn my views to a provision for what remains of
life in England."[31] Unlike most refugees, Hutchinson was wealthy enough to
cut a figure in the metropolis. The capital from several profitable investments,

together with his pension of £1,000 per annum, gave him a financial cushion denied to most exiles.[32] Everyone, he asserted, urged him to settle in England and, as the honors and invitations continued to flow, that prospect must have seemed enticing.[33]

After the outbreak of armed conflict, however, Hutchinson began to baulk as he found "the passion for my native country" returning. Events had overtaken his emphasis on reconciliation and, given the broad public support for the Revolutionaries in the colonies, his diagnosis of the crisis was clearly flawed. The relevance of his views on colonial affairs paled, the utility of his connections evaporated, and the novelty of his presence wore off with the arrival of fresh waves of refugees. As a result, the former governor saw his standing decline precipitously. Although his fellow exiles still consulted him, he was increasingly ignored by the administration. After a year and a half he declared candidly, "We Americans are plenty here, and very cheap. Some of us at first coming, are apt to think ourselves of importance, but other people do not think so, and few, if any of us are much consulted, or enquired after."[34]

As his alienation grew, Hutchinson waxed nostalgic for Massachusetts. As for many Creole diaspora exiles, the former colonies remained "home." "My thoughts day and night are upon New England," Hutchinson wrote. "New England is wrote upon my heart in as strong characters as Calais was upon Queen Mary's." Trapped in England among his fellow Massachusetts refugees and barred from returning to a transformed New England, Hutchinson increasingly retreated to the world of the past. He focused his energies on completing his *History of Massachusetts-Bay,* declaring "from my situation at this time of life, so unexpected to me, three thousand miles from my country and friends, so that every scene has the appearance of a dream, rather than a reality." In 1780, Hutchinson died, still living in London.[35]

Hutchinson's exile experience demonstrates how many prominent Tories became increasingly disillusioned with metropolitan life. Despite their initial high hopes, they exercised minimal influence over government policy during the war years. Surprisingly, given their standing and loyalty to the Crown, they played little part in the British Atlantic's reconfiguration. Despite their attachment to metropolitan institutions and values, they were actually the American Revolution's real displaced victims. Struggling to find a role in exile, these Tories never really came to terms with new political realities.

Émigrés from less privileged backgrounds—both white and black—not metropolitan refugees like Hutchinson or Thompson, were the real agents in the British Atlantic's reconfiguration. Whether as traders or settlers, they played the lead role in the new British empire. The Scottish immigrant, James Parker, and his family provide one striking example of their postwar commercial activities. A successful merchant in pre-Revolutionary Norfolk, Virginia, Parker became a stalwart supporter of the British cause. After fighting alongside Governor Dunmore in Virginia, he participated in several subsequent military campaigns. Following a stint in a French prison, Parker followed Hutchinson's route into exile in London during 1783. Unlike the Massachusetts governor, however, Parker was not a leading Tory office-holder or notable. Despite his mercantile background, he fell into the Loyalist coalition's broad middling ranks. Parker also arrived in England later than Hutchinson. Illustrating the importance of timing in the Loyalist diaspora, his bitter experience of war had hardened his reaction to the American Revolution. It irrevocably severed any emotional or cultural ties that he had with the former colonies—which may in any event have been weaker, or more ambiguous, given his Scottish descent. Unlike the Massachusetts governor, Parker did not retain any lingering nostalgia for American life nor did he harbor any illusions about the metropolitan establishment. The United States, as far as he was concerned, was weak, unstable, and faction-ridden: it harbored a people who lacked virtue, commitment, and consistency. Meanwhile, the British leadership had proved itself both incompetent and vacillating. Spurning both, Parker dedicated himself to a private agenda that revolved around reviving his fortunes and ensuring his family's future prosperity.[36]

Parker was aggressive in pursuing compensation for himself and his associates. Moving in the same circle as more prominent Tories like James Chalmers and William Franklin, Parker became an active member of the Loyalist émigré community and was appointed to the refugees' principal lobbying group, the Board of Loyalist agents, in 1787.[37] Beyond these efforts on behalf of his fellow émigrés, however, his main priorities did not lie in the public sphere. Instead, he was intent on reuniting his scattered family and restoring their economic fortune. Having gained employment as an underwriter at Lloyd's to supplement his Treasury pension,[38] Parker then encouraged his Virginia-born wife, Margaret, to join him in London. Though reluctant to leave America, she eventually made the voyage to England, only to die within a year of her arrival in 1785.[39]

Undeterred Parker turned to launching his two young sons, Patrick and Charles Stewart, upon commercial careers. His efforts reveal the options open to mercantile Loyalist families within and beyond the British empire, the utility of the Parkers' predominantly Scottish network of contacts, the some-times contrasting fortunes of second-generation exiles, and the tensions that could arise between them and their parents. Patrick and Charles Stewart's paths took profoundly different trajectories. After initially contemplating serving as an Indian army cadet and then working as a clerk in a Glasgow counting house, Patrick's ambition became to return to Virginia.[40] Disobeying his father, he traveled to the Chesapeake in 1785, where he set up as a dry goods merchant.[41] Although most of Parker's business associates had either returned to Scotland or fled to the Caribbean and Canada, some native Virginian acquaintances did remain in the vicinity. These maternal family ties were strong enough to secure the prospect of trade, but they ultimately proved insufficient to underpin Patrick's business. By 1794 his commercial ventures had run into trouble and he died bankrupt in 1795 en route for England.[42]

Patrick's career represented a major blow to James Parker's ambitions for his family, which he anticipated being fulfilled exclusively within the British empire. Given his detestation of the Americans and bitter resentment of their independence, James had no desire to see his elder son become a citizen of the republic. He was angry that Patrick had ignored his advice and, in effect, rebelled. There was a rather crude equation in his mind between the colonists' and his son's disobedience. "If heaven had granted my warmest wish it was that my sons might be independent[,] have fortitude, industry, stubborn integrity," he declared, "but you have abandoned me[,] become an Alien & made choice of a society whose principles every honest man abhors."[43]

The career of James's other son, Charles, stayed within the boundaries that he had mapped out: boundaries that show the potential strength of the com-mercial networks the family could draw upon. After leaving school, Charles worked at the Port Glasgow customs house before being sent to Spain to learn a language that was obviously useful in the Caribbean and South American trades.[44] Using his old Chesapeake connections, James then asked James Campbell, a fellow Loyalist and former business partner, to get Charles a post in the strategically placed colony of Grenada, where Campbell now lived. Charles first served as a clerk under another Scottish merchant, George Robert-son, who had taken advantage of Grenada's recently acquired free port status to trade with Caracas and New Granada.[45] A copartnership with commercial interests in Demerara as well as Grenada was then formed in 1790 between them and Daniel Gordon. In 1792, after a dispute with Gordon, this was dis-solved and a new partnership launched. This firm initially ran into trouble owing to the outbreak of war with France. "[T]he hardships we experience from this storm are not trifling & keep our minds in the most cruel state of anxiety," Charles maintained, "altho' we hope from the ampleness of our funds that we shall still weather it out."[46]

His confidence was justified. He subsequently prospered both as a merchant involved in the re-export trade with the Spanish colonies and as a planter producing cotton on slave-worked estates situated in the fertile, underutilized lands of Demerara and Essequibo. As a result, like other "soujourners," Charles was eventually able to retire to Scotland.[47] Ironically he had achieved the independence and security that had perhaps inspired James himself some forty years earlier as he ventured across the Atlantic to Virginia.[48] Moreover, Charles had accomplished these goals within the British empire, away from the rebellious Americans, and in accordance with his father's wishes. For this reason, their personal relations were smooth. James, in fact, probably revelled in his son's accomplishment. Meanwhile Charles always struck the right deferential note, paying due heed to James's advice on matters such as his marriage in 1797 to a fellow Scot.[49] Evidently the family were sufficiently close that the aging Loyalist even went to live with them in Scotland during his declining years. For him, this had probably always constituted "home."[50]

The Parker family's fate during the postwar years demonstrates the patchy fortunes of exiled mercantile Tories as they sought to re-establish themselves by exploiting their commercial, personal, and political connections within and, in Patrick's case, beyond the British empire. The Parkers' network was unsurprisingly composed predominantly of Scots and had developed in the years prior to the imperial crisis. But the American Revolution had, of course, severely disrupted this social web in the former colonies. Under these changed circumstances, Patrick's choice of Virginia as a base was unwise. Regardless of his trading ability, he would have struggled because of his diluted personal ties there. By contrast, Charles was able to tap into the Scottish network in the Caribbean, which had been reinvigorated following the Loyalist diaspora and was particularly dense in recently acquired territories like Grenada and Demerara.[51] This, in part, accounts for his commercial success and rapid ascent.

Because of the unevenness of the available source material, poorer white Loyalists are far more difficult to track and their motivations harder to evaluate than either Hutchinson's or the Parkers.' Against the odds, poorer Loyalists still managed to re-establish themselves in the wake of the war. Samuel Williams, a small planter from Anson County, North Carolina, came from a less wealthy background than James Parker.[52] However, he became an active Loyalist. Williams raised a militia company in early 1776 and fought in North Carolina's first Revolutionary battle at Moore's Creek Bridge. After that defeat, he fled to Georgia together with his four sons. The family then migrated to East Florida in 1778. Williams renewed his activity on behalf of the Loyalist cause there by commanding another company that skirmished along the Georgia border. He and two of his sons, Henry and Jacob, later fought in the backcountry after the British reconquest of Georgia and were living in Savannah at the war's end. By this point another son, William, and Henry's wife and children had joined them. When the British evacuated the city, they all returned to East Florida. Meanwhile, after seeing service with the imperial forces, the other brother, Samuel Jr., finished the war in New York.

Unlike the Parkers, the family never got back together again. Little else is known about the father, who died at some point before 1787 and therefore only had a brief exile experience. The sons, however, pursued nearly every option open to settler Loyalists in their quest to find a new home. Following the British evacuation of New York in 1783, Samuel Jr. went to New Brunswick. Like many others, he later chose to move west to the upper St. Lawrence Valley. Henry and William migrated to the Bahamas in 1784 and succeeded in becoming planters. For them, the Caribbean became a land of opportunity. Like Patrick Parker, Henry probably returned to the United States: In 1807 a Henry Williams owned land near the family's pre-Revolutionary home in Anson County. Finally, Jacob traveled to London in a futile attempt to obtain compensation. Like other poorer Loyalists without the necessary connections, however, he was unable to pursue the claim effectively and eventually died in a London workhouse.

The Williams family narrative demonstrates the range of the poorer Loyalists' diaspora from the South, the main sphere of British operations in the war's final phase. Ultimately members of the clan found their way to Canada, the Bahamas, and Britain, as well as back to the United States. They played a role in the Maritime Provinces' transformation from a social and cultural extension of New England to becoming home to a rich assortment of exiles, including American-born poorer whites, ex-planters, free blacks, slaves, and discharged soldiers. The Williamses also participated in the Loyalist outflow to the northern fringes of the Caribbean. Not only did settlement expand in the minor outpost of the Bahamas, but the arrival of exiles like Henry and William also prompted an economic transition. Long dependent on shipbuilding, fishing, and other maritime activities, the Bahamas developed a plantation economy based on cotton cultivation and slavery.[53] Settlers like the Williamses played a significant role in this postwar reconfiguration.

Black Loyalists also fled the colonies in large numbers. Though subject to imperial direction like poorer whites, these fugitives, of course, retained their own motives and ambitions. As war proved a transforming experience for them, they probably entered the diaspora with heightened expectations for the future. Given their rather ambiguous connection with the American colonies, they also quickly identified themselves, in effect, as "Black Britons"—a status that gave them, as they saw it, the moral and physical leverage to make demands on the authorities. Their priorities, however, were shaped by their distinctive culture, the complex amalgam identified by Graham Hodges as "black republicanism," which acted as the prism through which they viewed their dispersal. "Black republicanism," the ex-slaves' settler ideology, centered on the notion of propertied independence underpinned by landholding. But this fundamental tenet was combined with an egalitarian streak, a propensity toward evangelical religion, and a tendency toward cultural separatism. The black Loyalists' relocation disseminated these values into the various regions of the British empire that became their destinations.[54]

If this black exodus had a single starting point, it was probably when Lord Dunmore, James Parker's patron, proclaimed freedom to all "indented servants [and] negroes . . . willing to serve His Majesty's forces to end the present rebellion" in November, 1775.[55] Responding to this call, black fugitives in Virginia, Maryland, and North Carolina joined his Ethiopian Regiment and, following his defeat, fled with him to New York. As the war progressed, army movements and British promises of freedom attracted numerous other African-Americans seeking an escape from slavery. Estimates of the number of black fugitives range up to 100,000. Although this is probably an exaggeration, slaves did flee their owners in the thousands. This constituted the largest black escape from slavery in the history of North America until the Civil War.[56] By participating in the evacuations of Savannah, Charleston, New York, and East Florida, they then became part of the Loyalist influx into Nova Scotia and New Brunswick where they were joined by others, like Jacob Ellegood's slaves, who still remained as bondsmen and women belonging to white Tories and British officers.

While the British seemed to embrace black hopes of freedom during the war, no consistent or explicit policy regarding the status of the fugitives emerged. However, defeat precipitated some crucial decisions. This was particularly true in New York, the last British stronghold in the former thirteen colonies. Here the black Loyalists found a patron in Guy Carleton, the commander-in-chief. Carleton affirmed that fugitives who had arrived behind army lines before November 30, 1782, and who claimed their liberty via the various proclamations, such as Sir Henry Clinton's Philipsburg Declaration of 1779, were free.[57] They were therefore entitled to imperial protection and transportation to Nova Scotia. He also went some way toward meeting several of the black Loyalists' other key demands. Each was to receive a certificate, a legal document, attesting to their refugee status. Also, several army corps were placed on the payroll until their departure, confirming their status as veterans. This was something that the black Loyalists saw as central to their new identity as "Britons." Another important goal—economic independence founded on landholding—was promoted by Carleton's recommendation that they be awarded allocations in Nova Scotia.[58]

Among the over three thousand black Loyalists fleeing New York for Nova Scotia in 1783 was Thomas Peters.[59] His career highlights the problems that black Loyalist refugees confronted as they struggled to fulfil their goals within the empire. Like the more renowned Olaudiah Equiano,[60] Peters provides a vivid illustration of the rise of the black Atlantic. Born into the Yoruba, he moved during his lifetime between five countries and undertook four oceanic voyages. Peters was first seized by African traders and purchased by French slavers who shipped him to Louisiana. He was then sold to an English colonist before being transferred in 1770 to William Campbell, a Scot residing in Wilmington, North Carolina.[61] Peters, like the white exiles, was then caught up in the imperial crisis. This affected him in two ways. First, he probably encountered Revolutionary rhetoric during the early 1770s. Second, under wartime pressures, cracks opened in the institution of slavery. In March 1776, taking advantage of the British presence in the Cape Fear region, Peters escaped with several fellow blacks. The fugitives were organized into the company of Black Pioneers and Peters fought with them for the remainder of the war. He was present at the siege of Charleston and the capture of Philadelphia. In an indication of his leadership, he was promoted to sergeant.[62]

After the war, Peters and his family were evacuated. Following a brief stay in Bermuda, they went to Nova Scotia. Peters first tried to settle in Digby near Annapolis Royal, home to over a thousand Loyalists.[63] The refugees faced some difficult conditions, especially scarce provisions and inadequate accommodation. More seriously there was an inevitable delay in parceling out land to them.

"Discontent and uneasiness have arisen in several of the New Settlements now forming in this Province," Governor John Parr acknowledged in 1784, "because they have not hitherto received Grants for the Lands which have been assigned to them."[64] The black Loyalists' unease was magnified when they learned that they would only receive twenty acres each instead of the one hundred acres they had been promised. To complicate matters, a deputy surveyor mistakenly laid out their lots in restricted school and glebe reserves.[65]

Peters emerged as a leader of the disgruntled black Loyalist community. In August 1784 he and a friend submitted a petition to the governor on behalf of their fellow Digby veterans. Drawing on Sir Henry Clinton's promise that black troops would receive the same allocations of land as "the Rest of the Disbanded Soldiers of His Majesty's Army," they urged that the general's commitment now be met.[66] Following further petitions and delays, a discouraged Peters joined the migration to New Brunswick in search of unallocated tracts. He met with little success there and, still landless, worked as a millwright.[67] By 1790 Peters had concluded that the black Loyalists "would have to look beyond the governor and his surveyors to complete their escape from slavery and to achieve the independence they sought."[68] Supported by over two hundred families, Peters drafted a petition to the secretary of state outlining the landless black Loyalists' grievances and asking for new and better grants.[69]

Despite the risks, Peters carried the petition across the Atlantic. In London, Peters sought connections based primarily on racial identity. He first gravitated toward the city's poor black community, which included a large group of ex-slaves. He then obtained letters of introduction from his former commanding officer in the Black Pioneers. Peters possibly received further assistance from Ottobah Cugoano, a leader in the London black community, who had links with prominent white abolitionists including Granville Sharp. Sharp was already familiar with the plight of the black Loyalists. He gave his support to the petition, organized its presentation to the secretary of state, and introduced Peters to the directors of the Sierra Leone Company.[70]

The Sierra Leone Company had developed out of Sharp's work with poor blacks and aimed at discouraging the slave trade by boosting other forms of commerce. In 1787 it sponsored a coastal settlement, mainly drawn from free London blacks, but the colony's destruction increased the company's need for potential settlers.[71] An obvious source lay in the disgruntled black Loyalists that Peters represented. Peters may have been aware of the Sierra Leone project before his arrival in England. His petition did emphasize that the black Loyalists were "ready and willing to go wherever the Wisdom of Government may think proper to provide for them as free Subjects of the British Empire."[72]

After almost a year in London, Peters returned to Halifax to promote the proposal.[73] The company had persuaded the imperial government to provide free transport for any black Nova Scotians who wanted to resettle. It promised that on their arrival in Africa, they would receive twenty acres per man, ten for each wife, and five for each child. The scheme represented a potentially significant turning point in the black Loyalist diaspora. However, it met with opposition from the provincial authorities and white settlers. Peters was harassed in both Nova Scotia and New Brunswick. At Digby, he was assaulted by a white resident who feared he was luring away cheap black labor. Other whites forged indentures and work contracts or refused to settle back wages in an effort to prevent emigration. But, despite white resistance and obstructionism, black enthusiasm for resettlement grew. Eventually about twelve hundred joined the venture.[74] The settlers were a diverse group with a wide range of prior experiences. Some were ex-Black Pioneers like Charles Wilkinson. Others were religious leaders like David George or Moses Wilkinson. Many, however, came from humbler backgrounds like the eighty-year-old laborer, Richard Herbert. What united them was a desire to find a place where they might enjoy economic and social autonomy.[75]

The migrants reached Africa in March 1792. Sierra Leone, however, proved another disappointment. Provisions quickly ran short and accommodation was inadequate. Compounding these problems, fever raged among the settlers. By September, only about one thousand remained alive. Political grievances then resurfaced. White domination was as pronounced in Sierra Leone as it had been in the Maritimes. Colonial administration was in the hands of John Clarkson, the settlement's superintendent, assisted by an all-white council. While Clarkson had some sympathy for the Nova Scotians, his councilors did not. Their opposition and mutual jealousies helped erode the trust that the superintendent had cultivated among the black migrants.[76] The collection of quit-rents for recently acquired lands, despite earlier promises that they would be deferred for ten years, was the principal flash point. Peters became the disaffected settlers' leader. Complaining of racism and incompetence, he asserted that such practices infuriated those "who had just emerged from Slavery and who were therefore jealous of every action, nay of every look that came from White Men, who were put in authority over them." A number of Nova Scotians even urged Peters to seize power. Clarkson regained control of the situation by calling a meeting of the settlers and asking them to choose between himself and Peters.[77] After being rejected the black Loyalist then suffered a rapid downfall. He was later reprimanded by an all-black jury for taking money from a dead man and died shortly afterwards.[78]

During his lifetime Peters strove for a modicum of personal freedom and security. Residing in locales from French Louisiana to Sierra Leone, he crossed the Atlantic repeatedly. Once free of slavery, Peters and his fellow Loyalists struggled against barriers that limited their prospects in both the Maritimes and Sierra Leone. Arguably Peters and his fellow ex-slaves exerted more influence over government policy and the contours of empire than a more privileged, metropolitan-based Loyalist like Thomas Hutchinson had done. They were instrumental in encouraging the British authorities to acknowledge their obligations to those displaced by the War of Independence regardless of their color. Also, fugitives like Peters helped bind the histories of black peoples in North America, the Caribbean, and Africa together, creating vital channels for the transmission of culture, news, and Revolutionary sentiment across the Atlantic world.

Refounding the British Empire

These case studies together help clarify the meaning of the Loyalist diaspora for those involved and highlight some of its central characteristics. Beyond that, they focus attention on several important features of the late eighteenth-century British Atlantic world. They span the histories of the Revolutionary American republic and the British empire and show how, despite the formal severing of the Anglo-American political connection, these constellations still impinged upon and shaped each other. Indeed, they clearly demonstrate the ways in which the Loyalist diaspora acted as the critical bridge between the two—one reinforced by the determination of some exiles, including members of the Parker and Williams families, to shuttle back and forth between the remaining British colonies and the United States. Political and territorial boundaries were permeable for these transients in a way that some historians have ignored or forgotten—a point also demonstrated by Charles Stewart Parker's involvement in Spanish American trade.

They also underline the force of William H. Nelson's observation that Loyalism was particularly attractive to ethnic, religious, and racial minorities, poised as they were between the relative tolerance and paternalism of the

British authorities and the potentially aggressive, fragile national ethos of the fledgling republic.[79] The émigré population that resulted was a diverse assemblage of peoples and this was reflected in the areas they settled. One Anglican clergyman, for example, aptly characterized his neighbors in the Annapolis Valley, Nova Scotia as "a collection of all nations, kindreds, complexions and tongues assembled from every quarter of the globe and till lately equally strangers to me and to each other."[80] This heterogeneity, in turn, forced upon the metropolitan authorities an appreciation that the empire they administered could no longer be seen principally as an extension of the metropolis, or even a displaced version of the pre-war American colonies. Instead, it had to be viewed as a new multiethnic and multinational polity.

With Hutchinson as the exception, these stories also prove that it is inappropriate to see these various Loyalist minorities simply as victims. Despite the obstacles confronting them, they became active agents in the late eighteenth-century reconfiguration of the British empire. The types of community they established may have varied depending on the size of the population flow involved, the migrants' composition (in terms of regional origins, socioeconomic background, ethnicity, race, and gender), and the density and mentality of the receiving population. In some areas like Upper Canada and the Bahamas, Loyalists arguably became the dominant element. In others, notably Nova Scotia, Grenada, Jamaica, and Sierra Leone, they constituted enclaves amidst an established settler or indigenous population. Finally, in provincial Britain, Loyalists dispersed and were eventually absorbed into the wider society. Overall, however, Loyalist settlers extended the empire's geographical boundaries as they pushed into frontier regions or filled other sparsely occupied areas.

Through their various activities, they also assisted in establishing or reinforcing the ties that bound the empire together. The American Revolution, then, did not mark the end of a British-Atlantic world, but merely its reorientation. As J. G. A. Pocock has recently reminded us, the creation of the American Republic was not the Revolution's only outcome. "Caribbean and Canadian histories," he points out, "claim a parity of esteem, derived from the sheer facts of their existence and their complicated continuity, and they still figure in a British history conceived as a history of empire in more than one sense of the term."[81] Finally, although the imperial government played a crucial role in organizing and sponsoring their migration, the subsequent Loyalist experience reveals a world that still lay largely outside metropolitan direction. It highlights the importance of the multiple relationships developing between the inhabitants of Britain's many and varied provinces and colonies—relationships that the émigrés themselves helped to forge. Studying these exiles thus provides an unexpected opportunity to venture beyond the underlying assumptions of core-periphery analysis to develop new perspectives on the British empire's imperatives.[82]

CHAPTER THIRTEEN

Early Slave Narratives and the Culture of the Atlantic Market

James Sidbury

Markets and the cultures of markets played complicated and unreliable roles in the lives of black people victimized by the Atlantic slave trade. On the most obvious level, enslaved blacks were ripped out of the societies (and thus cultures) into which they were born because they were literally commodified by the markets and market cultures of Europe and the Americas. As objects of European markets, slaves sold into the Americas suffered the brutal consequences of those markets' success at governing human action according to questions of profit and loss. These destructive influences of the market continued to affect black people once they arrived in the Americas, where they and their children continued to be bought and sold, and where laws were passed legalizing the killing of slaves by their masters, laws which explicitly rested on the assumption that slaves were property with market value rather than legally recognized persons. Slaves, and black people fortunate to have escaped from slavery in the Americas, had every reason to develop hostile reactions to the Atlantic market and to the cultures that grew under the umbrella of that market.

In some ways they did. The texts produced by the first generations of black anglophone writers are replete with condemnations of the inhumanity of

Europeans responding to market incentives. Olaudah Equiano, the author of *The Interesting Narrative of the Life of Olaudah Equiano or Gustavus Vassa the African* and the most accomplished of the first generation of slave narrators, expressed this sentiment forcefully after noting that whites divided siblings and friends unnecessarily in West Indian slave marts: "O, ye nominal Christians! . . . Is it not enough that we are torn from our country and friends to toil for your luxury and lust of gain? Must every tender feeling be likewise sacrificed to your avarice?"[1] Not surprisingly, other black authors joined Equiano in decrying the ways that the market distorted humane impulses and degraded the black people who became its objects.

Less predictably, these negative feelings toward the market and market relations, while present in many of these texts, almost never constitute the whole story. Several authors, most notably Equiano and the American author Venture Smith, included passages in their autobiographical narratives in which they described their petty mercantile activities in terms reminiscent of Benjamin Franklin's autobiography. In some ways Equiano's path toward freedom began when, while an enslaved sailor traveling among the islands of the Caribbean, he "endeavoured to try . . . [his] luck and commence merchant" (*IN*, 116). Beginning with a "single half bit," he reported having doubled his money by buying a glass tumbler in St. Eustatia and selling it in Montserrat. Having found success in trading glasses, he reported branching out into the gin trade, by buying a "jug of Geneva" on a later trip back to St. Eustatia and selling it upon his return to Montserrat. At the end of that series of exchanges he claimed that his "capital . . . amounted in all to a dollar" (*IN*, 116). He continued to reinvest his profits in petty trade, finally earning enough money to buy himself from his Quaker master and—also a consumer—to invest in "a suit of superfine cloathes to dance in at my freedom" (*IN*, 134). As a free man Equiano remained for some time a sailor in the Caribbean traveling from port to port accumulating a small sufficiency through petty mercantile activity.[2] The very market that had once enslaved Equiano had become a source first of freedom and then of prosperity.

Equiano did, in fact, achieve real prosperity. When he died he left his daughter an estate of close to £1,000.[3] But that prosperity did not come directly from his career as a petty "merchant," nor did it come from his labor as sailor, overseer or personal servant. It came instead when he engaged in a different market, the market in books. By writing and publishing the narrative of his life, he, like the other black authors discussed in this chapter, participated in the marketplace of ideas that had developed in eighteenth-century western Europe. As members of the first generation of people of African descent to play active roles in the production and exchange of ideas in "enlightened" Europe, these men had to negotiate barriers created by the emergence of racial thought in Britain, Germany, France and, after 1776, the United States.[4] The path that Equiano, especially, had to follow to win a hearing for his antislavery ideas and to sell his book created precedents that other black writers could and would use to influence public opinion and to earn money as authors. But if the narrators' more obvious involvement with the market entailed a set of ironies rooted in their transformation from objects of the slave trade to petty entrepreneurs seeking to escape slavery, a different set of ironies came into play when formerly enslaved people sought to sell their lives—now as narratives—on a different market.

Market and Nation

In what terms, then, did these early victims of Atlantic slavery discuss the capitalist markets of the Atlantic economy and the cultures that they spawned? How should we understand the apparently coexisting pictures they painted of the brutality of market relations juxtaposed against the liberatory possibility of empowerment through engagement with those very markets? Several of these early black writers offered a coded key to this question by portraying an imagined projected history of transformed market relations in Africa. I have argued elsewhere that one project in these early black texts was the elaboration of a shared history through which black people in Africa, Europe, and the Americas could overcome the cultural diversity of sub-Saharan Africa and understand themselves to be "Africans." Like any coherent historical vision, this interpretation rested on an attempt both to structure stories of the past and to project them into the future; in this case, Equiano and his friend and collaborator Quobna Ottobah Cugoano sought to project a future that would give shape to the narrative trajectory of the African people they were calling into existence. Christianity and the Bible most forcefully shaped that narrative, and the peoples of sub-Saharan Africa would have to move from paganism to Christ in order to become "Africans" worthy of inclusion in the modern world.[5] But like other eighteenth-century Protestants these authors connected civilization to Christianity, and markets—good markets, at any rate—simultaneously served as civilizing forces and as signs of civilization.[6] In the contrast between the brutal and illegitimate ways in which black victims of the slave trade were swept into the barbaric market in humans, and the transformed market relations that several early authors sought to bring to the coast of Africa, a history of commercial development was projected onto Africa. Within that history the market, allied with Christianity, was a universal and universalizing force that would create a just world in which "Africans" would emerge as a unified people.

An initial step in projecting this history of commercial development onto Africa involved stories of the African slave trade. In such stories early anglophone blacks confronted in the starkest terms the barriers they faced as they sought to forge an "African" identity, for several of these authors had been born on the continent of Africa and enslaved by people Europeans called "Africans." The moment of enslavement, then, stands on several levels as the baseline from which the projection of an African people into history begins. It was one of *the* key moments in the personal histories of those—like Equiano, Cugoano, James Albert Ukawsaw Gronniosaw, and Venture Smith—who experienced it, and each was aware that his path toward the authorial presence embodied in his narrative began with enslavement.[7] In addition, and more importantly for my current purposes, the moment of enslavement stands in their texts as the epitome of the unjust and illegitimate market that had to be eradicated if Africa was to be properly transformed.[8] And finally, the experience of having been sold would serve as the base from which Equiano especially would enter the literary marketplace to re-sell his life, this time as text.

None of this is to say that these authors portrayed their native societies as characterized by illegitimate market cultures. Instead each described his enslavement in ways that showed the local traditional market relations of his village to have been perverted or infringed upon in some way by trade with Europe and the Americas. Equiano, for example, described the traditional markets that he had once frequented with his mother, and described the legitimate trade in enslaved people that took place there: the "strictest account" was taken, he said, of the "manner of procuring" slaves, and only those who were "prisoners of war, or . . . had been convicted of kidnapping, or adultery" or other heinous crimes were "suffered to pass" (*IN*, 37). The people of his native village Essaka did, in fact, enslave prisoners of war, but Equiano insisted that slavery in Essaka differed fundamentally from American slavery: "with us they do no more work than other members of the community," their material lives resembled those of free people, and they could own property (*IN*, 40).[9] Most other authors passed on describing traditional slavery in Africa, but several described their own enslavement and experiences as slaves in Africa in ways that complicate Equiano's idyllic vision.

Equiano, Gronniosaw, Cugoano, and Smith all portrayed themselves as having been illegitimately enslaved. Equiano and Cugoano, author of *Thoughts and Sentiments on the Evil and Wicked Traffic of the Slavery and Commerce of the Human Species,* both reported having been kidnapped by marauding bandits; Gronniosaw joined a merchant traveling to the coast in hopes of seeing more of the world, only to find himself transformed into a commodity and sold into the Atlantic world; and Smith and his village fell victim to a "numerous army . . . instigated by some white nation" that attacked his people, killed and tortured his father, and took Smith himself "and the women prisoners."[10] If some of the authors described some time spent in traditional African familial slavery—Equiano, for example, described being sold to a goldsmith who had "two wives and some children, and they all used me extremely well" (*IN,* 48)—all reported being brutally transported from their homes to the coast in response to market forces pulling them into the Atlantic world. Whether victims of brutal armies, unscrupulous merchants, or evil bandits, each of these men portrayed an Africa in which the forces of international commerce had transformed men into monsters who cheated and stole without concern for right or wrong in their efforts to feed European and American demand.

For Equiano and Cugoano, both of whom were engaged in a project of calling into existence an "African" people, the color of their enslavers raised important questions about the way European commerce combined with the cultural diversity of sub-Saharan Africa to hinder the rise of an "African" nation.[11] Equiano provided no physical description of his kidnappers, but he did note that he passed through "different nations" while being transported from Essaka to the slave-trading baracoon on the coast, and he referred to the slave-traders responsible for his journey as "those sable destroyers of human rights" (*IN,* 51). Cugoano demonstrated how much he thought was at stake in this question by approaching it indirectly. He first asserted that it "matter[ed] not" whether his kidnappers were black or white (*TS,* 12), but it obviously did matter to him, because he later acknowledged that "to the shame of my own countrymen . . . I was first kid-napped and betrayed by some of my own complexion" (*TS,* 16).[12] Both men pointed out the role that European demand played in transforming Africa's slave trade, but they used the role of African residents in the trade to highlight the problems of an

Africa perverted by contact with Europe but untransformed by the universalizing principles of Christianity and legitimate commerce.

Through their experiences within the Atlantic world economy these authors learned of the supposedly beneficial effects of markets, though ironically the lessons of market beneficence were often taught most convincingly by white failures to respect the market's rules. Equiano again provided the most subtle and engaging picture of this process when he described his career as a petty merchant seeking to scratch out enough of a stake to purchase his freedom. On several occasions he paid a price for believing the market's conceit that each buyer or seller entered into exchanges as an equal whose personal qualities—race, wealth, religion—were rendered irrelevant by universal market forces. During the four years that he spent as a slave trader in the Caribbean, he "experienced many instances of ill usage, and . . . saw many injuries done to other negroes" in their "dealings with whites." On one island all of the trade goods of Equiano and a friend were taken by white ruffians. When Equiano and his friend complained, their antagonists threatened to flog them, and complaints to local authorities only brought a "volley of imprecations" and another threatened flogging (*IN*, 117–18). Venture Smith had an analogous experience when, while still enslaved, he "hired out a sum of money to" a white man, only to have his creditor's brother break "open my chest containing" the note and destroy it.[13] In these and countless other cases, the authors accepted the rules of the market that had turned them into commodities and behaved in the way that the market dictated.[14] Their black skins, however, made them vulnerable to unscrupulous whites in Europe and the Americas, and they were denied the rewards that they had earned.

Despite these setbacks the authors of these early texts did succeed at using the market to gain their freedom. Through this process they reversed the earlier action of the market, purchasing themselves as commodities—as objects—on the market and transforming themselves into owners of commodities or subjects. Such a transformation could not be worked through the unfettered mechanism of the market; the laws that created the framework in which British Atlantic commerce proceeded did not recognize slaves' right to own property, so British law did not recognize the right of enslaved people to use money to purchase themselves.[15] Instead, slaves living in British polities or in the United States relied on their masters to grant them the privilege of owning property and the privilege of self-purchase. This requirement loomed over their attempts to win freedom. Even though Robert King had promised to sell

Equiano his freedom when the slave acquired enough money to pay a previously agreed purchase price, Equiano remained anxious lest King revoke the promise. And Equiano claimed that King would, indeed, have been so inclined had he not been convinced to honor his word by the ship captain under whom Equiano had been serving. The market, then, provided a path along which the enslaved could pursue freedom, but so long as racism and the law of slavery distorted the universal formal equality that was, in theory, the essence of market culture, the path remained unsure.

On its simplest level, removing the barriers that hindered blacks from traveling that path freely meant abolishing slavery and the slave trade, and Equiano and Cugoano, both as authors and as political activists, sought to convince the British to take this step. But as Equiano's narrative made clear, many of the hindrances that blocked black progress resulted from racial prejudice as much as from slavery. Thus he continued to be physically threatened and economically cheated after he purchased his freedom, as did Gronniosaw and many other more anonymous free people of color in Britain and the Americas. So long as Africa remained outside of the West's concept of history, so long as Africans remained a *nonpeople,* such oppression would continue and the beneficial effects of the market would flow unreliably if at all to black people. Denied entry into the culture of the market, blacks would remain outsiders to the Atlantic market, subject at worst to being commodified as objects and at best to struggling on the market's margins.

Cugoano and Equiano suggested that overcoming these obstacles required the complete social and religious transformation of Africa's residents and of the peoples of its diaspora. Christianity was the key to this transformation, and virtually all of the early slave narrators hoped to encourage missionaries to spread the "Truth" of Christianity among the black peoples of Africa and the Americas. Such missionary activity would also require that Europeans recognize the ways that slavery and the slave trade violated the spirit of Christianity and thus that they begin to live up to the universalist promise of Christ's offer of salvation. While twenty-first-century readers might be troubled by the way in which such a project encouraged the elimination of "traditional" West African spiritual traditions, few probably find these authors' advocacy of such a program surprising.

The future social transformation envisioned by two of these authors is more startling.[16] Equiano and Cugoano developed an interpretation of the history of "African" people that inserted them into Western history. Christianity offered the shared past that they needed, allowing the authors to see the diversity of sub-Saharan Africa as rooted in an ancient diaspora that could be explained, ultimately, by reference to the Old Testament.[17] And the Bible also foretold one of the projected futures that history requires, a future in which Africans would come together as a Christian people of a modern diaspora. But these authors also turned to the market and its capacity to transform society in order to project a *secular* future for "Africans" in the world of Western nation-states.

In and of itself, melding secular and sacred visions of national identity was neither unusual nor original. England and then Britain had nurtured long-established traditions in which "freeborn Englishmen" saw themselves as an "Elect Nation."[18] And historians have spilled vast amounts of ink arguing about the interpenetration of market relations and religious belief as, to use Richard Bushman's classic formulation, Puritan New Englanders' children became Yankees.[19] But if many groups in the eighteenth-century English-speaking world saw themselves embedded in both biblical archetypal narratives and seemingly secular processes of social progress, each idiosyncratic combination of these idioms reveals much about those who created the mix. Such is the case for the historical vision that emerged among early black writers.

Equiano offered only an abbreviated version of this history. Having called for support of missionary efforts in Africa and of the British colony at Sierra Leone, he turned to the need to integrate the peoples of West Africa as equals into the West's empire of commerce. This would involve the elimination of the "inhuman traffic of slavery," and its replacement by "a system of commerce . . . in Africa" (*IN*, 233). Thus in a single sentence Equiano denied that the inhuman trade in people belonged in a legitimate commercial system, while appealing to Britons' greed ("the demand for manufactures would most rapidly augment") and sense of secular civilizing mission ("the native inhabitants would insensibly adopt the British fashions, manners, customs, &c."). Promising that merchants and manufacturers could do well by doing good, he assured them that a "commercial intercourse with Africa" would open "an inexhaustible source of wealth to the manufacturing interests of Great Britain" (*IN*, 234). Abolition of the slave trade and the integration of Africa into England's commercial empire offered an "immense, glorious, and happy prospect—the clothing, &c. of a continent ten thousand miles in circumference, and immensely rich in productions of every denomination in return for manufactures" (*IN*, 235). Intent on winning the political support of British merchants and manufacturers, he did little to specify the way Africa and Africans would be transformed by this market revolution.

Cugoano was more explicit than Equiano, offering a vision of the transformation of Africa that appears to have drawn explicitly on Great Britain's settler societies in the Americas. He shared with Equiano the belief that the first step was to stop Europe's illegitimate exploitation of Africa, and he argued that this could only happen if the slave traders' misrepresentations of the "character of the inhabitants on the west coast of Africa" were countered and the slave trade was abolished (*TS*, 172). If "noble Britons" were to accomplish this change and begin to deal with West Africans "in a friendly manner," then the progress of learning and commerce would transform the coast. "As the Africans became refined and established in light and knowledge, they would imitate their noble British friends, to improve their lands, and make use of that industry as the nature of their country might require," bringing far more wealth to England than could slavery. Africa, then, "would become a kind of first ornament to Great-Britain" (*TS*, 172–73). Enlightened through Christianity and secular learning, civilized through commerce and industry, Africa and Africans would rise as fully equal participants in the West's narrative of universal history.

Doing so entailed both accepting the culture of the Atlantic world market and being accepted into it. Olaudah Equiano and Ottobah Cugoano supported missionary programs that they believed would bring the residents of West Africa willingly to the culture of the market. Such a transformation for Africa was worthwhile not only because it would end the iniquitous traffic in human beings but because Equiano and Cugoano both implicitly accepted Enlightenment historical ethnography, which understood human societies to pass through set stages of progress, and both believed African societies existed at more primitive stages of development than those that prevailed in Europe and the Americas.[20] Both men also believed, however, that European exploitation of Africa violated the rules of the market and the bounds marking off the civilized from the barbaric. Integrating Africa into the market would, at once, raise Africa out of primitivism, help create Africans as a people, and further the progress and civilization of Great Britain specifically and of mankind more generally. Just as the masters of several of these authors had, by granting them the privilege of self purchase, permitted them to transform themselves from object to subject, so Britain, by fostering the commercial development of Africa, would permit the peoples of Africa and the diaspora—"Africans"—to transform themselves into a nation. This new people would then be able to take its proper place on the stage of world history.

The analogy between individual manumission and the liberation and creation of a people, however, cut in more than one direction. Equiano and Cugoano, the two authors who explicitly participated in this discourse, could be understood to be asking for British charity toward Africa and Africans, but that is a simplification. While Equiano expressed gratitude toward Robert King, the master who manumitted him, he made it clear that freedom came from something more fundamental than King's benevolence. Equiano had sought commercial success in order to be ready to exploit the chance for freedom when God presented it, but he explained passing up an earlier chance to run to freedom by insisting that if God wanted him to become free, He would offer a legal and legitimate path to freedom. Thus, King offered Equiano his freedom not only out of benevolence but because it was part of God's plan.

Equiano and Cugoano were equally certain that the rise of an African people was a part of God's plan, and thus their request for British aid implied a cost should the British fail to live up to their obligations. Commercial development was, after all, a universal law only because God made it so, and should those in power on Earth fail to follow divine prescription, then there would be a price to pay. Equiano, clearly the voice of conciliation in the collaborative project of the two men, left the threat of vengeance wholly implicit in his narrative, but his friend Cugoano was explicit. Should the British block the divinely mandated march of progress on Earth—should, in other words, Europeans turn their backs on God's benevolent plans for "Africans" and the rest of mankind— then a just God would punish the wicked offenders: "The voice of our complaint implies a vengeance, because of the great iniquity that you have done, and because of the cruel injustice done unto us Africans, . . . and if it is not hearkened unto, it may yet arise with a louder voice, as the rolling thunder, and it may encrease in the force of its volubility, not only to shake the leaves of the most stout in heart, but to rend the mountains before them, and to cleave in pieces the rocks under them" (*TS,* 111). Africans would be brought into existence as a people, either in man's time through their incorporation into the culture of the market, or in God's time when true justice would be brought to the world.

Selling Lives

There are two further ways that early slave narrators, especially Equiano and Cugoano, involved themselves in markets. First, by writing self-consciously persuasive texts, they entered into the then-emerging marketplace of ideas that has come to be labeled, following Jürgen Habermas, the "public sphere." On some level this appeal to a marketplace of ideas inheres in all authors' entry into print in the age of the Enlightenment and thus in all of the narrators. Equiano and Cugoano much more than the others, however, explicitly set forth arguments that they hoped their readers would find persuasive and to which they hoped their readers would respond by advocating antislavery. In other words, they sought to convince those who consumed their texts in private to take public stands on public issues. Equiano did this with greater tact than Cugoano, but only a willfully perverse reader could finish either man's book without recognizing its antislavery appeal.

Habermas notes that the growth of long-distance trade in luxury goods helped to create the public market for news, novels, and ideas more generally.[21] The Atlantic slave trade emerged in response to that same luxury trade, which creates yet another of the seemingly endless ironies that surround these slave narratives. Not only did the same market that enslaved these authors when they were children in Africa permit them as adults to buy their freedom in the Atlantic world, it also created the bourgeois public sphere into which they entered in their attempt to bring the iniquitous trade in people—a "luxury" they believed humanity could no longer afford—to an end.

The irony turns on itself one more time. A working marketplace in ideas, just like a working market in other commodities, rests upon the presumption that it is the quality of the idea—the commodity—rather than the identity of the seller that determines value. This was, as noted earlier, often a rule honored in the breech in the commercial world of the Atlantic market, especially when black sellers sought to collect payment from their white customers. Equiano, Venture Smith, and Gronniowsaw all recorded incidents in which whites violated the supposed anonymity of market relations with impunity, incidents that complicated these men's efforts to move from slavery to freedom. As they moved into the marketplace of ideas, however, they themselves sought as authors to subvert the conceit of depersonalization so central to theories of the market.

This was more than a theoretical question. The basic rules governing the unimportance of a seller's identity pertained when ideas rather than goods were offered for sale, and eighteenth-century political writers often paid allegiance to those rules by writing under pseudonyms that laid claim to virtuous qualities. The evidence of this virtue was, of course, the text itself. The pseudonym announced the context in which the author hoped to be read, but anonymity guaranteed that the reader would evaluate the ideas without reference to the writer. The most famous example in U.S. history is the decision of James Madison, Alexander Hamilton, and John Jay to publish all of the *Federalist* essays under the single signature of "Publius," but theirs was a completely conventional decision.[22] Whether or not one wrote under a pseudonym, the existence of a public sphere was to ensure that ideas received a fair hearing (and nothing more than a fair hearing), regardless of who proposed them.[23]

The use of pen names was not so ubiquitous as to have become expected, so there is nothing surprising in the fact that early slave narrators signed their texts. However, early black writers went well beyond placing their names on title pages. Not only were the narratives signed—in Equiano's case with an additional "Written by himself"—but on the title pages of their books the authors asserted authority through claims to specific historical pasts rather than through the "quality" of their ideas: Equiano was "Gustavus Vassa, the African," Cugoano and Venture Smith each signed as "A Native of AFRICA," and James Albert Ukawsaw Gronniosaw was "AN AFRICAN PRINCE."[24] Similarly, black authored books often included an engraving of the author on the frontispiece as a visual sign of blackness.[25] This was in part because the very fact that "Africans" wrote these texts served as a key part of the argument by putting the lie to claims that blacks were too "savage" or "uncivilized" to write books. And while one can imagine pseudonymous claims to African identity (say, "Africanus"),[26] such pen names would almost certainly have elicited denials of black authorship, given the frequency with which some whites questioned the "authenticity" of signed texts. Regardless, though, of the choices these narrators could have made, the choices that they did make initiated what became a convention of the genre by trumpeting their authorship and identity as both selling point and substance of the text.

Such claims to authority through heritage and experience altered the place of these texts within the public realm. Rather than disembodied opinions entering the marketplace of ideas where they would find their proper place, these were ideas whose meanings and persuasive power inhered in the bodies that offered them. And because so much meaning was attached to the fact that black bodies could produce such texts, the texts became emblems of the possibilities of "Africans." It is hardly surprising that the personal narrative or autobiographical account became the dominant genre through which black people could enter into the marketplace of ideas: while the interest or importance of Equiano's offering of *The Interesting Narrative* of his own life was not self-evident in the eighteenth-century world, it was a much smaller stretch for white readers to accept his authority in that realm than to accept the value of Cugoano's *Thoughts and Sentiments*. No one had, after all, ever questioned that blacks had lives, even potentially interesting lives, but to assert that they had thoughts or sentiments worthy of publication was something else again. And this leads to a final and remarkably persistent problem about the way in which early black authors engaged with the market.

What did it mean that former slaves began selling their "lives" to book buyers throughout Britain? On the one hand, given the contradiction in a notion of anonymous autobiography, selling the self practically inheres in the genre and has since the emergence of the modern notion of the author and the copyright over the course of the seventeenth and eighteenth centuries.[27] But if every author who sold his or her "life" engaged in a complicated process of objectification by turning that life and its experiences into a commodity to be sold, the implications of that process were not the same for everyone. This is true on the most obvious level simply because the selling of the self must have meant something quite different for people who had, in fact, been sold, than it did for politicians, preachers, lay converts, or fiction writers. It may have been concern over this dynamic that made Cugoano so hesitant to include an autobiographical narrative within his *Thoughts and Sentiments*—he adds a bit about his life story in a short passage added to the beginning of the text upon the request of "some friends" who thought such details might cause his ideas to be "more effectually taken into consideration."[28] He surely recognized the implicit racism in the belief that his experiences, more than the power of his ideas, would render his *Thoughts and Sentiments* worthy of consideration.

Authors of autobiographical texts faced a different version of this problem. The very form of their books laid claim to authority through experience, and the conventions of autobiographical writing subordinated formal argument to narrative and thus implicitly rooted persuasion in an appeal to personal experience. Slave narrators offered readers "the slave's" experience in a firsthand account, and the immediacy of the account created the authority that made such narratives a staple of abolitionism. Not surprisingly, one effective way to assert this claim was to travel and lecture—to present to the buying public the very black body that authorized the written text.

Equiano pioneered a process that would become standard for slave narrators during the nineteenth century. He began by taking unusual control of the production of his book. Publication of the first edition of the *Interesting Narrative* was subsidized by an extensive subscription list of patrons who committed to buying the book before it appeared. Upon publication Equiano registered his copyright to the story, laying legal claim to his own written life. When still a slave, Equiano had learned how to win powerful patrons, and his initial marketing plan relied on some of those skills. Once the first edition was published he continued to solicit new subscriptions, but he supplemented his old plan by traveling throughout the British Isles to promote his book and the abolitionist cause that it espoused. By the standards of the market—by almost any standards—he achieved great success. He sold enough books to run through nine editions during his lifetime, and he secured for himself and his family a solidly middle class economic existence. His newfound wealth and respectability probably played a role in his ability to marry and start a family.[29] It was certainly what allowed him to leave that family on comfortable material footing when he died.

There is no record that Equiano ever stopped to examine the way in which his greatest triumphs over slavery—his emergence as an important anti-slavery activist and his resulting ascendance to prosperity—came from his dedicated and industrious efforts to commodify and market his life. It would have been remarkable had he done so, since the path he chose allowed him to accomplish so much both personally and politically. And there is, of course, an enormous difference between being made a commodity and sold into slavery, and choosing to make one's life story a commodity and selling it as a book. But that very real difference does not erase the equally real resemblance, a resemblance whose importance is reinforced if one remembers the way that Equiano and the other early narrators relied upon their "authenticity"—their blackness and their African births—to authorize their texts.

Neither Equiano nor other narrators chose trading upon their black bodies instead of fighting within an ideal public sphere for recognition of their ideas. As Habermas takes pains to point out, it was a bourgeois public sphere; one could only gain access to the marketplace of ideas if one's ideas could be packaged in salable form.[30] Educational disadvantages combined with hardening Western assumptions about black intellectual ability to raise much higher barriers to the sorts of formal expository argument offered by Cugoano than to the "moving" and "authentic" life story. Given the success with which writers as gifted as Equiano could convey social criticism and political ideas through autobiography, there is little wonder that they chose to do so. It was the literary form through which black intellectuals could most effectively participate in and influence an unsympathetic dominant culture.

Considering the enormous richness and vitality of the literary traditions that have emerged from the slave narrative, the celebratory tone of most scholarship on narratives is entirely appropriate. But there are implications less worthy of celebration in the centrality of the trope of authenticity to "black" expression in the eighteenth and nineteenth centuries. The need to assert the authors' "African" or black identity on the title pages of these early texts, the need to prove that the text emanated somehow from an authentic black body, and the way in which, following Equiano, that was proved by displaying those black speaking bodies on lecture tours, all of this served to delineate issues about which blacks could legitimately speak (or write).

But in doing that, it also set firm boundaries on those things about which blacks could legitimately speak or write, limits that retain remarkable power in the twenty-first century. A black body and personal experience with slavery could authorize Equiano—or, later, Frederick Douglass, or William Wells Brown—to speak about racial issues and abolition, but it opened up that space without recognizing the validity of his or their opinions outside of that realm.[31] Olaudah Equiano and other slave narrators appealed through autobiography to authentic experience in order to authorize their advocacy of abolition. This allowed them to sidestep, but not overcome, the racially restricted public sphere that emerged when Europeans (and Euro-Americans) projected a "universal" trajectory of world history that ignored or excluded people of color. Numerous historians and critics have justly honored the way in which slave narrators wrote themselves into Western history and into humanity. To recognize the way in which the market forced them to sell themselves and their ideas as peculiarly "black," and thus the way in which it segregated their ideas and limited the legitimate scope of those ideas, underscores the very high barriers that they faced. It also helps to explain why the victories they won by clearing those barriers have remained so incomplete.

CHAPTER FOURTEEN

The British Caribbean in the Age of Revolution

Edward L. Cox

Historians have generally defined the "Age of Revolution" as spanning the period from roughly 1760 to about 1830.[1] During those years, hardly any institution was safe from the onslaught of radical ideas permeating the Western world. In North America, by successfully asserting their independence, thirteen colonies replaced British control and monarchical control with a republican system. In France, a republican government also emerged in place of the monarchy. The watchwords of the French Revolution, "Liberty, Fraternity, and Equality," carried in their wake powerful concepts that challenged principles on which society had long rested. On the French colony of St. Domingue, *petit blancs* (lesser whites) intensified their campaign for political representation. Free coloreds seized the watchwords of the revolutionary ideology and demanded equal rights with whites. Slaves capitalized on divisions within the free population to launch a successful revolt in 1791 that resulted in the establishment of the black republic of Haiti in 1804.[2]

The Haitian Revolution posed direct threats to the existing social order in the Greater Caribbean. Of all the British Caribbean colonies, Jamaica was the closest to St. Domingue and the one therefore most open to the effects of the revolution. Other British Caribbean islands, particularly those with a history of French presence, were obvious targets for revolutionary ideology. As fighting escalated on St. Domingue and as the leftward drift of the French Revolution became evident by 1793, a growing number of French revolutionaries arrived in the Caribbean. Their mission was to ensure that the white planters on St. Domingue carry out the decisions of the French National Assembly promoting rights of petit blancs and free people of color. Members of the French National Assembly were fearful that British victories in the European wars would severely threaten the revolution's gains both in France and in the West Indies. Under the leadership of Victor Hugues, the revolutionaries were instructed to create dissent among the nonwhite population on the British islands. This diversionary tactic would severely limit Britain's ability to devote undivided attention to the European theater.[3]

While scholars have long recognized the direct nexus between the French and Haitian revolutions, only recently have they ventured beyond the narrow nationalistic confines to explore the impact of these revolutions on British and Spanish Caribbean colonies, particularly those with a sizable population of French extraction.[4] The present study aims at partly rectifying this imbalance. Through an examination of the social and political situation in fin de siècle British Caribbean, it seeks to cast light on British Caribbean societies when local administrators sought to maintain tranquility and political stability amid stirrings for equality during a period that has been described as "a turbulent time."[5]

Revolutionary Contagion

By the end of the eighteenth century, the British Caribbean colonies constituted mature slave societies that had already experienced the "golden age" of sugar cultivation.[6] The emergence of a sugar monoculture meant that the islands had become increasingly dependent on slave imports for plantation agriculture. A small and dwindling white population maintained control over the islands' major sociopolitical institutions and controlled the growing number of slaves who worked on the sugar plantations. The third major population group consisted of free people of color who, though free, occupied a societal position lower than whites.

White planter elites in the British Caribbean controlled the colonies' major sociopolitical institutions. Drawing on British political traditions, they exercised power through elected assemblies that had generally accompanied the first settlers. They were responsible for passing laws and for generally providing for the maintenance and upkeep of government. Staunchly committed to recreating in the Caribbean societies they left behind in Europe, their behavior, dress, and diet were ill-suited to the tropics. A governor and appointed Council shared power unequally with the Assembly. While ideally both houses should work to promote the well being and prosperity of the colonies, occasionally friction arose because of the Assembly's jealous guarding of the power of the purse. In this regard, their actions closely resembled those of their North American cousins whose power by mid-eighteenth-century British authorities belatedly sought to curtail.

Like their North American relatives, British Caribbean planters took seriously their responsibility for governing and controlling the colonies. Their prime concern by 1700 was to provide an adequate framework and structure for the control of slaves and to maintain their hegemony on the islands. They invariably expressed considerable anxiety at the prospect of slaves from other islands—particularly those under foreign control—stimulating insurrection locally. There were, however, a number of highly publicized instances when slave rebellions occurred without any external stimulants. When, therefore, a massive slave insurrection started on the French colony of St. Domingue in 1791, British Caribbean colonists quivered at the prospect of its spread to their borders.

Revolutionary rumblings among St. Domingue's servile and free colored population at the end of the eighteenth century sent shock waves throughout the Caribbean world. Free coloreds and blacks recognized the importance of the "Haitian" influence even before the French colony of St. Domingue had officially become the independent republic of Haiti in 1804.[7] While newspapers and private letters might have been the major source of information for whites and some free people of color, black seamen orally transported to various Caribbean colonies news of events unfolding in St. Domingue from 1791 onward.[8] These accounts undoubtedly fostered a "spirit of insubordination" among slaves and free coloreds throughout the British colonies. According to Robert Renny, even before Toussaint L'Ouverture had become governor of St. Domingue in 1800, Jamaican slaves sang of the activities and triumphs of the Haitian revolutionaries with the words, "One, two, tree, all de same; Black, white, brown, all de same."[9]

Jamaica felt the impact of the revolutionary activities almost immediately and perhaps most profoundly with the outbreak of the Second Maroon War of 1796. The slightly less than one thousand Maroons then on the island had enjoyed a semi-autonomous state since 1739. Obviously aware of civil and military conflicts on St. Domingue, they seized the opportunity to secure their freedom and expel the British from the island. British policymakers were unwilling to take any chances. They therefore initiated a massive build-up of forces on the island to suppress Maroon activities and to guard against the outbreak of servile insurrection and the possible spread of revolutionary ideology. With the aid of hunting dogs from the Spanish on Santo Domingo, authorities eventually outnumbered, outmaneuvered, and tricked the Maroons, who were finally overcome in 1796. Committed to ridding the island once and for all of what they perceived to be a menace to British settlement, the authorities sent the remaining Maroons to Nova Scotia from where they were to be shipped to Sierra Leone.[10]

Upwards of five thousand Caribs inhabited the northern part of St. Vincent.[11] Their presence had antedated British seizure of the island from the French in 1763. When the French briefly occupied St. Vincent between 1779 and 1783 as the American Revolution escalated into a major European maritime conflict, the Caribs openly welcomed them. Such action caused the British, after regaining possession of the island in 1784, to question the Caribs' loyalty to the British Crown. The presence on St. Vincent of so many potentially "hostile" Caribs meant that overall whites were numerically disadvantaged. Moreover, the free population on St. Vincent and other Windward Islands consisted of an indeterminable number of persons with French connections and sympathies on whom British authorities felt they could not depend in the event of a war with France.

Some islands, especially the Leeward Islands and Barbados, were wrongly considered to be immune from revolutionary disturbances. The reasoning was that the white and free colored inhabitants, who had imbibed the best of British cultural traditions and assumptions, were unlikely to find the revolutionary ideology appealing. Authorities believed that the slaves would have been similarly disposed. In 1791, for example, a British naval commander had noted that the fully cultivated islands of Barbados, Antigua, and St. Kitts were relatively safe and unlikely to experience any ill effects of the Haitian and French revolutions. The reason for this, he argued, was the presence on the first two islands of a fairly large and stable white population that had fully internalized the British monarchical principles and forms of government. Antigua's naval base and Moravian missionaries reportedly also provided that island with the military apparatus and moral/religious imperative to keep the slaves in subjection. On St. Kitts, the fort of Brimstone Hill likewise supposedly provided adequate physical and psychological protection for whites. Further, all three islands lacked uncultivated lands where runaway slaves could conceal themselves for an extended period and from which they could effectively plan large-scale revolts.[12]

Naval commanders did not adequately consider that the geostrategic location of St. Kitts rendered it highly accessible to French activists. St. Kitts and other Leeward Islands were natural stopping off points for insurrectionists journeying from St. Domingue to Guadeloupe and Martinique. While Antigua's naval station was headquarters for the British fleet in the West Indies, other islands were not. On none of them, moreover, could adequate steps be taken to prevent the entry of persons exposed to the French revolutionary ideology. Administrators assumed their borders were secure.

Such feelings of immunity from insurrectionary activities proved to be misguided. Antigua and St. Kitts authorities received a rude shock when, in 1793 and 1795 respectively, the capture on their shores of individuals from the French islands exposed the porous nature of their safety network. The first case involved that of Morillon Desfosses, a man from Guadeloupe who had been seized at Antigua and charged with spying. Desfosses had reportedly been "despatched by the Committee of Safety at Guadeloupe to the different English islands, for the purpose of watching the Motion of the loyal French Emigrants there, and of exciting an Insurrection of the free Gens de Coleur and slaves."[13]

Equally troubling to local authorities was the capture on St. Kitts in 1795 of five free colored persons from the neighboring French islands. Among them was Jean François de Cotte, a revolutionary from Guadeloupe who had intended "to stir up sedition among the free colored people . . . to follow the example of those in the French islands" to demand their rights by any means necessary. De Cotte's visit to the island was not an isolated event. What was most startling to the authorities, however, was that De Cotte and other free coloreds had intended "to attack St. Kitts and put to death all white inhabitants, women, and children."[14] Local whites undoubtedly felt a profound sense of unease over the possibility of externally generated insurrection and killings.

The actions of both Desfosses and De Cotte were part of a carefully calibrated scheme in which French authorities sought to destabilize the British Caribbean in furtherance of their geopolitical goals. As the leftward drift of the French Revolution had become unmistakable by 1793, the Republican government in France had sent to the region emissaries under the direction of Victor

Hugues with the stated purpose of undermining British authority and creating trouble for local authorities. Fostering servile and civil insurrection was uppermost in the minds of these revolutionaries. The goal was that, by forcing the British to devote much-needed manpower in defense of their Caribbean possessions, revolutionary France would likely be relatively safe from British invasion. The French also probably hoped to make their Caribbean possessions unattractive to their rival.

Counter-Revolutionary Measures

Some colonies self-interestedly passed laws to provide a greater degree of internal social control and thus minimize the possibility of unrest. From 1792 onward, almost every island sought to ascertain the number of foreigners resident on its shores and to halt the entry of others. Although no island went as far as South Carolina in enacting legislation to detain black seamen whose ships had visited Haiti, the impact of the measures was the same.[15] Nonresident slaves and free coloreds arriving in the British Caribbean were now subject to severe scrutiny.

Equally important was the state of military preparedness each island experienced as war clouds descended ominously. In late 1792 the British government augmented the size of each company stationed in its Caribbean possessions.[16] Slaves were increasingly used to work on the islands' fortifications. Ensuring troop complements was now a matter of the highest priority. In 1794, Sir Charles Grey, commander of British forces in the West Indies, noted that "sword and climate" had diminished the size of his effectives. Advocating reinforcements, he stressed that every island needed additional troops and artillery in varying proportions.[17] In some instances, British troops were augmented by the addition of locally recruited forces from among the slave population. These developments ultimately threatened the fragile relationship that traditionally existed between civil and military authorities in the British Caribbean.[18]

Despite the passage of restrictive immigration laws, some colonies nonetheless experienced considerable political and social unrest. Grenada and St. Vincent were the scenes of various forms of social upheaval that threatened their slave societies. On both islands, authorities deemed it necessary to adopt stringent measures to monitor and curtail the movements of white "new subjects" and all free coloreds.[19] As early as November 1791, Secretary of State Earl

Grenville had asked the various governors "to prevent communications of an improper or dangerous nature with the French West Indian Islands." Governor James Seton reported his intention to "watch very particularly the temper and disposition of the slaves under my government." However, he had "every reason to hope that no disturbance whatsoever is likely to happen amongst the slaves in the colony."[20] Such sentiments mirrored the views expressed by Grenada's authorities, who in early 1792 optimistically reassured their superiors in Britain that the local situation was generally under control and there was no need for alarm.[21]

Barely two weeks after he had expressed such optimism about St. Vincent's internal safety, Seton found it necessary to amend his remarks. On January 12, he reported that the white residents had been "somewhat alarmed on account of a supposed intended revolt amongst the slaves on the leeward side of the island." After a "very strict investigation by the principal magistrates," Seton concluded that the reports were groundless. To be sure, there had been "a little refractory behaviour on one or two plantations and very different ideas held by the negroes than has been hitherto known."[22] Seton believed that he had the situation firmly under control. After all, he had already taken steps to curtail communication with the French islands.

A continuing source of concern for authorities on St. Vincent and Grenada was the disposition of the whites of French extraction and free coloreds. It was more difficult to restrict the movement of these free persons than of slaves. Equally important was the fact that free coloreds from neighboring islands could travel to both islands fairly easily. In January 1793, Seton issued a proclamation restraining the admission into St. Vincent of all free coloreds from the French islands. A later one applied to "foreigners of every description." The first edict was aimed specifically at persons holding "illegal meetings, clubs, and associations in the various quarters of the island; and who hold and carry illegal and treasonable correspondence with divers persons in the French islands." It required aliens to appear within six days before the governor and take an oath of loyalty before being permitted to reside on the island. Justices of the Peace could apprehend and bring before the governor and could possibly discipline those who failed to take such action.[23] A Vagrant Act provided imprisonment for anyone residing on the island less than twelve months without gubernatorial permission.[24] Although this proclamation dealt with individuals who were already on the island, it failed to address specifically the larger issue of the motive for the arrival of these foreigners. Royalists, especially free coloreds, who fled Martinique in the wake of the revolutionary upheavals there, sought refuge in St. Vincent. Once they had landed, they became indistinguishable from their Jacobin counterparts.

A similar situation existed on Grenada. In 1792, an official remarked that the arrival of at least one thousand foreigners, mostly free coloreds, within the previous six months augured ill for the island's safety. The situation was especially acute because of the supposedly doubtful attachment to the British Crown of French-speaking individuals of every race and class.[25] Although Lieutenant-Governor Ninian Home reported in 1794 that he had granted entry to some white foreigners whose "sufferings are great ... and principles good," he refused to permit any free coloreds or slaves to enter. Home defended his decision on the grounds that by publicly airing egalitarian doctrines many foreign free coloreds were potential threats to the well-established principles on which plantation society had long rested.[26]

Free Coloreds

Free coloreds in the British Caribbean were traditionally portrayed as opportunists intent on self-interestedly advancing their cause, regardless of whether they were loyal to the Crown or embraced French Republican ideals. Of the former group were Louis La Grenade and an assimilationist group of free coloreds who wrote to the British government disavowing any intention of embracing the revolutionary ideology or seeking to subvert the political system.[27] At the other end of the spectrum was the vast body of free coloreds during the revolutionary era who willingly or unwillingly gravitated toward Hugues because the Republican agenda seemed to promise them a greater semblance of equality with whites than they could hope to achieve under the British.

A third alternative, of questionable practicality and attractiveness, was available to and apparently pursued for a while by some free coloreds. In early 1791, there was in circulation "a narrative addressed Incognito to the Coloured People collectively in the different Islands" that purportedly came from U.S. President George Washington. The document apparently held out the prospect of setting up a separate state or country for British Caribbean free coloreds where they would enjoy full civil and political rights. Expressing their readiness "to embrace [the sentiments of the document] the moment they have a certainty in the Validity thereof," Grenada's free coloreds sought validation that Washington was indeed the document's author or that the contents had his support.[28] Whether or not Washington or anyone acting under his authority was the author of this interesting document is uncertain. Evidently Grenada's free coloreds found its contents appealing. How the document reached the region, or the response of free coloreds in other islands to it, is only a matter of conjecture.[29]

La Grenade and his assimilationist group of free coloreds were quick to affirm their attachment to the Crown.[30] La Grenade had converted from Roman Catholicism to Anglicanism, frequently led groups of slaves in search of runaways, and had received from the legislature a sword as a token of his loyalty and service. Such individuals were hardly likely to take any action that would possibly jeopardize their societal standing.

Despite government's restrictive policies, Grenada's free coloreds under the leadership of Julien Fédon started an unsuccessful rebellion in March 1795 that would have handed the island over to the French.[31] The fact that the French—both white and free colored—had for some forty years been accorded second class citizenship by the British had been a source of considerable angst for many. Fédon and his associates found the revolutionary rhetoric and ideology particularly appealing. For some fifteen months, white and free colored inhabitants who had remained loyal to the Crown remained holed up in the capital town of St. George's while Fédon and his associates ravaged the countryside. Only when external military aid arrived in mid-1796 was the rebellion crushed. The failure of their effort proved to be an immediate major embarrassment for the island's free coloreds, who were the prime movers in the uprising. Most of the guilty received the death sentence, which was later commuted to banishment. Guilty whites who received death sentences were later pardoned. From 1797 until the end of the Napoleonic Wars, officials imposed even more stringent measures aimed at monitoring the free colored and new white populations, curtailing the entry of foreigners, and better controlling the slaves.

It was difficult for authorities to prevent free colored contacts with their brethren in the Caribbean as a whole. Even after Fédon's Rebellion on Grenada had cast a heavy net of suspicion over the actions of free coloreds in most colonies, evidence emerged of questionable free colored cooperation and collaboration on an interisland and even transnational basis. In 1800, Council President Drewry Ottley reported the discovery in St. Vincent of "a correspondence carried on between some free colored Persons of this island, Martinique, and Antigua, of a very improper, and perhaps Seditious nature." At the center of the activities was a mulatto man named Tyley, who worked as a painter at the Botanical Gardens where he lived. His accomplice was William Dowding, who was at the center of activities on Grenada regarding the missive to George Washington. The writings of Tyley and Dowding were "grossly abusive of the White Inhabitants of the West Indies and of the Laws & Courts of Judicature." Ottley was of opinion that the lack of unanimity among the free coloreds regarding a proposed mode of action for effecting change stemmed more from "our vigilance and strength, and their weakness, than to any real attachment, on their part, to the existing Government under which they live." Such an opinion, argued Ottley, was justified "by the constant and unvaried tenour of their writings since the commencement of the French Revolution."[32]

Such reportedly "subversive" free colored activity was accompanied by troubling constitutional maneuvers. At about the same time Tyley's writings had been discovered, an Antiguan free colored man named Brenner had journeyed to England to seek from Parliament political advancement for his brethren throughout the British Caribbean. "A man of suspected character in the Commercial line, from his conduct as Chief Clerk to a considerable House which has failed in that island," Brenner "was supported at this moment in London by a Society of coloured People." An integral part of Brenner's agenda was "to get them [free coloreds] placed upon a footing of equality with the Whites, and thereby to enable them gradually to incorporate themselves in our Society and to become our Companions both in Public and in private Life." Ottley had "no hesitation in declaring that if this system were once to be adopted, and the distinction of Colour forgotten, both We and they should soon be involved in one common Ruin by the powerful exertions of the Negroes."[33] Such remarks clearly reveal the extent to which the revolutionary era had energized free coloreds to seek by constitutional and extralegal means political equality and rights which their counterparts on the French colonies enjoyed.

Carib Uprising

On St. Vincent, though, authorities encountered an uprising not from the free coloreds or slaves, but rather from the Caribs. In April 1793, Seton had expressed concern that the French from Martinique and Guadeloupe were fostering discontent among the Caribs of St. Vincent in order to undermine British authority on the island and minimize the potential for British forces in the region to strike a decisive blow against the revolution. To better deal with this incipient problem, he had met with twenty of the Carib chiefs, to whom he "strongly urged the bad policy of putting themselves under French influence, representing to them it was contrary to their real interests which they appeared at the time to be sensible of." Seton had taken the additional steps of prohibiting the chiefs, "under pain of H. M. greatest displeasure, from having any intercourse whatever with the French islands, to which they all solemnly agreed to confirm." He had also promised to give them protection and a substantial reward for any white person they turned in to government as having been within their boundary without a pass. Seton apparently believed that the chiefs were content with that arrangement. Two days later, however, he lamented the fact that "two of those perfidious Chiefs and about fifty other Charaibs" went to Martinique as "emissaries of the French Democratic Party here."[34] Because the Caribs lived at the island's northern extremity, it was difficult for Seton to monitor their activities. His only option was to hire a vessel to patrol the northern waterway in hopes of intercepting any correspondence and Caribs moving between St. Vincent and St. Lucia.

The situation, however, was quickly getting out of hand. In July 1793, Seton reported that "since the unfortunate attempt of the Royalists at Martinico, we have every reason seriously to dread the preponderancy of the other Party [Republicans] amongst the Charaibs of this Island. At Martinico and St. Lucia I understand they are fitting out a considerable number of Privateers to be ready to put to sea when the Hurricane months commences [sic]."[35] Seton was in a state of near desperation because of what he termed "the truly alarming and dangerous situation." This state of affairs was aggravated by the actions of "an internal set of subjects, savage in their Natures, prone to plunder and ready for every kind of Mischief, excited to acts of Rebellion by Emissaries distributing money amongst them from the Persons at present in Command at Martinico." Over the previous three days, there had arrived on the island a number of persons who "whatever their Professions may be, have for some time past, certainly been in habits inimical to good order in Civil Society." Under the circumstances, the island's legislature requested that General Bruce, then commanding British forces in the region, order the return to St. Vincent of the Flank and other companies of the 48th Regiment that had recently been moved to Dominica.[36]

Such reports of movements of Republican forces from the French Caribbean to neighboring British islands were hardly unique. Later that year Seton informed his superiors that a schooner had captured a French privateer, *La Liberté*, three days out of Point-à-Pitre, Guadeloupe, and bound for Trinidad. According to one prisoner's testimony, the object of the vessel's journey was "to procure men, above 2000 persons white and of colour, who had been sent off from the conquered islands, being there waiting for vessels to convey them to Point-à-Pitre." It also appears that two days earlier about one hundred French white men had traveled from Trinidad to Point-à-Pitre on a vessel flying alternatively Spanish and French colors.[37] The presence in the waters around St. Vincent of so many privateers compounded the security problem for local authorities.

Matters soon came to an unexpected head on St. Vincent. Fearful for the island's safety after receiving word on March 5, 1795, of civil insurrection on Grenada, Governor Seton immediately caused the general alarm to be sounded. He also repaired to Fort Charlotte with whatever members of the militia he could assemble. According to Seton, he "ordered the Charaib Chiefs in the usual manner to attend me in Council; which order had been on all former occasions punctually obeyed." He lamented, however, having "received for answer from Chatoué [Chatoyer] their chief, that the message came too late, and that they would not attend." Confessing that he was fully aware of the Caribs' intentions, Seton dispatched an urgent message to Sir John Vaughn and Vice Admiral Caldwell at Martinique apprising them of his situation in hopes that they would provide him with military and naval relief. On the morning of March 8, 1795, he learned that "a considerable number of armed Charaibs and French were joining in a particular Quarter" of the island. Seton, therefore, ordered a party of militiamen and "trusted" slaves to surprise them in their haunts in the woods. This group returned with Carib and French prisoners, as well as "Proofs that left no doubt of their Guilt."[38] Seton's worst fears of internal insurrectionary activity by Caribs and French had become a reality.

The denouement came within four days. On March 9, 1795, planters on the windward part of the island started abandoning their estates and, with their families, sought refuge in Kingstown. Some twenty volunteer horsemen who had joined the militia in that part were forced to beat a hasty retreat in the face of a superior number of hostile Caribs. Emboldened by the relative lack of resistance he encountered, on March 12 Chatoyer took charge of the military post at Dorsetshire Hill, overlooking Kingstown, where he and his followers "hoisted a National Flag and began to fortify themselves." Seton had every reason to fear for the island's safety. The insurgents had killed all the white prisoners they had taken and had destroyed and set fire to buildings and plantations. Seton concluded that, as had been the case with Fédon in Grenada, the insurgents' intention was to burn the city of Kingstown, attack the fort, and take over the entire island after they had received outside succor. Once Seton received assistance from General Vaughn, he launched a three-pronged retaliatory attack in which the insurgents were dislodged. Among those killed were Chatoyer and twenty other Caribs and an indeterminable number of Frenchmen. About twenty-five persons were wounded, and fifty were taken as prisoners. More than half of the 120 whites and 250 Caribs who took part in the action escaped.[39]

The routing of the insurgents at Dorsetshire Hill did not lead to the immediate surrender of other groups of Caribs and Frenchmen. At the end of March 1795, bands of Caribs, appearing within two to three miles of their former stronghold at Dorsetshire Hill, continued to "burn and destroy everything that had before escaped their devastations." Some even appeared again at Dorsetshire Hill, though they dispersed whenever government sent militia and armed slaves against them.[40] Seton finally admitted that he had previously underestimated the number of insurgents, whom government had unsuccessfully attempted to remove from a stronghold overlooking Calliaqua. One month later he remarked that some were "seen coming down in two separate bodies, to the number of 400 or upwards, marching in good order, well armed, and headed by five or six Frenchmen."[41] By May 1795, the insurgents' numbers had increased even further, while their depredations continued almost unabated. Frustrated, Seton reported that "they appeared in bodies of upwards of 700–800, near our post at Calliaqua, apparently intending to surround it and cut it off. They sent a message to the commander asking him to surrender."[42] One year after hostilities had commenced, Seton admitted his disappointment that the Carib insurgents "still occupy nearly the same ground they did at the beginning of June last, within a few miles of Kingstown, and in considerable force."[43] Eventually, government's conclusion of separate terms of surrender for the French left the Caribs isolated and without major military support. By October 1796, all the Carib chiefs had surrendered. Over time, large numbers of their followers turned themselves in to the authorities. In November 1796, about forty-seven hundred Carib insurrectionists were held as prisoners on the tiny island of Balliceaux off the southeastern end of St. Vincent.[44]

Such action lessened rather than completely curtailed the Caribs' actions. An indeterminable number who escaped the authorities' clutches remained on the island and apparently maintained contact with the French. In April 1798, Governor Bentnick reported the capture in the woods of "one of the Charaib Chiefs, called Augustine, and nine others." Bentnick acceded to Augustine's request of a pardon for "those yet in the mountains." The pardon was applicable only to those who surrendered by April 12. Admitting that the number of

Caribs still on the island was "much greater than we thought," Bentnick promised to send forces in search of those who had not availed themselves of his offer of a pardon. He regretted that those at large still maintained "constant communication with Guadeloupe through the runaway negroes who fly to the woods." Augustine's first question after being captured had been if the French had already landed in England.[45] Eventually, with their wives and families and barely enough food to last the duration of the voyage, the Caribs were transshipped to Roatan Island off Honduras. When the last forty-five Caribs surrendered in 1805, Governor Beckwith reported that the war had finally ended with the "unconditional surrender of all these people in the course of the last month."[46] All that remained was the apportionment to whites for settlement of the more than thirty thousand acres of land the Caribs previously occupied.[47]

The new British subjects and Frenchmen who participated in the insurrection did not fare much better. As has been noted earlier, they had played a major role in the Carib war through the information, weaponry, and presumably tactical support they supplied. After the commencement of hostilities, large numbers that arrived from Martinique joined them. In May 1795, for instance, two prisoners claimed to have been part of a company of 150 men who had landed on the island a few days earlier. They had brought with them ten barrels of gunpowder, 100 spare muskets, and 100 spikes. Moreover they had expected two frigates to follow two days later with twenty-five pieces of cannon, ammunition, and stores.[48] After the signing of the articles of surrender in June 1796, local authorities sought to get even with the French insurrectionists and their supporters.

The manner in which government treated the new British subjects reflected the extent of British prejudice toward anyone with French connections. Even before the insurrection had ended, Governor Seton had concluded that "all the French inhabitants within this Government were more or less concerned in fomenting & supporting" the uprising. He had, therefore, "ordered the greatest part of them to be apprehended, and to be confined on board Vessels in Kingstown Bay till they could be otherwise disposed of." The nine British subjects that Seton appointed to investigate into the cases of the French presented him with a list of seventy-four persons "whom they found most inimical to the safety of the Colony, and whom in their opinion it was necessary to ship for England. The rest they considered as less criminal and recommended their being indulged with being sent to North America." Seton duly sent to England the seventy-four assigned for that country, and ordered the others to leave the island immediately.[49]

Because members of neither group had received trial in a court of law, Seton's actions were particularly suspect. Officials in England, however, apparently sanctioned his behavior on the grounds of state interest. By 1798, four members of the group that had been sent to England unsuccessfully appealed the nature of proceedings against them. According to them, they had not violated their oath of allegiance to the Crown. No charge of disloyalty or rebellion had been brought against them. Of immediate concern to these individuals who were then lodged at Stapleton Prison near Bristol was the fact that, having been treated in a manner similar to prisoners of war, they could be exchanged as such. Their request to remain in England until they could prove their innocence and return to their property on the island was also denied.[50] In keeping with established British policies, St. Vincent authorities had used banishment and exile as the preferred method to deal with both Caribs and new subjects whose activities apparently ran counter to British interests.

The cruel repression and eventual banishment by the British of the Caribs on St. Vincent, like that of the Jamaican Maroons and the Grenada insurrectionists led by Julien Fédon, reflected the understandable fears whites had entertained about the potential consequences of the spread within their borders of revolutionary ideology. First unleashed by the American Revolution and finding further expression in the French and Haitian revolutions, this ideology had stimulated notions of liberty and equality that threatened existing social order and norms. Through challenges they made to established authority, the Caribs had shown that liberty applied to them just as much as to the British. Despite the banishment of supposedly untrustworthy inhabitants, whites in the British Caribbean were probably in a weakened position than they had been before the American Revolution. Their inability to maintain their hegemonic position without reverting to the home country for military and other support had exposed their increasing dependence on Great Britain if the social order was to remain intact.

Mobilizing Slaves

As British Caribbean officials sought to put down insurrections, they quickly recognized the inadequacy of their militia and other troops then stationed within their borders. In 1794, for example, Sir Charles Grey reported that total troop strength in the British Caribbean stood at only 5,298; he actually needed 10,800 for the effective defense of the islands.[51] As emergencies arose, the answer lay in increasingly recruiting slaves locally to perform some of the necessary military and paramilitary duties. In addition, black regulars had also been recruited for the British West India Regiments for service in the region.[52] One of the arguments supporting the creation of these regiments was the belief that Africans could better withstand malaria, yellow fever, and other epidemics that contributed significantly to an abysmally high mortality rate for white British troops. Thus, the use of Black Troops could conceivably increase the longevity and improve the quality of life for the whites.

As Roger Norman Buckley has pointed out, British officials increasingly relied on these regiments during the Napoleonic Wars as a whole.[53] The Black Troops' presence on the islands had an important impact on the ongoing debate over slavery. Their legal and civil status formed the basis of a fairly lengthy correspondence between officials on St. Vincent and their superiors in England. In the process, officials on both sides of the Atlantic came closer to recognizing the need to resolve definitively a situation that they had long avoided. At the same time, they took the first tentative though important steps to redress some of the basic inequities that confronted slaves and free coloreds in the Caribbean.

On St. Vincent in 1799, a case arose of a black member of the 4th West India Regiment who, in a quarrel, wounded a free man who died subsequently though not of the wounds he received. Precisely how the soldier was to stand trial became a contentious issue that had serious repercussions for society as a whole. According to local law, slaves charged with murder were to undergo trial by two magistrates. Military law, however, suggested otherwise. Members of the king's Black Troops were regarded as free persons, received treatment in the same facilities as their white counterparts, and were subject to the same discipline. A conflict between civil and military officials immediately became evident. Attorney General Archibald Gloster argued that the Black Troops were in fact slaves and thus subjected to local laws. While recognizing the limited influence his opposition to the deployment of Black Troops in the Caribbean might have on British policy, he provided an opening for those who wished "to place them in the clear light of free people." They could be manumitted by deed, or freed either by the colonial legislature or by an act of the British parliament.[54] While the immediate case was satisfactorily resolved locally, Governor Bentinck asked his superiors for a definitive ruling on the status of the

Black Troops. He rightly noted that "this Question is likely to accrue very often, and as the aversion to the Black Corps is daily increasing I apprehend it may at some period become the cause of serious disputes among the Inhabitants, the Military, and the Negroes."[55] From his viewpoint, it was now time for action.

In the interim, Drewry Ottley, then temporarily in command of the island's government, had championed the cause of the Black Troops. For him, it seemed perfectly appropriate and easy for the king to issue a declaration enhancing the status of the Black Troops whom he had purchased. The fitting course of action would be a statement asserting that "from the Moment of their being enrolled in any Regiment, [such persons] shall to all intents and purposes, be considered as Free except as to their Military Services." They would therefore "become entitled to the Rights and Privileges, enjoyed by other Free Negroes and Coloured People." This action would make them eligible for trial by jury and other civil rights that free coloreds then enjoyed. Ottley stressed the need for a speedy resolution of the matter, concluding that manumission of the Black Troops was "more consistent with their Military Character, and more consonant with the Ideas of Government." Ottley, however, was quick to point out that he was not advocating granting them or other free coloreds equality with whites.[56]

Committed to the continued use of the Black Troops in the Caribbean, the home secretary cautioned Bentinck against "listening to the objections which the local and ancient prejudices of the Island may suggest to the establishment of Negro Corps." Recognizing the invaluable role the Black Troops had played in the islands' security, the minister warned the legislature not to expect only Europeans (whites) to defend them. He had to await, however, the opinion of the law officers on the civil status these soldiers would occupy. The legal opinion was that military service did not exempt Black Troops from the operation of local laws. Manumission was necessary if they were to be excluded from the operation of slave laws against them. Even then, they would still be subject to the same disabilities that free coloreds faced. The law officers left unanswered the larger political question as to whether or not the British government should pass a law releasing the Black Troops from the operation of colonial laws.[57]

As late as 1801, the British government had failed to make a definitive ruling on the status of the Black Troops who had served them so well in the Caribbean as a whole. Indeed, its indecision is apparent from the fact that at the end of that year the Earl of Hobart, then holding the seal of the War Office, requested a legal opinion on the very points that his predecessor had raised two years earlier.[58] He received essentially the same response, to the effect that Black Troops were subject to the operation of local laws. Momentarily, at least, planters could rest on their oars. The various rulings validating the existing practice of viewing black soldiers as special slaves assured them that society would remain intact.

Implicit in the frequent requests that officials in both London and the Caribbean were making for guidance in determining the status of Black Troops was their desire to implement change. The only realistic option open to them by the end of 1801 was parliamentary intervention. The end of the war with France and suppression of internal insurrections, however, meant that these troops were no longer as necessary or unpopular locally as had been the case during the war. Yet the mutiny by Black Troops on Dominica in 1802 stemmed largely from their immense fear of being once more reduced to slavery when the troops were disbanded.

By 1807, the British government finally took action. Incorporated into the Mutiny Act for that year was a clause stating that members of the Black Troops were to all intents and purposes free citizens.[59] Local prejudices notwithstanding, Black Troops who had seen service in the Caribbean during the late eighteenth and early nineteenth centuries had now obtained an improvement in their civil position. Reached despite considerable opposition from local planters, this decision was indicative of the contradictory position that blacks occupied in the colonies during the revolutionary period. It also pointed to planters' declining power in the face of their increasing dependence on Britain for maintaining their internal security. Despite the American Revolution's rhetoric of the colonists' right to liberty and self-government, military exigencies of the revolutionary era exposed the dependence of the British West India colonies on the mother country for their protection and internal security. In an age when abolitionist pressure was escalating in Great Britain, it would soon become increasingly difficult for British Caribbean planters to defend the institution of slavery when the parliamentary campaign for abolition intensified.

Missionaries

If the military dependence of the colonists on Great Britain threatened their ability to withstand the external assaults on slavery, this institution was gradually being undermined from within. The period after 1790 witnessed an intensified effort to halt the Atlantic slave trade. Part of the reasoning was that over-dependence on the trade had contributed to slave revolts. The important part played by African slaves in the Haitian Revolution had been fully recognized. Many gradual reformers saw an increasing role in the British Caribbean for Christian missionaries. As part of the efforts made to ameliorate the condition of slaves and lessen the dependence on imported Africans, these missionaries would help "prepare" slaves for inevitable freedom that many felt was not too far off. Simultaneously, they would instill in the slaves an ethical sense that would ultimately make them better workers for the time being. Almost with a sense of inevitability, British Caribbean planters grudgingly received these missionaries in the late eighteenth and early nineteenth centuries.

Missionary teachings ultimately and unintentionally enhanced the slaves' sense of self-worth and led them to increasingly question their oppressed societal position. In the eyes of local whites, some missionaries were directly responsible for the increased spirit of subversion among the slaves. The reported discovery on Tobago in 1802 of "a most serious and alarming plot . . . of an intended Insurrection of the Negroes throughout the island" to kill all the island's white inhabitants on Christmas Day convinced authorities that missionary teachings and revolutionary rhetoric had prompted the slaves' actions.[60] Likewise on Barbados, Methodist missionaries were widely viewed as being involved in the 1816 slave and free colored disturbances of 1816. Some years later, the Reverend John Smith was prosecuted in British Guiana for allegedly encouraging slaves to rebel. Finally, Jamaican missionaries were implicated in slave uprisings on that island in 1831. Everywhere the pattern seemed unmistakable. Whatever might be the merit of the arguments supporting them in the region, the missionary presence was perceived as disruptive of the status quo in the short run. Their presence and activities eventually led to an undermining of the system of slavery.[61]

Such missionary activities also affected the consciousness and actions of free coloreds. As early as 1800 one individual had noted that missionary influence "from the phraseology" of letters and petitions free coloreds were writing. "From a mixture of Religious and Political Sentiments, and from their [free coloreds'] respective expressions toward the Methodist Missionaries in the West Indies" he feared that Methodist preachers had inculcated "principles of insubordination and discontent." The missionaries, he remarked, ought to have been "confining their discourses to those topics of Religion which they were sent to teach."[62] In the first quarter of the nineteenth century free coloreds increasingly emerged in major leadership roles in a number of churches.

Rather than being assimilationists, they used their position, education, and connections to call into question a system that continued to discriminate against them by virtue of their ethnicity.

Revolutionary Legacies

Slavery remained firmly entrenched in the British Caribbean in the early nineteenth century. But there were subtle changes in the condition of servitude during and after the revolutionary wars. For the slaves, as for the free population, hostilities produced unanticipated temporary food shortages. Their work regimen probably increased in the wake of the destruction that the era witnessed, especially in St. Domingue. Price increases on the European market for sugar induced planters to expand production or work their slaves harder to capitalize on the opportunity for enhanced profit making.

Yet steps were taken to ameliorate the daily conditions of slaves. Partly because of abolitionist lobbying, some colonies passed laws eliminating Sunday markets and providing for religious instruction for slaves. The laws also approved minimum standards of clothing and food, regulated punishments, and prohibited the break-up of families through sales. After the Slave Trade Abolition Act of 1807 denied planters access to traditional sources of African labor, they took additional steps toward amelioration. By this time, too, they were having second thoughts about the efficacy of maintaining too Africanized a slave population. In the wake of revolutionary upheavals at home and abroad, legislators grudgingly considered it in their interest to ameliorate the condition of their slaves lest they be driven to open revolt.

In profound ways, then, all population groups in the British Caribbean still felt in the 1820s and 1830s the effects of the "Age of Revolution." Emboldened by the manner in which colonial St. Domingue had been transformed into an independent Haiti, slaves and many free coloreds became increasingly assertive for their liberty and rights. Property destruction and fear of internal revolts shattered whites' self-confidence. Increasingly dependent on Great Britain militarily and ever hopeful of occasional relaxed policies that would permit them to trade with the United States, British West Indian planters could ill afford to antagonize the mother country. When, therefore, British colonial policymakers finally agreed to ameliorate the condition of slaves and free coloreds and to abolish slavery, the weakened and impoverished planters could put up only token resistance.[63]

CHAPTER FIFTEEN

Freedom, Migration, and the American Revolution

Trevor Burnard

Did the Revolution change the nature of migration to the United States? This chapter argues that the Revolution advanced rather than retarded the cause of unfree labor in the United States. Americans increasingly differentiated between forms of labor based on race—whites had to be free, blacks had to be controlled. The Revolution's impact on the cause of freedom was thus highly ambivalent: the freedom of white men was heightened but the subjugation of people not of European descent was continued, even advanced. Britons, on the other hand, came to believe in the post-Revolutionary period that all forms of unfree labor were undesirable, even if their imperial system remained predicated on the maintenance of strict racial hierarchies. From the perspective of a white Anglo-American patriot, the impact of the Revolution on freedom was immense. For a slave embarking from West Africa for South Carolina, or a Massachusetts Loyalist relocated to Canada, or an English convict incarcerated under the Hulks Act on a ship on the Thames, the emancipatory potential of the Revolution was more limited.

Slavery and Freedom

The effect of the Revolution on migration patterns within the polities of British America varied from region to region. In New England and British North America, migration was limited. Immigrants before 1776 represented only a small portion of populations growing rapidly through natural increase. Little changed after the Revolution.[1] The Middle Colonies and the Chesapeake varied in their commitment to slavery and plantation agriculture but both attracted similar sets of migrants. Slave importations declined considerably over time, virtually ceasing by the 1760s. The Revolution completed the process.[2] Before the Revolution, Europeans—mostly servants or convicts—rather than Africans dominated migration.[3] The Revolution saw a decisive break in migration patterns. Transportation of convicts halted and indentured servitude declined.[4] People in both regions also questioned the morality of slavery. Pennsylvania passed the first legislative act in the Western world against slavery in 1780. New York and New Jersey followed suit in 1799 and 1804 respectively. Delaware, Maryland, and Virginia were not prepared to abolish slavery but evinced notable antislavery sentiment. Manumissions became more frequent, especially in Delaware and Maryland. By 1820, 43 percent of blacks in Maryland and Delaware were free. Chesapeake political leaders played a leading role in ensuring that the slave trade to the United States as a whole was abandoned from 1808.[5] Yet this shift to free labor was more apparent than real. In New York and New Jersey, the slave population continued to grow in the last two decades of the eighteenth century. The abolition of slavery led to a revival of indentured servitude, which was on its last legs at the Revolution. Employers continued to control the labor of blacks but under more flexible conditions than under slavery.[6] Moreover, antislavery sentiment in the Chesapeake was shallowly based. Few slave owners followed George Washington's lead in manumitting slaves and freedom was tinged with considerable restrictions.

In the part of the United States most committed to unfree labor—South Carolina—the Revolution entrenched slavery. The extent of South Carolinians' commitment to coerced labor was evident in the Philadelphia Convention to ratify the Constitution when they threatened to leave the Union if the slave trade was not continued.[7] None of their three late-eighteenth-century constitutions contained any declaration that all men were by nature born free. As C. C. Pinckney exclaimed, "we should make that declaration with a very bad grace when a large part of our property consists in men who are actually born slaves."[8] Manumission rates remained the lowest in mainland America. Slaves were most commonly freed because they were the children of slave owners—50 percent of slaves manumitted in the 1780s were mulattoes—with nearly a quarter of manumissions arising from black self-purchase. Few were freed as a result of Revolutionary fervor.[9] Once the Revolution was over, South Carolinians resumed importing slaves as quickly as they could, from Africa and from other American states. Nearly twenty thousand Africans were landed in South Carolina in the 1790s. The high-water mark was reached just between 1804 and 1807 when forty thousand slaves landed in Charleston, entrenching slavery in the backcountry. The slave population in the low country nearly doubled in half a century, increasing from 53,257 in 1760 to 110,711 in 1810. Natural increase and internal slave importation kept slave populations stable.[10] Africans arrived in societies dominated by planters determined at all costs to maintain the institution of slavery. Moreover, planters established themselves firmly in control of local political processes and had a strong presence nationally. Both state and federal laws and the federal Constitution guaranteed slave owners' rights. Most importantly, no countervailing power existed that worked against slavery and slave owners. In addition, low country South Carolina's heavily outnumbered whites were bolstered by a large influx of settlers from northern areas moving into the backcountry. After the Revolution, "multitudes from Europe and the middle and eastern states of America, poured into South Carolina."[11]

Thus, only in the Middle Colonies and the Chesapeake was there evidence of a shift toward largely free migration. Residents in these regions signaled their growing ambivalence about chattel slavery by accentuating pre-Revolutionary tendencies toward free migration.[12] But even in these regions the shift from unfree to free labor was not all that great. Elsewhere, regional migration patterns that pertained before the Revolution continued after it. More importantly, migration patterns in the various regions of the United States resembled patterns in similar regions that had remained within the empire. If the Revolution had changed migration from being mainly unfree to being mainly free, then we would expect a greater commitment to free migration and to freedom in general in the United States than in areas that remained in the British Empire. In particular, New England should have been more committed to free labor than British North America and the Lower South should have advanced the cause of freedom more than the British West Indies. But in neither case did the American region outdistance its imperial counterpart.

By 1790, the overwhelming majority of New England's 17,000 slaves were nominally free, following the passing of gradual emancipation acts in the early 1780s.[13] Slavery was not formally abolished in British North America until 1834. Moreover, the influx of American Loyalists into British North America rapidly increased the number of slaves in that region, even if slavery remained a functionally unimportant institution and even if most blacks moving to British North America came as free men. Only one British North American province, Upper Canada, passed an act against slavery and that merely forbade future imports and did not free a single slave.[14] Yet differences in antislavery sentiment between the two regions were limited. British North Americans were at the forefront of ambitious schemes to resettle blacks in Sierra Leone and Jamaican Maroons in Nova Scotia. Public sentiment was firmly against slavery, not least because Canadians associated the institution with the United States, and an indigenous Canadian abolitionist movement won major victories limiting slavery between 1793 and 1808. Abolitionism remained powerful in Canada throughout the first half of the nineteenth century and Canada was a favored destination for fugitive American slaves.[15]

A more important comparison is between low country South Carolina and Jamaica, two British American colonies with a deep commitment to slavery and to the slave trade. South Carolinian migration patterns after the Revolution resembled those into Jamaica. Significantly, the majority of migrants after the Revolution into South Carolina from outside the United States were Africans; most African migrants to the United States went to South Carolina and the Lower South. Slave importations into Jamaica dwarfed imports elsewhere in the English-speaking world. Jamaica imported 348,723 slaves between 1776 and 1807, increasing its annual importations to an all-time high of 23,018 in 1793. As in South Carolina, the number of white migrants (almost all of whom were free) increased in the late eighteenth century, allowing the white population to grow from 12,737 in 1774 to 30,000 in 1807, a growth rate of 135 percent.[16] Nevertheless, as in South Carolina, African migration far outstripped European migration: in the 1790s, Jamaica imported more Africans in any two year period than there were Europeans living on the island.

But similarities in migration statistics mask major differences. South Carolinian planters' victory in the Revolutionary conflict strengthened their power and entrenched slavery more firmly than before. Jamaican planters, however, became increasingly beleaguered in the late eighteenth and early nineteenth centuries as abolitionism grew to become a significant movement of reform in

Britain. The differences between the two sets of planters were magnified after the abolition of the slave trade into the British Empire in 1807 and into the United States in 1808. Low country South Carolina planters felt sufficiently powerful to provoke their own doom by engineering the American Civil War. Jamaican planters, on the other hand, faded away into bankruptcy and political irrelevancy. For these two sets of planters, the American Revolution mattered enormously. It shored up slaveholders' power in the United States when that power was being circumscribed throughout the British Empire.

The result of the Revolution left low country planters in a powerful position, especially after they ensured federal protection for slavery and the slave trade. Their position became virtually inviolate after 1808 when they stitched up an historic compromise with potential rivals in the backcountry. The Compromise of 1808 was a victory for low country planters and a triumph for political aristocracy. The new system of representative apportionment kept political power firmly in the hands of low country representatives by ensuring that the ownership of slaves gave slave owners a disproportionate share of the franchise. Half of the seats in the legislature were allotted on the basis of population, half on the basis of taxes paid, most of which were on slaves. The 1808 compromise, in short, provided South Carolina with a tougher version of the three-fifth clause in the Constitution that allowed slave owners a greater share of the national government than their numbers warranted. It allowed South Carolina to withstand the democratizing pressures that transformed other Southern states' political systems during the Jacksonian period. Theoretically, South Carolina was the most democratic society in the world as it had eliminated property qualifications for voting on white adult males. But, in practice, it had a remarkably aristocratic political system. The planters who engineered the Compromise of 1808 placed numerous constraints on popular politics and made sure that planter interests would be paramount in the system of apportioning representation, in property requirements for officeholders, and in legislative control of appointments and elections. The planter elite had a virtual monopoly on the governor's office, congressional seats, and national senate positions. Their control of the legislature was especially important. "The legislature," exulted political leader James Hammond in 1845, "has all power. The Executive has none. The people have none beyond electing members of the legislature, a power very negligently exercised from time immemorial."[17]

Low country planter power was not total; planters still had to negotiate very carefully with white yeomen who valued their independence as fiercely as did planters themselves.[18] But the extent of their political independence was formidable. They did not have to deal with free blacks as political equals, as Jamaican whites were forced to do after 1830. Nor did they suffer interference from the federal government in determining how they could treat their slaves. Their power over dependents—slaves, women, and poorer whites—was so absolute that it encouraged them to recalcitrant opposition when they felt their interests even slightly threatened. That intransigence came to the fore in the nullification dispute of the early 1830s and in the secessionist movement of late 1860. Indeed, low country planters' determination to brook no interference— real or inferred—with their commitment to a slave republic is a central theme in American history, leading as it did to America's greatest conflagration.

Nineteenth-century Jamaican planters could only look at South Carolina with envy. In the eighteenth century, Jamaican planters had been notoriously jealous of their liberties and had been the most fervent defenders in British America of colonial rights against metropolitan privilege.[19] In the aftermath of the American Revolution, Jamaican planters found their power and liberties greatly circumscribed. Between 1788 (the start of serious abolitionist pressure) and 1865 (Morant Bay) planters were assailed from every side. The nineteenth-century planter was a mere shadow of his former self. In retrospect, Jamaican planters should have endeavored to join their mainland friends in opposing British rule. By staying within the empire, Jamaica severed its longstanding cultural ties to areas that became part of the United States. Consequently, her political, material, and cultural dependence upon Britain was heightened. Unfortunately for Jamaican planters, such heightened dependence occurred at a time when escalating attacks on slavery challenged fundamental values of white Creole Jamaican culture.[20] From a white planter's perspective, Jamaican history between 1788 and 1865 was one long retreat. Of course, from an African slave's perspective, this period is one of continual, if not constant, progress from slavery to freedom. That black aspirations were eventually quashed after the Morant Bay Revolt of 1865 did not altogether negate the remarkable advances they had made since the American Revolution. Nor did it reverse the curbs on planter pretensions and planter power that had occurred in the same period.

Jamaican planters faced numerous challenges after 1788. The most important was the growth of abolitionism in Britain, a phenomenon that became a mass movement of reform in the immediate aftermath of the American Revolution. The strength of abolitionism took Jamaican planters completely by surprise and shattered their complacent belief in their economic indispensability to Britain.[21] Even before the slave trade was abolished in 1807 planters were forced to alter their customary treatment of slaves and were required to make efforts to ameliorate slave conditions. Their plantations remained profitable, however, until the abolition of the slave trade. Their economic difficulties, induced by what Seymour Drescher calls an act of imperial "econocide" unprecedented in the annals of imperial enterprise, were aggravated by the efforts of the British Navy to keep illegal slave imports from entering the island, by the activities of missionaries intent on revealing planter abuses of slaves, by metropolitan humanitarian reformers who regarded planters as notable backsliders, and by slaves who took advantage of planter weakness to make violent bids for freedom, notably in the Baptist War of 1831–32.[22] By the 1820s, whites understood that their longstanding insistence that only propertied whites were able to be political citizens was no longer tenable. Moreover, the West Indian political interest in London faded away as West Indian economic importance to the empire lessened.[23]

Planters increasingly felt alone in a hostile world. The influential Creole Jamaican politician Richard Barrett said as much when introducing a bill in favor of colored people to the Jamaica Assembly in 1823. Colored people needed to be given additional privileges because "we were called on by the threatening dangers of our situation, and by the uncommon character which the plans of our enemies had assumed, to establish our security on a broader basis than that on which it had hitherto rested."[24] Most whites resisted Barrett's clarion call in 1823 but by 1830, facing intense pressure from the Colonial Office, the House agreed to pass a restrictive franchise for free blacks and coloreds and Jews. Whites hoped that Jews and free blacks and coloreds would join them in the fight against abolition but they had acted too slowly. Their delay had alienated people of color from their interest. The antagonism between the plantocracy and newly franchised groups continued until Morant Bay in 1865. White planters fought a generally losing battle against black and brown politicians and against an imperial order opposed to their interests. By 1865, Jamaican planters were defeated. In order to maintain vestiges of white supremacy and keep people of color from attaining political power, they willingly abrogated the Jamaican constitution and agreed to become politically neutered.[25] South Carolina planters also faced defeat in the same year but the different route by which they reached their denouement suggests self-immolation rather than defeat from the outside.

Significantly, colored assemblymen in Jamaica distinguished themselves from white planters by claiming that they were the group most committed to Jamaica and its future. By contrast, planters increasingly appeared to be temporary sojourners. One way in which colored people proved their patriotism was in regard to immigration. Planters wanted immigration in order to increase population so that a more favorable balance between land and labor could be created. A side benefit would be that more docile migrant workers, whom planters could command, would replace "unreliable" Creole Afro-Jamaicans. Afro-Jamaicans protested vigorously about the introduction of "uncivilized" East Indian and African laborers whom they believed would undercut the wages of local workers. Eventually, their protests were successful. From the mid-1840s, British officials cut back drastically on immigration funding, accepting Afro-Jamaican arguments that the use of public funds to foster private interests was unjustifiable.[26]

From this perspective, therefore, the push to replace slavery with indentured labor was not only a sign of planters' continuing commitment to unfree labor (although that is certainly part of the story) but also was evidence of the extent to which ex-slaves were able to dictate the process of emancipation. In Barbados, where black population was increasing, where planters maintained power, and where conditions were unfavorable for the creation of an independent landed peasantry, indentured laborers were unnecessary: ex-slaves had little choice but to return to work on plantations. Consequently, very few people moved to Barbados as indentured laborers. Instead, Barbados had a net outflow of people as poorly paid plantation workers were forced to move elsewhere in search of work.[27] Jamaican planters, on the other hand, eagerly sought indentured laborers, ideally from Africa but also from India and China, to replace black Jamaican peasants whom they could no longer effectively control. But despite the arrival of 25,000 indentured laborers between 1834 and 1865, the Jamaican plantation economy went into free fall. It was only in the most newly acquired of Britain's Caribbean territories that indentured labor was very important. Both Trinidad and British Guiana imported large numbers of indentured servants, mainly Indians, in the nineteenth century. Significantly, however, the sugar industry's demand for labor in these two colonies encouraged employers to treat their laborers relatively well so that laborers would be enticed to extend their contracts. Moreover, colonial officials regulated employment conditions, withholding laborers from abusive employers, allowing migrants to change employers, and even allowing indentured servants to return home early. Only in Jamaica did the indentured labor system come to resemble slavery—perhaps one reason why it failed so dismally there.[28]

South Carolinian planters found it easier than their Jamaican counterparts to obtain the labor they needed, under conditions they desired, both during slavery and afterwards. The abolition of the slave trade in 1808 did not end their need for new slaves but they were able to get what slaves they needed from an extensive internal slave trade.[29] Only during Reconstruction did South Carolinian planters face constraints upon their power to command black labor. The challenge planters faced during Reconstruction was severe as American freedmen briefly "enjoyed an unparalleled opportunity to help shape their own destiny."[30] For the first time, Southern planters were unable to heighten their own freedom through circumscribing the freedom of African-Americans. But planters' loss of power did not last long. Their postwar "search for a substitute for slavery" was successful. By the late nineteenth century, Southern planters had enmeshed blacks in a comprehensive system of segregation, disfranchisement, peonage, and poverty. The apogee of postwar planter control over black labor came with the development of convict leasing. It was not slavery, yet it had most of the requisites of slavery: blacks working in gangs, subjected to constant supervision, and under the discipline of the lash. But convict leasing also had the advantages of free labor. The Southern convict labor supply was remarkably elastic, as lessees had only minimal investment in any individual convicts and could replace convicts easily if they were released, pardoned, or died. Southerners found it easy to reassert their old understandings that paupers, dependents, and vagrants had to be compelled to work by using the new language of contract.[31]

British Emancipation

The rise of universal white manhood suffrage in the nineteenth century did not end the link between black dependence and white freedom. Only mature adults were entitled to freedom: children, women, and uncivilized races lacked the capacity for independent judgment that was the foundation of freedom.[32] Increasingly, Southern Americans denied that Africans shared a common humanity with Europeans. Their inferiority, it was asserted, was due not to condition but to nature. Such racialist beliefs were more pernicious than what had preceded them, precisely because they were no longer linked to a belief in natural subordination, and were able to survive both slavery and emancipation largely unscathed.[33]

Late eighteenth- and nineteenth-century Britons generally shared American views about the linkages between intellectual capacity and freedom, although without a Revolution to encourage them they did not throw away their beliefs in the rightness and inevitability of natural subordination nor develop a full-blooded philosophy of racial hierarchies.[34] But after the American Revolution, Britons did reconsider the relationship between migration and freedom in ways that significantly narrowed their acceptance of unfree labor in the British Empire. The result was that it was in the British Empire rather than in the United States that the most severe challenges to unfree labor occurred. American free blacks recognized the extent to which Britain led America in advancing the progress of freedom by pointedly celebrating the anniversary of West Indian emancipation rather than the anniversary of the Declaration of Independence.[35] American humanitarians living in northern cities were no less hostile to slavery than their British counterparts. But the nature of American politics after the Revolution—the country remained a loose confederation of quasi-sovereign states rather than an integrated polity—did not allow reformers the same scope as was possible in the highly centralized and relatively authoritarian British Empire to target the abolition of slavery in far-distant places.

Christopher Brown has traced the process by which a few visionary imperial thinkers began to rethink the relationship between empire and coerced labor in the 1770s, challenging, for the first time, prevailing assumptions about the customary associations of slavery with imperial wealth and power. The genesis of these ambitious schemes for developing an empire that did not have slaves came in part because the writers were typical Enlightenment intellectuals who wanted to guide American plantation societies into conformity with civilized norms. But they principally arose from the practical consequence of incorporating an unprecedented number and variety of peoples within British imperial control. British imperial officials had to face after the Seven Years' War the reality of an empire that was remarkably multiethnic and polyglot and had to consider the question of to what extent these new subjects who pledged their allegiance to the monarch should enjoy the same rights as natural born subjects.

British re-evaluations of the place of slavery within the empire occurred at the same time as imperial officials rethought the nature of the political relationship that ought to exist between metropolis and colonial dependencies. That a few people began to reconsider the rightness of slavery at the same time as Britain in general attempted to reassert political authority in the Americas was not coincidental. Imperial insiders such as Maurice Morgann, who wrote one of the first British schemes for the emancipation of the slaves, saw both enslaved Africans and American colonists as imperial subjects. In doing so, he implicitly denied the pretensions of the latter to be the equal of metropolitan Britons while envisioning the former as potential allies rather than internal enemies. If his plan had been accepted, Africans would have had a substantial increase in their freedom and American colonists would have had their customary liberties severely curtailed. Advancing emancipation thus necessitated a sustained effort to enforce colonial subordination. Opposition to colonial autonomy could deepen hostility to American slavery and vice versa.[36]

Brown pays particular attention to an unpublished work written in the early years of the Revolutionary crisis by the Reverend James Ramsay, later to become a leading antislavery campaigner in the 1780s. In a lengthy text composed in 1778, Ramsay explicitly linked reforms of colonial governance that would greatly enhance centralized authority with his opposition to slavery as an imperial institution. He perceived, correctly, that the British practice of treating American slavery as outside of imperial oversight and as local customs that established private rights upon which metropolitan governments did not intrude had given American slaveholders license to act as unrestrained tyrants. He detested what he termed the "Kingdom of *I*" where Caribbean grandees abused their excessive liberties by oppressing less fortunate slaves. Ramsay's preferred imperial philosophy was that of enlightened authoritarianism, resembling the absolutist arguments first made by Jean Bodin in the late Renaissance: only an all powerful state, presided over by an all powerful but benevolent monarch (or colonial governor) could support the poor and unfortunate against the tyrants of the Kingdom of *I*.[37]

Brown thinks Ramsay atypical and that the scope and novelty of such ambitions were undone and discouraged by the results of the American Revolution. He sees Ramsay, Morgann and others as quixotic visionaries whose ideas fell on barren soil, even if their schemes prefigured "the nineteenth-century imperial mission that lauded Christianity, civilization, and commerce." For Brown, ambitious plans to abolish slavery were dismissed by ministers who learned from their disastrous attempt to impose imperial discipline upon white colonists that discretion and a respect for customary rights of local autonomy, especially over slavery, were the better part of valor. Brown's conclusions—that reformers were forced to shift to attacking the slave trade rather than slavery per se when they realized how powerfully slave owners could defend their right to legislate over their slaves—may be correct for the established colonies of the

Western hemisphere, although his argument that the result of the Revolution prevented metropolitan interference with slavery in the British Empire for a further half-century is overstated. But the twin ideas of Ramsay and other reformers—abolishing colonial slavery while shoring up metropolitan authority in the empire—were typical rather than atypical in imperial thinking for how *new* territories should be settled and governed.[38]

In the 1780s, Britain embarked on several projects that were quite different from any planned while the thirteen colonies were still part of the British Empire. Schemes of settlement envisioned in the 1780s intersected with the two great issues that dominated the thinking of progressive Britons in the period immediately before the American Revolution: what was to be the status of blacks in the empire and what was the best form of penal discipline. Ideas about black freedom circulated widely in the 1780s and overlapped with ideas about what to do with convicts, who could no longer be sent from Britain to the Chesapeake. Both discourses intersected with ideas about migration and led to interesting new projects, designed in part to cope with the massive rearrangements of population in the British Empire resulting from the Revolution.[39] These projects were a short-lived settlement of displaced British settlers from Spanish territory in Central America to the Gulf of Honduras; an expedition of free blacks to Sierra Leone; and the transshipment of British convicts to Botany Bay in Australia. In each project, we can see how British commitment to unfree migration as essential to colonial settlement had been undermined by the 1780s.[40]

The Honduras experiment was the most explicitly radical of the new schemes and the most unsuccessful. It was also very much the creation of one man, who wanted to use the coercive powers of a powerful state in order to impose freedom on both blacks and whites. Men were to be molded into humanitarianism by benevolent authoritarians—Bodin's theories, in short, put into practice. Colonel Edward Despard, superintendent at Honduras, was a Bodin-like forward-thinking despot. He was determined to control everything at Honduras, from the distribution of land to the treatment of blacks to the exercise of justice.[41] His views on who should have what were decidedly unconventional. He wanted all settlers, rich and poor, black and white, male and female, to have equal rights to land. In short, he wanted Honduras to be a radical experiment in racial and gender democracy. Movement to Honduras was, in his opinion, enough to dissolve previous ties and conditions, including conditions of unfreedom. Moreover, he brooked no opposition to his plans, as the leading men of the colony lamented when they commented both on his "leveling principles" and on "his passion for despotic authority." Despard had a passion for equality that was so strong that he was determined to impose it regardless of the opinions of established white settlers. But depriving planters unilaterally of their property in slaves and turning upside down settled notions of the superiority of whites over blacks led settlers to claim that Despard was violating the liberties of Britons. Settlers complained that their "society had been dissolved" as "all Men . . . were on an equal footing." The Home Secretary, Lord Sydney, agreed: "people of Colour, or Free Negroes . . . [were not] considered upon an equal footing with People of a different Complexion." Despard had overreached himself by not respecting the "natural Prejudices" of British citizens. After Sydney resigned, Despard lost his job and eventually his sanity: he was executed in 1803 after his scheme to assassinate George III was discovered.[42]

Freedom imposed by authoritarian dictate was just as important in the envisioning of civil society in Sierra Leone. The brainchild of abolitionist Granville Sharp, the Sierra Leone project appealed to the British government as a means of dealing with the problem of black poor people living in Britain and with free blacks in Nova Scotia and Jamaica. For abolitionists, the Sierra Leone settlement was a welcome step toward the larger emancipation of blacks and toward the abolition of race as a primary differentiator of status in the empire. Sharp saw his colony as a "Province of Freedom" where "the law of natural right and justice" would prevail "for a race of men supposed to be uniformly open to the persuasions of reason." His vision soon faltered: six months after the colonists had landed at Granville Town, Sharp wrote that he had "had but melancholy reports of my poor little ill-thriven swarthy daughter, the unfortunate colony of Sierra Leone." But his insistence that Sierra Leone was to be a haven for freedom prevailed, although not in the form that Sharp and his successors in the Sierra Leone Company wanted. Enlightened despotism faltered in the face of resolute efforts by black refugees from Nova Scotia and other settlers to determine what freedom they would have. As in Honduras, the lesson of Sierra Leone was the one that should have been learned from the American Revolution: the unwillingness of people accustomed to pre-colonial customs of colonial autonomy to accept limitations on the exercise of their historical liberties.[43]

The most important settlement project initiated in Britain in the aftermath of the American Revolution, however, concerned not free migrants but convicts. The American Revolution precipitated a crisis in penal policy by ending the practice of transporting convicted felons to the Chesapeake. Britain needed to find a new place to dispose of its unwanted criminals. They found it across the other side of the world, in Botany Bay on the eastern coast of Australia.[44] At first glance, the transportation of convicts to Australia seems a reinforcement of previous patterns of migration. In the popular imagination, Australia was founded as a police state with its raison d'être the enforced labor of unfree former citizens of Britain. Indeed, one popular history of transportation to Australia sees Botany Bay as a South Seas' Gulag composed of groaning white slaves tyrannized by ruthless authoritarian masters.[45]

Yet the people who imagined the early settlement of Botany Bay were more concerned with implanting freedom in a new land than with reinforcing and enhancing unfreedom. As Alan Atkinson has argued, in the mid-1780s "New South Wales was envisaged as a land of Englishmen where the rights . . . of liberty would prevail."[46] Lord Sydney, home secretary and a man sympathetic both to Country Whig ideology and to the ideals that motivated American resistance to Britain in the Revolutionary conflict, was the prime mover. Influenced by contemporary models of authority such Jean-Jacques Rousseau's *The Social Contract,* and Daniel Defoe's *Robinson Crusoe,* where stranded Englishmen created "Government and Laws" and "a Kind of Common-Wealth among themselves," Sydney believed that the convicts removed across the world would become free on arrival, able to form a government of their own devising. Australia was to be a self-governing civil society full of free people, who were unable to return to Britain but who were otherwise unrestrained by arbitrary authority.

Sydney's vision for Australia depended on what was by the 1780s an increasingly old-fashioned view that transportation was the final punishment that a convicted felon suffered for his or her offence. People convicted of a felony might ask for a sentence of transportation in order to avoid hanging but from the point of embarkation the punishment for the convict was complete. Henceforth, they were freeborn Britons, free from penal restraint as long as they remained abroad. By this logic, convicts transported to Australia could do as they pleased—and Sydney hoped that they would be able, even in the most exotic of circumstances, to organize themselves into a band of brothers, governed by the principles of British liberty. Australia was thus from the start intended to be a free society rather than a penal colony, let alone a slave society.[47]

How Sydney understood what the status of convicts in Australia would be stood in marked contrast to British American attitudes toward convict laborers. Over the course of the eighteenth century, the status of convicts in the

Chesapeake became increasingly degraded. From being seen as inferior kinds of indentured servants, convicts began to be assimilated, in the second half of the eighteenth century, with slaves. In 1748, convicts in Virginia were prohibited from giving evidence in courts of law, in terms similar to those used disqualifying blacks and Indians. They were also excluded from the franchise and in Maryland from 1769 had to register their names with local authorities, even after finishing their terms of servitude. The trend was clear: a progressive equation of convicts with slaves and a characterization of both groups as morally disqualified from membership in civil society.[48] Sydney wanted to halt the whittling away of convicts' rights that had occurred in the Chesapeake: an unsurprising concern for a man passionate about defending the traditional constitutional liberties of Englishmen. Sydney's solicitude toward the rights of convicts seemed dreadfully old-fashioned to the new theorists of penology who wished to see convicts as a people set apart from civil society. Sydney was concerned that the American colonists, whose commitment to their own liberties he otherwise much admired, had abrogated the rights of free English people (which he considered transported convicts to be). He insisted that the convicts sent to New South Wales in 1788 were to arrive with all their rights intact. Indeed, for some years in New South Wales convicts were technically allowed the status of free people when they appeared in court, appearing not as "convicts" but as "laborers" or "settlers."[49] In a sense, Sydney's attempt to reaffirm older, more extensive models of liberty made Australia, as Atkinson notes, "the last great initiative of what is called the first British Empire."[50]

Lord Sydney's vision of Botany Bay as a place where Rousseau's social contract could be worked out in a real experiment was modified, if not contradicted, by experience in Australia. Within a very short time, nearly all of the rights of convicts in New South Wales had been reduced to those of people in servitude.[51] Captain Arthur Phillip, another forward-thinking despot, believed that convicts ought to be "servants of the Crown till the time for which they are sentenced is expired." Although strictly enjoined to "emancipate" convicts, to "discharge [them] from their servitude," and to grant them freehold title, Phillip ignored his instructions. He believed that convicts should not be given any substantial independence until after they had served the terms to which they had been condemned. Phillip's actions soon superseded Sydney's intentions for Australia and placed the authority of the state as superior to the liberties of the people. Humane authoritarianism triumphed over ancient notions of commonwealth.[52]

But even if practice deviated from theory, the technical fiction that convicts went to Australia of their own volition and that they were free men and women on arrival was immensely important in shaping early Australian society. New South Wales, like Honduras and Sierra Leone, and like later British settlements overseas, was founded as a free society where slavery, in particular, was banned. Even Phillips, a firm advocate of centralized state authority, was determined that slavery would not be exported to Australia, stating "That there can be no slavery in a free land and consequently no slaves."[53] As "servants of the Crown," convicts were not exactly free but they were not slaves or even indentured servants. They were closer to wage laborers than to servants, even if their labor was coerced rather than voluntary. A private employer paid convicts a quasi-wage, a mix of maintenance in kind and money, for convicts allocated by the state-controlled labor market. Incentives and rewards rather than the whip governed the extraction of work by convicts and skilled workers received wages commensurate with their talents.[54] In its continuing distaste for uncompensated unfree labor, New South Wales was therefore a different type of British colony from the British American colonies that preceded it. All people in Australia, even convicts, were supposed to be free. This was a victory for liberty, although an ambivalent victory: in order to give liberty to all, Aborigines had to be excluded not only from citizenship but also from existence altogether. Aborigines could not be enslaved because they existed entirely outside society as a people with no systematic pattern of relationships nor any rights that Europeans need recognize.[55]

Two Empires of Liberty

British experience in founding new societies in British America profoundly influenced how they conceived of colonization projects in the second British Empire. One lesson they learned was that metropolitan authority had to be stronger in peripheral areas than when earlier settlements had been founded in the seventeenth century. Governance in the nineteenth century was increasingly based upon coercion and control rather than upon consent and cooperation, even if settlers continued to dispute metropolitan claims achieved by coercion.[56] The strengthening of imperial institutions after 1783 and especially the subjecting of nonwhite populations to direct rule without consent suggests that British imperialists de-emphasized liberty in the British Empire. It is this increasingly authoritarian form of governance—quite the opposite lesson intended by the American Revolutionaries whose revolt was a violent plea for imperial latitude—that makes the founding of the United States seem an advance in the course of liberty.[57]

Yet Britons always resisted American claims to priority in the national bragging contest about who was most devoted to freedom. Britons were forced to reformulate many of their ideas about imperialism in the aftermath of the American Revolution but they did not abandon their conception of themselves as a people peculiarly obsessed with liberty.[58] Increasingly, Britons distinguished themselves from Americans by contrasting their own willingness to force British liberties on non-European peoples throughout the world with white American tendencies to confine their much-vaunted liberty only to themselves. The second consequence of the American Revolution on British imperial thinking was to produce among Britons "a much keener awareness of Britain's character as a multinational empire."[59] It was Britain's responsibility, or burden, to bring civilization to non-European peoples. Humanitarian campaigns to abolish the slave trade and slavery as well as attempts to wipe out "heathenish" practices in India and Africa fitted within this perception of responsibility. Ironically, this fervent commitment to expanding liberty's reach was accompanied by increasingly authoritarian forms of governance. Imperial officials in the early nineteenth century circumscribed the powers of white settlers over dependent peoples in order to "protect" people deemed inferior from being exploited by Europeans. One lesson learned by humanitarian reformers from American and West Indian intransigence against imperial authority in the eighteenth century is that the freedom white settlers insisted upon for themselves included the freedom to oppress and enslave "lesser" peoples.

Such obsession with spreading liberty throughout the world influenced British views on colonization, migration and the United States. The United States remained the major point of comparison to Britain when Britons began seriously thinking about colonization and migration once again in the 1830s. The United States, however, was less positive example than negative warning. Although colonial theorists admired American commitment to democracy and universal white male suffrage, the United States was mostly a disappointment. Its material prosperity was not matched by moral strength. In particular, the continuing commitment that Southerners evinced to black chattel slavery made a mockery of American protestations that their land was a land of freedom.

Thinkers on migration and colonization in the 1830s shared Adam Smith's view that colonization in British America was a failure because it was based so heavily on slavery. Smith's *Wealth of Nations* was as much a critique about the deficiencies of slavery as a moral and economic system as it was an attack on mercantilism.[60] British thinkers accepted both Smith's attacks on mercantilism and his strictures about slavery as axiomatic. The most ingenious colonization schemes were attempts to "find some artificial substitute for the slave and convict labour, by which our colonies have hitherto been rendered productive."[61] Moreover, increased interest in colonization occurred at an expansive period in British history and at a time when Britons felt immensely proud of their world-leading role in abolishing slavery. "Nothing can detract," the mid-Victorian colonial theorist Herman Merivale stated, "from the merit of that crowning measure, almost a solitary instance, in the history of many centuries, of a national act of disinterested self-denial. To be the citizen of a state which has accomplished it, may be a higher title of distinction than to be the countryman of the conquerors of the East, or of the commercial sovereigns of the West."[62]

By the early decades of the nineteenth century, the vast majority of migrants to America were free migrants. Given that Britain was still sending convicts to Australia, Bermuda, and Gibraltar and by the middle of the century began importing indentured servants from Asia to plantations in the West Indies, Africa, and the Pacific, the claim advanced here that it was Britain rather than America that most fully re-evaluated the appropriateness of using unfree labor in overseas settlements may seem overstated. Yet we need to distinguish between 1780 and 1840, when belief in the superiority of free labor and the immorality of coerced labor, especially slavery, was universal among forward-thinking Britons, and the period of colonization in the late nineteenth century, when scientific racism was in full bloom and when the rights of non-European peoples were being steadily eroded. In the sixty years that followed the American Revolution, freedom was an essential characteristic of British colonial settlement and unfreedom was explicitly and systematically excluded from areas under British rule, as far as was possible.[63] Colonial reformers explicitly compared their commitment to free labor with American acceptance of slavery, "taunt[ing] them with the miseries which their institutions engender."[64] It was not just the economic inefficiencies of slavery that offended British reformers but it was the deleterious effect of slavery on a people's morals and behavior. Many of the ills that colonial reformers attributed to the United States arose from slavery. A host of early nineteenth-century British writers, from Fanny Kemble to Mrs. Trollope to Charles Dickens, condemned the United States in such a fashion. Edward Gibbon Wakefield, a devotee of Smith's four-stage analysis of the rise of civilization and the originator of systematic colonization schemes employed in the settlement of Canada, Australia, and New Zealand, spelled out the implications of societies based on slavery most forcefully, if idiosyncratically. He agreed with Mrs. Trollope that the United States was prone to fits of enthusiasm and that it exhibited marked barbaric tendencies. He tellingly compared the citizens of the United States to "the Tartar conquerors of China," who, "being themselves barbarous, consider[ed] all but themselves barbarians." The history of colonization in the United States was an example of cultural degeneration, based on the wide spatial dispersion of Americans and continuing shortages of labor that necessitated the implantation of chattel slavery in order to assure economic growth.

Wakefield's theories, in which land would be kept at artificially high prices in order to ensure the right balance between capital and labor, were predicated upon avoiding the evils that he believed had beset the United States, in particular the evil of slavery. His system, he argued, was the only means by which slavery could be abolished and the best way to allow free labor to play the role that slavery had played in the formation of the old plantations. Wakefield's schemes, of course, were not notably successful and were vigorously attacked, most memorably by Karl Marx who thought Wakefield had unwittingly given the capitalist game away. But Britons did not contest Wakefield's account of colonial American history nor his denunciation of American hypocrisy in condemning British political corruption when they "have remained mute and careless while groans echoed and whips clanked around the very walls of their spotless congress."[65]

Like Thomas Jefferson, Wakefield saw a bloody future for the United States, fearing "the not too distant thunder, which threatens to steep half the Union in blood, and to ruin the other half."[66] Wakefield imagined slave rebellion, not Southern secession, but his and Jefferson's fears did come to pass. For British colonial reformers, the American Civil War was final proof that Americans threatened freedom. For Irish economist J. E. Cairnes, Southern commitment to slavery necessitated aggressive territorial expansion in order to replenish exhausted cotton lands. The Civil War was just the first step by an archaic feudal planter class with totalitarian tendencies toward "a great slaveholding confederacy" that would include "the whole tropical region of the New World." For Cairnes, "the slave system in America is the greatest curse that has yet darkened the earth" and needed to be destroyed before it expanded southward. His mentor and admirer, John Stuart Mill (also an enthusiast for Wakefieldian ideas), agreed. There needed to be "a crusade of all civilized humanity" to crush the slave power, which had proven itself "such a pest to the world." Southern slave-owners were "enemies of mankind" who professed "the principles of Attila and Genghis Khan" and who, if not checked, would "propagate their national faith at the rifle's mouth" in Central America and the Caribbean.[67]

Mill's apocalyptic fears illustrated how far Britons had moved on from the views held by white Southerners in the decades after the American Revolution. If the thirteen colonies had remained British, South Carolinian planters would have heard voices such as Mill's much earlier than they did.[68] But confident in their political power and determined not "to abandon our country to become a black colony," as South Carolina congressman Francis Pickens declaimed, South Carolina managed to pass a series of congressional bills gagging discussion of antislavery after 1835. For a generation after the abolition of slavery in the West Indies, Southern slaveholders could ignore complaints about how they trampled on the liberties of black Americans. The result of the American Revolution was not only to sever the United States from Britain but was also to isolate the plantation states of the South from the humanitarian currents that transformed both Britain and its empire between 1780 and 1840. It took a bloody Civil War and a hundred years of struggle against segregation to bring the United States back into conformity with standards of freedom long established elsewhere.

Notes

Introduction

1. James Otis, *The Rights of the British Colonies Asserted and Proved* (1764; London, 1766), 61. On the role of the Seven Years' War in the coming of the American Revolution, see Jack P. Greene, "The Seven Years' War and the American Revolution: The Causal Relationship Reconsidered," *Journal of Imperial and Commonwealth History* 8 (1980), 85–105; Fred Anderson, *Crucible of War: The Seven Years' War and the Fate of Empire in British North America, 1754–1766* (New York, 2000).

2. Eric Hinderaker, *Elusive Empires: Constructing Colonialism in the Ohio Valley, 1673–1800* (New York, 1997); H. M. Scott, *British Foreign Policy in the Age of the American Revolution* (Oxford, 1990); John Brewer, *The Sinews of Power: War, Money, and the English State, 1688–1783* (New York, 1989).

3. For an early statement of the need for scholars of the American Revolution to heed the lessons of social history, see Edmund S. Morgan, "The American Revolution: Revisions in Need of Revising," *William and Mary Quarterly*, 3rd ser., 14 (1957), 3–15. The corpus that Morgan's essay helped inspire is far too expansive to mention in full here, but see Alfred F. Young, ed., *Beyond the American Revolution: Explorations in the History of American Radicalism* (DeKalb, Ill., 1993).

4. The classic statement is, of course, Bernard Bailyn, *The Ideological Origins of the American Revolution* (Cambridge, Mass., 1967). In challenging the ideological interpretation, John Philip Reid argues persuasively that American patriots were drawing on a constitutional discourse that was current throughout the British provincial world, most notably in Ireland, West Indies, and India. Reid, *Constitutional History of the American Revolution*, 4 vols. (Madison, Wisc., 1986–93); see also Jack P. Greene, *Peripheries and Center: Constitutional Development in the Extended Polities of the British Empire and the United States, 1607–1788* (Athens, Ga., 1986). On India, see P. J. Marshall, "The Whites of British India, 1780–1830: A Failed Colonial Society?" *International History Review* 12 (1990), 26–44.

5. See especially Lewis B. Namier, *England in the Age of the American Revolution*, 2nd ed. (New York, 1961); Jack P. Greene, "The Plunge of Lemmings: A Consideration of Recent Writings on British Politics and the American Revolution," *South Atlantic Quarterly* 67 (1968), 141–75.

6. For further discussion, see Eliga H. Gould, *The Persistence of Empire: British Political Culture in the Age of the American Revolution* (Chapel Hill, 2000). See also H. T. Dickinson, "Britain's Imperial Sovereignty: The Ideological Case against the American Colonists," in Dickinson, ed., *Britain and the American Revolution* (London, 1998), 64–96; Jack P. Greene, "Competing Authorities: The Debate over Parliamentary Imperial Jurisdiction, 1763–1776," *Parliamentary History* 14 (1995), 47–63.

7. Greene, *Peripheries and Center;* Richard Koebner, *Empire* (Cambridge, U.K., 1961).

8. Eliga H. Gould, "An Empire of Manners: The Refinement of British America in Atlantic Perspective," *Journal of British Studies* 39 (2000), 114–22; John Clive and Bernard Bailyn, "England's Cultural Provinces: Scotland and America," *William and Mary Quarterly,* 3rd ser., 11 (1954), 300–313; T. H. Breen, "An Empire of Goods: The Anglicization of Colonial America, 1690–1776," *Journal of British Studies* 25 (1986), 467–99; Susan O'Brien, "A Transatlantic Community of Saints: The Great Awakening and the First Evangelical Network, 1735–1755," *American Historical Review* 91 (1986), 811–32; Charles E. Clark, *The Public Prints: The Newspaper in Anglo-American Culture, 1665–1740* (Oxford, 1994).

9. Gould, "Zones of Law, Zones of Violence: The Legal Geography of the British Atlantic, circa 1772," *William and Mary Quarterly,* 3rd ser., 60 (2003), 471–510.

10. Gerald Stourzh, *Benjamin Franklin and American Foreign Policy,* 2nd ed. (1954; Chicago, 1969); Max Savelle, *The Origins of American Diplomacy: The International History of Angloamerica, 1492–1763* (New York, 1967).

11. Daniel Baugh, "Maritime Strength and Atlantic Commerce: The Uses of 'A Grand Marine Empire,' " Lawrence Stone, ed., *An Imperial State at War: Britain from 1689 to 1815* (London, 1994).

12. *Extracts from the Votes and Proceedings of the American Continental Congress, Held at Philadelphia, on the Fifth of September, 1774* (London, 1774), 30, 41.

13. See Peter S. Onuf, *The Origins of the Federal Republic: Jurisdictional Controversies in the United States, 1775–1787* (Philadelphia, 1983).

14. John Dickinson, "Arguments against the Independence of the Colonies," in Jack P. Greene, ed., *Colonies to Nation* (New York, 1975), 293. On Congress's deliberations see Jack Rakove, *The Beginnings of National Politics* (New York, 1979); Pauline Maier, *American Scripture: Making the Declaration of Independence* (New York, 1997).

15. Peter S. Onuf and Nicholas G. Onuf, *Federal Union, Modern World: The Law of Nations in an Age of Revolution, 1776–1814* (Madison, Wisc., 1993); David C. Hendrikson, *Peace Pact: The Lost World of the American Founding* (Lawrence, Kans., 2003).

16. Thomas Paine, *Common Sense,* in Greene, ed., *Colonies to Nation,* 278.

17. *Thoughts on Government* (Boston, 1776), reprinted in Robert J. Taylor, ed., *The Papers of John Adams,* 10 vols. to date (Cambridge, Mass., 1977–83), 4:86–93, at 92.

18. Willi Paul Adams, *The First American Constitutions: Republican Ideology and the Making of the State Constitutions in the Revolutionary Era* (Chapel Hill, 1980); Marc W. Kruman, *Between Liberty and Authority: State Constitution Making in Revolutionary America* (Chapel Hill, 1997).

19. Gordon S. Wood, *The Creation of the American Republic, 1776–1787* (Chapel Hill, 1969); C. Bradley Thompson, *John Adams and the Spirit of Liberty* (Lawrence, Kans., 1998).

20. For a good introduction to the ratification contests in the various states see Michael Allen Gillespie and Michael Lienesch, eds., *Ratifying the Constitution* (Lawrence, Kans., 1989).

21. On revolutionary American identities see Peter S. Onuf, *Jefferson's Empire: The Language of American Nationhood* (Charlottesville, 2000) and David Waldstreicher, *In the Midst of Perpetual Fetes: The Making of American Nationalism, 1776–1820* (Chapel Hill, 1997).

22. Jefferson to Edmund Randolph, Aug. 18, 1799, in Andrew A. Lipscomb and Albert Ellery Bergh, eds., *The Writings of Thomas Jefferson,* 20 vols. (Washington, D.C., 1903–4), 10:127–28.

23. See the Continental Congress's Plan of Treaties, July 18, 1776, in Worthington C. Ford, ed., *Journals of the Continental Congress,* 34 vols. (Washington, D.C., 1904–37), 5:576–89. For contrasting interpretations of the "new diplomacy" see Felix Gilbert, *To the Farewell Address: Ideas of Early American Foreign Policy* (Princeton, 1961), and the deflationary account in James Hutson, *John Adams and the Diplomacy of the American Revolution* (Lexington, Ky., 1980).

24. Frederick Marks, III, *Independence on Trial: Foreign Affairs and the Making of the Constitution* (Baton Rouge, 1973).

25. For a good introduction to the period see John R. Howe, Jr., "Republican Thought and the Political Violence of the 1790s," *American Quarterly* 19 (1967), 147–65. On the Federalist campaign against aliens see James Morton Smith, *Freedom's Fetters: The Alien and Sedition Laws and American Civil Liberties* (Ithaca, 1956).

26. Farewell Address, reprinted in Gilbert, *To the Farewell Address,* 145.

27. Simon Newman, *Parades and Politics of the Street: Festive Culture in the Early American Republic* (Philadelphia, 1997); Albrecht Koschnik, "Voluntary Associations, Political Culture, and the Public Sphere in Philadelphia, 1780–1830" (Ph.D. diss., University of Virginia, 2000).

28. John [Holroyd], Lord Sheffield, *Observations on the Commerce of the American States,* rev. ed. (1784; New York, 1970), 190–91.

29. On the importance of compromise in the politics of the early republic see Peter B. Knupfer, *The Union As It Is: Constitutional Unionism and Sectional Compromise, 1787–1861* (Chapel Hill, 1991).

30. [Madison], "Consolidation," *National Gazette,* Dec. 5, 1791, J. C. A. Stagg et al., eds., *The Papers of James Madison: Congressional Series,* 17 vols. (Chicago and Charlottesville, 1959–91), 14:137–39.

31. See Richard D. Brown, "The Emergence of Urban Society in Rural Massachusetts, 1760–1820," *Journal of American History* 61 (1974–75), 29–51, and "The Emergence of Voluntary Associations in Massachusetts, 1760–1830," *Journal of Voluntary Action Research* 2 (1973), 64–73.

32. Alexis de Tocqueville, *Democracy in America,* trans. Phillips Bradley (2 vols., orig. pub., 1835 and 1840; New York, 1945), 2:8–12, 98–101; Nathan Hatch, *The Democratization of American Christianity* (New Haven, Conn., 1989).

33. As François Furet observed of the French Revolution, the answer to this question can vary widely, depending upon how it is constructed. Furet, "The French Revolution Is Over," in Furet, *Interpreting the French Revolution,* trans. Elborg Forster (Cambridge, U.K., 1985).

34. Carl Lotus Becker, *The History of Political Parties in the Province of New York, 1760–1766* (1909; Madison, Wisc., 1968), 22; see also Eliga H. Gould, "Revolution and Counter-Revolution," in David Armitage and Michael Braddick, eds., *The British Atlantic World, 1500–1800* (New York, 2003).

35. On the Loyalists who went to Britain, see especially Mary Beth Norton, *The British-Americans: The Loyalist Exiles in England, 1774–1789* (Boston, 1972). By contrast, there has been far less attention paid to exiles who did not return to the metropolis. A partial exception are the Loyalists who emigrated to Upper Canada (present-day

Ontario); however, Canadian historians tend to emphasize their role as founders of a new colonial society (and proto-nation), typically passing over the fact that they were also refugees from a much older one.

36. Eliga H. Gould, "A Virtual Nation: Greater Britain and the Imperial Legacy of the American Revolution," *American Historical Review* 104 (1999), 476–89; Jaime E. Rodriguez O., "The Emancipation of America," *American Historical Review,* 105 (2000), 131–52; Lester E. Langley, *The Americas in the Age of Revolution, 1750–1850* (New Haven, Conn., 1996).

37. See also David Brion Davis, *The Problem of Slavery in the Age of Revolution, 1770–1823* (Ithaca, 1975).

o n e : Fears of War, Fantasies of Peace

1. Linda Colley, *Britons: Forging the Nation, 1707–1837* (New Haven, Conn., 1992), 5.

2. Paul Kléber Monod, *Jacobitism and the English People, 1688–1788* (Cambridge, U.K., 1989); J. E. Cookson, *The Friends of Peace: Anti-war Liberalism in England* (Cambridge, U.K., 1982).

3. E. P. Thompson, "The Making of a Ruling Class," *Dissent* 40 (1993), 377–82; Nicholas Rogers, *Crowds, Culture, and Politics in Georgian Britain* (Oxford, 1998).

4. Paul Langford, *A Polite and Commercial People: England, 1727–1783* (Oxford, 1989), esp. chaps. 2, 5, and 8; Kathleen Wilson, *The Sense of the People: Politics, Culture, and Imperialism in England, 1715–1785* (Cambridge, U.K., 1995).

5. Jack P. Greene, "'A Posture of Hostility': A Reconsideration of Some Aspects of the Origins of the American Revolution," American Antiquarian Society, *Proceedings,* 87 (1977), 27–68.

6. North's speech, as quoted in *London Evening Post,* Feb. 25, 1775, in R. C. Simmons and P. D. G. Thomas, eds., *Proceedings and Debates of the British Parliaments Respecting North America, 1754–1783,* 6 vols. (White Plains, N.Y., 1982–86), 5:436.

7. [John Wilkes], *Considerations on the Expediency of a Spanish War* (London, 1761), 27–32, 38.

8. *A Letter to a Member of the Honourable the House of Commons, on the Present Important Crisis of National Affairs* (London, 1762), 19.

9. [James Marriott], *Political Considerations; Being a Few Thoughts of a Candid Man at the Present Crisis* (London, 1762), 55.

10. *A Letter to a Member of the Honourable the House of Commons,* 19.

11. *Reasons for Keeping Guadaloupe at a Peace, Preferable to Canada* (London, 1761), 6.

12. [William Burke], *Remarks on the Letter Address'd to Two Great Men* (London, 1760).

13. *The Comparative Importance of our Acquisitions from France in America* (London, 1762), 8.

14. *A Letter from the Cocoa-Tree to the Country-Gentlemen,* 3rd ed. (London, 1763), 5.

15. [Israel Mauduit], *The Plain Reasoner: Or, Farther Considerations on the German War* (London, 1761), 19.

16. *A Compleat History of the Late War; or annual Register of it's Rise, Progress, and Events in Europe, Asia, Africa, and America* (Dublin, 1763), 329; a London edition appeared in 1765.

17. *A Letter to a Member of the Honourable the House of Commons*, 27.

18. [Josiah Tucker], *The Case of Going to War, for the Sake of Procuring, Enlarging, or Securing of Trade, Considered in a New Light* (London, 1763), 14, 37n.

19. Eliga H. Gould, *The Persistence of Empire: British Political Culture in the Age of the American Revolution* (Chapel Hill, 2000), chap. 3; Rogers, *Crowds, Culture, and Politics in Georgian Britain*, chap. 2.

20. [Samuel Johnson], "The Bravery of the English Common Soldier," *British Magazine* (1760), in Donald Greene, ed., *The Yale Edition of the Works of Samuel Johnson*, vol. 10 (New Haven, Conn., 1977), 284.

21. *A Letter to the Right Honourable the Earl of H***x*, 2nd ed. (London, 1763), 10.

22. *An Address to the People of Great-Britain and Ireland, on the Preliminaries of Peace, signed November 3, 1762, between Great-Britain, France, and Spain* (London, 1763), 10; *Some Reasons for Serious Candor in Relation to Vulgar Decisions Concerning Peace or War* (London, 1762), 5.

23. [William Knox], *The Present State of the Nation* (London, 1768), 42.

24. *An Impartial Examination of the Conduct of the Whigs and Tories, from the Revolution down to the Present Time*, 2nd ed. (London, 1764), 150.

25. [William Pulteney, Earl of Bath], *Reflections on the Domestic Policy, Proper to be observed on the Conclusion of a Peace* (London, 1763), 68.

26. See Nicholas Tracy, "The Gunboat Diplomacy of the Government of George Grenville, 1764–1765: The Honduras, Turks Island, and Gambian Incidents," *Historical Journal* 17 (1974), 711–35.

27. [Thomas Whately], *The Regulations Lately Made concerning the Colonies* (London, 1765), 31.

28. *The Political Balance, in Which the Principles and Conduct of the Two Parties Are Weighed* (London, 1765), 60.

29. "Extract of a letter from Boston, in New England," Aug. 5, 1765, in John Almon, ed., *A Collection of Papers Relative to the Dispute between Great Britain and America, 1764–1776* (1777; New York, 1971), 9.

30. Gould, *Persistence of Empire*, 123–26; Jack P. Greene, *Peripheries and Center: Constitutional Development in the Extended Polities of the British Empire and the United States, 1607–1788* (Athens, Ga., 1986).

31. James Otis, *The Rights of the British Colonies Asserted and Proved*, 2nd ed. (London, 1766), 61.

32. Richard Bland, *An Enquiry into the Rights of the British Colonies* (1766; London, 1769), 18 [i.e., 22; pagination error].

33. [Arthur Lee], *An Appeal to the Justice and Interests of the People of Great Britain, in the Present Disputes with America* (London, 1774), 3.

34. Letter to Dennis De Berdt, Jan. 12, 1768, in Thomas Hollis, ed., *The True Sentiments of America* (London, 1768), 73.

35. [John Dickinson], *A New Essay on the Constitutional Power of Great-Britain over the Colonies* (London, 1774), 63–64n. General Gage's father was Thomas Gage, first Viscount Gage.

36. Caroline Robbins, *The Eighteenth-Century Commonwealthman: Studies in the Transmission, Development and Circumstances of English Liberal Thought from the Restoration of Charles II until the War with the Thirteen Colonies* (Cambridge, Mass., 1959); Bernard Bailyn, *The Ideological Origins of the American Revolution* (Cambridge,

Mass., 1967); J. G. A. Pocock, *The Machiavellian Moment: Florentine Political Thought and the Atlantic Republican Tradition* (Princeton, 1975), chaps. 12–14.

37. Pocock, *Machiavellian Moment*, 427–36; Lois Schwoerer, *"No Standing Armies!" The Anti-Army Ideology in Seventeenth-Century England* (Baltimore, 1974); John Childs, *The British Army of William III, 1698–1702* (Manchester, U.K., 1987), chap. 8.

38. See, for example, *A Letter to the Author of An Enquiry into the Revenue, Credit and Commerce of France. Wherein the former and present State of the Power and Commerce of that Kingdom are fully consider'd and deduced from Authentic Accounts. By a Member of Parliament* (London, 1742), 71, where the author lamented that maintaining such troops encouraged ordinary men and women to look no further into the government's conduct of foreign affairs than "the Huzza's of the People of Ostend, upon the Landing of British Regiments."

39. George Farquar, *The Recruiting Officer* (1706), in Shirley Strum Kenny, ed., *The Works of George Farquar*, 2 vols. (Oxford, 1988), 2:41. The stage history comes from the editor's introduction (2:7–10).

40. [William Pulteney], *A Proper Answer to the By-Stander . . .* (London, 1742), 6.

41. *Seasonable and Affecting Observations on the Mutiny-Bill, Articles of War and Use and Abuse of a Standing Army* (London, 1750), 9–10.

42. P. G. M. Dickson, *The Financial Revolution in England: A Study in the Development of Public Credit* (London, 1967).

43. See, for example, Voltaire in *Letters on England,* trans. and ed., Leonard Tancock (New York, 1980), 51.

44. Swift, *The Conduct of the Allies* (1712), in Herbert Davis, ed., *The Prose Works of Jonathan Swift,* 14 vols. (Oxford, 1939–68), 6:42, 53.

45. "Of Public Credit" (1752), in Hume, *Essays: Moral, Political, and Literary,* ed. Eugene F. Miller (Indianapolis, 1985), 352. The passage quoted was only added in 1770; however, it is in keeping with Hume's argument in the rest of the essay.

46. *German Politicks, or The Modern System Examined* (London, 1744), 78.

47. [Thomas Carte], *A Full Answer to the Letter from a By-Stander* (London, 1742), 197.

48. *Craftsman,* no. 245 (March 13, 1730/1).

49. "Major D'Ofranville's Letter to the Right Honourable the Lord Viscount Townshend" (Oxford, Nov. 2, 1716), in *The Several Papers . . . laid before the Right Honourable the Lords Spiritual and Temporal in Parliament assembled, Relating to the Riots at Oxford* (London, 1717), 15.

50. [Pulteney], *A Proper Answer to the By-Stander,* 74.

51. [William Guthrie], *An Address to the Public, on the late Dismission of a General Officer* (London, 1764), 20.

52. *The Question of the Independency of Military Officers Serving in Parliament, Stated and Considered* (London, 1764), 50.

53. *A Letter Addressed to Two Great Men, on the Prospect of Peace* (London, 1760), 45–46.

54. [Samuel Bever], *The Cadet* (London, 1756), 182.

55. *An Address to the Electors of England* (London, 1756), 22.

56. [Richard Burn], *Observations on the New Militia Bill, Now under the Consideration of Parliament* (London, [1757]), 26; Eliga H. Gould, "To Strengthen the King's Hands: Dynastic Legitimacy, Militia Reform and Ideas of National Unity in England,

1745–1760," *Historical Journal* 34 (1991), 329–48; J. R. Western, *The English Militia in the Eighteenth Century: The Story of a Political Issue, 1660–1802* (1965; London, 1993).

57. Gould, *Persistence of Empire*, chap. 3; Rogers, *Crowds, Culture, and Politics*, chap. 2.

58. William Welby, Lt. Col. of the Lincolnshire Militia, to Charles Townshend, May 28, 1761, P.R.O. 20/8/76, 191–93. The officer hit the soldier's cartridge box.

59. Young, *A Letter from a Militia-Man to his Colonel* (London, 1760), 2.

60. *The Complete Militia-Man, or a Compendium of Military Knowledge* (London, 1760), vii.

61. George Townshend and William Windham, *A Plan of Discipline for the Use of the Norfolk Militia,* 3rd rev. ed. (London, 1768; orig. pub., 1759), xxx. For publication history in the colonies, see J. A. Houlding, *Fit for Service: The Training of the British Army, 1715–1795* (Oxford, 1981), 207n.

62. Simmons and Thomas, eds., *Proceedings and Debates,* 1:182–83, 237–38, 268–70, 301–3, 345–46, and 365–67; Stanley J. Pargellis, *Lord Loudoun in America* (New Haven, Conn., 1939), 355.

63. [Alexander Carlyle], *Plain Reasons for Removing a Certain Great Man from His M——y's Presence and Councils for ever . . . by O. M. Haberdasher* (London, 1759), 11–12.

64. William Donaldson, *North America. A Descriptive Poem* (London, 1757), 3.

65. Quoted in [Joseph Grove], *A Letter to a Right Honourable Patriot; Upon the Glorious Success at Quebec* (London, 1759), 25.

66. "An Essay to an Epitaph on . . . Major General Wolfe," *Annual Register* 2 (1759), 452.

67. Donaldson, *North America,* 17–18.

68. [Benjamin Franklin], *The Interest of Great Britain Considered, with Regard to Her Colonies, and the Acquisitions of Canada and Guadaloupe* (London, 1760), 13.

69. *An Examination into the Value of Canada and Guadaloupe, with an Impartial Account of the Latter* (London, 1761), 5; *Reasons for Keeping Guadaloupe,* 57–58.

70. *A Letter to the Right Honourable Ch——s T——nd, Esq.* (London, 1763), 18–19.

71. Pitt's speech on the army estimates for 1764, as quoted in ibid., 20.

72. [David Hartley], *The Budget. Inscribed to the Man, who Thinks Himself Minister,* 6th ed. (London, 1764), 9.

73. See, for example, Pitt's speech on the 1764 army estimates in Simmons and Thomas, eds., *Proceedings and Debates,* 1, 441.

74. *An Application of some General Political Rules, to the Present State of Great-Britain, Ireland and America* (London, 1766), 80.

75. *The Justice and Necessity of Taxing the American Colonies* (London, 1766), 10.

76. Otis, *The Rights of the British Colonies,* 65, 97–98; [Daniel Dulany], *Considerations on the Propriety of Imposing Taxes in the British Colonies* (London, 1766), 54–55, 59.

77. [John Dickinson], *Letters from a Farmer in Pennsylvania, to the Inhabitants of the British Colonies* (London, 1768), 65.

78. [William Knox], *The Claim of the Colonies to an Exemption from Internal Taxes Imposed by Authority of Parliament, Examined* (London, 1765), 26.

79. *Four Dissertations on the Reciprocal Advantages of a Perpetual Union between Great-Britain and her American Colonies* (London, 1766), 103.

80. "Anti-Sejanus: The 'Ingratitude of the Americans,'" *London Chronicle,* 19 (Jan. 28, 1766), in Edmund S. Morgan, ed., *Prologue to Revolution: Sources and Documents on the Stamp Act Crisis, 1764–1766* (1959; Chapel Hill, 1973), 134, 132.

81. *The Justice and Necessity of Taxing the Americans*, 10.

82. Grenville to Captain Samuel Hood, Oct. 30, 1768, quoted in P. D. G. Thomas, *The Townshend Duties Crisis: The Second Phase of the American Revolution, 1767–1773* (Oxford, 1987), 102

83. [John Cartwright], *American Independence the Interest and Glory of Great Britain* (London, 1774), 63. See also Peter S. Onuf, *Jefferson's Empire: The Language of American Nationhood* (Charlottesville, 2000); David C. Hendrickson, "The First Union: Nationalism versus Internationalism in the American Revolution" (in this volume).

84. William Allen, *The American Crisis: A Letter, Addressed by Permission of the Earl Gower, Lord President of the Council, on the present alarming Disturbances in the Colonies* (London, 1774), 26.

85. [Charles Lloyd], *A Short History of the Conduct of the Present Ministry, with Regard to the American Stamp Act*, 2nd ed. (London, 1767), 152.

86. Alexander Carlyle, *The Justice and Necessity of the War with our American Colonies Examined. A Sermon, preached at Inveresk, Dec. 12, 1776* (Edinburgh, 1777), 35–36.

87. Adam Smith, *An Inquiry into the Nature and Causes of The Wealth of Nations* (1776), ed. Edwin Cannan, with a new preface by George J. Stigler, 2 vols. in one (Chicago, 1976), 2:456.

88. Richard Price, *Observations on the Nature of Civil Liberty, the Principles of Government, and the Justice and Policy of the War with America* (London, 1776), 69–70.

89. Richard [Watson], *A Sermon Preached before the Lords Spiritual and Temporal . . . Jan. 30, 1784* (London, 1784), 19.

90. Thomas Day, "Fragment of an Original Letter on the Slavery of the Negroes" (1776), in Day, *Four Tracts* (London, 1785), 13 (paginated separately).

91. William Bolts, *Considerations on India Affairs*, 3 vols. (London, 1772–75), 1:75.

92. "Manifesto and Proclamation . . . by the Earl of Carlisle, Sir Henry Clinton, and William Eden," New York, Oct. 3, 1778, British Library Add. MSS 34,417, 38.

93. East Apthorp, *A Sermon on the General Fast . . . Dec. 13, 1776, for the Pardon of Sins, averting Judgements, imploring Victory, and perpetuating Peace to the British Empire* (London, 1776), 19.

T W O : The First Union

1. Jack P. Greene criticizes orthodoxies old and new in "The Problematic Character of the American Union: The Background of the Articles of Confederation," *Understanding the American Revolution: Issues and Actors* (Charlottesville, 1995), 128–63. The material in quotation is drawn, in rough sequential order, from Richard Morris, *The Forging of the Union, 1781–1789* (New York, 1987), 55–63; Joseph Story, *Commentaries on the Constitution of the United States* (New York, 1970 [1833]), Samuel H. Beer, *To Make a Nation: The Rediscovery of American Federalism* (Cambridge, Mass., 1993), 200–202; and Jack N. Rakove, *The Beginnings of National Politics: An Interpretive History of the Continental Congress* (Baltimore, 1982 [1979]). Morris has elaborated his conclusions in "The Forging of the Union Reconsidered: A Historical Refutation of State Sovereignty over Seabeds," *Columbia Law Review* 74 (1974), 1056–93. See also Curtis P. Nettels, "The Origin of the Union and of the States," Massachusetts Historical Society, *Proceedings* 72 (1957–60), 68–83, and Samuel H. Beer, "Federalism, Nationalism, and Democracy in America," *American Political Science Review* 72 (1978), 9–21.

2. John Locke, *Two Treatises on Government,* Peter Laslett, ed., (Cambridge, U.K., 1988), 2nd Treatise, XII, para. 146, p. 365; Nicholas Greenwood Onuf, *The Republican Legacy in International Thought* (Cambridge, U.K., 1998), 233; J. G. A. Pocock, "States, Republics, and Empires: The American Founding in Early Modern Perspective," in Terence Ball and J. G. A. Pocock, eds., *Conceptual Change and the Constitution* (Lawrence, Kans., 1988), 55–77.

3. "Thoughts on the State of the Contest with America," Feb. 1778, in E. C. Mossner and I. S. Ross, eds., *The Correspondence of Adam Smith* (Oxford, 1987), 383.

4. S. Rufus Davis, *The Federal Principle: A Journey through Time in Quest of a Meaning* (Berkeley, 1978), 3, 38.

5. L. H. Butterfield, ed., *Diary and Autobiography of John Adams,* 4 vols. (New York, 1964), 4:38–39.

6. *Letters from a Farmer in Pennsylvania,* in Forrest McDonald, ed., *Empire and Nation* (Indianapolis, 1999), 38. See also Jack P. Greene, *Negotiated Authorities: Essays in Colonial Political and Constitutional History* (Charlottesville, 1994).

7. See the illuminating discussion in Daniel Webster's speech on the Panama mission in 1826. Edward Everett, ed., *The Works of Daniel Webster,* 6 vols.(Boston, 1858), 3:195–96.

8. John Adams's Notes of Debates, Sept. 6, 1774, Paul H. Smith et al., eds., *Letters of Delegates to Congress, 1774–1789,* 25 vols.(Washington, D.C., 1976–98) 1:28.

9. John Adams to Abigail Adams, June 17, 1775, ibid., 1:497.

10. John Adams to Patrick Henry, June 3, 1776, in Robert J. Taylor et al., eds., *The Papers of John Adams,* 10 vols. to date (Cambridge, Mass., 1977–), 4:234–35. For a similar enumeration, see Adams to William Cushing, June 9, 1776, ibid., 244–45.

11. John Adams to Hezekiah Niles, Feb. 13, 1818, *The Works of John Adams, Second President of the United States: with a Life of the Author,* 10 vols. (Boston, 1850–56), 10:283.

12. The Declaration of Independence, in Merrill D. Peterson, ed., *Thomas Jefferson Writings* (New York, 1984), 19, 23–24.

13. Resolution on Required Texts, Minutes of the Board of Visitors of the University of Virginia, March 4, 1825, in Peterson, ed., *Jefferson Writings,* 479.

14. Jack P. Greene, *Peripheries and Center: Constitutional Development in the Extended Polities of the British Empire and the United States, 1607–1788* (Athens, Ga., 1986), 144.

15. See, e.g., Josiah Tucker, *A Letter to Edmund Burke,* in Robert Livingston Schuyler, ed., *Josiah Tucker: A Selection from His Economic and Political Writings* (New York, 1931), 381–84.

16. James H. Hutson, *John Adams and the Diplomacy of the American Revolution* (Lexington, Ky., 1980).

17. David Ramsay, "An Oration on the Advantages of American Independence . . . ," July 4, 1778, in Hezekiah Niles, *Principles and Acts of the Revolution in America* (New York, 1876), 381.

18. For a similar analysis, see Jerrilyn Greene Marston, *King and Congress: The Transfer of Political Legitimacy, 1774–1776* (Princeton, 1987); Peter S. Onuf, *The Origins of the Federal Republic: Jurisdictional Controversies in the United States, 1775–1787* (Philadelphia, 1983), 16; John M. Murrin, "1787: The Invention of American Federalism," in David E. Narrett and Joyce S. Goldberg, eds., *Essays on Liberty and Federalism: The Shaping of the U.S. Constitution* (College Station, Tex., 1988), 32. On the imperial

constitution as a "template" for federal union, see Peter S. Onuf, *Jefferson's Empire: The Language of American Nationhood* (Charlottesville, 2000).

19. Thomas Burke to the North Carolina Assembly, Oct. 25, 1779, *Letters of Delegates,* 14:109.

20. On the continuities between 1777 and 1787 in the authority allocated to Congress and the states, see Andrew C. McLaughlin, *The Constitutional History of the United States* (New York, 1935), 125; and Alexander H. Stephens, *A Constitutional View of the Late War Between the States,* 2 vols. (Philadelphia, 1868), 84–87.

21. Merrill Jensen, ed., *The Documentary History of the Ratification of the Constitution* (Madison, Wisc., 1976), 1:86. Merrill Jensen, *The Articles of Confederation: An Interpretation of the Social-Constitutional History of the American Revolution, 1774–1781* (Madison, Wisc., 1959), 137; Morris, *Forging of the Union,* 88. Rakove's nuanced and imaginative treatment still gives a greater importance to this amendment than in my judgment it deserves. Rakove, *Beginnings of National Politics,* 171.

22. "Thoughts on Government" (1776), *Papers of John Adams,* 4:92.

23. Emmerich de Vattel, *The Law of Nations, or the Principles of Natural Law Applied to the Conduct and to the Affairs of Nations and of Sovereigns,* ed. Charles G. Fenwick (Washington, 1916 [1758]), chap. 1, no. 10, p. 12. See also the discussion of Burlamaqui, Pufendorf, and Montesquieu in St. George Tucker, *View of the Constitution of the United States with Selected Writings* (Indianapolis, 1999 [1803]); and, more generally, the analysis in S. Rufus Davis, *The Federal Principle,* and Peter Onuf and Nicholas Onuf, *Federal Union: Modern World: The Law of Nations in an Age of Revolutions, 1776–1814* (Madison, Wisc., 1993).

24. Thomas Burke's "Notes on the Articles of Confederation," [ca. Dec. 18, 1777], *Letters of Delegates,* 8:435, and Jack N. Rakove, "The Articles of Confederation, 1775–1783," in Jack P. Greene and J. R. Pole, eds., *The Blackwell Encyclopedia of the American Revolution* (Cambridge, Mass., 1994), 292.

25. John Witherspoon's Speech in Congress, [July 30, 1776], *Letters of Delegates,* 4:584–87.

26. John Adams's Notes of Debate, July 30, 1776, *Letters of Delegates,* 4:568.

27. Benjamin Rush's Notes for a Speech in Congress, [Aug. 1, 1776], *Letters of Delegates,* 4:600–601.

28. Cf. Thomas Burke to Richard Caswell, March 11, 1777, *Letters of Delegates,* 6:427. See Jensen, *Articles of Confederation,* Joseph L. Davis, *Sectionalism in American Politics* (Madison, Wisc., 1977).

29. James Wilson's Summation and Final Rebuttal, Dec. 11, 1787, in Bernard Bailyn, ed., *The Debate on the Constitution,* 2 vols.(New York, 1993), 1:832–68, at 866; Benjamin Franklin to Ferdinand Grand, Oct. 22, 1787, in Jared Sparks, ed., *The Works of Benjamin Franklin,* 10 vols. (Boston, 1840), 9:619.

30. Entry for Sept. 17, 1774, *Diary and Autobiography,* 2:134–35.

31. John Adams to Abigail Adams, June 17, 1775, *Letters of Delegates,* 1:497; *Diary and Autobiography,* 3:321–22; Rossie, *Politics of Command,* 11–12. On sectional compromise, see Don Higginbotham, *The War of American Independence: Military Attitudes, Policies, and Practice, 1763–1789* (New York, 1971), 83. On regional differentiation more generally, see Jack P. Greene, *Imperatives, Behaviors, and Identities: Essays in Early American Cultural History* (Charlottesville, 1992); D. W. Meinig, *The Shaping of America: A Geographical Perspective on Five Hundred Years of History,* 3 vols. to date, Volume 1, *Atlantic*

America, 1792–1800 (New Haven, Conn., 1986); and David Hackett Fischer, *Albion's Seed: Four British Folkways in America* (New York, 1989).

32. George Washington to Richard Henry Lee, Aug. 29, 1775, cited in Rossie, *Politics of Command*, 28.

33. John Adams to Henry Knox, Sept. 29, 1776, *Letters of Delegates*, 5:260.

34. John Thomas to John Adams, Oct. 24, 1775, *Papers of John Adams*, 3:241.

35. John Witherspoon, *The Dominion of Providence over the Passions of Men* (Philadelphia, 1776), cited in H. James Henderson, *Party Politics in the Continental Congress* (New York, 1974), 71.

36. John Adams to Joseph Hawley, Nov. 25, 1775, *Letters of Delegates*, 2:385–86.

37. Richard Henry Lee to Patrick Henry, May 26, 1777, *Letters of Delegates*, 7:123–24.

38. See Henderson, *Party Politics in the Continental Congress*, and Davis, *Sectionalism in American Politics*.

39. Jefferson to William Fleming, June 8, 1779, Julian P. Boyd et al., eds., *The Papers of Thomas Jefferson*, 31 vols. to date, (Princeton, 1950–), 2:288.

40. Gerry to Congress, June 19, 1779, *Letters of Delegates*, 13:84n.

41. Christopher Gadsen to Samuel Adams, April 4, 1779, Richard Walsh, ed., *The Writings of Christopher Gadsen, 1746–1805* (Columbia, S.C., 1966), 161–64.

42. James Warren to John Adams, June 13, 1779, *Papers of John Adams*, 8:93–94.

43. See discussion in Merrill D. Peterson, *Adams and Jefferson: A Revolutionary Dialogue* (New York, 1976).

44. "Official Letter Accompanying Act of Confederation," Nov. 17, 1777, Elliot, *Debates*, 1:69–70.

45. See the review of this controversy in Kenneth M. Stampp, "The Concept of Perpetual Union," *The Imperiled Union: Essays on the Background of the Civil War* (New York, 1980), 3–36.

46. North Carolina Delegates to Richard Caswell, May 20, 1779, *Letters of Delegates*, 12:499.

47. Thomas Burke to the Assembly of the State of North Carolina, Oct. 31, 1779, *Letters of Delegates*, 14:119n.

48. "Circular Letter from Congress to their Constituents," Sept. 8, 1779, in Henry P. Johnston, ed., *The Correspondence and Public Papers of John Jay*, 4 vols. (New York, 1890), 1:229–30.

49. James Madison to Thomas Jefferson, Nov. 18, 1781, Boyd et al., eds., *Papers of Jefferson*, 6:131–32.

50. John Joseph Meng, *Despatches and Instructions of Conrad Alexandre Gérard, 1776–1780* (Baltimore, 1939), 763–67; Daniel of St. Thomas Jennifer's Notes on Franco-American Alliance, [July 4? 1779], *Letters of Delegates*, 13:145–48n.

51. David Ramsay to Nicholas Van Dyke, April 1, 1786, *Letters of Delegates*, 23:214.

52. See John Murrin, "A Roof Without Walls: The Dilemma of American National Identity," in Richard Beeman, Stephen Botein, and Edward C. Carter II, eds., *Beyond Confederation: Origins of the Constitution and American National Identity* (Chapel Hill, 1987).

T H R E E : War and State Formation in Revolutionary America

1. By the early eighteenth century, virtually every major European state seems to have been "invented": France, Spain, the Netherlands, Austria, Prussia, Russia, and

Britain. An applicable term for them is "composite" states. For national identity and the nationalization of culture, I have been especially influenced by Ernest Gellner, *National and Nationalism* (Oxford, 1983); Bruce D. Porter, *War and the Rise of the State* (New York, 1994); Benedict Anderson, *Imagined Communities: Reflections on the Origins and Spread of Nationalism,* rev. ed. (London, 1991); and Lawrence Stone, ed., *An Imperial State at War: Britain from 1689 to 1815* (London, 1994).

2. The best introduction to this literature and the controversies surrounding the subject is Clifford J. Rogers, ed., *The Military Revolution Debate* (Boulder, Colo., 1995).

3. Charles Tilly, ed., *The Formation of National States in Western Europe* (New York, 1975), and *Coercion, Capital, and the European States, AD 990–1990* (Oxford, 1990).

4. Geoffrey Parker, "In Defense of the Military Revolution," in Rogers, ed., *Military Revolution Debate,* 341. John A. Lynn, however, warns against oversimplifications about the connection between centralization, bureaucratization, and armies in the early modern era. For France, as an example, see his *Giant of the Grand Siecle: The French Army, 1610–1715* (New York, 1997), "Epilogue: Insights on State Formation."

5. Brian M. Downing, *The Military Revolution and Political Change in Early Modern Europe* (Princeton, 1992), examines the relationship between major wars and the political character of European states. See also Stone, ed., *Imperial State at War,* chaps. 1, 2, 3, 8.

6. Linda Colley, *Britons: Forging the Nation, 1707–1837* (New Haven, Conn., 1992); John Brewer, *The Sinews of Power: War, Money, and the English State, 1688–1783* (New York, 1989); Stone, ed., *Imperial State at War,* chaps. 3, 5.

7. Leonard W. Labaree, *Royal Government in America: A Study of the British Colonial System before 1783* (New Haven, Conn., 1930), esp. chaps. 3, 10; Jack P. Greene, *The Quest for Power: The Lower Houses of Assembly in the Southern Royal Colonies, 1689–1776* (Chapel Hill, 1963), 297–309.

8. William Pencak, *War, Politics, and Revolution* (Boston, 1981), xi, xii, 5, 6.

9. Jack P. Greene, *Negotiated Authorities: Essays in Colonial and Constitutional History* (Charlottesville, 1994), 178, 179.

10. Ibid., chap. 1; Mark Greengrass, ed., *Conquest and Coalescence: The Shaping of the State in Early Modern Europe* (London, 1991).

11. The best treatment of American Whigs' methods and tactics is Pauline Maier, *From Resistance to Revolution: Colonial Radicals and the Development of American Opposition to Britain, 1765–1776* (New York, 1972).

12. Detailed narratives of the dozen years before independence include ibid.; Lawrence Henry Gipson, *The Coming of the Revolution, 1763–1775* (New York, 1954); Bernard Knollenberg, *Origin of the American Revolution, 1759–1766* (New York, 1960) and *The Growth of the American Revolution, 1766–1775* (New York, 1975); Merrill Jensen, *The Founding of a Nation: A History of the American Revolution, 1763–1776* (New York, 1968).

13. Don Higginbotham, ed., *The Papers of James Iredell, 1767–1783,* 2 vols. (Raleigh, 1976), 2:19.

14. The rich literature on the evolution of American constitutional thinking includes Charles H. McIlwain, *The American Revolution: A Constitutional Interpretation* (New York, 1923); Andrew C. McLaughlin, *The Foundations of American Constitutionalism* (New York, 1932); Jack P. Greene, *Peripheries and Center: Constitutional Development in the Extended Polities of the British Empire and the United States, 1607–1788*

(Athens, Ga., 1986); Bernard Bailyn, *The Ideological Origins of the American Revolution,* enlarged ed. (Cambridge, Mass., 1992). The most prolific author in the last generation on constitutional issues is John Phillip Reid. A preliminary evaluation of his work is Jack P. Greene, "From the Perspective of Law: Context and Legitimacy in the Origins of the American Revolution. A Review Essay," *South Atlantic Quarterly* 85 (1986), 56–77.

15. Don Higginbotham, "The American Militia: A Traditional Institution with Revolutionary Responsibilities," in Don Higginbotham, ed., *Reconsiderations on the Revolutionary War* (Westport, Conn., 1778), 87–89, 92, 93, 95–96; William H. Nelson, *The American Tory* (New York, 1961), 17–20, 31–32; Jensen, *Founding of a Nation,* chaps. 18–24; Benjamin Woods Labaree, *The Boston Tea Party* (New York, 1964), chaps. 11–13; David Ammerman, *In the Common Cause: American Response to the Coercive Acts of 1774* (Charlottesville, 1974), chap. 8.

16. John Phillip Reid, *In a Defiant Stance: The Conditions of Law in Massachusetts Bay, the Irish Comparison, and the Coming of the American Revolution* (University Park, Pa., 1977), and *In a Rebellious Spirit: The Argument of Facts, the Liberty Riot, and the Coming of the American Revolution* (University Park, Pa., 1979).

17. Studies that offer a cautionary note as to claims for cultural and evolutionary national feeling in eighteenth-century America are S. N. Eisenstadt, *Revolution and the Transformation of Societies: A Comparative Study of Civilizations* (New York, 1978); and Yehoshua Arieli, *Individualism and Nationalism in American Ideology* (Cambridge, Mass., 1964).

18. Congress refused even to consider Joseph Galloway of Pennsylvania's proposed Plan of Union, which advocated intercolonial defense and control of Indian affairs, as well as a legislative union with Britain. The plan is analyzed in Julian P. Boyd, ed., *Anglo-American Union: Joseph Galloway's Plans to Preserve the British Empire* (Philadelphia, 1941). A recent reexamination of Congress's negative reaction to Galloway's proposal is in Paul H. Smith, ed., *Letters of Delegates to Congress, 1774–1789,* 27 vols. (Washington, D.C., 1976–98), 1:112–13, 116–17.

19. Jack N. Rakove, *The Beginnings of National Politics: An Interpretive History of the Continental Congress* (New York, 1979), chaps. 1–3; Ammerman, *In the Common Cause,* chaps. 1–3; Greene, *Peripheries and Center,* chap. 7; Jerrilyn Greene Marston, *King and Congress: The Transfer of Political Legitimacy, 1774–1776* (Princeton, 1987), chaps. 1–4.

20. The delegates resorted to both "assertiveness and deference" in their desperate effort "to combine empire and liberty." Neil L. York, "The First Continental Congress and the Problem of American Rights," *Pennsylvania Magazine of History and Biography* 122 (1998), 354–83, quotations on 376, demonstrates the difficulties that congressmen felt about asserting their principles without implying a threat to secede from the empire.

21. One scholar even calls the Second Continental Congress "a more conservative body than the first." Nelson, *American Tory,* 116–17.

22. John Adams to James Warren, July 6, 1775, in Smith, ed., *Letters of Delegates,* 1:589.

23. Rakove, *Beginnings of National Politics,* chaps. 5–6; John Ferling, *John Adams: A Life* (Knoxville, 1992), 123; Smith, ed., *Letters of Delegates,* 3:63–68, for Dickinson's proposed resolutions for negotiating with the king.

24. Emory M. Thomas, *The Confederate Nation, 1861–1865* (New York, 1979), 58–66; Richard E. Beringer et al., *Why the South Lost the Civil War* (Athens, Ga., 1986), 75–81; William C. Davis, *"A Government of our Own": The Making of the Confederacy* (New York, 1994).

25. Richard Henry Lee to Thomas Jefferson, Aug. 25, 1777, in Smith, ed., *Letters of Delegates,* 7:551.

26. McLaughlin, *The Foundations of American Constitutionalism,* chap. 6., and *A Constitutional History of the United States* (New York, 1935), chaps. 1–3, remain the most thoughtful accounts of American federalism from before 1763 to 1787.

27. Charles Royster, *A Revolutionary People at War: The Continental Army and American Character, 1775–1783* (Chapel Hill, 1979), chap. 1, describes the *rage militaire.* For quotation, see Peter S. Onuf, *The Origins of the Federal Republic: Jurisdictional Controversies in the United States, 1775–1783* (Philadelphia, 1983), 7.

28. H. Trevor Colbourn, *The Lamp of Experience: Whig History and the Intellectual Origins of the American Revolution* (Chapel Hill, 1965); Lois G. Schwoerer, *"No Standing Armies": The Antiarmy Ideology in Seventeenth-Century England* (Baltimore, 1974); Don Higginbotham, *George Washington and the American Military Tradition* (Athens, Ga., 1985), chap. 2.

29. Richard R. Johnson, "'Parliamentary Egotisms': The Clash of Legislatures in the Making of the American Revolution," *Journal of American History* 74 (1987), 338–62; Onuf, *Origins of the Federal Republic,* 21–22; Greene, *Peripheries and Center,* 164–65.

30. The last two paragraphs draw heavily on Gordon Wood, *The Creation of the American Republic, 1776–1787* (Chapel Hill, 1969), chap. 9; Rakove, *Beginnings of National Politics,* 133–215; Morris, *The Forging of the Union,* chap. 4; and Greene, *Peripheries and Center,* chap. 8.

31. David C. Hendrickson argues convincingly that Burke's amendment, contrary to the view of most historians, "was supremely unimportant" and merely repeated the conventional understanding of Congress's limited authority. See his "The First Union: Nationalism vs. Internationalism in the American Revolution," in this volume.

32. Samuel Johnston to Thomas Burke, April 19, 1777, Early University Papers, University of North Carolina at Chapel Hill.

33. "Gouverneur Morris' Proposals on Fiscal and Administrative Reform," [June–July? 1778], in Smith, ed., *Letters of Delegates,* 10:202–16, quotation on 208. Throughout the history of the Continental Congress and the Confederation, Morris offered penetrating commentaries on the federal government and the union. See also Mary-Jo Kline, *Gouverneur Morris and the New Nation, 1775–1778* (New York, 1978), 109–26.

34. Jefferson criticized the constitutional division of powers that enfeebled Virginia's chief executive in his *Notes on the State of Virginia,* ed. William Peden (Chapel Hill, 1954), Query XIII, "The Constitution of the State."

35. Charles E. Bennett and Donald R. Lennon, *A Quest for Glory: Major General Robert Howe and the American Revolution* (Chapel Hill, 1991), chap. 7; John S. Pancake, *This Destructive War: The British Campaign in the Carolinas, 1780–1782* (University, Ala., 1985), 63–67.

36. Richard H. Kohn, *Eagle and Sword: The Federalists and the Creation of the Military Establishment in America, 1783–1802* (New York, 1975), chap. 2; Kenneth Bowling, "New Light on the Philadelphia Meeting of 1783: Federal-State Confrontation at the Close of the War for Independence," *Pennsylvania Magazine of History and Biography* 101 (1977), 419–50; Richard B. Morris, *The Peacemakers: The Great Powers and American Independence* (New York, 1965), 440–48.

37. Don Higginbotham, "George Washington's Contributions to American Constitutionalism," in Higginbotham, *War and Society in Revolutionary America: The Wider Dimensions of Conflict* (Columbia, S.C., 1988), 193–213.

38. Merrill Jensen, *The New Nation: A History of the United States during the Confederation, 1781–1789* (New York, 1950), 54–84; E. Wayne Carp, "The Origins of the Nationalist Movement of 1780–1783: Congressional Administration and the Continental Army," *Pennsylvania Magazine of History and Biography* 107 (1983), 363–92. For the argument that there was no cohesive centralist movement in Congress in the early 1780s, see Rakove, *Beginnings of National Politics*, 307–24; and Lance Banning, "James Madison and the Nationalists, 1780–1783," *William and Mary Quarterly*, 3rd ser., 40 (1983), 227–55.

39. Jackson Turner Main, *Political Parties before the Constitution* (Chapel Hill, 1973), esp. chaps. 12–13.

40. Rakove, *Beginnings of National Politics*, chaps. 12–14; Richard B. Morris, *The Forging of the Union, 1781–1789* (New York, 1987), 95–97; Michael McShane Burns, "John Jay as Secretary for Foreign Affairs" (Ph.D. diss., University of North Carolina at Chapel Hill, 1974), chap. 6, esp. 284–87; Julian P. Boyd, "Two Diplomats Between Revolutions: John Jay and Thomas Jefferson," *Virginia Magazine of History and Biography* 67 (1959), 131–46.

41. Morris, *The Forging of the Union*, 194–204; Charles R. Ritcheson, *Aftermath of the Revolution: British Policy Toward the United States, 1783–1795* (Dallas, 1969), chaps. 4–5; Burns, "John Jay," chap. 4; Rakove, *Beginnings of National Politics*, chap. 14; Roberta Jacobs, "The Treaty and the Tories: The Ideological Reaction to the Return of the Loyalists" (Ph.D. diss., Cornell University, 1974).

42. For the military fortunes of the Confederation, see Don Higginbotham, *The War of American Independence: Military Attitudes, Policy, and Practice, 1763–1789* (New York, 1971), 438–52; and Harry M. Ward, *The Department of War, 1781–1795* (Pittsburgh, 1962), chaps. 7–9, Knox quotation on 80.

43. Burns, "John Jay," chap. 5; Morris, *Forging of the Union*, chap. 9; Onuf, *Origins of the Federal Republic*, chap. 7; Peter S. Onuf, "Anarchy and the Crisis of the Union," in Herman Belz et al., eds., *To Form a More Perfect Union: The Critical Ideas of the Constitution* (Charlottesville, 1992), 272–302.

44. Willi Paul Adams, *The First American Constitutions: Republican Ideology and the Making of the State Constitutions in the Revolutionary Era* (Chapel Hill, 1980), 86–93, 268–69, 273, 290; Onuf, *Origins of the Federal Republic*.

45. The secondary literature of Antifederalism has reached substantial proportions. Still quite valuable for an overview is Jackson Turner Main, *The Antifederalists: Critics of the Constitution, 1781–1788* (Chapel Hill, 1961). A new monograph that stresses Antifederalist thought and its place in the American political tradition is Saul Cornell, *The Other Founders: Antifederalism and the Dissenting Tradition in America, 1788–1827* (Chapel Hill, 1999).

46. Stanley Elkins and Eric McKittrick, *The Founding Fathers: Young Men of the Revolution* (Washington, D.C., 1961), an American Historical Association pamphlet; Main, *The Antifederalists*, 260n.

47. Main, *Political Parties*, 455.

48. Higginbotham, "George Washington's Contributions to American Constitutionalism," 208–9; Stuart Leibiger, *Founding Friendship: George Washington, James Madison, and the Creation of the American Republic* (Charlottesville, 1999), 60, 64,

67–68; Glen A. Phelps, *George Washington and American Constitutionalism* (Lawrence, Kans., 1993), 92–95. No single letter better captures Washington's apprehension than his missive to Henry Lee, April 4, 1786, in W. W. Abbot et al., eds., *The Papers of George Washington, Confederation Series,* 6 vols. (Charlottesville, 1992–97), 4:4.

49. Circular to the States, June 1783, in John C. Fitzpatrick, ed., *Writings of George Washington,* 39 vols. (Washington, D.C., 1931–44), 23:483–96; Merrill Jensen, et al., eds., *The Documentary History of the Ratification of the Constitution,* 18 vols. to date, not numbered consecutively (Madison, Wisc., 1976–), 13:60–61.

50. The recent study of the Washington-Madison alliance and Madison's overall role is Leibiger, *Founding Friendship,* chap. 3. A more detailed account of Madison's part in the writing and ratification of the Constitution is Lance Banning, *The Sacred Fire of Liberty: James Madison and the Founding of the Federal Republic* (Ithaca, 1995), chaps. 4–8. Monroe's interpretation of the outcome in Virginia is in Julian P. Boyd et al., eds., *The Papers of Thomas Jefferson,* 31 vols. to date (Princeton, 1950–), 13:351–52. For Jefferson's letter to Adams, Aug. 30, 1787, see Max Farrand, ed., *Records of the Federal Convention of 1787,* rev. ed., 4 vols. (New Haven, Conn., 1937), 3:76.

51. Peter Gay, *Voltaire's Politics: The Poet as Realist,* 2nd ed. (New Haven, Conn., 1988), quotations on 180, 181.

52. These remarks on Washington are drawn from my *George Washington: Uniting a Nation* (Lanham, Md., 2002), which examines his public life and imagery in the context of leadership in Europe and America in the Early Modern era.

53. Jacob E. Cooke, ed., *The Federalist* (Wesleyan, Conn., 1961), 250–57, for Madison's analysis.

54. Madison's Notes, in Farrand, ed., *Records of the Federal Convention,* 2:88.

55. Walter Millis, *Arms and Men* (New York, 1956), 41. See also Richard H. Kohn, "The Constitution and National Security: The Intent of the Framers," in Richard H. Kohn, ed., *The United States Military under the Constitution of the United States, 1789–1989* (New York, 1991), 61–94.

56. Kohn, *Eagle and Sword,* esp. chap. 14; Andrew R. L. Cayton, "'Separate Interests' and the Nation-State: The Washington Administration and the Origins of Regionalism in the Trans-Appalachian West," *Journal of American History* 79 (1992), 39–67, quotation on 47.

FOUR: John Adams, Republican Monarchist

1. Johns Adams [hereafter, JA], *A Defence of the Constitutions of Government of the United States,* 3 vols. (London, 1787–88); Charles Francis Adams, ed., *The Works of John Adams, Second President of the United States: with a Life of the Author,* 10 vols. (Boston, 1850–56; hereafter, Adams, *Works*), vols. 4–6.

2. *Discourses on Davila, Gazette of the United States* (serial publication, New York and Philadelphia, 1790–91); Adams, *Works,* 6:223–403, with marginal notes by JA up to 1813.

3. [JA], "Reply of the [Massachusetts] House [of Representatives] to [Governor Thomas] Hutchinson," Jan. 26 (first reply), and March 2 (second reply), 1773, in Robert J. Taylor et al., eds., *Papers of John Adams,* 10 vols. to date (Cambridge, Mass., 1977– ; hereafter, JA, *Papers*), 1:309–46.

4. *Letters of Novanglus,* Letter 7, March 6, 1775, JA, *Papers,* 2:314.

5. [JA], *Thoughts on Government* (Philadelphia, 1776), JA, *Papers,* 4:86–93.

6. [JA], *The Report of a Constitution or Form of Government for the Commonwealth of Massachusetts* (Boston, 1779), JA, *Papers*, 8:236–61.

7. *Thoughts on Government*, JA, *Papers*, 4:87.

8. Gordon S. Wood, *The Creation of the American Republic* (Chapel Hill, 1969), esp. chaps. 6, 9, 11, 13.

9. John R. Howe, *The Changing Political Thought of John Adams* (Princeton, 1966), esp. chap. 4; Wood, *Creation of the American Republic*, esp. chap. 14; Joyce O. Appleby, "The New Republican Synthesis and the Changing Political Ideas of John Adams," *American Quarterly* 25 (1973), 578–95.

10. "Clarendon to Pym," Letter 3, *Boston Gazette*, Jan. 27, 1766, JA, *Papers*, 1:167.

11. First and second "Reply of the House to [Governor] Hutchinson," JA, *Papers*, 1:315–30, 331–45.

12. James Wilson, *Considerations on the Nature and Extent of the Legislative Authority of the British Parliament* (Philadelphia, 1774); Thomas Jefferson, *A Summary View of the Rights of British-America* (Philadelphia, 1774).

13. *Letters of Novanglus*, Letter 7, March 6, 1775, JA, *Papers*, 2:314. Adams usually employed "republic" to indicate a government that balanced the principles of monarchy, aristocracy, and democracy. In *Novanglus*, however, he may also have meant an extended confederation of autonomous provinces under one head of state.

14. Published serially in the *Boston Gazette*, republished in one volume in 1768; see JA, *Papers*, 1:103–28.

15. J. G. A. Pocock, *Virtue, Commerce, and History: Essays on Political Thought and History, Chiefly in the Eighteenth Century* (Cambridge, U.K., 1985), esp. chap. 11; and Eliga H. Gould, *The Persistence of Empire: British Political Culture in the Age of the American Revolution* (Chapel Hill, 2000), chap. 6.

16. Pauline R. Maier, *American Scripture: Making the Declaration of Independence* (New York, 1997), 122–23 (quoting Adams to Timothy Pickering, Aug. 6, 1822, JA, *Works*, 2:514).

17. Adams to Lee, Nov. 15, 1775, JA, *Papers*, 3:307–8.

18. Adams to Penn, [ante March 27, 1776], ibid., 4:82.

19. Ibid., 4:89.

20. Adams to James Warren, May 12 and June 16, 1776, ibid., 4:182, 316.

21. Ibid., 8:228–71.

22. Ibid., 8:242.

23. Ibid. *The Report's* "Frame of Government," encompassing the provisions for the legislative, executive, and judicial powers, is at ibid., 8:242–57.

24. *The Report*, "Chap. III. Executive Power. Section I. Governor," arts. i, ii, v–xv, ibid., 8:249–50, 251–54.

25. Jack P. Greene, "Legislative Turnover in Colonial British America, 1696 to 1775: A Quantitative Analysis," *William and Mary Quarterly*, 3rd ser., 38 (1981), 442–63; Richard Alan Ryerson, "Portrait of a Colonial Oligarchy: The Quaker Elite in the Pennsylvania Assembly, 1729–1776," in Bruce C. Daniels, ed., *Power and Status: Officeholding in Colonial America* (Middletown, Conn., 1986), 106–35, 295–300.

26. See *The Report*, "Chap. II. The Frame of Government," "Section II. Senate," art. v, and "Section III. House of Representatives," art. iii, JA, *Papers*, 8:246, 248.

27. See ibid., 8:236, 368–69, 377–78; 9:136, 138, and many subsequent references (see index in vol. 10); JA, *Diary and Autobiography*, ed. L. H. Butterfield, 4 vols. (Cambridge,

Mass., 1961), 2:413; L. H. Butterfield et al., eds., *Adams Family Correspondence,* 6 vols. to date (Cambridge, Mass., 1963–93), 3:228, 349.

28. Abigail Adams to Mary Smith Cranch, Dec. 9, 1784; Abigail Adams to Royal Tyler, [Jan. 4, 1785], *Adams Family Correspondence,* 6:18, 45, 50.

29. See Appleby, "John Adams and the New Republican Synthesis," 194n. 8 (quoting JA to Samuel Perley, June 19, 1809, in which JA partly misremembers the past), on the Assembly of Notables; and Howe, *Changing Political Thought of John Adams,* 106–7, and JA to Thomas Jefferson, Nov. 30, 1786, in Lester J. Cappon, ed., *The Adams-Jefferson Letters: The Complete Correspondence between Thomas Jefferson and Abigail and John Adams,* 2 vols. (Chapel Hill, 1959), 1:156, on Shays's Rebellion.

30. JA began writing the *Defence* shortly after a visit to Holland in 1786 (Abigail Adams to Mary Smith Cranch, Sept. 12, 1786, Abigail Adams Correspondence, American Antiquarian Society; Abigail Adams to Cotton Tufts, Oct. 10, 1786, recipient's copy, Mannes School of Music, New York City, and draft, Adams Papers, Microfilms, reel 369; and JA to Thomas Jefferson, Sept. 11, 1786, in Cappon, ed., *Adams-Jefferson Letters,* 1:152–153). The best study of JA's *Defence* is C. Bradley Thompson, *John Adams and the Spirit of Liberty* (Lawrence, Kans., 1998).

31. Adams, *Works,* 4:379–80.

32. Abigail Adams to John Quincy Adams, March 20, 1787, Adams Papers, Microfilms, reel 369.

33. JA to Jefferson, Dec. 6, 1787, in Cappon, ed., *Adams-Jefferson Letters,* 1:213–14 (see also JA to Jefferson, Nov. 10, 1787, and Jefferson to JA, Nov. 13, 1787, in ibid., 1:210, 211–12).

34. The principal advocates of this view are John Howe, Gordon Wood, and Joyce Appleby; see notes 9 and 29, above.

35. Howe, *Changing Political Thought of John Adams,* chap. 4.

36. See JA to James Warren, Feb. 25, 1779, JA to the President of Congress, Feb. 27, 1779, JA, *Papers,* 7:427–31; JA to Abigail Adams, Feb. 20 (2nd letter), and 28 (1st letter), 1779, *Adams Family Correspondence,* 3:175, 181–82; and Howe, *Changing Political Thought of John Adams,* 108–12.

37. See William Pencak, "John Adams and the Massachusetts Provincial Elite," in Richard Alan Ryerson, ed., *John Adams and the Founding of the Republic* (Boston, 2001).

38. Zoltan Haraszti, *John Adams and the Prophets of Progress* (Cambridge, Mass., 1952); Daniel R. Coquillette, "Justinian in Braintree: John Adams, Civilian Learning, and Legal Elitism, 1758–1775" in Coquillette, ed., *Law in Colonial Massachusetts 1630–1800* (Boston, 1984); and Thompson, *John Adams and the Spirit of Liberty.*

39. J. G. A. Pocock, *The Machiavellian Moment: Florentine Political Thought and the Atlantic Republican Tradition* (Princeton, 1975), esp. 526.

40. Charles R. McKirdy, "Massachusetts Lawyers on the Eve of the American Revolution: The State of the Profession," in Coquillette, ed., *Law in Colonial Massachusetts,* 339.

41. Coquillette, "Justinian in Braintree," ibid., 359–418.

42. L. Kinvin Wroth and Hiller B. Zobel, eds., *Legal Papers of John Adams,* 3 vols. (Cambridge, Mass., 1965), 3:242 (Boston Massacre); JA, *Papers,* 1:252–309 (Independence of the Judges); 312–13, 335–36, 345 (reply to Hutchinson).

43. Pencak, "John Adams and the Massachusetts Provincial Elite."

44. McKirdy, "Massachusetts Lawyers," *Law in Colonial Massachusetts,* 337–58.

45. *Machiavellian Moment,* 526.

F I V E : Revising Custom, Embracing Choice

1. Charles James Faulkner, "Winchester Law School Notes and Legal Essays," Charles James Faulkner (1806–84), Law Practice/Winchester Law School Materials, (1825–26), Faulkner Family Papers, Virginia Historical Society, Richmond, Va.

2. J. R. Pole, "Reflections on American Law and the American Revolution," *William and Mary Quarterly*, 3rd ser., 50 (1993) 142–43.

3. Among the best and most thorough interpretations of Americans' unfavorable self-comparisons with England and the "culture of emulation" those feelings cultivated are Richard Bushman, *The Refinement of America: Persons, Houses, Cities* (New York, 1993), esp. 181–203 and 402–47; and Jack P. Greene, "Search for Identity: An Interpretation of Selected Patterns of Social Response in Eighteenth-Century America," *Journal of Social History* 6 (1970), 189–220.

4. For more on the development of notions of America as an exceptional place, see Jack P. Greene, *The Intellectual Construction of America* (Chapel Hill, 1993).

5. In his definitive work on the constitutional development of Anglo-America, Jack P. Greene has shown how Americans appropriated English laws from the late seventeenth century through the promulgation of the U.S. Constitution. See Jack P. Greene, *Peripheries and Center: Constitutional Development in the Extended Polities of the British Empire and the United States, 1607–1788*, 2nd ed. (New York, 1990). John Philip Reid has also written extensively on this subject. See *In Defiance of the Law: The Standing Army Controversy, the Two Constitutions, and the Coming of the American Revolution* (Chapel Hill, 1981).

6. David Lieberman has written a fine account of Mansfield's legal reforms in *The Province of Legislation Determined: Legal Theory in Eighteenth-Century Britain* (New York, 1989), 88–121.

7. See Perry Miller, "The Legal Mentality," in *The Life of the Mind in America: From the Revolution to the Civil War* (New York, 1965), esp. 156–204 and 239–68.

8. Faulkner, "Legal Essays."

9. Thomas Jefferson, "Autobiography," 1821, Paul Leicester Ford, ed., *The Works of Thomas Jefferson*, 12 vols. (New York, 1904–5), 1:50.

10. Faulkner, "Legal Essays."

11. James Wilson, "Comparison of the Constitution of the United States, with that of Great Britain," and "Of the Common Law," in Robert G. McCloskey, ed., *The Works of James Wilson*, 2 vols. (Cambridge, Mass., 1967), 1:311, 335.

12. Daniel J. Boorstin, *The Mysterious Science of the Law: An Essay on Blackstone's Commentaries Showing How Blackstone, Employing Eighteenth-Century Ideas of Science, Religion, History, Aesthetics, and Philosophy, Made of the Law at Once a Conservative and a Mysterious Science* (Cambridge, Mass., 1941), 3.

13. Sir William Blackstone, *Commentaries on the Laws of England*, Facsimile of the First Edition of 1765–69, 4 vols., ed. Stanley N. Katz (Chicago, 1979), 1:63–64.

14. Ibid., 85–86.

15. See, e.g., Hugh Henry Brackenridge, *Law Miscellanies: Containing an Introduction to the Study of the Law, Notes on Blackstone's Commentaries, shewing the Variations of the Law of Pennsylvania from the Law of England, and what Acts of Assembly might require to be Repealed or Modified; Observations on Smith's Edition of the Laws of Pennsylvania; Strictures on Decisions of the Supreme Court of the United States, and*

On Certain Acts of Congress, with Some Law Cases, and a Variety of Other Matters, Chiefly Original (Philadelphia, 1814), 70.

16. Wilson, "Letter to the speaker of the Pennsylvania house of representatives, Aug. 24, 1791," in McCloskey, *Works of Wilson*, 1:60–61.

17. See, for example, the MS Litchfield Law School notebooks of: Asa Bacon, 1794, 6; Daniel Sheldon, Jr., 1798, 5; Aaron Burr Reeve, 1802–3, 1:11; Ely Warner, 1808–9, 1:10. All of the above notebooks are located in the Ingraham Memorial Research Library, Litchfield Historical Society, Litchfield, Connecticut. See also anonymous notebook, 1813, 1:8–17, Special Collections Department, Earl G. Swem Library, College of William and Mary. For more on the states' adoption of English statutes, see Elizabeth Gaspar Brown, *British Statutes in American Law, 1776–1836* (Ann Arbor, 1964).

18. For the strength of English reliance on custom and its importance in governing themselves and one another, see such works as J. G. A. Pocock, *The Ancient Constitution and the Feudal Law: A Study of English Historical Thought in the Seventeenth Century*, rev. ed.(1957; New York, 1987); E. P. Thompson, *Customs in Common* (New York, 1993). There are numerous works that document the translation of these values to Anglo-America. Among the most prominent are: Jack P. Greene, *Pursuits of Happiness: The Social Development of Early Modern British Colonies and the Formation of American Culture* (Chapel Hill, 1988); James Horn, *Adapting to the New World: English Society in the Seventeenth-Century Chesapeake* (Chapel Hill, 1997); David Grayson Allen, *In English Ways: The Movement of Societies and the Transferal of English Local Law and Custom to Massachusetts Bay in the Seventeenth Century* (Chapel Hill, 1981); Warren M. Billings, "Transfer of English Law to Seventeenth-Century Virginia," in K. R. Andrews, N. P. Canny, and P. E. H. Hair, eds., *Westward Enterprise: English Activities in Ireland, the Atlantic, and America, 1480–1650* (Detroit, 1979). J. R. Pole gives an admirably succinct assessment of the relationship between community custom and the common law in "Reflections on American Law," 142.

19. Peter S. DuPonceau, *A Dissertation on the Nature and Extent of the Jurisdiction of the Courts of the United States, being a Valedictory address Delivered to the Students of the Law Academy of Philadelphia, at the close of the Academical Year, on the 22d April, 1824. To which are Added, a Brief Sketch of the National Judiciary Powers Exercised in the United States Prior to the Adoption of the Present Federal Constitution, by Thomas Sargeant, Esq., and the Author's Discourse on Legal Education, Delivered at the Opening of the Law Academy, in February, 1821* (Philadelphia, 1824), 91.

20. Ibid., vii.

21. Ely Warner, MS Litchfield student notebook, 1808–9, 1:21.

22. Blackstone, *Commentaries*, 1:76–79. American legists closely followed Blackstone's criteria for valid custom in their lectures and writings. See, for example, St. George Tucker, *Blackstone's Commentaries: With Notes of Reference to the Constitution and Laws of the United States and of the Commonwealth of Virginia* (Philadelphia, 1803) app. A, 1:74–79; James Riddle Law Notebook, 1815, Virginia Historical Society, Richmond, Va.; MS Litchfield Law School notebooks of Asa Bacon, 1794, 1; Daniel Sheldon, Jr., 1798, 2; Aaron Burr Reeve, 1802–3, 1:5.

23. Tucker, *Blackstone's Commentaries*, vol. 1, 76n.; vol. 3, app. A, 30. Tucker's definition of custom was taken from Blackstone, *Commentaries*, 1:74–79.

24. Ely Warner, MS Litchfield notebook, 1808–9, 1:9. Italics added.

25. Quotations are taken from Asa Bacon, MS Litchfield notebook, 1794, 3. Every Litchfield notebook I examined had nearly identical passages with regards to the argument about common law extending from the time of Richard I.

26. Origen Storrs Seymour, MS Litchfield student notebook, 1824–25, Yale University Law Library, 1:4. Underlining in original.

27. First found in Aaron Burr Reeve, MS Litchfield notebook, 1802–3, 1:22. This argument is also found in all subsequent notebooks examined, through George Flagg Mann's of 1825–26.

28. Stith's *History of Virginia*, 4, 8, quoted in Tucker, *Blackstone's Commentaries*, vol. 1, app. 383–84.

29. Tucker *Blackstone's Commentaries*, vol. 1, app. 383–84.

30. Blackstone, *Commentaries*, (7th ed., 1775), 1:106. *Calvin v. Smith*, also known as *Calvin's Case*, 7 Rep. 17, 1608. James Wilson refers to this edition of Blackstone's *Commentaries* in "Considerations on the Nature and Extent of the Legislative Authority of the British Parliament," McCloskey, ed., *Works of Wilson*, 2:739–40.

31. Tucker, *Blackstone's Commentaries*, vol. 1, app. 382.

32. Wilson, "Considerations on the Nature and Extent of the Legislative Authority of the British Parliament," McCloskey, ed., *Works of Wilson*, 2:739–40.

33. Barbara Black, "The Constitution of Empire: The Case for the Colonists," *University of Pennsylvania Law Review* 124 (1976), 1199–1200. In this article Black offers an innovative analysis of *Calvin's Case* and its importance to legal arguments about the Revolution. For colonial and Revolutionary-era debates over the question of whether America was a conquered territory, see Greene, *Peripheries and Center*, 24–28, and Reid, *In Defiance of the Law*, 79–80.

34. Blackstone, *Commentaries*, 1:44–46.

35. Zephaniah Swift, *A System of the Laws of Connecticut, in Six Books* (Windham, Conn., 1795), 1:37.

36. St. George Tucker, lecture notebook, note G, 28. St. George Tucker, unnumbered vol. 3, Special Collections Department, Earl G. Swem Library, College of William and Mary, Williamsburg, Va.

37. Blackstone, *Commentaries*, 1:74.

38. Tucker, note G, ms unnumbered 3:25.

39. Wilson, "Of Municipal Law," and "Of the General Principles of Law and Obligation," McCloskey, ed., *Works of Wilson*, 1:182, 102.

40. Hugh Henry Brackenridge, *Law Miscellanies*, 32, 40–43.

41. Swift, *System of the Laws in Connecticut*, 1:42.

42. Seth Staples, MS Litchfield student notebook, 1798, 5.

43. Asa Bacon, MS Litchfield student notebook, 1794, 6. See also the MS Litchfield student notebooks of Daniel Sheldon, Jr., 1798, 5; Aaron Burr Reeve, 1802–3, 1:13; Ely Warner, 1808–9, 1:11; Origen Storrs Seymour, 1824–25, 1:12.

44. Wilson, "Of the Common Law," McCloskey, ed., *Works of Wilson*, 1:356.

45. Ibid., 362.

46. DuPonceau, *Dissertation*, xvii.

47. James Wilson's charge to the grand jury, trial of John Singleterry and Gideon Henfield, July 22, 1793, as quoted in DuPonceau, *Dissertations*, xvii.

48. David Hoffman, *A Lecture Introductory to a Course of Lectures, Now Delivering in the University of Maryland* (Baltimore, 1825), 33.

49. Wilson, "Of the Common Law," McCloskey, ed., *Works of Wilson,* 1:345, 348.

50. Tucker, *Blackstone's Commentaries,* vol. 1, app. 394–401.

51. Ibid., 406–7.

52. Ibid., 411–12.

53. DuPonceau, *Dissertation,* x.

54. Nathaniel Chipman, *Sketches of the Principles of Government* (Rutland, Vt., 1793), 237–38.

55. Hugh Henry Brackenridge, *Law Miscellanies;* Tapping Reeve, *The Law of Baron and Femme; of Parent and Child; of Guardian and Ward; of Master and Servant; and of the Powers of Courts of Chancery. With an Essay on the Terms, Heir, Heirs, and Heirs of the Body* (New Haven, Conn., 1816); *A Treatise on the Law of Descents in the Several States of America* (New York, 1825); Peter S. DuPonceau, *A Dissertation on the Nature and Extent of the Jurisdiction of the Courts of the United States;* James Kent, *An Introductory Lecture to a Course of Law Lectures, Delivered November 17, 1794* (New York, 1794).

56. Tucker, *Blackstone's Commentaries.*

57. Kent, *Commentaries on American Law,* 4 vols. (New York, 1826–30), 1:442.

58. Ibid., 1:439, 2:326; David W. Raack, "To Preserve the Best Fruits: The Legal Thought of Chancellor James Kent," *American Journal of Legal History* 33 (1989), 336; Carl F. Stychin, "The Commentaries of Chancellor Kent and the Development of American Common Law," *American Journal of Legal History* 37 (1993), 448.

59. DuPonceau, *Dissertation,* 91.

s i x : The Ratification Paradox in the Great Valley of the Appalachians

1. The Great Valley of the Appalachians begins in what is today Quebec, crosses through New York and New Jersey before entering the Lehigh, Lebanon, and Cumberland valleys of Pennsylvania and the Shenandoah Valley and Great Valley of Virginia. Eighteenth century settlers spilled eastward into the North Carolina piedmont, but the Great Valley itself continues through Georgia to what is today Birmingham, Alabama. This study focuses mainly on the Pennsylvania valleys and the Shenandoah Valley in Virginia, the widest section of the Great Valley and the longest settled in 1787. Fast growing manufacturing and trading towns included Reading and Carlisle in Pennsylvania and Winchester in Virginia. The region already boasted two colleges: Dickinson in Carlisle, Cumberland County, Pennsylvania; Washington (now Washington and Lee) in Lexington, Rockbridge County, Virginia. The region could hardly be considered "frontier" in the sense of early westward development. Wayland F. Dunaway, "Pennsylvania as an Early Distributing Center of Population," *Pennsylvania Magazine of History and Biography* 55 (1931), 134–64; Carl Bridenbaugh, *Myths and Realities: Societies of the Colonial South* (Baton Rouge, 1952), 123–30; Robert D. Mitchell, *Commercialism and Frontier: Perspectives on the Early Shenandoah Valley* (Charlottesville, 1977), 16–19, 25–58, 104–6; James T. Lemon, *The Best Poor Man's Country* (Baltimore, 1972), 13–23, 43–49, 63–64; James G. Leyburn, *The Scotch-Irish: A Social History* (Chapel Hill, 1962), 185, 200, 205–8; George P. Donehoo, *Pennsylvania: A History* (New York, 1926), 425–29, 904–13; Warren R. Hofstra and Robert D. Mitchell, "Town and Country in Backcountry Virginia: Winchester and the Shenandoah Valley, 1730–1800," *Journal of Southern History* 59 (1993), 619–46; Thomas L. Purvis, "Politics of Ethnic Settlement in Late Eighteenth-Century Pennsylvania," *Western Pennsylvania Historical Magazine* 70 (1987),

107–22; Dietmar Rothermund, *The Layman's Progress: Religious and Political Experience in Colonial Pennsylvania, 1740–1770* (Philadelphia, 1961); Klaus Wust, *The Virginia Germans* (Charlottesville, 1969), 43–57; Mary M. Schweitzer, "America's First Midwest: The Great Valley of the Appalachians in the 18th Century," (unpublished manuscript); Warren Hofstra, *The Planting of New Virginia: Settlement and Landscape in the Shenandoah Valley* (Baltimore, 2004); Kenneth Keller, "Rural Politics and the Collapse of Pennsylvania Federalism," *Transactions of the American Philosophical Society* 72 (1982), part 6; A. G. Roeber, *Faithful Magistrates and Republican Lawyers: Creators of Virginia Legal Culture, 1680–1810* (Chapel Hill, 1981), 95–98, 113, 123–24, 135–58, 175–205, 243, 283–90.

2. In Pennsylvania, Northampton County, which included both the Lehigh Valley and the large region to the north occupied by Connecticut claimants, voted Federalist. Moving south, the next three counties in the Great Valley voted unanimously Antifederalist: Berks, Dauphin, and Cumberland counties. Franklin in Pennsylvania and Washington in Maryland split their votes evenly. All six counties of the Shenandoah Valley in Virginia voted Federalist: Berkeley, Frederick, Shenandoah, Rockingham, Augusta, and Rockbridge. The classic study of the geographic distribution of voting on the ratification of the Constitution can be found in Owen G. Libby, "The Geographical Distribution of the Vote of the thirteen States on the Federal Constitution, 1787–88," *Bulletin of the University of Wisconsin*, Economics, Political Science, and History Series, 1, no. 1, 1–116; esp. 27–29, 35–37, and 51–67.

3. Ronald P. Formisano, "Deferential-Participant Politics: The Early Republic's Political Culture, 1789–1840," *American Political Science Review* 68 (1974), 473–87.

4. Richard R. Beeman, *The Old Dominion and the New Nation, 1788–1801* (Lexington, Ky., 1972), 28–48; Charles S. Sydnor, *Gentlemen Freeholders: Political Practices in Washington's Virginia* (Chapel Hill, 1952), 18–26, 67–93; Dale Edward Benson, "Wealth and Power in Virginia, 1774–1776: A Study of the Organization of Revolt" (unpublished Ph.D. diss., University of Maine, 1970), 12, 22, 27; Robert Wheeler, "The County Court in Colonial Virginia," in Bruce C. Daniels, ed., *Town and County: Essays on the Structure of Local Government in the American Colonies* (Middletown, Conn., 1978), 111–33; Bernard Bailyn, "Politics and Social Structure in Virginia," in James Morton Smith, ed., *Seventeenth-Century America: Essays in Colonial History* (Chapel Hill, 1959), 90–115.

5. Bailyn, "Politics and Social Structure," 91–92, 111–12; Timothy H. Breen, *Tobacco Culture, The Mentality of the Great Tidewater Planters on the Eve of Revolution* (Princeton, 1985), 35–36; Sydnor, *Gentlemen Freeholders*, 1–10; Jack P. Greene, "'Virtus et Libertas': Political Culture, Social Change, and the Origins of the American Revolution in Virginia, 1763–1766," in Jeffrey J. Crow and Larry E. Tise, eds., *The Southern Experience in the American Revolution* (Chapel Hill, 1978), 55–108.

6. Sydnor, *Gentlemen Freeholders*, 67; Beeman, *Old Dominion and the New Nation*, 28–33; Roeber, *Faithful Magistrates*, 28, 112, 147–49; Jack P. Greene, "Society, Ideology, and Politics: An Analysis of the Political Culture of Mid-Eighteenth-Century Virginia," in Richard M. Jellison, ed., *Society, Freedom and Conscience: the American Revolution in Virginia, Massachusetts, and New York* (New York, 1976), 14–76; Benson, "Wealth and Power," 21–22; Albert H. Tillson, Jr., *Gentry and Common Folk: Political Culture on a Virginia Frontier* (Lexington, Ky., 1991), 17–21.

7. Wust, *Virginia Germans*, 35–42, 52, 74–77; Sydnor, *Gentlemen Freeholders*, 35.

8. Tillson, *Gentry and Common Folk*, 36–37, 64–77; Leyburn, *Scotch-Irish*, 209, 299; Sydnor, *Gentlemen Freeholders*, 28–29; Mitchell, *Commercialism and Frontier*, 106–8.

9. Alan Tully, *Forming American Politics: Ideals, Interests, and Institutions in Colonial New York and Pennsylvania* (Baltimore, 1994), 330–81; Mary M. Schweitzer, *Custom and Contract: Household, Government, and the Economy in Colonial Pennsylvania* (New York, 1987), 89–115.

10. Gary Nash, *Quakers and Politics: Pennsylvania, 1681–1726* (Princeton, 1968), 89–98; Alan Tully, *William Penn's Legacy: Politics and Social Structure in Provincial Pennsylvania, 1726–1755* (Baltimore, 1977); Lemon, *Best Poor Man's Country*, 42–70; Schweitzer, *Custom and Contract*, 89–115.

11. Lemon, *Best Poor Man's Country*, 150–83; Schweitzer, *Custom and Contract*, 21–88.

12. Schweitzer, *Custom and Contract*, 115–68; Lemon, *Best Poor Man's Country*, 54–61. See also Jacob Price, "Economic Function and Growth of American Port Towns in the Eighteenth Century," in Donald Fleming and Bernard Bailyn, eds., *Perspectives in American History* (Cambridge, Mass., 1974), 123–66.

13. Thomas M. Doerflinger, *A Vigorous Spirit of Enterprise: Merchants and Economic Development in Revolutionary Philadelphia* (Chapel Hill, 1986), 47–62; Arthur M. Jensen, *The Maritime Commerce of Colonial Philadelphia* (Madison, Wisc., 1963); Bernard L. Herman, *Townhouse: Architecture and Material Life in the American City, 1780–1830* (Chapel Hill, forthcoming), chap. 5: "The Merchant's Parlor."

14. Schweitzer, *Custom and Contract*, 194; Wayne L. Bockelman, "Local Government in Colonial Pennsylvania," in Daniels, ed., *Town and County*, 216–37; Richard Alan Ryerson, *"The Revolution is Now Begun": The Radical Committees of Philadelphia, 1765–1776* (Philadelphia, 1978), 9–13; Keller, "Rural Politics," 3.

15. Pennsylvania's legislature did not represent the same level of "inner gentry" that dominated provincial politics in Virginia. Greene, "Society, Ideology, and Politics," 16–17; Ryerson, *Revolution*, 9; Bockelman, "Local Government," 216–24; Keller, "Rural Politics," 3; Tully, *William Penn's Legacy*, 115–17.

16. Lucy Simler, "The Township: The Community of the Rural Pennsylvanian," *Pennsylvania Magazine of History and Biography* 106 (1982), 41–68; Bockelman, "Local Government," 223–24, 234; Tully, *William Penn's Legacy*, 115–17, Ryerson, *Revolution*, 44.

17. Benson, "Wealth and Power," 4, 146. For the continued dominance of the elite in Virginia government, during and after the Revolution, see Beeman, *Old Dominion and the New Nation*, xi–xii; Tillson, *Gentry and Common Folk*, 64, 79–81, 137; Greene, "Society, Ideology, and Politics," 102; Greene, "'Virtus et Libertas,'" 76; Roeber, *Faithful Magistrates*; John E. Selby, *The Revolution in Virginia* (Charlottesville, 1988), 317.

18. Benson, "Wealth and Power;" John David McBride, "The Virginia War Effort: 1775–1783: Manpower Policies and Practices" (unpublished Ph.D. diss., University of Virginia, 1977), 29, 42, 46–48; Tillson, *Gentry and Common Folk*, 45–58, 66–77, 87–88; James Titus, *The Old Dominion at War: Society, Politics, and Warfare in Late Colonial Virginia* (Columbia, S.C., 1991), 138–39.

19. Ronald Hoffman, "The 'Disaffected' in the Revolutionary South," in Alfred F. Young, ed., *The American Revolution: Explorations in the History of American Radicalism* (DeKalb, Ill., 1976), 276, 300–301; Formisano, "Deferential-Participant Politics," 483; Sydnor, *Gentlemen Freeholders*, 41–59; Rhys Isaac, *The Transformation of Virginia, 1740–1790* (Chapel Hill, 1982); Tillson, *Gentry and Common Folk*, 1–3, 78–79, 134–37; Titus, *Old Dominion at War*, 146; Beeman, *Old Dominion*, 33–45.

20. Tillson, *Gentry and Common Folk*, 64, 87–88, 101–7; Hoffman, "The Disaffected," 278.

21. Greene, "'*Virtus et Libertas,*'" 55–108; Tillson, *Gentry and Common Folk*, 78–79, 96–200; Hoffman, "The Disaffected," 275.

22. Jackson T. Main, "Sections and Politics in Virginia, 1781–1787," *William and Mary Quarterly*, 3rd Ser., 12 (1955), 96–112, esp. 97–98; Beeman, *Old Dominion and the New Nation*, 93; Freeman Hart, *The Valley of Virginia in the American Revolution* (Chapel Hill, 1942), 117, 127, 130, 149–69; Risjord, *Chesapeake Politics, 1781–1800* (New York, 1978), 126–38; Selby, *Revolution in Virginia*, 318; Risjord and Gordon DenBoer, "The Evolution of Political Parties in Virginia, 1781–1800," *Journal of American History* 60 (1974), 961–84; Leyburn, *Scotch-Irish*, 300.

23. E. James Ferguson, "Currency Finance: An Interpretation of Colonial Monetary Practices," *William and Mary Quarterly*, 3rd Ser., 10 (1953) 153–80; Risjord, *Chesapeake Politics*, 174–79; Mary M. Schweitzer, "State-Issued Currency and the Ratification of the U.S. Constitution," *Journal of Economic History* 49 (1989), 311–22.

24. Risjord and DenBoer, "Evolution of Political Parties," 955; Risjord, *Chesapeake Politics*, 240–43; Hart, *Valley of Virginia*, 149–69; Mary M. Schweitzer, "A New Look at Economic Causes of the Constitution: Monetary and Trade Policy in Maryland, Pennsylvania, and Virginia," *Social Science Journal* 26 (1988), 15–26; Hofstra, *Planting of New Virginia*.

25. Hart, *Valley of Virginia*, 173–74; Risjord, *Chesapeake Politics*, 295–96; Schweitzer, "Economic Causes," 15–26. For the abundance of Antifederalist and Federalist publications in Winchester, see the editors' notes in Merrill Jensen, John P. Kaminski, and Gaspare J. Saladino, eds., *Documentary History of the Ratification of the Constitution*, 17 vols. to date (Madison, Wisc., 1976–), 8:401–2, 467–68.

26. For the story of the first Frederick County vote, ibid., 8:91–92.

27. William Graham to Zachariah Johnston, Nov. 3, 1787, ibid., 8:143. William Graham was president of Washington College in Lexington, Rockbridge County.

28. Ibid., 8:165, 227, 10:1530–34, 1548–52; Beeman, *Old Dominion and the New Nation*, 3–4, 131.

29. Jensen et al., eds., *Documentary History*, 10:1720–23, 1732, 1744–46.

30. George W. Franz, *Paxton: A Study of Community Structure and Mobility in the Colonial Pennsylvania Backcountry* (New York, 1989), 34–40; Tully, *Forming American Politics*, 384–89.

31. Franz, *Paxton*, 43–79; Brooke Hindle, "The March of the Paxton Boys," *William and Mary Quarterly*, 3rd. ser., 32 (1946), 461–86.

32. Schweitzer, *Custom and Contract*, 4–17, 194–96, 209–216, 221–29; Jensen, *Maritime Commerce*, 130–52.

33. Robert Brunhouse, *The Counter-Revolution in Pennsylvania, 1776–1790* (Harrisburg, Pa., 1942), 12–14; Ryerson, *Revolution*, 24, 64; Douglas M. Arnold, *Political Ideology and the Internal Revolution in Pennsylvania, 1776–1790* (New York, 1989), 19–24.

34. Steven Rosswurm, *Arms, Country, and Class: The Philadelphia Militia and "Lower Sort" during the American Revolution, 1775–1783* (New Brunswick, N.J., 1987), 97, 99, 100–101, 136; Ryerson, *Revolution*, 117–22, 134, 141–47, 226–28; Laura L. Becker, "Diversity and Its Significance in an Eighteenth-Century Pennsylvania Town," in Michael Zuckerman et al., eds., *Friends and Neighbors: Group Life in America's First Plural Society* (Philadelphia, 1982), 212–13.

35. Rosswurm, *Arms, Country, and Class*, 100–104; Eric Foner, *Tom Paine and Revolutionary America* (New York, 1976), 63–65, 128–29, 132–33; Brunhouse, *Counter-*

Revolution, 14–15; Arnold, *Political Ideology*, 38–40, 46–53. The Cannon Reference is in Foner, *Tom Paine*, 128–29.

36. J. R. Pole, *Political Representation in England and the Origins of the American Republic* (New York, 1966), 271–76; Gordon S. Wood, *The Creation of the American Republic, 1776–1787* (Chapel Hill, 1969), 84–89, 137, 170, 226–27, 230–33, 249–50, 271, 430–45; Arnold, *Political Ideology*, 54–56; Robert N. C. Nix, Jr., and Mary M. Schweitzer, "Pennsylvania's Contributions to the Writing and the Ratification of the Constitution," *Pennsylvania Magazine of History and Biography* 112 (1988), 4–11; Brunhouse, *Counter-Revolution*, 11–15.

37. Brunhouse, *Counter-Revolution*, 40–44; Arnold, "Republican Revolution," 100–119, 173–81.

38. Bockelman, "Continuity and Change," 87–88, 109–20, 135, 210; Ryerson, *Revolution*, 4–5, 39–64, 177–206, 243–44, 252–56; Becker, "Diversity," 212–13.

39. Brunhouse, *Counter-Revolution*, 17, 28–32; Nix and Schweitzer, "Pennsylvania's Contributions"; Pole, *Political Representation*, 272; Arnold, *Political Ideology*, v, 42–43, 58–59, 69–99, 119, 139–47, 171–72, 179–84, 187–88, 194–95, 219–25, 234–40; Wood, *Creation of the American Republic*, 244–51; *A Candid Examination of the Address of the Minority of the Council of Censors* (Philadelphia, 1784).

40. Schweitzer, *Custom and Contract*, 115–68; Brunhouse, *Counter-Revolution*, 96, 150–51; Doerflinger, *Vigorous Spirit of Enterprise*, 302–10.

41. Ironically, Pennsylvania's would-be land barons bungled their speculative attempts badly. Robert Morris ended the 1790s a bankrupt, in debtors' prison. See Doerflinger, *Vigorous Spirit of Enterprise*, 219–24; Brunhouse, *Counter-Revolution*, 82–88; Norman Wilkinson, *Land Policy and Speculation in Pennsylvania, 1779–1800: A Test of the New Democracy* (New York, 1979); Elizabeth K. Henderson, "The Northwestern Lands of Pennsylvania, 1790–1812," *Pennsylvania Magazine of History and Biography* 60 (1936), 131–60; Schweitzer, "State-Issued Currency."

42. "Plain Truth" in the *Philadelphia Independent Gazetteer*, in Merrill Jensen, ed., *Documentary History of the Ratification of the Constitution*, vol. 2 (Pennsylvania), (Madison, Wisc., 1976), 292–93. "Address and Reasons of Dissent of the Minority of the Convention of Pennsylvania to their Constituents," ibid., 2:617–24; Rodger C. Henderson, "John Smilie, Antifederalism and the 'Dissent of the Minority,' 1787–1788," *Western Pennsylvania Historical Magazine* 71 (1988), 253–62; Arnold, *Political Ideology*, 242–46, 309–11.

43. "Address and Reasons of Dissent;" Arnold, *Political Ideology*, 250–64, 275–82.

44. Jensen et al., ed., *Documentary History*, 670–708; Saul Cornell, "Aristocracy Assailed: The Ideology of Backcountry Anti-Federalism," *Journal of American History* 76 (1990), 1148–72.

45. Jensen et al., ed., *Documentary History of Ratification*, 660–61, 694–96, 709–25; Brunhouse, *Counter-Revolution*, 212–14; *The Ordeal of the Constitution: The Antifederalists and the Ratification Struggle of 1787–1788* (Norman, Okla., 1966), 58.

46. Thomas P. Slaughter, *Whiskey Rebellion: Frontier Epilogue to the American Revolution* (New York, 1986), 96–105, 144–89; Kentucky protestors continued to refuse to pay the Whiskey Tax until it was repealed in 1805, and then accepted a negotiated settlement over their past dues. Mary K. Bonsteel Tachau, "The Whiskey Rebellion in Kentucky: A Forgotten episode of Civil Disobedience," *Journal of the Early Republic* 2 (1982), 239–59; on the resemblance to Shays's Rebellion, see J. R. Pole, "Shays's Rebellion: A

Political Interpretation," in J. P. Greene, *The Reinterpretation of the American Revolution* (New York, 1968), 416–34.

47. Slaughter, *Whiskey Rebellion*, 193, 228; Matthew Schoenbachler, "Republicanism in the Age of Democratic Revolution: The Democratic-Republican Societies of the 1790s," *Journal of the Early Republic* 18 (Summer 1998), 237–61.

48. For the Fries rebellion, see Slaughter, *Whiskey Rebellion*, 3, 175, 221; Keller, "Rural Politics," 25–36, 40. In the presidential election of 1800, Great Valley residents largely voted for McKean, although there were still many who distrusted his earlier support for the federal Constitution. Schoenbachler, "Republicanism in the Age of Democratic Revolution"; Roeber, *Faithful Magistrates*, 324. The Shenandoah supported Jefferson, but there seems to have been a great deal of personality politics involved.

49. Risjord and DenBoer suggest that few average Virginians enjoyed being actively involved in party politics. Risjord and DenBoer, "Evolution of Political Parties," 984. Roeber, *Faithful Magistrates*, 321–33, 330.

50. John C. Hudson, "North American Origins of Middlewestern Frontier Populations," *Annals of the Association of American Geographers* 78 (1988), 395–413.

51. William H. Phillips, "Patent Growth in the Old Dominion: The Impact of Railroad Integration before 1880," *Journal of Economic History* 52 (1992), 389–400.

S E V E N : Similarities and Continuities

1. Prince George's County Commissioners of the Tax, Almshouse and Pension Papers, 1820–1842, Maryland Hall of Records, C1153. Vermillion claimed under "an act to provide for certain persons engaged in the land and naval service of the United States, in the Revolutionary war," of the U.S. Congress March 18, 1818.

2. David Curtis Skaggs, *Roots of Maryland Democracy, 1753–1776* (Westport, Ct., 1973); Ronald Hoffman, *A Spirit of Dissension: Economics, Politics, and the Revolution in Maryland* (Baltimore, 1973); Woody Holton, *Forced Founders: Indians, Debtors, Slaves, and the Making of the Revolution in Virginia* (Chapel Hill, 1999); Michael A. McDonnell, *Popular Mobilization and Political Culture in Revolutionary Virginia* (Chapel Hill, forthcoming). My thanks to Mike for a copy of his manuscript.

3. Paul G. E. Clemons, *The Atlantic Economy and Maryland's Eastern Shore: From Tobacco to Grain* (Ithaca, 1980); Steven Sarson, "Wealth, Poverty, and Labor in the Tobacco Plantation South: Prince George's County, Maryland, in the Early National Era" (Ph.D. diss., Johns Hopkins University, 1998), 8, 445–46; Margaret Law Callcott, ed., *Mistress of Riversdale: The Plantation Letters of Rosalie Stier Calvert, 1795–1821* (Baltimore, 1991). I thank Robert J. Brugger and the Johns Hopkins University Press for permission to use the letters, Ann Wass of Riversdale's Historical Society for samples of the originals, and Nathalie Morello of the University of Wales Swansea for checking translations.

4. Jack P. Greene, *Understanding the American Revolution: Issues and Actors* (Charlottesville, 1995), especially 359–70.

5. One person could produce about 1,500 pounds of tobacco per year, requiring a minimum 40 to 50 acres of land (three acres in tobacco, the rest in food crops and fallow. The division between small and large yeomen assumes the labor of two free full-time household members and five slaves. Edward C. Papenfuse, Jr., "Planter Behavior and Economic Opportunity in a Staple Economy," *Agricultural History* 46 (1972), 303–6;

Allan Kulikoff, *Tobacco and Slaves: The Development of Southern Cultures in the Chesa-peake, 1680–1800* (Chapel Hill, 1986), 47–48; Lorena S. Walsh, "Slave Life, Slave Society, and Tobacco Production in the Tidewater Chesapeake, 1620–1820," in Ira Berlin and Philip D. Morgan, eds., *Cultivation and Culture: Labor and the Shaping of Slave Life in the Americas* (Charlottesville, 1993), 175.

6. These figures understate inequality because property was assessed at less than market value, owners failed to inform assessors when they acquired new property (asses-sors visited every three to five years), up to a third of county property is unaccounted for in these figures because it belonged to nonhousehold heads, nonresidents, or the yet undivided estates of the deceased, and many rich residents owned property outside the county. The figures are derived from county property assessments matched against the censuses of 1800, 1810, and 1820. Assessments are extant from 1794 and census popula-tion schedules for Prince George's and other southern Maryland counties for 1830 are lost. I converted all figures to dollars at £1.00 to $2.67 (tax assessments were in Maryland pounds until 1813). Steven Sarson, "Distribution of Wealth in Prince George's County, Maryland, 1800–1820," *Journal of Economic History* 60 (2000), 847–55; Lee Soltow, *Distri-bution of Wealth and Income in the United States in 1798* (Pittsburgh, 1989).

7. Prince George's County Land Records [PGCLR], March 2, 1811, JRM 14, 336–42; Nov. 4, AB 3, 434–36; Nov. 5, AB 3, 422–25; April 10, 1826, AB 4, 205–6; Oct. 24, 1836, AB 10, 510–13.

8. Jean Butenhoff Lee, "Land and Labor: Parental Bequest Practices in Charles County, Maryland, 1732–1783," in Lois Green Carr et al., eds., *Colonial Chesapeake Soci-ety* (Chapel Hill, 1988), 306–41.

9. Rosalie Eugenia Calvert [REC] to Henri Jean Stier [HJS], Nov. 19, 1803, and REC to HJS, Aug. 20, 1805, in Callcott, ed., *Mistress of Riversdale*, 59, 126.

10. REC to HJS, March 31, 1814, ibid., 265. See also REC to HJS, March 20, 1816, and to Charles Jean Stier [CJS], April 8, 1816, ibid., 291–92, 295–96.

11. REC to HJS, March 20, 1816, ibid., 292 and to CJS, April 8, 1816, ibid., 296.

12. REC to HJS, May 19, 1805, ibid., 117.

13. For labor-land ratios I discounted slaves under 8 years old, and counted slaves aged 8 to 14, and men over 45 and women over 36 as half-hands.

14. REC to HJS, Aug. 2, 1810; June 24, 1811; to CJS, Feb. 18, 1814; to HJS, March 20, 1815, Callcott, ed., *Mistress of Riversdale*, 223, 238, 263, 280.

15. Prince George's County Register of Wills [PGCRW], Inventories, April 3, 1838, PC 1, 411–17.

16. REC to HJS, Sept. 22, 1805; Oct. 7, 1805; Jan. 19, 1807; June 9, 1809, Callcott, ed., *Mistress of Riversdale*, 128, 129, 156, 206.

17. REC to HJS, April 1, 1809; June 5, 1820; ibid., 202, 360; PGCLR, Feb. 25, 1812, JRM 15, 575–77; June 7, 1813, JRM 15, 597–681; July 18, 1820, AB 1, 383–87; April 1, 1826, AB 2, 285–87.

18. Ronald Hoffman in Collaboration with Sally D. Mason, *Princes of Ireland, Planters of Maryland: A Carroll Saga, 1500–1800* (Chapel Hill, 2000), 77–79, 99–101, 163–68, 287–92, 299–309, 312–16; Whitman H. Ridgeway, *Community Leadership in Maryland, 1790–1840* (Chapel Hill, 1979).

19. REC to HJS, April 12, 1813, to HJS, Oct. 29, 1816, Callcott, ed., *Mistress of Rivers-dale*, 256, 307. Calvert invested $5,000 more in the turnpike for Henri Jean Stier, ibid., 218, 248, 257, 258, 323. The Maryland Assembly incorporated the turnpike company in

Dec. 1812: William Kilty, *Laws of Maryland, 1776–1818, Revised and Collected under the Authority of the Legislature* (Annapolis, 1820), 1812, chap. 78.

20. Hoffman with Mason, *Princes of Ireland, Planters of Maryland*, 98–130, 218–64, 334–50; Jack P. Greene, *Pursuits of Happiness: The Social Development of Early Modern British Colonies and the Formation of American Culture* (Chapel Hill, 1988), 86–87.

21. REC to CJS, July 23, 1810, Callcott, ed., *Mistress of Riversdale*, 222.

22. Fredrika J. Teute, "Land, Liberty, and Labor in the Post-Revolutionary Era: Kentucky as the Promised Land" (Ph.D. diss., Johns Hopkins University, 1988), 184–311; Lee Soltow, "Land Inequality on the Frontier: The Distribution of Land in East Tennessee at the Beginning of the Nineteenth Century," *Social Science History* 5 (1981), 275–91; "Kentucky Wealth at the End of the Eighteenth Century," *Journal of Economic History* 43 (1983), 617–33.

23. REC to HJS, April 1, 1809, Nov. [no date], 1810, Calcott, ed., *Mistress of Riversdale*, 201, 230.

24. REC to HJS, May 12, 1817, ibid., 317–18.

25. REC to HJS, March 13, 1819, ibid., 242.

26. REC to HJS, Dec. 12, 1808, ibid., 198.

27. PGCLR, FF 1, June 12, 1781, 135–37; FF 2, Sept. 27, 1785, 431–32; Maryland State Papers, Federal Direct Tax, Prince George's County, Maryland, 1798 [FDTPG], Eastern Branch and Rock Creek Hundreds, Particular List of Dwelling Houses, 4; Particular List of Lands, Lots, Buildings, and Wharves, 7; Prince George's County Tax Assessments [PGCTA], Real Property, 1800, 32; Personal Property, 1800, 38.

28. PGCRW, Inventories, April 3, 1838, PC 1, 411–17; Bayly Ellen Marks, "Economics and Society in a Staple Plantation System: St. Mary's County, Maryland, 1790–1840" (Ph.D. diss., University of Maryland, 1979), 377.

29. REC to HJS, March 26, 1807, Callcott, ed., *Mistress of Riversdale*, 161.

30. REC to CJS, Dec. 10, 1808, ibid., 196.

31. REC to HJS, May 12, 1817, ibid., 318.

32. REC to HJS, May 12, 1808; May 12, 1809; March [n.d.], 1810; June 15, 1810; Aug. 30, 1810, ibid., 190, 201, 217, 221, 228.

33. REC to MLS, Dec. 29, 1803, ibid., 70–71. See also 35–39, 137, 145, 147, 388; Marks, "Economics and Society in a Staple Plantation System," 362, 376–77; Rhys Isaac, *The Transformation of Virginia, 1740–1790* (Chapel Hill, 1982), 30–42, 52–57.

34. REC to CJS, Sept. 12, 1803; to HJS and MLS, Sept. 16, 1803, Callcott, ed., *Mistress of Riversdale*, 57, 58.

35. REC to HJS, Sept. 26, 1806; REC to HJS, Jan. [n.d.], 1807, ibid., 149, 159.

36. PGCTA, Real Property, 1800, 41.

37. FDTPG, Collington and Western Branch Hundreds, Particular List of Slaves, 1; Particular List of Dwelling Houses, 2; Particular List of Land, Lots, Buildings, and Wharves, 3.

38. PGCRW, Inventories, Jan. 15, 1801, ST 4, 88–100; Hoffman with Mason, *Princes of Ireland, Planters of Maryland*, 231–32, 345–46, 348–49.

39. Sarson, "Wealth, Poverty, and Labor," 88–112, 158–60, 222–50.

40. PGCTA, Real Property, 1800, 6; Personal Property, 1800, 6; FDTPG, Prince Frederick and Washington Hundreds, Particular List of Lands, Lots, Buildings, and Wharves, 16.

41. PGCRW, Wills, Feb. 18, 1800, T1, 450; Inventories, [n.d.], 1800, ST3, 347.

42. PGCTA, Real Property, 1800, 21; Personal Property, 25.

43. Prince George's County Levy Court [PGCLC], Proceedings, April 7, 1795, 1; Judgements, April Session, 1800, 467; Callcott, ed., *Mistress of Riversdale,* 54, 93, 112, 119, 128, 130, 131, 141, 164, 168, 200, 345.

44. PGCTA, Real Property, 1800, 2, 3, 17, 42; Personal Property, 1800, 2, 3, 20, 43; PGCLC, Proceedings, April 6, 1795, 1.

45. Lois Green Carr, "County Government in Maryland, 1689–1709," (Ph.D. diss., Harvard University, 1968), 581–97; Carville V. Earle, *Evolution of a Tidewater Settlement System: All Hallow's Parish, Maryland, 1650–1783* (Chicago, 1975), 206–12; Gregory A. Stiverson, *Poverty in a Land of Plenty: Tenancy in Eighteenth-Century Maryland* (Baltimore, 1977), xii; Russell R. Menard, *Economy and Society in Early Colonial Maryland* (New York, 1985), 51–77, 155–201, 302–20; James Horn, *Adapting to a New World: English Society in the Seventeenth-Century Chesapeake* (Chapel Hill, 1994), 147–60, 253–92, 328–33.

46. PGCTA, Real Property, 1800, 4.

47. PGCRW, Wills, Feb. 18, 1800, T1, 450; Inventories, [n.d.], 1800, ST3, 347.

48. PGCTA, Real Property, 1800, 6; Personal Property, 1800, 6; FDTPG, Prince Frederick and Washington Hundreds, Particular List of Lands, Lots, Buildings, and Wharves, 16.

49. PGCTA, Real Property, 1803, 8; 1804, 6; 1806, 6; 1808, 6; PGCRW, Inventories, Dec. 16, 1808, ST4, 59–61.

50. REC to HJS, Sept. 10, 1808, Callcott, ed., *Mistress of Riversdale,* 191–92.

51. PGCTA, Real Property, 1800, 30; Personal Property, 1800, 33; REC to HJS, June 1, 1811, Callcott, ed., *Mistress of Riversdale,* 237.

52. PGCLR, Nov. 9, 1804, JRM 10, 449–53; Dec. 8, 1804, JRM 10, 438–39.

53. REC to HJS, Sept. 26, 1806, Callcott, ed., *Mistress of Riversdale,* 149, 65.

54. REC to HJS, Dec. 7, 1807, ibid., 175.

55. PGCLR, April 2, 1814, JRM 16, 126–27; PGCTA, Real Property, 1815, 29; REC to HJS, June 5, 1820, Callcott, ed., *Mistress of Riversdale,* 360.

56. Edmund S. Morgan, *American Slavery, American Freedom: The Ordeal of Colonial Virginia* (New York, 1975).

57. Jean B. Russo, "Self-Sufficiency and Local Exchange: Free Craftsmen in the Rural Chesapeake Economy," Carr et al., eds., *Colonial Chesapeake Society,* 389–432; Christine Daniels, "'Getting his [or her] Livelyhood': Free Workers in Slave Anglo-America, 1675–1810," *Agricultural History* 71 (1997), 125–61.

58. PGCTA, Real Property, 1800, 28, 29, 43; Personal Property, 1800, 3, 31, 44; PGCRW, Wills, T1, April 12, 1797, 397 (Wootton); PGCTA, Real Property, 1800, 3, 12, 27, 42; Personal Property, 1800, 24, 30, 42 (Hill).

59. PGCTA, Personal Property, 1800, 30; PGCRW, Inventories, Jan. 12, 1802, ST4, 240–42.

60. Ibid., March 10, 1802, ST4, 266.

61. PGCLC, Levy Book, 1803, 613; 1805, 634; Levy List, 1805; Levy Book; Almshouse and Pension Papers, 1830.

62. "An Act for the temporary relief of the Poor in the several Counties in this State," Jan. 30, 1817, Kilty, *Laws of Maryland,* 1817, chap. 192; PGCLC, Proceedings, Feb. 21, 1817, 603; March 1, 604–16; March 17, 621–24; May 19, 626–29; July 7, 639–40; Aug. 6, 648; Steven Sarson, "'Objects of distress': Inequality and Poverty in Early Nineteenth-Century Prince George's County," *Maryland Historical Magazine* 96 (2001), 141–62.

63. Russell R. Menard, "From Servant to Freeholder: Status Mobility and Property Accumulation in Seventeenth-Century Maryland," *William and Mary Quarterly*, 3rd ser., 30 (1973), 37–64; Russell R. Menard, P. M. G. Harris, and Lois Green Carr, "Opportunity and Inequality: The Distribution of Wealth on the Lower Western Shore of Maryland, 1638–1705," *Maryland Historical Magazine* 69 (1974), 169–84; Lorena S. Walsh, "Servitude and Opportunity in Charles County, Maryland, 1658–1705," in Aubrey C. Land et al., eds., *Law, Society, and Politics in Early Maryland* (Baltimore, 1977), 111–33.

64. Bayly Ellen Marks, "The Rage for Kentucky: Emigration from St. Mary's County, 1790–1810," in Robert D. Mitchell and Edward K. Muller, eds., *Geographical Perspectives on Maryland's Past*, University of Maryland Occasional Papers in Geography 4 (1979), 108–28; Teute, "Land, Liberty, and Labor in the Post-Revolutionary Era," 184–311; Soltow, "Kentucky Wealth at the End of the Eighteenth Century," 617–33; idem, "Land Inequality on the Frontier," 275–91.

65. Donald R. Adams, Jr., "Prices and Wages in Maryland, 1750–1850," *Journal of Economic History* 46 (1986), 625–45; Lorena S. Walsh, "Land, Landlord, and Leaseholder: Estate Management and Tenant Fortunes in Southern Maryland, 1642–1820," *Agricultural History* 59 (1985), 381, 388–90; Stiverson, *Poverty in a Land of Plenty*, 45–53; Kulikoff, *Tobacco and Slaves*, 136–40.

66. Willard F. Bliss, "The Rise of Tenancy in Virginia," *Virginia Magazine of History and Biography* 58 (1950), 429, 430–33; Stiverson, *Poverty in a Land of Plenty*, 1–27; Walsh, "Land, Landlord, and Leaseholder," 374–77, 379–80, 386–87.

67. Steven Sarson, "Landlessness and Tenancy in Early National Prince George's County, Maryland," *William and Mary Quarterly*, 3rd ser., 57 (2000), 585–94.

68. Mary Clement Jeske, "Autonomy and Opportunity: Carrollton Manor Tenants, 1734–1790" (Ph.D. diss., University of Maryland, 1999); Bliss, "Rise of Tenancy," 436, 437, 438–39; REC to HJS, March 17, 1812, Calcott, ed., *Mistress of Riversdale*, 251.

69. Kulikoff, *Tobacco and Slaves*, 107–16; Sarson, "Landlessness and Tenancy," 594–97.

70. REC to HJS, Sept. 15, 1804, Calcott, ed., *Mistress of Riversdale*, 97.

71. REC to HJS, Nov. 24, 1805, ibid., 134.

72. Prince George's County General Court, Circuit Court Papers, Maryland Hall of Records, T-67, Box 18, Folder 15, 1810.

73. REC to HJS, Sept. 15, 1804, Callcott, ed., *Mistress of Riversdale*, 97.

74. REC to Isabelle van Havre [IvH], May 6, 1807, ibid., 168.

75. REC to IvH, Sept. 28, 1804, ibid., 100, 81.

76. REC to HJS, May 14, 1804, ibid., 85.

77. REC to IvH, May 6, 1807, ibid., 168, 136.

78. Russell R. Menard, "From Servants to Slaves: The Transformation of the Chesapeake Labor System," *Southern Studies* 16 (1977), 355–90.

79. REC to IvH, Oct. 25, 1816; REC to HJS, March 13, 1819, Callcott, ed., *Mistress of Riversdale*, 304, 343.

80. Skaggs, *Roots of Maryland Democracy*, 141–73; Hoffman, *A Spirit of Dissension*, 152–68; Holton, *Forced Founders*, 191–205; McDonnell, *Popular Mobilization and Political Culture*, chaps. 4, 5.

81. Holton, *Forced Founders*, 217–218; McDonnell, "Popular Mobilization and Political Culture in Revolutionary Virginia," *Journal of American History* 85 (1998), 978–81; Hoffman, *A Spirit of Dissension*, 208–22 (quotes on 210, 220).

82. Hoffman, *A Spirit of Dissension*, 243; Holton, *Forced Founders*, 215, 220.

E I G H T: The Irish Immigrant and the Broadening of the Polity in
Philadelphia, 1790–1800

1. J. Franklin Jameson, *The American Revolution Considered as a Social Movement*
(Princeton, 1926), 11; John K. Alexander, *Render them Submissive: Responses to Poverty
in Philadelphia, 1760–1800* (Amherst, Mass., 1980), 7, 32–33, 104–5, 120–21, 164–74. For
the "new Irish," see Maurice J. Bric, "Patterns of Irish Emigration to America,
1783–1800" in *Eire-Ireland* 36 (2001), 10–28.

2. Most of the Penal Laws were passed between 1695 and 1710 and attached religious
tests to the franchise, public office, the holding and inheritance of land, and access to
education and the professions. The organization and practice of religion was also
strictly controlled.

3. Richard Alan Ryerson, "Republican Theory and Partisan Reality in Revolutionary Pennsylvania: Toward a New View of the Constitutionalist Party," in Ronald Hoffman and Peter J. Albert, eds., *Sovereign States in an Age of Uncertainty* (Charlottesville,
1981), 104–5; William Hanna, *Benjamin Franklin and Pennsylvania Politics* (Stanford,
1964), 7–12. See also Douglas McNeil Arnold, *A Republican Revolution: Ideology and Politics in Pennsylvania, 1776–1790* (New York, 1989). Davies was the Irish attorney general
between 1606 and 1619 and is quoted from Karl S. Bottingheimer, *English Money and
Irish Land* (Oxford, 1971), 13. For the Penal Laws, see Sean J. Conolly, *Religion, Law and
Power: The Making of Protestant Ireland, 1660–1760* (Oxford, 1992).

4. Charles Francis Adams, ed., *The Works of John Adams, Second President of the
United States: with a Life of the Author*, 10 vols. (Boston, 1850–56), 8:209.

5. F. G. Franklin, "The Legislative History of Naturalization in the United States,
1776–1795," *Annual Report of the American Historical Association* 1 (1901), 305; Jonathan
Elliot, ed., *Debates on the Adoption of the Federal Constitution*, 5 vols. (Philadelphia,
1861) 5:389, 398. Franklin is quoted ibid., 5:399.

6. *General Advertiser (GA)*, April 5, 1793; *New York Packet*, Aug. 24, 1787.

7. These were the St. David's (Welsh) Society, founded in 1729, the St. Andrew's
(Scottish) Society, founded in 1747, the German Society, founded in 1764, and the
English Society of the Sons of St. George, founded in 1772.

8. John H. Campbell, *A History of the Society of the Friendly Sons of St. Patrick and
the Hibernian Society* (Philadelphia, 1892), introduction; *St. Andrew's Society of
Philadelphia. The Constitution and Rules* (Philadelphia, 1769), 4, 3; Alexander, *Render
them Submissive*, 7, 164.

9. Campbell, *Friendly Sons*, 153, 155; Martin to Mathew Carey, June 6, 1790, Lea &
Febiger Incoming Correspondence, Box 9 (1785–96), Historical Society of Pennsylvania (HSP).

10. *American Daily Advertiser (ADA)*, March 25, 1793; *Aurora*, March 20, 1799. The
last quotation is taken from the *Pennsylvania Packet*, Dec. 2, 1785.

11. Edgar S. Maclay, ed., *Journal of William Maclay* (New York, 1890), 12; Clark to
Jones, Oct. 15, 1794, U.C., Smith-William Jones Correspondence, HSP. Adams is quoted
in Ronald M. Baumann, "The Democratic-Republicans of Philadelphia: The Origins,
1776–1797" (Ph.D. diss., Pennsylvania State University, 1970), 403.

12. Richard G. Miller, *Philadelphia. The Federalist City: A Study of Urban Politics,
1789–1801* (Port Washington, N.Y., 1975), 62–63; *GUS*, Oct. 7, 11, 13, 27, 1794.

13. Norman Blanz, "Editors and Issues: The Party Press in Philadelphia, 1789–1801" (Ph.D. diss., Pennsylvania State University, 1974), 4; Miller, *Philadelphia*, 93, 70, 58–60.

14. Chambers to Carey, March 26, 1794, Lea & Febiger Incoming Correspondence, Box 4, (1775–96), John Chambers Folder (1792–96), HSP; (Belfast) *Northern Star (NS)*, Aug. 27, 1795, "Letter from Philadelphia."

15. *NS*, July 27, 1795; Mathew Carey to John Chambers, June 19, 1795, Lea & Febiger Collection, Letterbooks (1792–97), HSP; Miller, *Philadelphia*, 52. Lee is quoted in Eugene Perry Link, *Democratic-Republican Societies, 1790–1800* (New York, 1942), 88.

16. Carey (1760–1839) was publisher of the (Dublin) *Volunteer's Journal* and a leading figure in contemporary Irish radicalism. After his paper published an alleged libel on the speaker of the Irish house of commons, he fled to Philadelphia where he founded America's first daily newspaper, the *Pennsylvania Evening Herald* on Jan. 25, 1785.

17. Cobbett arrived in Philadelphia in 1796 and founded *Porcupine's Gazette*. Under the pseudonym of "Peter Porcupine," he also published a number of pamphlets that were highly supportive of Federalist policy.

18. Isaac Briggs to Carey, May 22, 1787, Lea & Febiger Incoming Correspondence, Box 2 (1785–96), HSP; William Cobbett, *The Life and Adventures of Peter Porcupine* (Philadelphia, 1796), 53.

19. [William Cobbett], *Detection of a Conspiracy Formed by the United Irishmen, with the Evident Intention of Aiding the Tyrants of France in Subverting the Government of the United States* in *Porcupine's Works* (London, 1801), vol. 8; Rosamund Jacob, *The Rise of the United Irishmen, 1791–4* (London, 1937); David Dickson et al., eds., *The United Irishmen: Republicanism, Radicalism and Rebellion* (Dublin, 1993).

20. Maldwyn Allen Jones, *American Immigration* (Chicago, 1960), 85; R. Barry O'Brien, ed., *The Autobiography of Theobald Wolfe Tone, 1763–1798*, 2 vols. (London, 1893), 1:211. See Marianne Elliott, *Wolfe Tone: Prophet of Irish Independence* (New Haven, Conn., 1989).

21. *National Gazette*, Dec. 15, 1792; *PG*, March 25, 1797. For the international dimension of the United Irishmen, see Marianne Elliott, *Partners in Revolution: The United Irishmen and France* (New Haven, Conn., 1982) and David A. Wilson, *United Irishmen, United States: Immigrant Radicals in the Early Republic* (Dublin, 1998).

22. *Detection of a Conspiracy*; *Aurora*, March 19, 1795; *GUS*, Nov. 19, 1798, Jan. 15, 18, March 7, 1799; *Porcupine's Gazette (PG)*, May 15 and Dec. 21, 1798; *Detection*, 203–4. Unless otherwise noted, all references to the American Society of United Irishmen are taken from the *Detection*.

23. [Carey], *To the Public . . .* , a broadside (Philadelphia, Feb. 5, 1799); *GUS*, Dec. 18, 1798; Carey to Cobbett, undated, Lea & Febiger Incoming Correspondence, Box 2 (July 1798–June 1799) HSP; *Carey's Recorder*, March 31, 1798.

24. *Aurora*, March 21, 1799.

25. *Aurora*, March 23, 1799.

26. John C. Miller, *Crisis in Freedom: The Alien and Sedition Acts* (Boston, 1951), 72; Peters to Pickering, Aug. 24, 30, 1798; Pickering to Peters, Aug. 27, 1798, Pickering Papers, vol. 23, Massachusetts Historical Society; *Aurora*, Feb. 27, 1798, "A Congress Man of '98."

27. The term "state prisoners" was applied to those leaders of the rebellions of 1796 and 1798, most of whom were detained in Kilmainham jail before transfer to holding stations in Britain, such as Fort George.

28. Marshall Smelser, "'Jacobin Phrenzy': Federalism and the Menace of Liberty, Equality and Fraternity," *Review of Politics* 13 (1951), 457–82; Robert Ernst, *Rufus King* (Chapel Hill, 1968), 261–62; King to Jackson, Aug. 28, 1799; King to Pickering, June 14, 1798, Charles R. King, ed., *The Life and Correspondence of Rufus King*, 6 vols. (New York, 1894–1900), 2:645–46; 2:348.

29. Nisbet to Marshall, "Letters of William Marshall, 1798–1800," *Journal of Presbyterian History* 39 (1961), 55.

30. James Thomas Flexner, *George Washington: Anguish and Farewell, 1793–1795* (Boston, 1969), 294; *GUS*, Jan. 29, 1799.

31. *Aurora*, Oct. 9, 1797, *PG*, Feb. 14, 1799; Miller, *Philadelphia*, 94–95.

32. *Aurora*, Oct. 12, 1797; *Journal of the Senate*, 8 (1798–99), 21–23, 111.

33. *PhG*, Jan. 22, 25, 1798. In Pennsylvania, the vote was confined to adult male citizens who were over 21 years of age, who had been in residence for at least two years and who had paid a state or county tax for at least six months before the relevant election. The sons of taxpayers could also vote. Citizens had to have either (a) been born or settled within America before July 4, 1776, or within Pennsylvania, before Sept. 28, 1776, or (b) immigrated on or before March 25, 1790. Voters who had immigrated between 1790 and Jan. 29, 1795, were obliged to take the required oaths under the naturalization acts. Those who entered the state after Jan. 29, 1795, needed five years residence before they could become citizens.

34. *PhG*, Feb. 2, 15, 1798.

35. *PhG*, Feb. 17, 15, 1798; *GUS*, Feb. 15, 1798, March 7, 1799.

36. *GUS*, Feb. 22, 1798; *ADA*, Feb. 21, 1798; Library Company of Philadelphia, Broadsides Collection Ab (1798)-23, "Questions to be Put to the Electors;" Ab (1798)-8, "Opinion of Chief Justice McKean." The results of the election were published in the *Aurora* on Feb. 24, 1798.

37. *GUS*, Feb. 20, 1798; *PG*, April 21, 1798.

38. *GUS*, Nov. 22, 1798; James Morton Smith, *Freedom's Fetters: the Alien and Sedition Laws and American Civil Liberties* (Ithaca, 1956), 162; Joseph Gales and W. W. Seaton, eds., *The Debates and Proceedings in the Congress of the United States (Annals of Congress)* 42 vols. (New York, 1834–56), 2nd Session, 1578, May 3, 1798; Ames to Christopher Gore, Dec. 18, 1798, in Seth Ames, ed., *Works of Fisher Ames with a Selection from his Speeches and Correspondence*, 2 vols. (Boston, 1854), 1:247.

39. Smith, *Freedom's Fetters*, 23; July 1, 1797, *Annals of Congress*, 1st Session, 423–26.

40. Samuel Eliot Morison, *The Life and Letters of Harrison Gray Otis*, 2 vols. (Boston, 1913) 1:107–8; May 2, 1798, *Annals of Congress*, 2nd Session, 1567–78.

41. May 2, 21 and 3, 1798 *Annals of Congress*, 2nd Session, 1568, 1778, 1572; Smith, *Freedom's Fetters*, 31. For the act, see *Statutes at Large* 1:566–69.

42. June 16, 1798, *Annals of Congress*, 2nd Session, 1961; April 25, 1798, ibid. (Senate), 548.

43. *Statutes at Large* 1:570–72; June 25, 1798, *Annals of Congress*, 1st Session, 1798; June 25, 1798, ibid., 2nd Session, 2035; *Statutes at Large*, 1:577–88.

44. Smith, *Freedom's Fetters*; Miller, Crisis in Freedom.

45. *Aurora*, Nov. 22, 1798; Frederick B. Tolles, *George Logan of Philadelphia* (New York, 1953); Library of Congress, Pennsylvania Broadsides (1799), "The Plea of Erin, or, The Case of the Natives of Ireland in the United States, Fairly Displaced."

46. All quotations in the two preceding paragraphs are taken from "The Plea of Erin." For the 1775 address, see Maurice J. Bric, "Ireland, America and the Reassessment of a Special Relationship, 1760–83," *Eighteenth-Century Ireland* 2 (1996), 88–119.

47. The quotations in the above paragraph are taken from [William Duane], *A Report of the Extraordinary Transactions which Took Place at Philadelphia in February 1799, in Consequence of a Memorial from Certain Natives of Ireland to Congress Praying a Repeal of the Alien Bill* (Philadelphia, 1799), 9, 24.

48. *A Report of the Extraordinary Transactions; Aurora,* Feb. 22, 1799.

N I N E : Dionysian Rhetoric and Apollonian Solutions

1. Jefferson to Edward Rutledge, June 24, 1797, in Paul Leicester Ford, ed., *The Works of Thomas Jefferson,* 12 vols. [Federal Edition] (New York, 1904–5), 8:318–19; Marshall Smelser, "The Federalist Period as an Age of Passion," *American Quarterly* 10 (1958), 391, 419; "The Jacobin Phrenzy: Federalism and the Menace of Liberty, Equality, and Fraternity," *Review of Politics* 13 (1951), 457–82; and "Jacobin Phrenzy: The Menace of Monarchy, Plutocracy, and Anglophobia, 1789–1798," *Review of Politics* 21 (1959), 239–58; John R. Howe, Jr., "Republican Thought and the Political Violence of the 1790s," *American Quarterly* 19 (1967), 147–65. The conventional interpretation is endorsed by Stanley Elkins and Eric McKitrick, *The Age of Federalism* (New York, 1993), 4.

2. Smelser, "Federalist Period as an Age of Passion," 396, 419; Howe, "Republican Thought and Political Violence," 150.

3. Richard Hofstadter, *The Idea of a Party System: The Rise of Legitimate Opposition in the United States, 1780–1840* (Berkeley, 1969), 130–69; quotations at 130, 149.

4. James M. Banner, Jr., *To the Hartford Convention: The Federalists and the Origins of Party Politics in Massachusetts, 1789–1815* (New York, 1970), ix, xi, 377.

5. On the problematic nature of the Revolutionary union, see John M. Murrin, "A Roof without Walls: The Dilemma of American National Identity," in Richard Beeman, Stephen Botein, and Edward C. Carter II, eds., *Beyond Confederation: Origins of the Constitution and American National Identity* (Chapel Hill, 1987), 333–48; Charles Royster, "Founding a Nation in Blood: Military Conflict and American Nationality," in Ronald Hoffman and Peter J. Albert, eds., *Arms and Independence: The Military Character of the American Revolution* (Charlottesville, 1984), 25–49; David Waldstreicher, *In the Midst of Perpetual Fetes: The Making of American Nationalism, 1776–1820* (Chapel Hill, 1997), 53–173; Peter S. Onuf, *Jefferson's Empire: The Language of American Nationhood* (Charlottesville, 2000), esp. chaps. 2, 4.

6. Alexander Hamilton, James Madison, and John Jay, *The Federalist,* ed. Benjamin Fletcher Wright (Cambridge, Mass., 1961), 108–11, 114–24.

7. John Marsh, *A Discourse Delivered at Wethersfield* (Hartford, 1784), 7; Murrin, "Roof Without Walls," 343. For more on this, see my "Republican Expectations: Revolutionary Ideology and the Compromise of 1790," in Donald R. Kennon, ed., *A Republic for the Ages: The United States Capitol and the Political Culture of the Early Republic* (Charlottesville, 1999), 3–35; Charles Royster, *Light-Horse Harry Lee and the Legacy of the American Revolution* (New York, 1981): 87–168; James E. Lewis, Jr., *The American Union and the Problem of Neighborhood: The United States and the Collapse of the Spanish Empire, 1783–1829* (Chapel Hill, 1998), 3–32.

8. Jefferson to James Madison, Nov. 17, 1798, in James Morton Smith, ed., *The Republic of Letters: The Correspondence between Thomas Jefferson and James Madison, 1776–1826*, 3 vols. (New York, 1995), 2:1080. The apportionment controversy is discussed by David P. Currie, *The Constitution in Congress: The Federalist Period, 1789–1801* (Chicago, 1997), 128–35; Richard Buel, Jr., *Securing the Revolution: Ideology and American Politics, 1789–1815* (Ithaca, 1972), 21–22; Drew McCoy, "James Madison and Visions of American Nationality in the Confederation Period: A Regional Perspective," in Beeman et al., eds., *Beyond Confederation*, 252–53.

9. John Laurance, Oct. 31, 1791, in *Annals of the Congress of the United States, 1789–1824*, 42 vols. (Washington, D.C., 1834–56), 3:148.

10. *Annals of Congress*, 3:179, 183, 186; Page, Vining, and Steele, Nov. 15, 1791.

11. Ibid., 3:191, 154, 170, 244; House vote, Nov. 15; Williamson, Nov. 3; Steele, Nov. 10, 1791.

12. Ibid., 3: 46–47, 244; Senate vote, Dec. 8; Findley, Dec. 12, 1791.

13. Ibid., 3:46–47, 201, 243, 244; Senate vote, Dec. 8, 1791; Laurance and Dayton, Nov. 21, 1791; Gerry, Findley, and Benson, Dec. 12, 1791. Adams cast the deciding vote in a deadlocked Senate on two separate occasions: first on Dec. 8, in favor of the Senate's substitute ratio of one to 33,000; and second on Dec. 15, in opposition to the motion that the Senate agree to the provisions of the House bill.

14. Ibid., 3:254–57, 262; Ames and Dayton, Dec. 19, 1791. Ames mistakenly said that the total would be 112 representatives. Applying the one to 30,000 ratio to the representable population of the United States, which was 3,408,752 (minus South Carolina, whose census returns were incomplete at this time), yields a total of 113 representatives. Under this plan, once South Carolina's population is included in the total, the maximum number of representatives for the nation increases to 120.

15. Ibid., 3:257–62; Ames, Dec. 19, 1791. Ames's calculations did not include South Carolina. With a representable population of 206,236, South Carolina was also entitled to an additional representative under Ames's proposal.

16. Ibid., 3:412, 264–65; Page, Feb. 16, 1792; Madison, Dec. 19, 1791; Memoranda of Consultations with the President, March 11-April 9, 1792, in Julian P. Boyd et al., eds., *The Papers of Thomas Jefferson*, 31 vols. to date (Princeton, 1950–), 23:264.

17. Madison to Jefferson, May 9, 27, 1789, in James Morton Smith, ed., *The Republic of Letters: The Correspondence between Thomas Jefferson and James Madison, 1776–1826*, 3 vols. (New York, 1995), 1:608, 614; *Annals of Congress*, 3:264–65; Madison, Dec. 19, 1791.

18. *Annals of Congress*, 3:243–44, 407, 268–69, 270–71, 408; Madison, Dec. 12, 1791; Feb. 16, 1792; Murray and Smith, Dec. 19; Venable, Feb. 16, 1792; Jefferson to Archibald Stuart, March 14, 1792, in Ford, ed., *Works of Thomas Jefferson*, 6:406.

19. *Annals of Congress*, 3:272, 273, 247, 263, 265; Sedgwick and Laurance, Dec. 19; Giles, Dec. 12; Dayton and Madison, Dec. 19, 1791.

20. Ibid., 3:191, 274; Nov. 15 and Dec. 19, 1791. On voting blocs in the First and Second Congresses, see Mary Ryan, "Party Formation in the United States Congress, 1789 to 1796: A Quantitative Analysis," *William and Mary Quarterly*, 3rd ser., 21 (1971), 523–42; H. James Henderson, "Quantitative Approaches to Party Formation in the United States Congress," ibid., 3rd ser., 30 (1973), 307–23.

21. *Annals of Congress*, 3:539, Washington's veto, April 5, 1792; Hamilton to Washington, April 4, 1792, in Harold C. Syrett, ed., *The Papers of Alexander Hamilton*, 27 vols.

(New York, 1961–87), 11:228–30; Memoranda of Consultations, in Boyd, ed., *Papers of Jefferson*, 23:264; Opinion on Apportionment Bill, April 4, 1792, ibid., 23:376–77.

22. *Annals of Congress*, 3:540–41, 543, 272; vote to override veto, April 6; Giles and final vote, April 9, 1792; Sedgwick, Dec. 19, 1791. Knowing that the 1/30,000 ratio resulted in a leftover fraction of 0.9 for their state may have influenced the votes of the South Carolinians.

23. Madison to Jefferson, May 9, 1789, in Smith, ed., *Republic of Letters*, 1:608; in Vining, Nov. 15, 1791, *Annals of Congress*, 3:187.

24. Jefferson to Washington, May 23, 1792, in Boyd, ed., *Papers of Jefferson*, 23:536–38; Jefferson to Archibald Stuart, March 14, 1792, in Ford, ed., *Works of Jefferson*, 6:406–7.

25. Boyd, ed., *Papers of Jefferson*, 23:538–39.

26. Substance of Conversation with the President, May 5, 1792, in Gaillard Hunt, ed., *The Writings of James Madison*, 9 vols. (New York, 1900–1910), 6:107–9; *Annals of Congress*, 3:271, in Smith, Dec. 19, 1791.

27. Substance of Conversation with President, May 5, 1792, in Hunt, ed., *Writings of Madison*, 6:109, 113; Jefferson to Washington, May 23, 1792, in Boyd, ed., *Papers of Jefferson*, 23:539.

28. James Morton Smith, *Freedom's Fetters: The Alien and Sedition Laws and American Civil Liberties* (Ithaca, 1956), 98; Jefferson to Madison, Dec. 28, 1794, April 12, May 10, 31, 1798, in Smith, ed., *Republic of Letters*, 2:867, 1035, 1048, 1054; Jefferson to Taylor, June 1, 1798, in Ford, ed., *Works of Jefferson*, 8:431.

29. Jefferson to Archibald Stuart, May 14, 1792, in Ford, ed., *Works of Jefferson*, 6:406–7; Jefferson to John Taylor, June 1, 1798, ibid., 8:432; Opinion on Apportionment, April 4, 1792, in Boyd, ed., *Papers of Jefferson*, 23:375; *Annals of Congress*, 3:105–6. By a vote of 20 to 7, the Senate rejected the explanatory amendment to which Jefferson alluded.

30. Jefferson to John Taylor, June 1, 1798, in Ford, ed., *Works of Jefferson*, 8:430–33; "Civis" [David Ramsay] to the Citizens of South Carolina, Feb. 4, 1788, in Bernard Bailyn, ed., *The Debate on the Constitution*, 2 vols. (New York, 1993), 2:149. In "Madison and Visions of American Nationalism," 226–58, McCoy discusses the logic of the southern "miscalculation" on population growth.

31. Jefferson to Madison, June 7, 1798, in Smith, ed., *Republic of Letters*, 2:1054, 1056–57; Frank Anderson, "Contemporary Opinions of the Virginia and Kentucky Resolutions," *American Historical Review* 5 (1899), 45–63, 225–52, quotations on 246, 247. James Roger Sharp, *American Politics in the Early Republic: The New Nation in Crisis* (New Haven, Conn., 1993), 187–97, argues that Jefferson's thinking underwent a fundamental change between June and November 1798.

32. Adrienne Koch, *Jefferson and Madison: The Great Collaboration* (New York, 1950), 209; Jefferson to Samuel Smith, Aug. 22, 1798, in Ford, ed., *Works of Jefferson*, 8:444; Kentucky Resolutions and Jefferson's drafts, ibid., 8:458–79; Smith, ed., *Republic of Letters*, 2:1080–84.

33. Jefferson to Madison, Jan. 30, Aug. 23, 1799, in Smith, ed., *Republic of Letters*, 2:1091, 1119; Koch, *Jefferson and Madison*, 199; Adrienne Koch and Harry Ammon, "The Virginia and Kentucky Resolutions: An Episode in Jefferson's and Madison's Defense of Civil Liberties," *William and Mary Quarterly*, 3rd ser., 5 (1948), 165–67; Elkins and McKitrick, *Age of Federalism*, 721.

34. Madison to Jefferson, Dec. 29, 1799, in Smith, ed., *Republic of Letters*, 2:1122; Report on the Resolutions, in Hunt, ed., *Writings of James Madison*, 6:349–50, 352.

35. Report on the Resolutions, ibid., 6: 350, 355, 357–58. See Pauline Maier, *From Resistance to Revolution: Colonial Radicals and the Development of American Opposition to Britain, 1765–1776* (New York, 1972), 27–48, for the radical Whig concept of a "just" revolution.

36. Report on the Resolutions, in Hunt, ed., *Writings of Madison*, 6:341–42, 374; [Henry Lee], *Plain Truth: Addressed to the People of Virginia* (Richmond?, 1799), 9; Madison, Notes for Debate on Commercial Regulation by Congress, Nov. 30–Dec. 1, 1785, in J. C. A. Stagg et al., eds., *The Papers of James Madison: Congressional Series*, 17 vols. (Chicago and Charlottesville, 1959–91), 8:432.

37. George Nicholas, *A Letter from George Nicholas, of Kentucky, to His Friend in Virginia* (Philadelphia, 1799), 22–24, 31.

38. [An Inhabitant of the North-Western Territory], *Observations on a Letter from George Nicholas to His Friend in Virginia* (Cincinnati, 1799), 26–27, 29–30.

39. Nicholas, *Letter from George Nicholas to His Friend*, 22; Jefferson to Madison, Nov. 17, 1798, in Smith, ed., *Republic of* Letters, 2:1080. The phrase "unifying element" appears in the Editor's Note to Koch and Ammon, "Virginia and Kentucky Resolutions," 146.

40. Smelser, "Federalist Period as an Age of Passion," 391, 419; Hofstadter, *Idea of a Party System*, 130; Jefferson to John Taylor, June 1, 1798, in Ford, ed., *Works of Jefferson*, 8:431. See Kenneth Stampp, "The Concept of a Perpetual Union," *Journal of American History* 65 (1978), 5–33, for the antebellum period.

T E N : Civil Society in Post-Revolutionary America

1. Daniel Doan, *Indian Stream Republic: Settling a New England Frontier, 1785–1842* (Hanover, N.H., 1997), 154–71.

2. Doan, *Indian Stream Republic*, 109–47, quotation at 119.

3. This thumbnail definition deliberately uses the past tense in order partly to situate it in the Revolutionary—early republic period, and partly to avoid issues raised by contemporary debate on "civil society." Political and social thought of the early republic differed radically from the context of current "civil society" debates, a point discussed in Adam Seligman, *The Idea of Civil Society* (New York, 1992), and Jean L. Cohen and Andrew Arato, *Civil Society and Political Theory* (Cambridge, Mass., 1992); see also John Ehrenberg, *Civil Society: The Critical History of an Idea* (New York, 1999). Contemporary American discussion centers on a relationship between complex patterns of interpersonal associations ("social capital") and individuals' reliance on government; much of this debate has coalesced around Robert Putnam, "Bowling Alone: America's Declining Social Capital," *Journal of Democracy* 6 (1995), 65–78, and *Bowling Alone: The Collapse and Revival of American Community* (New York, 2000).

4. My summary of these characteristics relies heavily on examples from the northern states. It is possible that procedures in southern states tended to legitimize actions stemming from less regularized or less publicly oriented procedures. Certainly this was the case regarding mobbing; see David Grimsted, *American Mobbing, 1828–1861: Toward Civil War* (New York, 1998), esp. 85–113.

5. Doan, *Indian Stream Republic,* 124, 163–69. The new assembly agreed to follow "all the former rules and regulations" of prior town meetings, 169. What those procedures were remains obscure; little is known about public-meeting procedure before the 1845 publication of Luther Cushing's guidebook for nonlegislative bodies; [Sarah Corbin Robert,] "Introduction," *Robert's Rules of Order Newly Revised* (Glenview, Ill., 1981), xxvii-xlii.

6. *Cleveland Whig,* Dec. 9, 1835. On ubiquity, and parameters, of meetings, see Mary P. Ryan, *Civic Wars: Democracy and Public Life in the American City during the Nineteenth Century* (Berkeley, 1997), 94–131.

7. First annual meeting report, Feb. 26, 1833, Ravenna Temperance Society Records, Dec. 10, 1830–Jan. 1838, Reed Memorial Library, Ravenna, Ohio. Transcriptions of these reports were sent to local newspapers by the secretary.

8. Conrad Edick Wright, *The Transformation of Charity in Postrevolutionary New England* (Boston, 1992), 58, 49–95, 134–42; Marc L. Harris, "Social Entrepreneurs: Economic Enterprisers and Social Reformers on Ohio's Western Reserve, 1795–1845" (Ph.D. diss., Johns Hopkins University, 1984), 293–328, and "The Process of Voluntary Association: Organizing the Ravenna Temperance Society, 1830," *Ohio History* 94 (1985), 158–70.

9. Pauline Maier, *From Resistance to Revolution: Colonial Radicals and the Development of American Opposition to Britain, 1765–1776,* paperback ed. (New York, 1974), 271–87; Dirk Hoerder, *Crowd Action in Revolutionary Massachusetts 1765–1780* (New York, 1977); Richard Alan Ryerson, *The Revolution Is Now Begun: The Radical Committees of Philadelphia, 1765–1776* (Philadelphia, 1978); Gordon S. Wood, *The Creation of the American Republic, 1776–1787* (Chapel Hill, 1969), 344–89.

10. David S. Shields, *Civil Tongues and Polite Letters in British America* (Chapel Hill, 1997); Peter Burke, *The Art of Conversation* (Ithaca, 1993), 112–20; Lawrence E. Klein, "Liberty, Manners, and Politeness in Early Eighteenth-Century England," *The Historical Journal* 32 (1989), 583–605; Margaret Jacob, *Living the Enlightenment: Freemasonry and Politics in Eighteenth-Century Europe* (New York, 1991).

11. Harris, "Process of Voluntary Association."

12. Rhys Isaac *The Transformation of Virginia, 1740–1790* (Chapel Hill, 1982); Christopher Grasso, *A Speaking Aristocracy: Transforming Public Discourse in Eighteenth-Century Connecticut* (Chapel Hill, 1999); Sandra M. Gustafson, *Eloquence is Power: Oratory and Performance in Early America* (Chapel Hill, 2000).

13. Grasso, *Speaking Aristocracy.*

14. Thomas W. Benson, ed., *Rhetoric and Political Culture in Nineteenth-Century America* (East Lansing, Mich., 1997); Stephen Oates, *With Malice Toward None: The Life of Abraham Lincoln* (New York, 1977), 3–60, esp. 16.

15. Peter Thompson, *Rum Punch and Revolution: Taverngoing and Public Life in Eighteenth-Century Philadelphia* (Philadelphia, 1997).

16. Alexis de Tocqueville, *Democracy in America,* 2 vols., trans. Phillips Bradley (New York, 1945), 2:114.

17. The term "meta-constitutional order" is adapted from Roger Sherman Hoar's analysis of the "supra-constitutional" context surrounding valid constitutional adoption and amendment, *Constitutional Conventions: Their Nature, Powers, and Limitations* (Boston, 1917).

18. Jack P. Greene, *The Quest for Power: The Lower Houses of Assembly in the Southern Royal Colonies, 1689–1776* (Chapel Hill, 1963), and *Peripheries and Center: Constitutional Development in the Extended Polities of the British Empire and the United States, 1607–1788* (Athens, Ga., 1986), 105–28; Wood, *Creation*, 162–96.

19. Wood, *Creation*, 306–43.

20. Thomas Paine, *Rights of Man*, Part I, in *Thomas Paine: Collected Writings*, ed. Eric Foner (New York, 1995), 467–68.

21. Samuel Eliot Morison, "William Manning's *The Key of Liberty*," *William and Mary Quarterly*, 3rd Ser., 13 (1956), 215–17.

22. The exact number depends on whether to count the Massachusetts constitution of 1777, written by the legislature but rejected by the towns. Connecticut and Rhode Island's legislatures made minor revisions in their respective royal charters. Willi Paul Adams, *The First American Constitutions: Republican Ideology and the Making of the State Constitutions in the Revolutionary Era*, trans. Rita and Robert Kimber (Chapel Hill, 1980), 63–98; Oscar and Mary Handlin, eds., *The Popular Sources of Political Authority: Documents on the Massachusetts Constitution of 1780* (Cambridge, Mass., 1966), 1–54.

23. Norman F. Cantor, *Imagining the Law: Common Law and the Foundations of the American Legal System* (New York, 1997); J. W. Tubbs, *The Common Law Mind: Medieval and Early Modern Conceptions* (Baltimore, 2000), esp. 186–95; James Q. Whitman, "Why Did the Revolutionary Lawyers Confuse Custom and Reason?" *University of Chicago Law Review* 58 (1991), 1321–68.

24. *Kamper v. Hawkins*, Virginia Reports 3 (1793), 20–108.

25. Ibid., 27–28.

26. Ibid., 69.

27. Ibid., 48.

28. *Calder v. Bull*, U.S. Reports 3 (1798), 386–400.

29. Ibid., 387–89, 395, 399. On Chase and Iredell, see Thomas C. Grey, "The Original Understanding and the Unwritten Constitution," in Neil L. York, ed., *Toward a More Perfect Union: Six Essays on the Constitution* (Provo, Utah, 1988), 145–68.

30. *Calder v. Bull*, 395. See also Ellen A. Peters, "Common Law Antecedents of Constitutional Law in Connecticut," *Albany Law Review* 53 (1989), 259–64.

31. Handlin and Handlin, *Sources*, 1–54; David P. Szatmary, *Shays' Rebellion: The Making of an Agrarian Insurrection* (Amherst, Mass., 1980), 38–39; Samuel Adams to John Adams, April 16, 1784, in Harry Alonzo Cushing, ed., *The Writings of Samuel Adams*, 4 vols.(New York, 1908), 4:296.

32. Samuel Adams to John Adams, Nov. 20, 1790, in Charles Francis Adams, ed., *The Works of John Adams*, 6 vols. (Boston, 1851), 6:420–21.

33. Wood, *Creation*, 306–43; Handlin and Handlin, *Sources*, Preamble to constitution, quote at 441.

34. Suzette Hemberger, "A Government Based on Representations," *Studies in American Political Development* 10 (1996), 289–332, esp. 319–23; Fisher Ames, speech in House of Representatives, Nov. 26, 1794, *Annals of Congress* 3:923, quoted in Hemberger, "Representations," 329.

35. Stanley Elkins and Eric McKitrick, *The Age of Federalism: The Early American Republic, 1788–1800* (New York, 1993), 485–88; David Waldstreicher, *In the Midst of Perpetual Fetes: The Making of American Nationalism, 1776–1820* (Chapel Hill, 1997).

36. Michael Phillips, "Blake and the Terror," *The Library*, 6th Ser., 16 (1994), 263–97.

37. In effect it substituted a sovereign moment for a sovereign person; see Hemberger, "Representations," on important innovations in representational theory arising from this substitution.

38. Elkins and McKitrick, *Age of Federalism;* Richard N. Rosenfeld, *American Aurora: A Democratic-Republican Returns* (New York, 1997). See also Simon P. Newman, *Parades and the Politics of the Street: Festive Culture in the Early American Republic* (Philadelphia, 1997).

39. Wright, *Transformation of Charity*, 34–35; 288n. Wright notes that many of these early charitable societies lapsed, though it is unclear why.

40. Steven C. Bullock, *Revolutionary Brotherhood: Freemasonry and the Transformation of the American Social Order, 1730–1840* (Chapel Hill, 1996); Wright, *Transformation of Charity*, 54–55, 73–74, 130–31; Ryan, *Civic Wars*, 58–131; Sean Wilentz, *Chants Democratic: New York City and the Rise of the American Working Class, 1788–1850* (New York, 1984).

41. Rosenberg, *American Aurora;* Linda K. Kerber, *Federalists in Dissent: Imagery and Ideology in Jeffersonian America* (Ithaca, 1970), 181–85.

42. Minor Myers, Jr., *Liberty without Anarchy: A History of the Society of the Cincinnati* (Charlottesville, 1983); Marc L. Harris, "'Cement to the Union': The Society of the Cincinnati and the Limits of Fraternal Sociability," *Proceedings of the Massachusetts Historical Society* 107 (1995), 115–40; Bullock, *Revolutionary Brotherhood;* Paul Goodman, *Towards a Christian Republic: Antimasonry and the Great Transition in New England, 1826–1836* (New York, 1988).

43. Paul A. Gilje, *The Road to Mobocracy: Popular Disorder in New York City, 1763–1834* (Chapel Hill, 1987), 97–119, 227; Maier, *From Resistance to Revolution*, 280–87; Charles Royster, *Light-Horse Harry Lee and the Legacy of the American Revolution* (Baton Rouge, 1981), 156–58.

44. Leonard L. Richards, *"Gentlemen of Property and Standing": Anti-Abolition Mobs in Jacksonian America* (New York, 1970); Grimsted, *American Mobbing*, 35–38, 56; "Temperance," n.d., Darius Lyman Family Papers, MSS 3364, Container 8, Folder 1, Western Reserve Historical Society, Cleveland, Ohio.

45. Grimsted, *American Mobbing*, 19–59, quote at 29.

46. Marvin E. Gettleman, *The Dorr Rebellion: A Study in American Radicalism: 1833–1849* (New York, 1973), 2–29.

47. Address of the State Suffrage Committee, July 1841, quoted in Gettleman, *Dorr Rebellion*, 43. The address was prepared by a committee of the Suffrage Association.

48. Gettleman, *Dorr Rebellion*, 30–165; William M. Wiecek, "Popular Sovereignty in the Dorr War—Conservative Counterblast," *Rhode Island History* 32 (1973), 3–51, and "'A Peculiar Conservatism' and the Dorr Rebellion: Constitutional Clash in Jacksonian America," *American Journal of Legal History* 22 (1978), 237–53; George M. Dennison, "The Dorr War and the Triumph of Institutionalism," *Social Science Journal* 15 (1978), 39–58.

ELEVEN: Religion, Moderation, and Regime-Building in Post-Revolutionary America

The author acknowledges with gratitude a grant from the University of North Carolina–Greensboro Research Council, a Senior Fellowship from the Pew Endowment

Christian Scholars Program, University of Notre Dame, and discussion with the Triangle Early American Seminar.

1. For theoretical outlines of an implicit bargain, see Robert Green McCloskey, ed., *The Works of James Wilson* (Cambridge, Mass., 1967), 71–72 and sermons by Samuel Cooper, Israel Evans, David Tappan, and John Smalley in Ellis Sandoz, ed., *Political Sermons of the American Founding Era, 1730–1815* (Indianapolis, 1991), 644–45, 1062–65, 1106–13, and 1431–38. For its factual outline, see Marc W. Kruman, *Between Liberty and Authority: State Constitutions in Revolutionary America* (Chapel Hill, 1997), 45–46; Thomas J. Curry, *The First Freedoms: Church and State to the Passage of the of the First Amendment* (New York, 1986), 218–22. Frank Lambert, *The Founding Fathers and the Place of Religion in America* (Princeton, 2003), 246–53, is skeptical of the existence of civil-religious reciprocity.

2. Fred J. Hood, *Reformed America: The Middle and Southern States, 1783–1837* (University, Ala., 1980), 7.

3. John C. Fitzpatrick, ed., *The Writings of George Washington*, Vol. 35, *March 30, 1796–July 31, 1797* (Washington, D.C., 1940).

4. Ernst Troeltsch, *The Social Teachings of the Christian Churches* (New York, 1928), 331–54, 691–990.

5. Jaroslav Pelikan, *The Christian Tradition: A History of the Development of Doctrine*, Vol. 5, *Christian Doctrine and Modern Culture since 1700* (Chicago, 1989), 89–117, 156–60; and Curtis D. Johnson, *Redeeming America: Evangelicals and the Road to the Civil War* (Chicago, 1993), 94–104. Roman Catholicism, of course, was, and historically remained, an original Primitive church. During the early republic, Catholics began to explore their relationship to American constitutionalism, see Patrick W. Carey, *An Immigrant Bishop: John England's Adaptation of Irish Catholicism to American Republicanism* (New York, 1982) and Robert M. Calhoon, *Religion and the American Revolution in North Carolina* (Raleigh, 1976), 69–73.

6. James Turner, *Without God, Without Creed: The Origins of Unbelief in America* (Baltimore, 1985), 45.

7. Mark A. Noll, *Princeton and the Republic, 1768–1822: The Search for a Christian Enlightenment in the Era of Samuel Stanhope Smith* (Princeton, 1989), 51.

8. Jack Scott, ed., *An Annotated Edition of Lectures on Moral Philosophy by John Witherspoon* (Newark, Del., 1982), 144.

9. Robert M. Calhoon, *Evangelicals and Conservatives in the Early South, 1740–1861* (Columbia, S.C., 1988), 86–87.

10. Winthrop D. Jordan, *White over Black: American Attitudes toward the Negro, 1550–1812* (Chapel Hill, 1968), 486–88.

11. Mark A. Noll, *Princeton and the Republic*, 123.

12. James M. Banner, *To the Hartford Convention: The Federalists and the Origins of Party Politics in Massachusetts, 1789–1815* (New York, 1970), 54.

13. Jonathan D. Sassi, *A Republic of Righteousness: The Public Christianity of the Post-Revolutionary New England Clergy* (New York, 2001), 21–51.

14. Lester H. Cohen, *The Revolutionary Histories: Contemporary Narratives of the American Revolution* (Ithaca, 1980), 108; John R. Fitzmier, *New England's Moral Legislator: Timothy Dwight, 1752–1817* (Bloomington, 1998) 131.

15. John L. Brooke, "A Deacon's Orthodoxy: Religion, Class, and the Moral Economy of Shays's Rebellion," in Robert A. Gross, ed., *In Debt to Shays: The Bicentennial of an Agrarian Rebellion* (Charlottesville, 1993), 208–10.

16. Sassi, *A Republic of Righteousness,* 133–36.

17. Calhoon, *Evangelicals and Conservatives,* 163–66.

18. Buckley, *Church and State in Revolutionary Virginia, 1776–1787* (Charlottesville, 1977), 35.

19. J. G. A. Pocock, "Religious Freedom and the Desacralization of Politics: From the English Civil Wars to the Virginia Statute," in Merrill D. Peterson and Robert C. Vaughan, eds., *The Virginia Statute for Religious Freedom: Its Evolution and Consequences for American History* (New York, 1988), 61.

20. Buckley, *Church and State in Revolutionary Virginia,* 190.

21. Pocock, "Religious Freedom and the Desacralization of Politics," 60–70.

22. Constance B. Schulz, "'Of Bigotry in Politics and Religion': Jefferson's Religion, the Federalist Press, and the Syllabus," *Virginia Magazine of History and Biography* 91 (1983), 84.

23. Paul Conkin, "Priestley and Jefferson: Unitarianism as a Religion for a New Revolutionary Age," in Ronald Hoffman and Peter J. Albert, eds., *Religion in a Revolutionary Age* (Charlottesville, 1994), 295–304.

24. Thomas J. Buckley, "The Political Theology of Thomas Jefferson," Peterson and Vaughan, eds., *The Virginia Statute,* 77.

25. Lance Banning, "James Madison, the Statute for Religious Freedom, and the Crisis of Republican Convictions," in Peterson and Vaughan, eds., *The Virginia Statute,* 115–30.

26. Daniel L. Dreisbach, "A New Perspective on Jefferson's Views on Church-State Relations: The Virginia Statute for Establishing Religious Freedom in its Legislative Context," *American Journal of Legal History* 35 (1991), 187–97; Dreisbach, *Thomas Jefferson and the Wall of Separation between Church and State* (New York, 2002), 81–94.

27. Banning, "James Madison, the Statute for Religious Freedom, and the Crisis of Republican Convictions," 116. As part of the codification of Virginia law and a conciliatory legislative tactic, the package of bills pertaining to religion included the Virginia Statute for Religious Freedom as Bill #82 along with Bill #83 on protecting Episcopal property, Bill #84 on observance of the Sabbath, and Bill #86 on civil marriage, see Dreisbach, "A New Perspective."

28. Robert Rutland et al., eds., *The Papers of James Madison,* Vol. 8, *10 March 1784–28 March 1786* (Chicago, 1973), 301.

29. Pelikan, *Christian Tradition,* Vol. 1, *The Emergence of the Catholic Tradition, 100–600* (Chicago, 1971), 108–20.

30. J. C. D. Clark, *English Society, 1660–1832,* 2nd ed. (Cambridge, U.K., 2000), x, 52–66.

31. John Dunn, *The Political Thought of John Locke* (Cambridge, U.K., 1969), 49n. 2.

32. Buckley, *Church and State in Revolutionary Virginia,* 131.

33. Eliga H. Gould, *The Persistence of Empire: British Political Culture in the Age of the American Revolution* (Chapel Hill, 2000), 18–20.

34. Rhys Isaac, *The Transformation of Virginia, 1740–1790* (Chapel Hill, 1982), 59–60; and Calhoon, *Evangelicals and Conservatives,* 30; and generally, Sandra Rennie, "Virginia's Baptist Persecution, 1765–1778," *Journal of Religious History* 12 (1982), 48–59.

35. Mark Beliles, "The Christian Communities, Religious Revivals, and Political Culture in the Central Virginia Piedmont, 1737–1813," in Garrett Ward Sheldon and Daniel L. Driesbach, eds., *Religion and Political Culture in Jefferson's Virginia* (Lanham, Md., 2000), 18–27.

36. In a ham-handed effort at fairness, the 1784 Assessment Bill allowed Quaker and Mennonite laity to receive direct financial support from the state because these sects did not have identifiable clerical leadership. In *Memorial and Remonstrance*, Madison seized on this well-meaning provision as prime evidence that governmental overtures to churches would spawn destructive religious tensions. Calhoon, *Evangelicals and Conservatives in the Early South*, 90.

37. Henry J. Young, "Treason and its Punishment in Revolutionary Pennsylvania," *Pennsylvania Magazine of History and Biography* 90 (1966), 278–91; and Young, "The Treatment of the Loyalists in Pennsylvania" (unpublished Ph.D. diss., The Johns Hopkins University, 1955), 82–93.

38. One such enclave was the Christianized portion of the Cherokee Nation; see William G. McLoughlin, *Cherokees and Missionaries, 1789–1839* (New Haven, Conn., 1984) and *Champions of the Cherokees: Evan and John B. Jones* (Princeton, 1990).

39. Stephen A. Marini, *Radical Sects in Revolutionary New England* (Cambridge, Mass., 1982), 82–84.

40. Ellen Eslinger, *Citizens of Zion: The Social Origins of Camp Meeting Revivalism* (Knoxville, 1999), 238.

41. Marion Nelson Winship, "Kentucky in the New Republic: A Study of Distance and Connection," in Craig Thompson Friend, ed., *The Buzzel about Kentuck: Settling the Promised Land* (Lexington, Ky., 1999), 108–9.

42. See Robert M. Calhoon, "The Evangelical Persuasion," in Hoffman and Albert, eds., *Religion in a Revolutionary Age*, 156–57.

43. Eslinger, *Citizens of Zion*, 223–24.

44. *The Psalms, Hymns, and Spiritual Songs of the Rev. Isaac Watt* (Boston, n.d.), 71.

45. For an early instance, see Stephen A. Marini, "Religion, Politics, and Ratification," in Hoffman and Albert, eds., *Religion in a Revolutionary Age*, 184–86.

46. See Nathan O. Hatch, *The Democratization of American Christianity* (New Haven, Conn., 1989).

47. Rhys Isaac, "'The Rage of Malice of the Old Serpent Devil': The Dissenters and the Making and Remaking of the Virginia Statute for Religious Freedom," in Peterson and Vaughan, eds., *The Virginia Statute*, 152; "Religious Petitions, 1774–1802, Presented to the General Assembly of Virginia," Virginia State Library, Richmond, Buckingham County Petition, Oct. 27, 1785.

48. Rachel N. Klein, *Unification of a Slave State: The Rise of the Planter Class in the South Carolina Backcountry, 1760–1808* (Chapel Hill, 1990); and Stephanie McCurry, *Masters of Small Worlds: Yeoman Households, Gender Relations, and the Political Culture of the Antebellum South Carolina Low Country* (New York, 1995), 131–35.

49. Cynthia Lynn Lyerly, *Methodism and the Southern Mind, 1770–1810* (New York, 1998), 132.

50. Hatch, *Democratization of American Christianity*, 105.

51. Jon Butler, *Awash in a Sea of Faith: Christianizing the American People* (Cambridge, Mass., 1990), 247–52.

52. Sylvia R. Frey and Betty Wood, *Come Shouting to Zion: African American Protestantism in the American South and the British Caribbean to 1830* (Chapel Hill, 1998); Janet Duitsman Cornelius, *Slave Missions and the Black Church in the Antebellum South* (Columbia, S.C., 1999), 4–12; Mechal Sobel, *Trabelin' On: The Journey to an Afro-Baptist Faith* (Princeton, 1988 [originally published by Greenwood Press in 1979]), 140;

Margaret Washington Creel, *"A Peculiar People": Slave Religion and Community Culture among the Gullah* (New York, 1988), 293–94; and Ann Taves, *Fits, Trances, and Visions: Experiencing Religion and Explaining Experience from Wesley to James* (Princeton, 1999), 80–81, 89–107.

53. "Your Sirvent, Sir" to John Fort, June 26, 1821, Neill Brown Papers, Duke University Library, printed in Robert M. Calhoon, "The Evangelical Persuasion," in Hoffman and Albert, eds., *Religion in a Revolutionary Age*, 182–83.

54. Tryphena Mock, "For the Message," *The Weekly Message*, April 24, 1858; Cheryl F. Junk, "Strangers in a Strange Land: The Church and the World in *The Weekly Message*, 1851–1871," Southern Historical Association, Nov. 6, 1999, Fort Worth, Texas.

55. Walter H. Conser, *Church and Confession: Conservative Theologians in Germany, England, and America* (Macon, Ga., 1984), chaps. 6–7.

56. Quentin Skinner, *The Foundations of Modern Political Thought*, Vol. I, *The Renaissance*, and Vol. II, *The Age of the Reformation* (Cambridge, U.K., 1978).

57. Robert M. Calhoon, "Lutheranism in Early Southern Culture," in Robert M. Calhoon and H. George Anderson, eds., *"A Truly Efficient School of Theology": The Lutheran Theological Southern Seminary in Historical Context, 1830–1980* (Columbia, S.C., 1981), 11–16.

58. Robert M. Calhoon, "Jacob Stirewalt and the Doctrine of Ministry," *Lutheranism with a Southern Accent, Proceedings of the Lutheran Historical Conference* (1998), 85–100.

59. David Henkel, *Carolinian Herald of Liberty, Religious and Political; Or, a Testimony against Attempted Measures to Lead to the Establishment of Popery among Protestants* (Salisbury, N.C., 1821), 1 and Lawrence R. Rast, "Cultivating the Holy Religion of Jesus: The Ministry and Ministries according to David Henkel and the Tennessee Synod," *Lutheranism with a Southern Accent*, 101–22.

60. Gottlieb Shober, *Review of a Pamphlet . . . by David Henkel* (Salisbury, N.C., 1821), 4.

61. Calhoon, "Lutheranism in Early Southern Culture," 16; Raymond M. Bost and Jeff Norris, *All One Body: The Story of the North Carolina Lutheran Synod, 1803–1993* (Salisbury, N.C., 1994), 221–22.

62. Robert Bruce Mullin, *Episcopal Vision/American Reality: High Church Theology and Social Thought in Evangelical America* (New Haven, Conn., 1986), 31.

63. Blackwell P. Robinson, "The Episcopate of Levi Silliman Ives," in Lawrence F. London and Sarah M. Lemmon, eds., *The Episcopal Church in North Carolina, 1701–1959* (Raleigh, 1987), 186–219; and "Is Bishop Ives Mad?" and "The Early Life of Bishop Ives," *Southern Churchman*, May 3 and 10, 1853.

64. Diana Hochstedt Butler, *Standing against the Whirlwind: Evangelical Episcopalians in Nineteenth-Century America* (New York, 1995), 71, emphasis added.

65. Robert M. Calhoon, "Moderates in Conflict: Primitive and Enlightened Scottish Calvinists in South Carolina, 1750–1860," Omohundro Institute Conference on Early American History, Glasgow, Scotland, June 12, 2001.

66. Abbeville District Petition, 1838, Race and Slavery Petitions Project, University of North Carolina at Greensboro.

67. "To the Public, Due West, S.C., October 1, 1850," Broadside Collection, South Caroliniana Library, University of South Carolina, Columbia, S.C.; Robert M. Calhoon, "Scotch Irish Calvinists in Conflict: The South Carolina Slave Literacy Controversy, 1838–1860," *Journal of Scotch Irish Studies*, forthcoming.

68. Gordon S. Wood, "Evangelical America and Early Mormonism," *New York History* 61 (1980), 379–80; Daniel L. Dreisbach, ed., *Religion and Politics in the Early Republic: Jasper Adams and the Church State Debate* (Lexington, Ky., 1996), 113–21.

69. Jack P. Greene, "A Fortuitous Convergence: Culture, Circumstance, and Contingency in the Emergence of the American Nation," in Greene, *Imperatives, Behaviors, and Identities: Essays in Early American Cultural History* (Charlottesville, 1992), 290–309.

T W E L V E : The American Loyalist Diaspora and the Reconfiguration of the British Atlantic World

I would like to thank the British Academy for the financial assistance received in support of this project.

1. This evocative phrase comes from Vincent T. Harlow, *The Founding of the Second British Empire, 1763–93*, 2 vols. (London, 1952–64), 1:62.

2. Stephen Conway, *The British Isles and the War of American Independence* (Oxford, 2000); Eliga H. Gould, *The Persistence of Empire: British Political Culture in the Age of the American Revolution* (Chapel Hill, 2000); Andrew Jackson O'Shaughnessy, *An Empire Divided: The American Revolution and the British Caribbean* (Philadelphia, 2000).

3. See, for example, Mary B. Norton, *The British-Americans: The Loyalist Exiles in England, 1774–1789* (London, 1974), 9.

4. Peter Marshall highlights some of these questions in his "British North America, 1760–1815," in P. J. Marshall, ed., *The Oxford History of the British Empire: The Eighteenth Century* (Oxford, 1998), 372–93.

5. For the figures, see Jack P. Greene, *Pursuits of Happiness: The Social Development of Early Modern British Colonies and the Formation of American Culture* (Chapel Hill, 1988), 7.

6. The estimate comes from Norton, *The British-Americans,* 8.

7. Robert M. Calhoon, Timothy M. Barnes, and George A. Rawlyk, eds., *Loyalists and Community in North America* (Westport, Conn., 1994), 6–9.

8. On Nova Scotia Loyalism, see Neil MacKinnon, *This Unfriendly Soil: The Loyalist Experience in Nova Scotia, 1783–1791* (Kingston and Montreal, 1986); James W. St. G. Walker, *The Black Loyalists: The Search for a Promised Land in Nova Scotia and Sierra Leone, 1783–1870* (London, 1976), 1–93. On New Brunswick Loyalism, see Ann Gorman Condon, *The Envy of the American States: The Loyalist Dream for New Brunswick* (Fredericton, NB, 1984).

9. William S. Wallace, *The United Empire Loyalists: A Chronicle of the Great Migration* (Boston, 1972), 86–111.

10. Wilbur H. Siebert, *Loyalists in East Florida; The Most Important Documents Pertaining thereto, Edited with an Accompanying Narrative,* 2 vols. (Boston, 1972), 1:61. Also see, Carole Watterson Troxler, "Refuge, Resistance, and Reward: The Southern Loyalists' Claims on East Florida," *Journal of Southern History* 55 (1989), 563–96; and, J. Barton Starr, *Tories, Dons, and Rebels: The American Revolution in British West Florida* (Gainesville, 1976).

11. Siebert, *Loyalists in East Florida,* 1:130.

12. Ibid., 101, 208, 181–210.

13. See Robin Cohen, *Global Diasporas: An Introduction* (London, 1997).

14. John McLeod, *Beginning Postcolonialism* (Manchester, U.K., 1998), 207.

15. Avtar Brah, *Cartographies of Diaspora: Contesting Identities* (London, 1997), 184.

16. Paul Gilroy, *The Black Atlantic: Modernity and Double Consciousness* (London, 1993).

17. North to Haldimand, Aug. 8, 1783, quoted in David Milobar, "Conservative Ideology, Metropolitan Government, and the Reform of Quebec, 1782–1791," *International History Review* 12 (1990), 51.

18. For a discussion of those imperatives, see Greene, *Pursuits of Happiness,* esp. chaps. 1 and 2.

19. For the role of migration in the initial formation of the British Atlantic, see Alison Games, *Migration and the Origins of the English Atlantic World* (Cambridge, Mass., 1999).

20. The phrase comes from William H. Nelson, *The American Tory* (Oxford, 1961), 91.

21. Gould, *The Persistence of Empire,* 211. See also Stephen Conway, "From Fellow-Nationals to Foreigners: British Perceptions of the Americans, circa 1739–1783," *William and Mary Quarterly,* 3rd ser., 59 (2002), 65–100.

22. Christopher A. Bayly, *Imperial Meridian: The First British Empire and the World, 1780–1830* (New York, 1989), 8–15.

23. Milobar, "Conservative Ideology, Metropolitan Government, and the Reform of Quebec." However, the interpretation offered here differs from his.

24. John Kendle, *Federal Britain: A History* (London, 1997), 18.

25. Eliga H. Gould, "American Independence and Britain's Counter-Revolution," *Past and Present* 154 (1997), 107–41. Gould uses the term "counter-revolutionary hegemon" critically in his "Revolution and Counter-Revolution" in David Armitage and Michael J. Braddick, eds., *The British Atlantic World, 1500–1800* (New York, 2002), 212.

26. John Eardley-Wilmot, *Historical View of the Commission for Enquiring into the Losses, Services, and Claims of the American Loyalists, at the Close of the War between Great Britain and her Colonies, in 1783* (Boston, 1972), 99.

27. It is reproduced in ibid., vi.

28. Cohen, *Global Diasporas,* esp. ix–xii.

29. Bernard Bailyn, *The Ordeal of Thomas Hutchinson: Loyalism and the Destruction of the First British Empire* (London, 1974), see 274–89.

30. Peter O. Hutchinson, ed., *The Diary and Letters of His Excellency Thomas Hutchinson, Esq.,* 2 vols. (Boston, 1884–1886), 1:157–87.

31. Hutchinson, ed., *Diary and Letters,* 1:215, 231.

32. Bailyn, *The Ordeal of Thomas Hutchinson,* 290.

33. Ibid., 1, 290.

34. Hutchinson, ed., *Diary and Letters,* 1:215, 231; 2:40.

35. Ibid., 1:351, 356; 2:156.

36. Keith Mason, "A Loyalist's Journey: James Parker's Response to the Revolutionary Crisis," *Virginia Magazine of History and Biography* 102 (1994), 139–66.

37. See Norton, *The British-Americans,* 305.

38. Ibid., 54.

39. Patrick Parker to James Parker, Norfolk, Aug. 20, 1785, 920 Parker Papers, Liverpool Record Office (PAR), I 40/24.

40. Patrick Parker to James Parker, Edinburgh, July 5, 1782, 920 ibid., I 40/5.

41. See correspondence between Patrick Parker and his father in 920 ibid., I 40/5.

42. James Parker to Charles Stewart Parker, London, Feb. 3, 1796, 920 ibid., III 10/15.

43. James Parker to Patrick Parker, Port Glasgow, Oct. 20, 1787, 920 ibid., I 41.

44. Charles Stewart Parker to James Parker, Port Glasgow, Jan. 18, 1787, 920 ibid., III 1/20; Charles Stewart Parker to James Parker, Xeres de la Frontera, May 27, 1788, 920 ibid., III 1/29.

45. James Campbell to James Parker, Grenada, July 27, 1789, 920 ibid., I 45.

46. Charles Stewart Parker to James Parker, Grenada, June 19, 1793, 920 ibid., I 47/19.

47. For Charles Stewart Parker's subsequent career, see the correspondence between him and his father in 920 ibid., I 47, 48, 49; III, 1, 4, 10.

48. On the meaning of independence to Scottish migrants, see Alan L. Karras, *Sojourners in the Sun: Scottish Migrants in Jamaica and the Chesapeake, 1740–1800* (Ithaca, 1992), 211–15.

49. Charles Stewart Parker to James Parker, Glasgow, Nov. 20, 1797, 920 PAR I 47/16; Charles Stewart Parker to James Parker, Criech, Dec. 4, 1797, 920 ibid., I 47/33.

50. Charles Stewart Parker to James Parker, Criech, Dec. 14, 1797, 920 ibid., I 47/35.

51. On Scottish networks in the Caribbean, see Karras, *Sojourners in the Sun,* esp. 202.

52. For the Williams family, see Carole Watterson Troxler, *The Loyalist Experience in North Carolina* (Raleigh, 1976), 38.

53. Michael Craton, *A History of the Bahamas* (London, 1969), esp. 162–202.

54. Graham R. Hodges, ed., *The Black Loyalist Directory: African Americans in Exile after the American Revolution* (New York, 1996), xv.

55. Sylvia Frey, *Water from the Rock: Black Resistance in a Revolutionary Age* (Princeton, 1991), 63, 67, 114.

56. Benjamin Quarles, *The Negro in the American Revolution* (Chapel Hill, 1960), 18–31; Frey, *Water from the Rock.*

57. Nov. 30, 1782, was the date that the Provisional Peace Agreement was signed between Britain and the United States. It included a provision that the British should not take "any Negroes or other Property of the American Inhabitants" on their departure. Carleton interpreted this to mean only confiscated slaves or those who had arrived behind British lines after the agreement was reached.

58. Walker, *The Black Loyalists,* 10–12.

59. Hodges, *The Black Loyalist Directory,* 1–214.

60. On Equiano's identity and background, see Vincent Carretta, "Olaudah Equiano or Gustavus Vassa? New Light on an Eighteenth-Century Question of Identity," *Slavery and Abolition* 20 (1999), 96–105.

61. Gary B. Nash, "Thomas Peters: Millwright and Deliverer," in David G. Sweet and Gary B. Nash, eds., *Struggle and Survival in Colonial America* (Berkeley and Los Angeles, 1981), esp. 69–85.

62. Ibid., 74.

63. Ibid., 77.

64. Quoted in Walker, *The Black Loyalists,* 20.

65. Nash, "Thomas Peters," 77.

66. Quoted in Walker, *The Black Loyalists,* 25.

67. Nash, "Thomas Peters," 77–78.

68. Quoted ibid., 78.

69. On the petition, see Walker, *The Black Loyalists,* 25.

70. Nash, "Thomas Peters," 78–79.

71. Stephen J. Braidwood, *Black Poor and White Philanthropists: London's Blacks and the Foundation of the Sierra Leone Settlement, 1786–1791* (Liverpool, 1994).

72. Walker, *The Black Loyalists*, 112–14.

73. Ibid., 94–107.

74. Walker, *The Black Loyalists*, 124.

75. Ibid., 123–24; Nash, "Thomas Peters," 82.

76. Nash, "Thomas Peters," 79–83.

77. Walker, *The Black Loyalists*, 145–47.

78. Ibid., 151.

79. Nelson, *The American Tory*, 91.

80. Quoted in J. M. Bumsted, "The Cultural Landscape of Early Canada," in Bernard Bailyn and Philip D. Morgan, eds., *Strangers within the Realm: Cultural Margins of the First British Empire* (Chapel Hill, 1991), 383.

81. J. G. A. Pocock, "The New British History in Atlantic Perspective: An Antipodean Commentary," *American Historical Review* 104 (1999), 498.

82. For similar attempts from rather different angles from those explored in this paper, see Elizabeth Mancke, "Another British America: A Canadian Model for the Early Modern British Empire," *Journal of Imperial and Commonwealth History* 25 (1997), 1–36; Patrick Griffin, "America's Changing Image in Ireland's Looking-Glass: Provincial Construction of an Eighteenth-Century British Atlantic World," ibid. 26 (1998), 28–49.

THIRTEEN: Early Slave Narratives and the Culture of the Atlantic Market

1. Olaudah Equiano, *The Interesting Narrative and Other Writings*, ed. Vincent Carretta (New York, 1995), 61. Carretta's editions of eighteenth-century black anglophone writers have quickly become the standards. For other black writers from that century, see Quobna Ottobah Cugoano, *Thoughts and Sentiments on the Evil of Slavery*, ed. Carretta (New York, 1999); Ignatius Sancho, *Letters of the late Ignatius Sancho, an African*, ed. Carretta (New York, 1998); and Carretta, ed., *Unchained Voices: An Anthology of Black Authors in the English-Speaking World of the 18th Century* (Lexington, Ky., 1996). Quotations from Equiano's *Interesting Narrative* and Cugoano's *Thoughts and Sentiments* will be cited in the text as *IN* and *TS* respectively.

2. Not surprisingly, given the patterns of trade then prevailing in the Americas, some ships on which Equiano worked engaged in the inter-American slave trade.

3. *IN*, 355n. 5.

4. Ivan Hannaford, *Race: The History of an Idea in the West* (Washington, D.C., and Baltimore, 1996).

5. James Sidbury, "Toward Africa: The Emergence of African Identity in Sacred and Secular Time" (unpublished essay).

6. Such connections were conventional in eighteenth-century Anglo-American thought. See, for example, David Brion Davis, *Slavery and Human Progress* (New York, 1984); Sacvan Bercovitch, "The Typology of America's Mission," *American Quarterly* 30 (1978), 135–55 (esp. 146–47); Ernest Lee Tuveson, *Millennium and Utopia: A Study in the Background of the Idea of Progress* (Berkeley, 1949); Anthony J. Barker, *The African Link: British Attitudes To the Negro in the Era of the Atlantic Slave Trade, 1550–1807* (London, 1978), 95–96; Ronald L. Meek, *Social Science and the Ignoble Savage* (Cambridge, U.K., 1976).

7. Vincent Carretta, "Olaudah Equiano or Gustavus Vassa? New Light on an Eigh-teenth-Century Question of Identity," *Slavery and Abolition* 20 (1999), 96–105, shows that Equiano may have been born in South Carolina and thus that his story of enslave-ment may have been fictional. Because I am analyzing the portrayal of the market in his text, I will treat Equiano's assertions as factually accurate. My argument would not change whether we knew Equiano to have been born in Africa or America.

8. They were writing when the slave trade was increasingly coming to be seen as an illegitimate form of commerce in "enlightened" Anglo-American thought. See Thomas Bender, ed., *The Antislavery Debate: Capitalism and Abolitionism as a Problem in His-torical Interpretation* (Berkeley, 1992); also see Christopher L. Brown, "The Empire without Slaves: British Concepts of Emancipation in the Age of the American Revolu-tion, *William and Mary Quarterly*, 3rd ser., 55 (1999), 273–306; David Brion Davis, *The Problem of Slavery in the Age of Revolution, 1770–1823* (Ithaca, 1975), esp. chaps. 1, 2, 5, 8; Seymour Drescher, *Capitalism and Antislavery: British Mobilization in Comparative Perspective* (New York, 1986), chaps. 1–4.

9. Cugoano likewise states that "some of the Africans in my country keep slaves . . . but those which they keep are well fed, and good care taken of them, and treated well" (150). Many modern historians concur with this view of the influence of the Atlantic slave trade on traditional African slavery. See Patrick Manning, *Slavery and African Life: Occidental, Oriental, and African Slave Trades* (Cambridge, U.K., 1990) for an analysis that agrees; compare John Thornton, *Africa and Africans in the Making of the Atlantic World, 1400–1680* (Cambridge, U.K., 1992), chaps. 2 and 3.

10. Venture Smith, *A Narrative of the Life and Adventures of Venture, A Native of Africa: But resident above Sixty Years in the United States of America*, in *Unchained Voices*, 373. Smith's story fits the "gun-slave cycle" interpretation of the slave trade. See Thorn-ton, *Africa and Africans*, 113–16 for a critical discussion of this historiography.

11. The meaning of "nation" in these texts is complicated. These authors, like others at the time, borrowed the term from the King James Version of the Bible that maintains that God "made of one blood all the nations of men for to dwell on the face of the earth" (Acts 17:26). Equiano explicitly cites this (p. 45) as do numerous other black authors from the nineteenth century. How to understand the way these authors translated this bibli-cal idea—or, more properly, this seventeenth-century English translation of a biblical idea—into the world of eighteenth-century nation-states is a question that requires fur-ther work. Benedict Anderson's discussion of "Creole Pioneers" and the emergence of nationalism in the Americas provides the starting point; see *Imagined Communities: Reflections on the Origin and Spread of Nationalism* (1983; London, 1991), chap. 4.

12. Roxanne Wheeler, "'Betrayed by Some of My Own Complexion': Cugoano, Abo-lition, and the Contemporary Language of Racialism," in Vincent Carretta and Philip Gould, eds., *Genius in Bondage: Literature of the Early Black Atlantic* (Lexington, Ky., 2001), 17–38, for a reading of this passage that focuses on the meanings of color.

13. *Unchained Voices*, 379. Gronniosaw likewise told stories of being cheated because he was a black man (*Unchained Voices*, 45, 46, and more ambiguously 51).

14. For other examples see *IN*, 139, 157, 172, 218.

15. This was not true in all American slave societies. See Thomas N. Ingersoll, "Free Blacks in a Slave Society: New Orleans, 1718–1812," *William and Mary Quarterly*, 3rd ser., 48 (1991), 173–200 for a discussion of the Spanish legal institution of *coartación*, which allowed slaves to have a magistrate set a price that they could pay for their freedom.

16. For example, see Geraldine Murphy, "Olaudah Equiano, Accidental Tourist," *Eighteenth-Century Studies* 27 (1994), 551–68, who notes that with "postcolonial hindsight, we wince at" Equiano's faith in free trade, though she adds helpfully that "Equiano did not have classic underdevelopment in mind for his homeland" (p. 561).

17. I have developed this argument in "Toward Africa: The Emergence of African Identity in Sacred and Secular Time" (unpublished essay).

18. Linda Colley, *Britons: Forging the Nation, 1707–1835* (New Haven, Conn., 1992), chap. 1 (esp. pp. 29–32, 37–38).

19. Richard Bushman, *From Puritan to Yankee: Character and the Social Order in Connecticut, 1690–1765* (Cambridge, Mass., 1967). This issue goes back in the historiography to Max Weber. For an introduction to the controversies and an important contribution to the debate, see Stephen Innes, *Creating the Commonwealth: The Economic Culture of Puritan New England* (New York, 1995), 25–38.

20. Meek, *Social Science and the Ignoble Savage*.

21. Jürgen Habermas, *The Structural Transformation of the Public Sphere: An Inquiry into a Category of Bourgeois Society*, trans. Thomas Burger with the assistance of Frederick Lawrence (1962; Cambridge, Mass., 1989), 15.

22. Of course pseudonyms could also be used to shield the identity of the proponent of unpopular or prohibited ideas. The principle behind the pseudonym is the same in either case. Interestingly, Benjamin Franklin wrote under the pseudonym "Historicus" in a late editorial attacking slavery (Paul Baepler, ed., *White Slaves, African Masters: An Anthology of American Barbary Captivity Narratives* [Chicago, 1999], 8)

23. *Structural Transformation*, 45–51. For a useful short gloss on some of these issues see Roger Chartier, *The Cultural Origins of the French Revolution*, trans. Lydia G. Cochrane (Durham, N.C., 1991), chap. 2. William E. Forbath provides a clear analysis of Habermas's thought and a critique of his acceptance of the conceit of depersonalization in the marketplace of ideas in "Habermas's Constitution: A History, Guide, and Critique," *Law and Social Inquiry* 23 (1998), 969–1016 (1004–7 for Forbath's critique of Habermas on access to the marketplace of ideas; this criticism logically extends to depersonalization).

24. See the title pages to Equiano's *Narrative* and Cugoano's *Thoughts and Sentiments. Unchained Voices*, 32 (Gronniosaw), 369 (Smith). Gronniosaw's text was written down by an amanuensis, so one cannot know whether he or someone else chose to assert his African birth. To compare the ways in which narratives relating white slavery in North Africa were signed—the author's place of origin was rarely included—see Baepler, ed., *White Slaves, African Masters*, esp. 73, 149, 161, 188.

25. See, for examples, the famous engraving of Equiano reproduced in *IN*, 2, and of Sancho in *Letters of the Late Ignatius Sancho*, 2.

26. As Catherine Molineux first pointed out to me, Ignatius Sancho signed several letters to a newspaper "Africanus." Sancho, *Letters of the Late Ignatius Sancho*, 81–82, 113–14, 214–15.

27. There is a large and growing literature on copyright and author's rights. For an introduction see John Feather, *A History of British Publishing* (London, 1988); Feather, *The Provincial Book Trade in Eighteenth-Century England* (Cambridge, U.K., 1985); David Saunders, *Authorship and Copyright* (London, 1992), chaps. 1–2; Feather, "From Rights in Copies to Copyright: The Recognition of Authors' Rights in English Law and Practice in the Sixteenth and Seventeenth Centuries" in Martha Woodmansee and Peter

Jaszi, eds., *The Construction of Authorship: Textual Appropriation in Law and Literature* (Durham, N.C., 1994), 191–209; Marlon B. Ross, "Authority and Authenticity: Scribbling Authors and the Genius of Print in Eighteenth-Century England" in *The Construction of Authorship*, 231–57. For autobiography, see G. Thomas Couser, *American Autobiography: The Prophetic Mode* (Amherst, Mass., 1979); Patricia Meyer Spacks, *Imagining a Self: Autobiography and Novel in Eighteenth-Century England* (Cambridge, Mass., 1976). None of these texts make the point about selling the self explicitly, but their analyses illustrate the process. The closest approaches to this point that I have found are in the literature on female authorship. See especially Felicity A. Nussbaum, *The Autobiographical Subject: Gender and Ideology in Eighteenth-Century England* (Baltimore, 1989) and Catherine Gallagher, *Nobody's Story: The Vanishing Acts of Women Writers in the Marketplace, 1670–1820* (Berkeley, 1994).

28. *TS*, 7. This passage is set off from the proper beginning of the text and introduced with an "*N. B.*"

29. Vincent Carretta, "'Property of Author': Olaudah Equiano's Place in the History of the Book," in *Genius in Bondage*, 130–50, and James Green, "The Publishing History of Olaudah Equiano's *Interesting Narrative*," *Slavery and Abolition* 16 (1995), 362–75, analyze Equiano's publishing strategy, including estimates of how much he probably cleared on different editions. For more general information on Equiano while selling his book, including a discussion of the promotion tours, see James Walvin, *An African's Life: The Life and Times of Olaudah Equiano, 1745–1797* (London, 1998), chap. 13; also Carretta, "Introduction," in *IN*, xiv-xvi, app. E, 347.

30. See Forbath, "Habermas's Constitution," esp. 981–84 and 1004–12, for a historical and theoretical discussion of the issues raised by questions of access to the public sphere.

31. The persistence of this effect is remarkable. Black Civil Rights workers during the 1950s and '60s could earn the right to hold forth on segregation and racism by putting their bodies on the line at lunch counters or in front of dogs and firehoses, but even a Nobel Peace Prize could not fully legitimate Martin Luther King Jr.'s opinions regarding the Vietnam War. And closer to home for those in the academy, a cycle has developed in which attempts to diversify faculties are often informed by assumptions that prospective black faculty members study "black" subjects, an assumption that can hardly be without effect on graduate students deciding on dissertation topics. Unfortunately, the current political environment has so endangered all efforts to diversify the academy that there is little room to experiment with alternate approaches.

FOURTEEN: The British Caribbean in the Age of Revolution

1. R. R. Palmer, *The Age of the Democratic Revolution: A Political History of Europe and America, 1760–1800*, 2 vols. (Princeton, 1959–64); Lester D. Langley, *The Americas in the Age of Revolution, 1750–1850* (New Haven, Conn., 1996); David Brion Davis, *The Problem of Slavery in the Age of Revolution, 1770–1823* (Ithaca, 1975). The revolutionary action and settlements of the period were hardly accompanied by the installation of democratic institutions. Franklin W. Knight, *The Caribbean: The Genesis of a Fragmented Nationalism*, 2nd ed. (1978; New York, 1990), 160.

2. C. L. R. James, *The Black Jacobins: Toussaint L'Ouverture and the San Domingo Revolution*, 2nd ed., rev., (New York, 1963); David Geggus, *Slavery, War, and Revolution:*

The British Occupation of Saint Domingue, 1793–98 (New York, 1981); Carolyn Fick, *The Making of Haiti: The Saint Domingue Revolution from Below* (Knoxville, 1990); Thomas O. Ott, *The Haitian Revolution, 1789–1804* (Knoxville, 1972); Franklin W. Knight, "The Haitian Revolution," *American Historical Review* 105 (2000), 103–15.

3. On this, see Ott, *Haitian Revolution*, op. cit.

4. For examples of this new trend, see David Barry Gaspar and David Patrick Geggus, eds., *A Turbulent Time: The French Revolution and the Greater Caribbean* (Bloomington, 1997), especially the essays by Geggus, Gaspar, and Roger Buckley.

5. Gaspar and Geggus, eds., *A Turbulent Time*.

6. Richard B. Sheridan, *Sugar and Slavery: An Economic History of the British West Indies, 1623–1775* (Baltimore, 1974), 452–59. The major exceptions were perhaps Trinidad and British Guiana.

7. David Patrick Geggus, "Slavery, War and Revolution in the Greater Caribbean in the Greater Caribbean, 1789–1815," in Gaspar and Geggus, eds., *A Turbulent Time*, 12–13.

8. Julius S. Scott, "Crisscrossing the Empires: Ships, Sailors, and Resistance in the Lesser Antilles in the Eighteenth Century," in Robert L. Paquette and Stanley L. Engerman, eds., *The Lesser Antilles in the Age of European Expansion* (Gainesville, 1996), 128–43; W. Jeffrey Bolster, *Black Jacks: African American Seamen in the Age of Sail* (Cambridge, Mass., 1997) 68–101.

9. Robert Renny, *A History of Jamaica*, (London, 1807), li, as quoted in Michael Craton et al., eds., *Slavery, Abolition, and Emancipation: Black Slaves and the British Empire* (London, 1976), 138.

10. Mavis C. Campbell, *The Maroons of Jamaica: A History of Resistance, Collaboration and Betrayal* (South Hadley, Mass., 1988), 209–49.

11. Seton to Portland, Nov. 16, 1796, Colonial Office, Public Record Office (CO) 260/14. There were actually two distinct groups of Caribs: the Red Caribs and the Black Caribs. On this, see J. Paul Thomas, "The Caribs of St. Vincent: A Study in Maladministration, 1763–1773," *Journal of Caribbean History* 18 (1984), 60–73.

12. Michael Duffy, "The French Revolution and British Attitudes to the West Indian Colonies," in Gaspar and Geggus, eds., *A Turbulent Time*, 82.

13. Stanley to Dundas, Nov. 15, 1793, CO 152/74; "Translation of the Confession of Morillon Desfosses," [1795], Francis Hart Collection, Massachusetts Historical Society.

14. Stanley to Portland, May 27, 1795, CO 152/74.

15. On Southern reaction to the Haitian Revolution, see Alfred N. Hunt, *Haiti's Influence on Antebellum America: Slumbering Volcano in the Caribbean* (Baton Rouge, 1988), 107–46

16. Dundas to Seton, Dec. 8, 1792, CO 260/12; Seton to Dundas, Jan. 14, 1793; Seton to Dundas, March 8, 1793.

17. Grey to Dundas, (secret), July 17, 1794, CO 319/5.

18. Roger Norman Buckley, *The British Army in the West Indies: Society and Military in the Revolutionary Age* (Gainesville, 1998), 173–202.

19. "New subjects" is the term used to refer to whites of French background who resided on the islands prior to their cession to the British. According to the terms of the 1763 treaty by which France handed over the islands to the British, these residents were to become British subjects, under certain circumstances.

20. Seton to Dundas, Dec. 20, 1791, CO 260/11; Dundas to Seton, March 8, 1792.

21. Matthew to Grenville, Jan. 7, 1792, CO 101/31.

22. Seton to Dundas, Jan. 12, 1792, CO 260/11.

23. Seton to Dundas, March 8, 1793, CO 260/12.

24. Seton to Dundas, Jan. 14, 1793, CO 260/12.

25. Williams to Dundas, July 4, 1792 CO 101/32; Williams to Dundas, Dec. 28, 1792, CO 101/33.

26. Home to Dundas, Feb. 9, 1793 and Aug. 1, 1794, CO 101/33.

27. Matthew to Dundas, Jan. 10, 1792,(with enclosure), CO 101/32.

28. "Grenada—To His Excellency George Washington Esq., Captain General and Commander in Chief in and over the United States of America, etc. etc. Done in the Town of St. George's, Grenada, this Second day of June 1791, By Wm Dowding," CO 260/16.

29. A free colored man, Dowding wrote the letter to Washington on June 2, 1791. He reportedly had entered St. Vincent in May 1800 "under false pretenses and therefore permitted by me to land." Later evidence revealed that he had "been just banished from Matinique after having been condemned to the Pillory, and to pay a fine by the Supreme Court for some violent outrage committed." Ottley to Portland, June 5, 1800, CO 260/16.

30. I had previously erroneously assumed (Edward L. Cox, *Free Coloreds in the Slave Societies of St. Kitts and Grenada, 1763–1833* [Knoxville, 1983], 83–84) that La Grenade and his cohorts merely wished to blunt the efforts of a radical branch of the local free colored community. This response to the document purportedly written by Washington indicates that the 1792 petitioners were aware of Dowding's actions.

31. Information in this paragraph draws on material in Cox, *Free Coloreds,* 76–91.

32. Ottley to Portland, June 5, 1800, CO 260/16.

33. Ibid.

34. Seton to Dundas, April 2, 1793, CO 260/12.

35. Seton to Dundas, July 13, 1793, CO 260/12.

36. Ibid, "To His Excellency James Seton, Esquire, Captain General & Governor in Chief of the Island of St. Vincent and its Dependencies, . . . The Humble Address of the Council and Assembly of the Said Island."

37. Seton to Portland, Dec. 15, 1794, CO 260/13.

38. Seton to Portland, March 16, 1795, CO 260/13.

39. Ibid.

40. Seton to Portland, March 30, 1795, CO 260/13.

41. Seton to Portland, April 22, 1795, CO 260/13.

42. Seton to Portland, May 8, 1795, CO 260/13.

43. Seton to Portland, March 29, 1796, CO 260/13.

44. Seton to Portland, Oct. 12, Nov. 16, and Nov. 20, 1796, CO 260/14.

45. Bentnick to Portland, April 9, 1798, CO 260/15.

46. Beckwith to Camden, June 10, 1805, CO 260/19.

47. For suggestions on why and how to divide the Carib lands among white settlers, see Ottley to Portland, Oct. 5 and Dec. 8, 1801, CO 260/17.

48. Seton to Portland, May 8, 1795, CO 260/13.

49. Seton to Portland, May 14, 1795, CO 260/13.

50. Petition signed by D. Raquet, J. Nigel Priest, J. N. Priddie, and Jacques Raquet to Dundas, Jan. 2, 1798, CO 260/15.

51. Grey to Dundas, July 17, 1794, CO 319/5.

52. Roger Norman Buckley, *The British Army in the West Indies: Society and the Military in the Revolutionary Age* (Gainesville, 1998), 128–271.

53. Roger Norman Buckley, *Slaves in Red Coats: The British West India Regiments, 1795–1815* (New Haven, Conn., 1979).

54. Gloster to Bentinck, Jan. 10, 1799, in Bentinck to Portland, Jan. 17, 1799, CO 260/16.

55. Bentinck to Portland, Jan. 17, 1799, CO 260/16. See the essay by Julius Scott on this issue in Gaspar and Geggus, eds., *A Turbulent Time.*

56. Ottley to Portland, Aug. 22, 1799, CO 260/16.

57. John Scott and John Milford to Portland, March 11, 1799, CO 324/63.

58. Hobart to Attorney and Solicitor General, Nov. 30, 1801, CO 324/119.

59. On this, see Buckley, *Slaves in Red Coats,* 70–79.

60. Ottley to Hobart, Jan. 10, 1802, CO 260/17; Trigge to Hobart, Jan. 1, 1802, CO 318/19; Keith Laurence, "The Tobago Slave Conspiracy of 1801," *Caribbean Quarterly* 28 (1982), 1–9.

61. For examples of the role of Christian missionaries, see Elsa V. Goveia, *Slave Society in the British Leeward Islands at the End of the Eighteenth Century* (New Haven, Conn., 1965); Robin Blackburn, *The Overthrow of Colonial Slavery, 1776–1848* (London, 1988); Mary Turner, *Slaves and Missionaries: The Disintegration of Jamaican Slave Society, 1787–1834* (Urbana, 1982); Emilia da Costa, *Crown of Glory, Tears of Blood: The Demerara Slave Rebellion of 1823* (New York, 1994).

62. Ottley to Portland, Jan. 5, 1800, CO 260/16.

63. For a general treatment on the abolition of slavery in the British Caribbean, see Michael Craton, *Sinews of Empire: A Short History of British Slavery* (New York, 1974). On British Caribbean response to the American Revolution, see Andrew Jackson O'Shaughnessy, *An Empire Divided: The American Revolution and the British Caribbean* (Philadelphia, 2000).

FIFTEEN: Freedom, Migration, and the American Revolution

1. Peter Marshall, "British North America, 1760–1815," in P. J. Marshall, ed., *The Oxford History of the British Empire: The Eighteenth Century* (Oxford, 1998), 391.

2. Gary B. Nash and Jean R. Soderlund, *Freedom By Degrees: Emancipation in Pennsylvania and its Aftermath* (New York, 1991), 74–98.

3. A. Roger Ekirch, *Bound for America: The Transportation of British Convicts to the Colonies 1718–1775* (Oxford, 1987), 114–16.

4. Ibid., 227–36; Farley W. Grubb, "The End of European Immigrant Servitude in the United States: An Economic Analysis of Market Collapse, 1772–1835," *Journal of Economic History* 54 (1994), 794–824.

5. Stephen Whitman, "Diverse Good Causes: Manumission and the Transformation of Urban Slavery," *Social Science History* 19 (1995), 333–70; Richard S. Dunn, "Black Society in the Chesapeake, 1776–1810," in Ira Berlin and Ronald Hoffman, eds., *Slavery and Freedom in the Age of the American Revolution* (Charlottesville, 1983), 49–82; William W. Freehling, "The Founding Fathers and Slavery," *American Historical Review* 77 (1972), 81–93.

6. Nash and Soderlund, *Freedom By Degrees,* 173–86.

7. Jack P. Greene, *Imperatives, Behaviors, and Identities: Essays in Early American Cultural History* (Charlottesville, 1992), 338–39.

8. Jonathan Elliot, ed., *The Debates in the Several State Constitutions on the Adoption of the Federal Constitution,* 5 vols. (Philadelphia, 1896), 4:316.

9. Philip D. Morgan, "Black Society in the Lowcountry, 1760–1810," in Berlin and Hoffman, eds., *Slavery and Freedom*, 115.

10. Sylvia Frey, *Water from the Rock: Black Resistance in a Revolutionary Age* (Princeton, 1991), 213; Patrick S. Brady, "The Slave Trade and Sectionalism in South Carolina, 1787–1808," *Journal of Southern History* 38 (1972), 601–20; Allan Kulikoff, "Uprooted Peoples: Black Migrants in the Age of the American Revolution," in Berlin and Hoffman, eds., *Slavery and Freedom*, 143–71.

11. John Drayton, *A View of South-Carolina as Respects Her Natural and Civil Concerns* (Charleston, 1802), 102–3.

12. Aaron Fogleman, "From Slaves, Convicts, and Servants to Free Passengers: The Transformation of Immigration in the Era of the American Revolution," *Journal of American History* 85 (June 1998), 61–62.

13. Arthur Zilversmit, *The First Emancipation: The Abolition of Slavery in the North* (Chicago, 1967), 109–24.

14. Robin Winks, *The Blacks in Canada: A History* (New Haven, Conn., 1971), 28–46, 96–113.

15. Ibid., 61–95, 112, 233–71.

16. Richard B. Sheridan, "The Slave Trade to Jamaica," in B. W. Higman, ed., *Trade Government and Society in Caribbean History, 1700–1920* (Kingston, 1983) 12; David Eltis et al., *The Transatlantic Slave Trade: A Database on CD-ROM* (Cambridge, U.K., 2000).

17. William W. Freehling, *The Road to Disunion: Secessionists at Bay, 1776–1854* (New York, 1990), 222–23, 591; Rachel N. Klein, *Unification of a Slave State: The Rise of the Planter Class in the South Carolina Backcountry, 1760–1808* (Chapel Hill, 1990), 238–68; Stephanie McCurry, *Masters of Small Worlds: Yeoman Households, Gender Relations, and the Political Culture of the Antebellum South Carolina Low Country* (New York, 1995), 240–46.

18. McCurry, *Masters of Small Worlds*, 251–56.

19. Jack P. Greene, "The Jamaica Privilege Controversy, 1764–66: An Episode in the Process of Constitutional Definition in the Early Modern Empire," *Journal of Imperial and Commonwealth History* 22 (1994), 16–53.

20. Thomas C. Holt, *The Problem of Freedom: Race, Labor, and Politics in Jamaica and Britain, 1832–1938* (Baltimore, 1992), 91; Edward Braithwaite, *The Development of Creole Society in Jamaica, 1770–1820* (Oxford, 1971), 100.

21. See Bryan Edwards, *A Speech delivered at a Free Conference . . . Concerning the Slave Trade* (Kingston, 1789). For Jamaica's continued importance, see P. J. Marshall, "Britain without America—A Second Empire?" in Marshall, ed., *Oxford History of the British Empire: The Eighteenth Century*, 584; Andrew Jackson O'Shaughnessy, *An Empire Divided: The American Revolution and the British Caribbean* (Philadelphia, 2000), 210.

22. Seymour Drescher, *Econocide: British Slavery in the Era of Abolition* (Pittsburgh, 1977); B. W. Higman, *Slave Population and Economy in Jamaica, 1807–1834* (Cambridge, U.K., 1976); J. R. Ward, *British West Indian Slavery, 1750–1834* (Oxford, 1984); Mary S. Turner, *Slaves and Missionaries: The Disintegration of Jamaican Slave Society, 1787–1834* (Urbana, 1982).

23. B. W. Higman, "The West India 'Interest' in Parliament, 1807–1833," *Historical Studies: Australia and New Zealand* 13 (1967), 1–9.

24. *The Jamaica Journal*, Nov. 22, 1823, cited in Gad J. Heuman, *Between Black and White: Race, Politics, and the Free Coloreds in Jamaica, 1792–1865* (Westport, Conn., 1981), 44.

25. Holt, *The Problem of Freedom*, 215–308; Heuman, *Between Black and White*, 44–196.

26. Holt, *The Problem of Freedom*, 198–202. For similar attempts to attract white and Asian migrants to the South, see James L. Roark, *Masters Without Slaves: Southern Planters in the Civil War and Reconstruction* (New York, 1977), 165–69.

27. J. H. Galloway, *The Sugar Cane Industry: An Historical Geography from Its Origins to 1914* (Cambridge, U.K., 1989), 146–54.

28. Holt, *Problem of Freedom*, 202; David Northrup, *Indentured Labor in the Age of Imperialism, 1834–1922* (New York, 1995), 20–25, 33, 108; Monica Schuler, *"Alas, Alas, Kongo": A Social History of Indentured African Immigration into Jamaica, 1841–1865* (Baltimore, 1980), 9.

29. Kulikoff, "Uprooted Peoples," 143–71.

30. Eric Foner, *Nothing But Freedom: Emancipation and Its Legacy* (Baton Rouge, 1983), 73.

31. Matthew J. Mancini, *One Dies, Get Another: Convict Leasing in the American South, 1866–1928* (Columbia, S.C., 1996), 220–38; Amy Dru Stanley, "Beggars Can't Be Choosers: Compulsion and Contract in Postbellum America," *Journal of American History* 78 (1992), 1288–93.

32. Eric Foner, "The Meaning of Freedom in the Age of Emancipation," *Journal of American History* 81 (1994) 439–44.

33. Davis, *The Problem of Slavery in the Age of Revolution*, 299–306; Winthrop D. Jordan, *White over Black: American Attitudes toward the Negro, 1550–1812* (Chapel Hill, 1968).

34. Holt, *The Problem of Freedom*, 307–9.

35. Foner, "Meaning of Freedom," 452.

36. Christopher Brown, "Empire without Slaves: British Concepts of Emancipation in the Age of the American Revolution," *William and Mary Quarterly*, 3rd ser., 56 (1999), 273–306.

37. Ibid., 297–303; Henry Heller, "Bodin on Slavery and Primitive Accumulation," *Sixteenth Century Journal* 25 (1994), 53–65.

38. Ibid, 276, 301, 305. See also Eliga H. Gould, "American Independence and Britain's Counter-Revolution," *Past and Present* 154 (1997), 107–41.

39. Alan Atkinson, *The Europeans in Australia: The Beginning* (Melbourne, 1997), 44–45.

40. Precursors of these schemes were the Palatine projects (1709–10); the settlement of Georgia (1732); and the founding of Nova Scotia (1749). A. G. Roeber, *Palatines, Liberty, and Property: German Lutherans in Colonial British America* (Baltimore, 1993); Jack P. Greene, "Travails of an Infant Colony: The Search for Viability, Coherence, and Identity in Colonial Georgia," in Harvey H. Jackson and Phinizy Spaulding, eds., *Forty Years of Diversity: A Symposium on Colonial Georgia* (Athens, Ga., 1984), 278–309; Elizabeth Mancke, "Another British America: A Canadian Model for the Early Modern British Empire," *Journal of Imperial and Commonwealth History* 25 (1997), 1–36.

41. Atkinson, *Europeans in Australia*, 45–46.

42. "Committee of Honduras settlers to London merchants," Aug. 27, 1787, Colonial Office Papers, Public Record Office (CO) 123/5/128–48; Lord Sydney to Edward Despard, Feb., 1788, CO 123/6/99.

43. John Peterson, *Province of Freedom: A History of Sierra Leone, 1787–1870* (London, 1969), 21–44.

44. A. Roger Ekirch, *Bound for America: The Transportation of British Convicts to the Colonies, 1718–1775* (Oxford, 1987), 229–37.

45. Robert Hughes, *The Fatal Shore* (New York, 1986), xvi, 2.

46. Atkinson, *Europeans in Australia,* 58.

47. Atkinson, *Europeans in Australia,* 40–41,47–58; idem, "The Free-Born Englishman Transported: Convict Rights as A Measure of Eighteenth-Century Empire," *Past and Present* 144 (1994), 93–98.

48. Atkinson, "Freeborn Englishman Transported," 98–107; Kenneth Morgan, "English and American Attitudes toward Convict Transportation," *History,* 72 (1987), 425–26; Ekirch, *Bound for America,* 154–56.

49. Atkinson, *Europeans in Australia,* 52–56, 90.

50. Ibid., xii.

51. Atkinson, "Free-born Englishman Transported," 111.

52. Atkinson, *Europeans in Australia,* 59–78.

53. Ibid., 62.

54. Stephen Nicholas, ed., *Convict Workers: Reinterpreting Australia's Past* (Melbourne, 1988), 8–12, 111–66.

55. Henry Reynolds, *The Law of the Land* (Ringwood, Vic., 1992), 7–14, 51–54.

56. P. J. Marshall, "Empire and Authority in the Late Eighteenth Century," *Journal of Imperial and Commonwealth History* 15 (1987), 105–22; Marshall, "Britain Without America—A Second Empire?," 587–95; Gould, "American Independence and Britain's Counter-Revolution"; H. V. Bowen, "British Conceptions of Global Empire, 1756–1783," *Journal of Imperial and Commonwealth History* 26 (1998), 19–21. The exception was Ireland, which achieved legislative authority coeval to Britain. Jack P. Greene, *Peripheries and Center: Constitutional Development in the Extended Polities of the British Empire and the United States, 1607–1788* (Athens, Ga., 1990), 208.

57. Fogleman, "From Slaves, Convicts, and Servants to Free Passengers," 60–66; Gordon S. Wood, *The Radicalism of the American Revolution* (New York, 1992), 145, 184.

58. Jack P. Greene, "Empire and Identity from the Glorious Revolution to the American Revolution," in Marshall, ed., *Oxford History of the British Empire: The Eighteenth Century,* 229–30.

59. Gould, "American Independence and Britain's Counter-Revolution," 140.

60. Jerry Z. Muller, *Adam Smith: In His Time and Ours* (Princeton, 1993), 120, 136.

61. Herman Merivale, *Lectures on Colonization and Colonies* (London, 1861), 271.

62. Ibid., 91.

63. A notable exception was South Africa, where slavery remained entrenched. Robert C.-H. Shell, *Children of Bondage: A Social History of the Slave Society at the Cape of Good Hope* (Hanover, N.H., 1994).

64. Ibid., 302.

65. M. F. Lloyd Prichard, ed., *The Collected Works of Edward Gibbon Wakefield* (Auckland, 1969), 461–97 (quotation on 471); and Bernard Semmel, *The Rise of Free Trade Imperialism: Classical Political Economy, the Empire of Free Trade and Imperialism, 1750–1850* (Cambridge, U.K., 1970), 110–18.

66. Prichard, ed., *Collected Works of Wakefield,* 489.

67. Bernard Semmel, *The Liberal Ideal and the Demons of Empire: Theories of Imperialism from Adam Smith to Lenin* (Baltimore, 1993), 33–38.

68. David Brion Davis, "American Slavery and the American Revolution," in Berlin and Hoffman, eds., *Slavery and Freedom in the Age of the American Revolution,* 262–80.

Index

May '14

卌 卌
卌 卌
卌 |||

Made in the USA
Middletown, DE
19 July 2016